'OHU'OHU NĀ MAUNA O 'E'EKA

'OHU'OHU
NĀ MAUNA O 'E'EKA

Place Names of Maui Komohana

Cody Kapueola'ākeanui Pata

North Beach-West Maui
Benefit Fund Inc.

Lahaina, Maui, Hawai'i

ISBN 978-1-9524-6105-7 (pbk : alk. paper)

Published by the North Beach-West Maui Benefit Fund, Inc.
P O Box 11329
Lahaina, Hawai‘i 96761

Distributed by University of Hawai‘i Press
2840 Kolowalu Street
Honolulu, HI 96822-1888

Every effort has been made to trace copyright holders
and to obtain their permission for the use of copyright material.
The publisher apologizes for any errors or omissions and
would be grateful if notified of any corrections that
should be incorporated in future reprints or editions of this book.

This book is printed on acid-free paper and
meets the guidelines for permanence and durability
of the Council on Library Resources.

Print-ready files provided by North Beach-West Maui Benefit Fund, Inc.

CONTENTS

FOREWORD

This book is another project of the HK West Maui Community Fund. As the late Native Hawaiian historian Edward Kanahele explained, "A place tells me who I am and who my extended family is. A place gives me my history, the history of my clan and the history of my people. I am able to look at a place and tie in human events that affect me and my loved ones. A place gives me a feeling of stability and of belonging to my family, those living and dead. A place gives me a sense of well-being and of acceptance of all who have experienced that place" (cited in Van 1991).

This project is intended to support a sense of well-being for Native Hawaiians and of acceptance of all who have experienced the places of West Maui. It is also intended to assist others in "self-reflection rather than asserting modernity's dominant temporal and spatial imaginaries" (Shapiro 1997).

The HK West Maui Community Fund expresses its profound gratitude to the North Beach-West Maui Benefit Fund for agreeing to publish this important work for a general, public audience. Both organizations hope this project will continue to deepen interest in the study and understanding of West Maui and its peoples as well as the collecting of traditional place-names throughout Hawai'i.

Lance D. Collins

PREFACE

Naming in Hawaiian culture is, as in all cultures, a very important act. It is said that the act of naming places is a way to control and infuse space with particular belief systems and values. Place names are our memory-scapes. In the twenty-first century we have come to understand that we need to examine the known, or uncover the forgotten or replaced, place names of Hawaiʻi. Place names reveal the complex history of Hawaiʻi—and too, there is importance in making connections between Hawaiian place names and Hawaiian cultural identity.

Let me share a personal example of what I just wrote. I was born in Lahaina in 1954, and in my youth, played in Lahaina's largest park: Maluʻuluolele. People from Olowalu to Honokōhau met there to enjoy the park's expanse and engage in various American sports activities. Sports teams from other parts of Maui, as well as the islands of Molokaʻi and Lānaʻi, were also hosted, creating the sense of a shared history of the place. However, during those Territorial and early Statehood eras, unbeknownst to me and many others who were using the park during those times, we were playing in, and on, a very sacred space. The story of that space and some of its attendant place names, the Mokuhinia wetland pond and its kapu (sacred) island Mokuʻula, for example, were "disappeared" in American pre- and post-Statehood efforts to erase almost anything related to Hawaiʻi and its culture. Lahaina became the "Whaling Capital"—a whitewashed version of what it was thought important to remember. And those actions were not only a figurative cover-up. The wetland pond was literally filled in—covered over—in 1918 to create a "ball park" in the United States' claimed Territory of Hawaiʻi.

The sacred space itself was disappeared!

Thankfully, when it came time to name the park, there were some in the community who knew Lahaina's Hawaiian cultural history. The name Maluʻulu-olele is a poetic reference to the old name Lele (for Lahaina and its environs), which had numerous breadfruit trees—so numerous it was said one could walk the length of Lele completely in the shade! Over time, as I came to know the place names associated with the sacred space I once played on, it was also shaping my cultural identity as a Hawaiian.

Learning—uncovering—the story of a place name takes research, time, and sometimes a little luck. And yes, regrettably, a place name's story is sometimes irretrievably lost. Yet to get to the story, one has to first know the place name. It is indeed our good luck that Pueo has researched those names and also included many of the stories associated with the many, many place names he has collected. Pueo is a former Hawaiian language student of mine, and I am proud of his accomplishments. His cultural revitalization work in the Hawaiian and Nomlāqa communities is extraordinary. This quote, lifted directly from his Instagram account, gives insight to the breadth and depth of his interests and how he sees himself: "Eclectic indigenous traveler, teacher, & student…oh, & kumu hula, entertainer, & artisan." I would certainly agree with his self-assessment, self-effacing as it may be. As a retired professor of Hawaiian language, I do regret that I will not be able to direct students in my classes to this book. Yet, as a former board member of the HK West Maui Community Fund, I am very pleased projects like this are being undertaken. Certainly, this text should take its rightful place with other important Hawai'i-related reference books.

S. Kī'ope Raymond

Acknowledgments

He hoʻīlina nō no kuʻu poʻe kamalei ʻohana a kaiaulu, a he aloha nui hoʻi no ko Maui Komohana a me ka poʻe akeakamai a ʻimi naʻauao o kēia au nei a me ko kēia mua aku.

Me ka naʻau hoʻomaikaʻi wale i kuʻu poʻe loea a kumu nō hoʻi: ʻo Nona Mahilani Kaluhiokalani (1952–2002), ʻo Diane Nāpua Amadeo (1938–2005), ʻo George Lanakilakeikiahialiʻi Nāʻope (1928–2009), ʻo Keʻala Kūkona (1954–2009), ʻo Jay Jay Ahulau Akiona (1966–2007), ʻo Eleanor Kaʻupu Makida (1932–2003), a ʻo Hilda Keanaʻāina (1926–2011).

Me ka mahalo he ʻauʻa ʻole nō iā: Keoni Kuoha, Ric and Debbie Pata, ko Ka Malama Mahilani, Gordon Apo, Lance Collins, North Beach-West Maui Benefit Fund, Honua-Kai West Maui Fund, Kīʻope Raymond, Frank Kaʻiuokalani Damas, Hōkūao Pellegrino, Dr. Ronald Williams, Jr., a me Sigrid Southworth.

INTRODUCTION

If it has a Hawaiian name, it has a Hawaiian story.

—Diane Nāpua Amadeo (1938–2005)

In Hawaiian toponymy, place names are succinct forms of moʻolelo—information-ladened utterances meant to be successively transmitted across generations. In delving into this project, I had to constantly remind myself that the task was to *only* compile inoa ʻāina of the three moku of Maui Komohana. Too often, I struggled to avoid becoming completely *luhe wale iho i ka lau uluhe*—entirely overwhelmed by the multitude of place names that sprawl like uluhe ferns across the land.

The overwhelming feeling had nothing to do with the number of names, but instead with the seemingly infinite possibilities and implications that exist within those names as moʻolelo. As I encountered a name, I would automatically start logging down anything and everything that I could find, seeking possible stories, connecting dots, and on and on until I would eventually remember my actual task: place name compilation. So often I would suffer a tinge of anxiety and regret from feelings of neglectfulness in not being able to give each name my undivided attention. Thankfully during those times, respite for my angst came from remembering that there are other resources available for those interested in researching the broader contexts of the inoa ʻāina, their rains and winds, as well as regional histories and ʻōlelo noʻeau.

Although "Just focus on the place names, brother!" eventually became my mantra, I still found myself quite often peering up from beneath a lush canopy of lau uluhe after allowing myself to be engulfed in the Hawaiian stories—documented, probable, plausible, or imagined—of each Hawaiian name.

STRUCTURE OF THE BOOK

The inoa ʻāina compiled within this book are those found for the kalana, ahupuaʻa, ʻili, land parcels, houses, sites, shoreline points, beaches, surfs, peaks, hills, streams, and other place-based features of each of the three moku of Maui Komohana.

The vast majority of the names featured are in the Hawaiian language. A few superimposed names of foreign origin have also been included, but only when their Hawaiian language predecessors and/or counterparts are known and listed. The place names have been compiled alphabetically within the five chapters of this book.

The first chapter, "Maui Komohana," lists place names common to the entire western region of Maui, as well as a list of place names which may provide insight into some of the regional vocabulary preferences of kūpuna and Hawaiian-language speakers of Maui Komohana. The next three chapters, "Lahaina Moku," "Kāʻanapali Moku," and "Wailuku Moku," feature place names compiled for each individual moku.

The last chapter, "Papa Kuhikuhi," serves as an index for place names that have been grouped into the individual ahupuaʻa and kalana of each of the three moku. The listings begin with the moku of Lahaina (commencing from the ahupuaʻa of Ukumehame and continuing northwest until the kalana of Lahaina), then the moku of Kāʻanapali (commencing from the ahupuaʻa of Honokōwai and continuing north and east to the kalana of Kahakuloa), and ends with the moku of Wailuku (commencing from the ahupuaʻa of Waiheʻe and continuing south to the ahupuaʻa of Waikapū).

METHODOLOGY

Because the names given to places reflect culture and history,
students of Hawaiian place names, like dictionary writers,
are confronted by subject matter as diverse as archaeology,
folklore, geography, history, language, and surfing.

—Mary Kawena Pukui, Samuel H. Elbert,
and Esther T. Mookini, *Place Names of Hawaii*

Research during a pandemic comes with many challenges. Blessedly, online resources regarding the subject of Hawaiian place names are quite prolific, and content continues to grow. Nonetheless, I truly look forward to a time when I can physically visit archives with resources yet undigitized.

My methodology of research and compilation for this project are the results of my classical trainings in the two formal ʻoihana from which I graduated: Hula, under Nona Mahilani Kaluhiokalani (1952–2002) and George Lanakilakeikiahialiʻi Nāʻope (1928–2009); and Haku Mele, under Eleanor

Ka'upu Makida (1932–2003). As such, the content and format for each entry is what I find valuable when researching inoa 'āina in the pursuits of my 'oihana. It is my hope that this project will be of service to our beloved community.

Me ka ha'aha'a,
Pueo

The general guide for the moku boundaries within this project was the "Hawaiian Government Survey: Maui, Hawaiian Islands" map of 1885. Completed during the reign of Kalākaua, this map exhibits information available to Hawaiian Kingdom-era surveyors, which was accepted as relevant by the last two ruling monarchs of Hawai'i, until at least the time when the map was "brought up to date in 1903 by John M. Donn." Altogether, dozens of maps—hard copies, online, publication insets/graphics, etc.—were meticulously analyzed, 47 of which contributed to the listings in this book.

Other resources, in order of serviceability, included: the Māhele indices of awards and documents; the Papakilo Database; Hawaiian-language newspapers; the Ulukau Hawaiian Electronic Library; Elspeth Sterling's *Sites of Maui*; various books, online publications, articles, and reports; Hawaiian language recordings; and personal communications.

Entry Format

Entries are not intended to be presented in an authoritative manner. Although modern diacritical markings are provided for place-name forms, they are not asserted. When the name is found within the main body of an entry, the spelling preferred by the author is used. (However, official name versions should perhaps be the kuleana of a board or council, the vetted members of which should be renowned for their expertise and qualifications.)

There have been ongoing discussions regarding the formalizing of place names into a standardized, one-name format. Examples from within this book include "Pu'u Kīlea" and "Pōhaku o Kā'anapali." Just as the Hawai'i mountain name "Maunakea (Mauna + Kea)" is now formally written as one word, so too could "Pu'u Kīlea" be written as "Pu'ukīlea," and "Pōhaku o Kā'anapali" as "Pōhakuokā'anapali." As stated above, however, the author will leave such assertions to an official board or council, as the main directive of this book was simply to compile and record place names. As such, for the most part, the place names found herein reflect their most common variants found in the various media consulted.

An example of the layout for an entry is:

1. **Lahaina**
2. Lahaina / Lāhainā
3. Lahaina / Lā-hainā
4. Pronunciation and meaning undetermined, perhaps: "lahaina n. 1. A variety of sugar cane, usually free tasseling, heavy stooling, and with rather semierect to recumbent growth; large, long heavy tops...2. A variety of sweet potato...3. Poising; leaping." /HD/; or, lā hainā—merciless sun.
5. The name of one of three moku of Maui Komohana. Lahaina is also the name of the kalana found in the moku of Lahaina. From 1820 to 1845, Lahaina was the capital of the Hawaiian Kingdom.

   Although scholars provide evidence that an older pronunciation for Lahaina was "Lāhainā," most modern-day scholars choose the spelling that reflects modern-day pronunciation, "Lahaina." Even in the vast majority of her works, native Hawaiian speaker and renowned scholar Mary Kawena Pukui chose to represent this place name without diacrtical markings, as have other contemporary scholars. This is likewise reflected in the pronunciations of residents, kūpuna, and in recordings of mānaleo.
6. "...ua waiho kapalua wale iho no o Lahaina i ka lai, ma kona hoopuni ia ana e na mokupuni, nolaila mai kekahi inoa ona, oia hoi na Honoapiilani, a me he mea la, ekolu inoa o keia kulanakauhale, he oiaio no, ekolu wale inoa, o Lele kona inoa kahiko, o Lahaina, he inoa hou ia, a o na Honoapiilani, he inoa mua no ia. [...*Lahaina in the calm is bordered on two sides as it is surrounded by the islands; that's where one of its names comes from, Nāhonoapi'ilani, and it's as if this town has three names, it's true, only three names; Lele is its ancient name, Lahaina is a new name, and Nāhonoapi'ilani is a former name.*]" /*Ke Au Okoa*, Buke 7, Helu 28, 26 'Okakopa 1871/
7. **Variants:** Lāhainā, Lāhaina, Raheina.

1. **Entry heading.** Most common form of the place name without modern diacritical markings. This form allows for researchers to perform searches of the same form.
2. **Place name with possible modern diacritical markings.** For some entries, multiple possible forms of the same name are separated by a

forward slash (/). Because the purpose of this project was to compile place names, it did not fall upon the author to assert an authoritative version of the name.

3. **Hyphenated form.** Hyphens are inserted between each possible linguistic component of a name which lends to the overall proposed definition of the place name, or its possible forms. Multiple possible hyphenated forms are separated by a forward slash (/).

4. **Proposed definition of the place name.** The phrase "Meaning undetermined, perhaps:" is used when it's likely that there is only one spelling, but the definition is not clear, or when there can be multiple meanings to the name.

   The phrase "Pronunciation and meaning undetermined, perhaps:" is used when there are no obvious clues provided for a name as to the exact pronunciation or meaning of a place name, or when the pronunciation and meaning are indiscernible based on orthography, misspelling, origin, or unavailable context. Some spellings recovered in this project may be reflective of colloquial pronunciations, degradations, contractions, and/or elisions. Although, due to the lack of contexts, these notes reflect a good amount of conjecture, should a pattern of colloquial elision or abbreviation in place names eventually become more discernable, such knowledge may influence the naming practices of future generations of Hawaiian-language speakers.

   For entries with more than one possible form, proposed definitions are provided for each form. For entries with quotable translation sources, expanded meanings are provided. Literal translations and definition quotations come from *Place Names of Hawaii, Hawaiian Dictionary*, and/or the dictionaries of Andrews and Parker. Citations for quotations are found between two forward slashes (/___ /) at the end of the quotation. Expanded dictionary quotations are included to provide a wider context to researchers, Hawaiian-language speakers, and students. Some parts of a dictionary quotation not considered relevant to the definition of the place name have been omitted. Relevancy was determined based upon the context of topography, geography, or geology of land, area, or region; and/or to reflect contexts of available moʻolelo and/or mele.

   Bracketed notes found after a definition reflect additional information about the place name such as the preferred pronunciations of descendants of certain places; families who have the same family names as a place; or to delineate relations to related names, or variations, given for the same area.

In some instances, variants of names led to proposed definitions of a place name. An example is for the ahupuaʻa of Poelua (Kahakuloa, Kāʻanapali), which has been conjectured in other resources to possibly represent *poʻe lua*—"lua-fighting people." However, a variant of this name is "Polua (Pō + -lua)." As such, the name may represent *pō ʻelua*—"two nights."

5. **General description.** The description of the place name, and the ahupuaʻa or kalana in which it is found.

Additional information that can be found in some entries also includes:

6. **Supporting quotations and/or notes.** Selected quotations provide definition support, additional context, and/or information possibly useful to other researchers. Basic citations are found at the end of a quotation between two forward slashes (/___ /). Italicized English translations for all Hawaiian language texts are provided by the author unless otherwise noted.

7. **Place name variants.** Variants of a place name are provided to allow researchers to perform their own searches on variant spellings.

"**Variant**" entries include variations of place names that were compiled in research, but which may be misspellings, misrepresentations, or less common/uncommon forms. Variant entries may allow for expanded searches by descendants and researchers. An example of an entry for a name variant is "Haaiwo," which is found in the 1929 transcription of the Māhele indices. By following the Land Commission Award (L.C.A.) number, researching other available documents for this L.C.A., along with cross-referencing the documents for the L.C.A. of the surrounding kuleana, it was determined that "Haaiwo" is a misspelling/misrepresentation of "Kuaiwa."

Also in this section may be found versions of ahupuaʻa and ʻili names appended by "-iki (lesser)," "-ʻuʻuku (smaller)," and "-nui (main)," as well as numbers (beginning with "i/I"), which indicate that further subdivision of land units has taken place but that the subdivisions retained the original name.

Other variant forms of place names can be researched and cross-referenced as found in moʻolelo, mele, articles, publications, reports, and on maps of various origins.

PERSONAL AND PROPER NAMES FOUND IN PLACE NAMES

Some names contain identifiable personal or proper names, and have been defined accordingly. An example would be:

8 Auwaiawao
ʻAuwaiawao
ʻAuwai-a-Wao

Literally, Wao's ditch.

A ditch, and the flatland area through which it runs, in the ahupuaʻa of Kelawea, in the kalana of Lahaina....

––––––––

Variant: Auwaiowao.

Additionally, place names like Kanahā, Mauʻoni, Maluʻihi, and Kaipuʻula have been translated literally in some contemporary publications, but are actually the proper names of the people for whom these places were named. However, when supporting context is not available, place names such as these have been translated literally.

Commonly Used Abbreviations and Citations

Andrews	Andrews' *A Dictionary of the Hawaiian Language* (2003 [1865])
HD	Pukui and Elbert's *Hawaiian Dictionary* (1986)
HPN	Clark's *Hawai'i Place Names: Shores, Beaches, and Surf Sites* (2002)
(KPA)	Papakilo Database, "Māhele 'Āina Index" collection database
Land Index (HSA)	Papakilo Database, collection database
Parker	Parker's revision of *A Dictionary of the Hawaiian Language* (1922)
Place Names (ULUK)	papakilodatabase.com, collection database
PNOH	Pukui et al.'s *Place Names of Hawaii* (1974)
(SHPD)	Papakilo Database, "State Inventory of Historic Places" collection database
SOM + #	Elspeth Sterling's *Sites of Maui* [The number of each SOM reference corresponds to the entry number of the appropriate *moku* chapter. (Example: From the "Lahaina Moku" chapter of this book, "Kai-o-Haui, sea from Lahaina to Maalaea. /SOM 5/." In this citation, "/SOM 5/" refers to entry #5 in the Lahaina chapter of *Sites of Maui*.)]

Commonly Used Hawaiian Language Land Terms

The following terms are defined as they apply to the contents of this book. Expanded definitions, as may apply for other regions, can be easily found in Hawaiian-language dictionaries or in other Hawaiian land term–based publications and resources.

Moku   Primary land division of an island; district. The three moku featured within this book are Lahaina Moku, Kāʻanapali Moku, and Wailuku Moku.

Ahupuaʻa   Primary land division into which a moku is subdivided.

ʻIli   Primary land division into which an ahupuaʻa is subdivided.

ʻIli loko   An ʻili which contains, or which consists entirely of, a freshwater or brackish inland pond.

ʻIlikū   "Short for *ʻili kūpono*" /HD/; "A nearly independent *ʻili* land division within an *ahupuaʻa*, paying tribute to the ruling chief and not to the chief of the *ahupuaʻa*. Transfer of the *ahupuaʻa* from one chief to another did not include the *ʻili kūpono* located within its boundaries." /HD/

Kalana   Large land division within a moku that consists of various ahupuaʻa. Each of the three moku within this book has one kalana; they are: Lahaina Kalana (in Lahaina Moku), Kahakuloa Kalana (in Kāʻanapali Moku), and Waiehu Kalana (in Wailuku Moku).

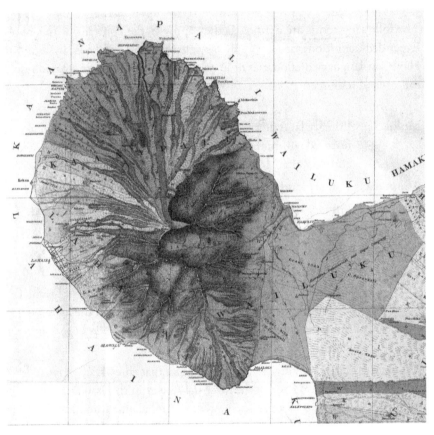

Map of Maui Komohana

CHAPTER I

MAUI KOMOHANA

'Ohu'ohu nā mauna o 'E'eka—
'A'ahu i ke kapa no'eno'e,
Kīpuni makalapua wehiwehi—
Lehua inoa hiehie wale nō.

The mountains of 'E'eka are bedecked—
Enshrouded in a finely printed mantle,
Arrayed in enfolding beauty—
Elegantly ladened with names.

na Cody Pueo Pata[1]

Maui Komohana historically came to be carved into what are the three moku of Lahaina, Kā'anapali, and Wailuku. Each of these three moku contain one kalana, several ahupua'a, and all of the smaller increments of land units of the moku system.

In the first section of this chapter will be found names for the places that unite Maui Komohana. The last section of this chapter includes place names from within this book that provide insight into variants of words once more commonly spoken in Maui Komohana.

---

1. A description of Maui Komohana, as seen upon W.D. Alexander's "Maui Hawaiian Islands" map of 1885, comparing the scripts of names, streaks, lines, and colors to a finely printed mantle of kapa.

I

1 Eeka
ʻEʻeka

"ʻEʻeka Same as ʻEka 2, a wind" /HD/; or, "ʻeka 1. nvs. Dirty, foul, fecal; filth, dirt, soil." /HD/

Name for the highest region of the mountain range of Maui Komohana. This name appears on the 1838 map drawn by Samuel P. Kalama of Lahainaluna. The term "ʻeʻeka" may refer to a personal name, or to the bog region atop Puʻu Kukui. Additionally, "ʻeʻeka" may be a reduced form of "ʻekaʻeka" which has been translated as "smoky gray, as clouds agitated by the onset of a storm...." /Nuʻuhiwa, 5 June 2021/

"Nā mauna o ʻEʻeka [*the mountains of ʻEʻeka*]" is a collective epithet for the entire mountain range. An alternative name that begins to appear more strongly in the early 1900s is "(mauna o) ʻEʻeke."

[NOTE: In 1954, the United States Board on Geographic Place Names officially decided that the names "Eke," "Eke Crater Peak," "Mauna Eeka," "Mauna o Ecka (*sic*)," "Mauna o Eeka," and "Mauna o Eka" would all be replaced by "Eke Crater."

It should be noted with ʻEke Crater at 4,449 feet in elevation, and Puʻu Kukui at 5,788 feet, there is a difference between the two of 1,339 feet in elevation.]

"No ka la Kuokoa ma Waihee Maui... I ka hiki anaʻku i ka pili o ke ao o ka la 28 o Nov, oiai au e kuu pau ae ana i na lehe ike a na maka ma ka lewa nuu o ka lani, ua hoopoluluhi ia me na ao kaalelewa, e kipu a hoolai malie mai ana no ka ua i ka lalani mauna o Eeka e hali mai ana hoi ka ohu i ka piko o Lihauanu.... [*Regarding Independence Day at Waiheʻe Maui... When we arrived at dawn on the 28th of Nov, while my eyelids strained themselves while peering into the heights of the sky, it was gloomy with drifting clouds, the rain was enfolding and gently settling upon the rows of mountains of ʻEʻeka* (ka lālani mauna o ʻEʻeka) *gathering the mists upon the top of Lihauanu....*] /Ka Nupepa Kuokoa, Buke 16, Helu 49, 8 Kēkēmapa 1877/

"Aia hoi na ao polohiwa e uhi ana ma ka piko o na mauna o Eeka, Olokui, Maunalei a me Konahuanui.... [*Clouds were covering the top of the mountains of ʻEʻeka, Olokuʻi, Maunalei and Konahuanui....*] /Ko Hawaii Pae Aina, Buke 13, Helu 31, 9 ʻAukake 1890/

"No 'na Hono a Piilani,' Maluna o ke Celaudina... Loaa mai i na lio e kai ia mai ana, motio pololei no Wailuku a hoohiki loa i ka ua-hoeha-ili o Waiehu i ka hoara [*sic*] 8 A. M. oia ka la 13 o Aperila, he oluolu no keia aina, no ke kokoke loa i na mauna o Eeka e iho mai ana ma ke alo pali me ka hui iniki i ka ili. [*Regarding 'the Bays of Piʻilani,' On Board the Claudine... We were picked up by the horses being led our way, dashed straight for Wailuku and we were brought to the Hōʻehaʻili rain of Waiehu at 8 a.m. that was on the 13th of April, this land is pleasant, because it is so close to the mountains of ʻEʻeka* (nā mauna o ʻEʻeka), *which descend along the the faces of the cliffs accompanied by chilled tingling of the skin.*]" /Ka Nupepa Kuokoa, Buke 31, Helu 19, 7 Mei 1892/

"Ma ke Kalaudina no na Wai-Eha…He mau leo hoohauoli o na kita e hoonanea ana i na paa mare me na makamaka. Ke malu ae la ke ao, ke kokolo iho la ka ohu i ke alo o na mauna o Eeka. Hoomanao ae la ka mea kakau he wahi mele i paa mau ia Maui nei, ʻAluna au o Eeka / Haa ana ka lehua i ka wai.' Hui pu hoi me ka lakou nei hoonioni i lalo pono nei o ke kumu o ka mauna. Ko ka mea kakau hoi e iho la no ia, o hanini e mai ua wai nei o Eeka. Ua ko keia halia a ka mea kakau, ua ninini io ia mai ua wai nei o luna o Eeka. Pulu pono na makamaka e nanea ana i ka lanai ahaaina…O ka mea kakau kekahi i kono ia mai e ke Kahu Kula Sabati Nui o Maui waena. He haʻohaʻo koʻu, elua Kahu Kula Sabati Nui o na Maui-waena nei. No kela aoao e pili la i ka Mauna Haleakala kekahi, no keia lehelehe e pili nei i na Mauna o Eeka kekahi. Ua kuhihewa paha au. Ea! Ae. ʻElua io no.'…Ke pepepe loa iho la ka la, ke kikoo iho la i na mauna o Eeka, hoomanao ae la ka mea kakau e haa hou mai no paha auanei ka lehua iloko o ke kiowai e kau mai la iluna o na Mauna o Eeka, a hanini hou mai no. Oiai ke halu iho la ke ao, ke kilou ae la ka opua i ke alo pali. [*The guitars had pleasant sounds causing the married couple and their guests to relax. The clouds began to cover, the mists crept across the face of the mountains of ʻEʻeka. The author recalled a certain song memorized by Maui, 'I was upon ʻEʻeka / The lehua blossoms danced upon the water.' They gathered together as they moved all the way down to the base of the mountain. What the author did was retire early, lest the water of ʻEʻeka soon pour down. The author's premonition was fulfilled, the water from upon ʻEʻeka certainly did pour forth. The guests enjoying themselves in the party pavilion were thoroughly soaked…The author was also invited by the Head Sunday School Director of central Maui. I was surprised; there are two Head Sunday School Directors of the places here called central-Maui. One from that side near Mount Haleakalā, and one from this lip near the Mountains of ʻEʻeka as well. Maybe I was wrong. But, you know what! Yes. 'Definitely two.'… The sun pressed down, the mountains of ʻEʻeka extended, the author thought that the lehua will soon dance again within the pond set up upon the Mountains of ʻEʻeka, and spill forth again. While the clouds deflate themselves, the cloud bank becomes caught upon the face of the cliff.*] / Ka Nupepa Kuokoa, Buke 38, Helu 2, 13 Ianuali 1899/*

"I ka makili ana ae o ka la a kiekie, ua piha-u ae la na kahakai i na makaainana, o ka paa no ia mai ka uluniu o Mala a hala ma kela peʻa o Olauniupoko, ke hele ala na kanaka a koliuliu, a ponalonalo, ka ua mea he hewa i ka wai ka nui o na kane, na wahine and children. I ke kiekie loa ana ae o ka la i ka hapalua like o kaupoku o ka mauna o Eeka, aia hoi, o ka wa ia i lohe ia aku ai o ka hookanikani pihe mai o ka leo o na kanaka ma naʻe mai o ka Loko o Mokuhinia. [*As the sun peered forth and ascended high, the shores were completely filled with the commoners, the area was packed from the coconut grove of Mala all the way past the boundary of ʻŌlauniupoko, the people grew into one huge mass, swarming, due to the men, women and children who overflowed like water. When the sun ascended to the middle of the roof of the mountain of ʻEʻeka, that's the time when the loud raucous of the people's voices were heard along the eastern side of the Pond of Mokuhinia.*] / Kuokoa Home Rula, Buke 10, Helu 40, 3 ʻOkakopa 1912/*

"Maui, the island next to the west, has one summit, Haleakala, exceeding 10,000 feet, (10,217,) and another, Eeka, 6130 feet…A slight subsidence of Maui would make it two distinct islands: and sinking it 5000 feet, Haleakala would still stand 5000 feet in elevation, and a sea which would be styled unfathomable would separate it from Eeka... The western peninsula consists of a mass of peaks and ridges, apparently without order or system; yet all evidently belong to a single region of igneous action. The highest point, Eeka, is 6130 feet in altitude... The proof is beyond doubt, both from tradition and topographical features, that on Maui, Hale-a-kala was in action long after Eeka, as already shown...." /Dana, 1849/

"West Maui has many sharp peaks and ridges, which are divided by deep valleys, and which, in descending towards the sea, open out and form sloping plains of considerable extent on the north and south sides; Mauna o' Eeka, the highest peak of West Maui, is only 6130 feet above the sea." /Rosser, 1870/

" 'Tis Maui's boast—unrivalled yet; / On earth its like can not be met. / Eeka caps our Maui West / Whose mists its lofty head invest. / Its pinnacles are beds of ooze / Whose treacherous mire a host may lose...." /Bailey, 1879/

"Between these mighty mountain peaks of Mauna Eeka, on West Maui, lies hidden the remarkable valley of Iao." /Newell, 1885/

"The mountain of Haleakala, House of the Sun, rose majestically before us. It is the largest extinct volcano in the world, its terminal crater being nineteen miles in circumference, its summit rising more than ten thousand feet above the level of the sea. This huge volcanic upheaval, with its spurs, slopes, and clusters of small craters, forms the entire portion of what is known as East Maui, while West Maui is a picturesque group of the Eeka Mountains. These are united by a desert strip of land, making an island about forty-eight miles long and thirty broad... From the veranda in front I caught a fine view of the Eeka Mountains, and from my window in the rear I could see the green slopes of Haleakala, and the wicked, restless ocean." /Mather, 1891/

"West Maui is composed mainly of the picturesque group of the Eeka mountains... Lahaina is thoroughly beautiful and tropical looking, with its white latticed houses peeping out from under coco palms, breadfruit, candlenut, tamarinds, mangoes, bananas, and oranges, with the brilliant green of a narrow strip of sugar-cane for a background, and above, the flushed mountains of Eeka, riven here and there by cool green chasms, rise to a height of 6000 feet... After some time the scene shifted, and through glacial rifts appeared as in a dream the Eeka mountains which enfold the Iao valley." /Bird, 1906/

"In the eastern portion of Maui the huge mass of Haleakala rises to rather over 10,000 feet; whilst Mount Eeka, in West Maui, rises in bulk to some 6,000 feet... There are some particularly wet mountains, and amongst these may be placed the high table-land of Kauai (4,000 feet) and the flat summit of Mount Eeka (6,000 feet) in West Maui. Here in a region of eternal mist we have developed a special bog-flora. Hillebrand describes the flat top of Mount Eeka as 'wrapt in a cloud of mist nearly the whole year.' " /Guppy, 1906/

Regarding an endemic sedge varietal from this region recorded by William Hillebrand in 1888, which bears the name "*Carex montis-eeka*" (with "*Carex*" denoting the sedge, and "*montis-eeka*" meaning "Eeka mountain"):

"In conversation with Rev. J.M. Lydgate I learn that the Eeka locality of Dr. Hillebrand is the point now generally known as Puu Kukui, and so recorded on the official maps. This fact is of considerable importance to the student of Hawaiian botany because the two localities have similar though slightly different floras. Eeka is given by Hillebrand as the type locality for some of his species, while in reality Puu Kukui is the place where the plants were collected. It is practically impossible to reach Eke from Puu Kukui; and I very much doubt if Hillebrand ever visited the locality. There may be some question as to whether Eke and Eeka are the same place." /(footnotes) Forbes, 1918/

Variants: Eeke, Mauna Kahalawai, West Maui Mountains.

2 Eeke
'E'eke

" 'e'eke 1. Redup. of 'eke… 'eke 2. vi. To cringe, shrink from, draw away from, flinch, wince; to become smaller, shrink." /HD/

An alternative name, which appears to have become more popular in the early 1900s, for " 'E'eka," the highest region of the mountain range also known by the superimposed name of foreign origin, "West Maui Mountains." The most common variant of this name in Native Hawaiian writings is "Mauna o 'E'eke"; During the early 1900s, " 'E'eke" also began to be used synonymously for Pu'u 'Eke in the kalana of Kahakuloa and ahupua'a of Honokōhau in the moku of Kā'anapali.

[NOTE: In 1954, the United States Board on Geographic Place Names officially decided that the names "Eke," "Eke Crater Peak," "Mauna Eeka," "Mauna o Ecka (*sic*)," "Mauna o Eeka," and "Mauna o Eka" would all be replaced by "Eke Crater."

It should also be noted that with 'Eke Crater at 4,449 feet in elevation, and Pu'u Kukui at 5,788 feet, there is a difference between the two of 1,339 feet in elevation.]

"He loa keia kula a makou e pae nei, he ihona wale no; huli papu aku la ke alo o Kalani, a me ka huakai imua, ke waiho mai la na Waieha i ka nani, nana aku o ka uliuli mai o ke ko, a me ka uluwehi o na laau, a e pu-a mai ana ka uwahi, a me ka mahu o na hale wiliko; a aia ke kiei mai la na puu, a me na lalani kuahiwi o Lihau, mauna Eeke, a o na pali o Iao ma ke kua…. [*Long was the open country upon which we mounted, only a descent; the face of the King (Kalākaua), and those journeying with him, turned forward unobstructed, the nā Wai'ehā region laid forth in beauty, we looked out over the greenness of the sugarcane, and the verdance of the plants, and the smoke rose, along with the steam of the mills; and, there the hills peered down upon us, along with the rows of mountains of Līhau, mount 'E'eke, and the cliffs of 'Īao in back….*]" /Ka Lahui Hawaii, Buke 2, Helu 3, 13 Ianuari 1876/

"I ko laua noho a kane a wahine ana, hanau mai la ka laua keiki, he keiki kane, oia ka mea nona ka moolelo a kakou e kamailio nei. Aka, i kekahi manawa, loaa iho la ka hihia ia Eeke, no ka mea, ua ike aku la o Eeke i ka wahine maikai o Puuwaiohina, no Kauaula ia, a ua hana laua i ka hewa. No ia mea, manao iho la o Lihau e umi i ke keiki, a hele pu aku no hoi i ke kalohe; a noia mea, hoopaapaa ae la laua. Lawe ae la o Eeke i ke keiki na kona makuahine e hanai, oia hoi o Maunahoomaha. Ma ia hope iho hookapu mai la ko lakou akua, o Hinaikauluau, aole e noho pu laua, aole hoi e launa aku me kekahi mea e; aka he anahulu mahope iho o keia olelo, haule hou iho la o Eeke i ka hewa, me Puuwaiohina, oia kela mea mua i hai ia ae nei, a o ko Lihau muli iho nohoi ia. No ia mea, hoopai mai la ua akua nei o lakou, a hoolilo ia o Eeke i mauna, a o Puuwaiohina hoi i kualapa, oia no kela kualapa i Kauaula e ku mai la. A aia ma ka welau o ua pali la malalo iho, he puka; ina e kani ana ua puka nei, oia iho la ka wa e pa ai ke kauaula, aole o kana mai. Mahope iho oia manawa, kupu mai ke aloha ia Lihau no ka laua kamalei; nonoi mai la ia ia Maunahoomaha, e ike mai i kana keiki. He mea oluolu ia i kona makuahonowai, a ike ia i kana keiki, alaila, oluolu kona manao. [*As they ('E'eke and Lihau) lived together as husband and wife, their child was born, a boy, he (Lāina) is the one for whom the tale about which we are talking belongs. But, at a certain time, 'E'eke became entangled in scandal, because 'E'eke saw the beautiful woman named Pu'uwaiohina, she was from Kaua'ula, and they perpetrated a sin. For this reason, Lihau thought to strangle the child, and go about in adultery as well; and for this reason, the two of them argued. 'E'eke took the child to be raised by his mother; she was Maunaho'omaha. Right after that their god, Hinaikauluau, placed restrictions upon them, the two of them were not to live together, and they were not to fornicate with anyone else; but ten days after this proclamation, 'E'eke fell again into sin, with Pu'uwaiohina; she's the one told of above, and she was indeed Lihau's younger sister. For this reason, their god punished them, and 'E'eke was changed into a mountain, and Pu'uwaiohina into a ridge; that's the ridge standing there at Kaua'ula. And there, right below the tip of this ridge, is a hole; if that hole is issuing forth a sound, that is the time when the Kaua'ula wind will blow, without limit. Right after this time, fondness welled up within Lihau for their beloved child; she requested of Maunaho'omaha to see her child. This was agreeable to her mother-in-law, and she saw her child; then, her mind was contented.*]" /Fornander, V, 535/

"Waikahe ma Maui—Na Awawa o Maalaea he Lokowai. Na ka mokuahi *Maunaloa* i lawe mai he nuhou i keia kapitala i ke kahuli ana o ke poiwai o Kulanihakoi ma ka pae mauna o Eeke, i Maui. Na keia wai i hanini mai ua halana pu ia aku la na oawa okai o Makena e ka wai a ka ua o Kulanihakoi.... [*Flood on Maui—The Gulches of Ma'alaea were Lakes. The steamship* Maunaloa *brought news to this capital about the overturning of the basin of Kūlanihāko'i on the mountain range of 'E'eke (pae mauna o Eeke), on Maui. This water poured forth and the lowland gulches of Mākena were flooded with the rainwater of Kūlanihāko'i....*]" /*Ka Nupepa Kuokoa*, Buke 40, Helu 20, 16 Mei 1902/

"Mahope iho o ka hookuu ana ae o Keoni Bulu ia Hanale, ia manawa i kani kikiko'u mai ai kela manu kamahao o na lalani mauna o Oolokui [*sic*], a hoonanea ae la na keonimana ame na lede i ke kani ana a ua manu nei. I ka hooki ana ae hoi o ua manu nei i kana kani ana, ia wa i kani hoehoene mai ai na oo hulu melemele o na lalani mauna o Eeke. I ko laua hooki ana ae hoi.... [*After John Bull released Henry (fullness replaced hunger), at that time that marvelous bird of the rows of mountains of Oloku'i sang with deep-toned resonance, and the gentlemen and ladies enjoyed the singing of this bird. As this bird finished his singing, it was then that the yellow-featherd ʻōʻō birds of the rows of mountains of ʻEʻeke sang forth sweetly. As they finished....*]" /*Ka Nupepa Kuokoa*, Buke 56, Helu 48, 29 Nowemapa 1918/

"Iao Valley back of Wailuku town and the Koolau gulches offer tropical scenery that cannot be surpassed. Mount Eeke, at the western end, is nearly 6,000 feet high, while Haleakala at the eastern end raises its dome 10,3000 feet above the sea...." /*The Maui News*, 18 July 1903/

Variants: Eeka, Mauna Kahalawai, West Maui Mountains.

3 Kahoolewa
Kahoʻolewa
Ka-hoʻo-lewa

Literally, the hoʻolewa ("Hoolewa 1. To cause to swing; to vibrate; to float in the air. 2. To lift up and carry, as between two persons; to carry in a manele or palanquin. 3. To carry a corpse in a funeral procession. 4. To cause a swinging or rotary motion, as in certain forms of dancing." /Parker, 172/).

———

Ridge which serves as a partial boundary between the moku of Lahaina, Kāʻanapali, and Wailuku.

In the moku of Lahaina, Kahoʻolewa separates the ahupuaʻa of Panaʻewa and Paʻūnāʻū in the kalana of Lahaina from the back of ʻĪao Valley [Wailuku].

In the moku of Kāʻanapali, Kahoʻolewa serves as the uppermost boundary for the most of the moku with the exception of the kalana of Kahakuloa which terminates in the ʻEke region.

For the moku of Wailuku, Kahoʻolewa separates the inland regions of the ahupuaʻa of Wailuku from portions of the two moku of Lahaina and Kāʻanapali.

Mispronunciation of the name "Kahoʻolewa" has been conjectured to be the source of the "Kahālāwai" in "Mauna Kahālāwai."

4 Maui Komohana

Literally, West Maui.

———

Term used for the three moku surrounding nā mauna o ʻEʻeka: Lahaina, Kāʻanapali, and Wailuku. However, in more recent times, this term has been used in reference the lands of the entire moku of Lahaina, and the western portion of the moku of Kāʻanapali to the ahupuaʻa of Honokōhau.

———

"He hauoli koʻu, no ka mea, ua lohe mai nei au, i keia la, ua hoomakaia ka hana ana i keia alanui, ma ka hana aupuni. E hooikaika oukou, e ko Maui Hikina, a ko loa keia hana. Ko Maui Komohana alanui koe, mai Ukumehame a Kamaalaea; i keia manawa, he ino loa ke alanui. [*I am glad because I just heard today that the work on this road has begun, as government work. Work hard, all of you of East Maui, until this task is completed. All that's left to be done for West Maui's road is from Ukumehame to Kamā'alaea; at this time, the road is very bad.*]" /*Ka Elele Hawaii*, Buke 1, Helu 3, 6 Mei 1844/

"E ike auanei oukou a pau e na kanaka ke nana mai i keia Olelo Hoolaha, owau o ka mea nona ka inoa malalo nei, no kuu Kuleana Aina nona ka inoa i kapaia o Pohakuo-kauhi, ma Wailuku, Maui Komohana, nona ka Helu 3360, ma ka Palapala Sila Nui, ua lilo loa ia'u ma ke ano Alodio.... [*Know all who are looking at this Announcement, I, the one to whom belongs the name below, regarding my Land Property to which belongs the name called Pōhakuokauhi, in Wailuku, West Maui, to which belongs the number 3360 in the Royal Patent Documents, it has become totally mine in the form of Alodial title....*]" /*Ka Nupepa Kuokoa*, Buke 1, Helu 47, 18 'Okakopa 1862/

"O na wahi haiki o ka aina kokoke moku i ke kai, ua kapaia he puali, elike me ka puali o Kamaomao mawaena o Maui Hikina ame Maui Komohana, ame ka puali o Panama e eli ia mai la a moku a lilo aku i kowa pookela no ka honua nei.... [*The narrow places which are almost separated by the sea are called isthmuses, like the isthmus of Kama'oma'o between East Maui and West Maui, and the isthmus of Panama being dug today until it breaks through and becomes the best channel for the world....*]" /*Ka Lanakila*, Buke 1, Helu 8, 2 Kepakemapa 1909/

5 Mauna Eeka
See Eeka.

6 Mauna Eeke
See Eeka & Eeke.

7 Mauna Kahalawai
Mauna Kahālāwai
Mauna Kahālāwai / Mauna Ka-hālāwai

Literally, Kahālāwai Mountain/The meeting mountain.

———————

Name in common usage for the mountain range also known as "(nā Mauna o) 'E'eka," "(nā Mauna o) 'E'eke," or by the superimposed name of foreign origin "West Maui Mountains." The name "Mauna Kahālāwai" may have originated from, or become popularized by, Maui author Barbara Lyons in the 1950s. This name has also been con-jectured to be a misrepresentation of Kaho'olewa Ridge.

———————

"Long ago there lived in Kahakuloa Valley a brother and sister. Their home was near the tip of that section of Mauna Kahalawai that lies like an arm flung out upon the water. Kahalawai stood for 'the junction between heaven and earth,' and was the ancient name for what we now call the West Maui Mountains.... Kaili and Nailima lost no time. Bidding

Pueo a grateful farewell, they set out for the far reaches of Mauna Kahalawai. Before the men had returned, in anger at having been fooled, the children were well on the way to a safe hiding place in a remote valley." /Lyons, *The Honolulu Advertiser*, 4 August 1957/

"'Iao Valley is centrally situated in the Mauna Kahalawai range of mountains, now called West Maui, over looking the County Seat of Wailuku town and the Central Maui plain and facing majestic Mauna Haleakala, House of the Sun, on East Maui. Facing 'Iao at its entrance, Mauna Ka-ne is to the right and Mauna Leo is to the left of the highway." /Ashdown, *Honolulu Star-Bulletin*, 24 July 1960/

"Slowly she [Pele] turned and walked up the steep grade of the mountain on whose slopes the volcanic cone, Pu'u Laina, stood. This was Mauna Kahalawai, the Meeting Place between Heaven and Earth—a range of towering peaks, and valleys with sheer ridged walls on which grew the pale-leafed kukui tree and the silvery koa." /Lyons, 1973/

"55. Mauna Kahalawai (Lyons 1962:19). Probably a variant spelling of Kano'olewa [*sic*] Ridge in *Atlas*." /(footnotes) Nimmo, 1987/

Variants: Eeka, Eeke, Mauna Kahalewai, West Maui Mountains.

8 Mauna Kahalewai

See Mauna Kahalawai.

9 Nalowale

"nalo.wale. vs. Lost, gone, forgotten, vanished, missing, hidden, extinct, disappeared (especially if unaccountably so)." /HD/

———

Name assigned to several archaeological sites in Maui Komohana for which the original names have been lost (nalowale).

10 Puali Komohana
Pū'ali Komohana

Literally, west side (of the) isthmus.

———

Collective epithet for the region on the western side of the central isthmus of Maui.

Some confusion may exist over this term based on Māhele records that place Waiehu and Waihe'e (of the moku of Wailuku) in Pū'ali Komohana.

———

"A no ka lilo ana o Kaleihaohia ke kahu nana e hanai ke keiki, a nana hoi e malama i ka manawa uuku; a nolaila, ua hoakaawale [*sic*] ia ka puali Hikina o Maui, no ka mea, o Kaleihaohia, oia iho la no ka Haku aina nona o Maui Hikina; a o ka puali Komohana hoi o Maui, oia no ka puali i koe ia Kakaalaneo a me kona mau alii a pau. [*Since Kalei-haohia* (Kālaihaohia) *became the guardian who would raise the child, and who would care for him while small, the east-side-of-the-isthmus region of Maui was separated because Kaleihaohia was the Lord to whom belonged East Maui; and the west-side-of-the-isthmus region of Maui, that was the side left to Kāka'alaneo and all of his chiefs under him.*]" / *Ka Nupepa Kuokoa*, Helu 2, Buke 41, 10 'Okakopa 1863/

"Ua poai puni ia ka puali Hikina o Maui, e na halekuai o na kanaka maoli, ke ku hoolai nei ma Honuaula, ma Kula, ma Makawao, ma Koolau, ma Hana, a ma Kaupo hoi. Ma ka puali Komohana, ke hoala nei, ma Waikapu a me Wailuku, o ke aiwa loa aku ia, no ka mea, aia mailaila na lua gula a na kanaka e eli nei, ua kukulu ia keia mau halekuai malalo o ke kumu manao 'Lokahi.' [*The east-side-of-the-isthmus region of Maui is completely encircled by the stores owned by Native Hawaiians; they are standing peacefully in Honua'ula, in Kula, in Makawao, in Ko'olau, in Hāna, and in Kaupō. On the west-side-of-the-isthmus region of Maui, they are rising, in Waikapū and in Wailuku; it's truly fantastic, because that's where the gold mines are that the people are digging; these stores were built under the value of 'Unity.'*]" / *Ke Au Okoa*, Buke 1, Helu 44, 19 Pepeluali 1866/

"Wi ma Kahakuloa.—He nui ka wi ma keia awawa, o ka Puali komohana o Maui nei i keia mau la; ke hahana loa nei ka wi; ke *uouo* nei na kama'ina no ka pololi. [*Famine at Kahakuloa.—There is a great famine in this valley, on the west-side-of-the-Isthmus region here on Maui these days; the famine is very intense; the residents cry out due to hunger.*]" / *Ka Nupepa Kuokoa*, Buke 6, Helu 8, 23 Pepeluali 1867/

"E halawai ana ka Ahahui Kula Sabati o Maui Komohana, ma ka luakini o Honokōhau, ke hiki aku i ka Poaono mua o Aperila 5, 1890, e makaala ae na Kula Sabati Apana, na Hope, na Kumu Papa, ke Kahu Kula Sabati nui, a me na Kahu Ekalesia o ia puali komohana. I laila oukou e lohe ae ai i ka oukou pane no ka hoopau ana aku i na pilikia i koe o kela hoike nui o ka la 1 o Ianuari i hala ma Wainee, Lahaina, malu i ka ulu. [*The Sunday School Association of West Maui is going to meet at the church of Honokōhau when we come to the first Saturday, April 5, 1890; the District Sunday Schools, the Assistants, the Class Teachers, the head Sunday School Supervisor, and the Church Pastors of that west-side-of-the-isthmus region will be ready. That is where you all will hear your response regarding the remaining issues of that big performance of the 1st of this past January at Waine'e, Lahaina, shaded by the breadfruit trees.*]" / *Ka Nupepa Kuokoa*, Buke 29, Helu 12, 22 Malaki 1890/

"Auwe kuu aloha e—a ke hoomanao poina ole nei au i ka ihona o Puuhele, e pii aku ai a hiki i Monowainui [*sic*], i ka pali o Aalaloloa, ka helena aku a Papalaau e hiki aku ai i Ukumehame, ka helena o Olowalu a hiki aku i Launiupoko, hoea aku i ka Malu Ulu o Lele i ka lepo ula o Lahaina, aloha wale ia wahi a maua e pili ai. Ua kaapuni ia e maua ka puali komohana o Maui. Aloha no kuu hoapili, luuluu wale.... [*Alas my beloved ē—I am recalling without forgetting the descent of Pu'uhele, to ascend until Manawainui, along the cliffs of 'A'alaloloa, going until Papalā'au to arrive at Ukumehame, traveling through Olowalu to arrive at Launiupoko, arriving at the Breadfruit Shade of Lele amidst the red dirt of Lahaina, fond memories of the place where we were together. The west-side-of-the-isthmus region of Maui was encircled by us and our travels. Affections for my beloved companion, truly bereaved....*]" / *Ke Aloha Aina*, Buke 7, Helu 34, 24 'Aukake 1901/

Variants: Maui Komohana, West Maui.

11 Puu Kukui

Pu'u Kukui

Meaning undetermined, perhaps: light hill, candlenut hill, or, Kukui (star) hill.

Highest peak (5,788 feet) of nā Mauna o 'E'eka.

"DIMENSIONS OF IAO VALLEY, MAUI. Length (from Wailuku), about 5 miles. Width of valley, 2 miles. Depth, near head, 4,000 feet. Elevation of Puu Kukui, above head of Valley, 5,788 feet. Elevation of Crater of Eke, above Waihee Valley, 4,500 feet." /Thrum, 1912/

"In conversation with Rev. J.M. Lydgate I learn that the Eeka locality of Dr. Hillebrand is the point now generally known as Puu Kukui, and so recorded on the official maps. This fact is of considerable importance to the student of Hawaiian botany because the two localities have similar though slightly different floras. Eeka is given by Hillebrand as the type locality for some of his species, while in reality Puu Kukui is the place where the plants were collected. It is practically impossible to reach Eke from Puu Kukui; and I very much doubt if Hillebrand ever visited the locality. There may be some question as to whether Eke and Eeka are the same place." /(footnote p. 55) Forbes, 1918/

"Some ruthless people have drained the bog of Puukukui on West Maui, by the method known as 'Louisiana drain' which will change the entire vegetation of that mountain summit and will gradually denude its slopes of the existing tree growth, through rapid erosion which must ensue sooner or later, as the water which under normal condition was absorbed by the vegetation at the summit, is carried off at once in torrents. Such actions on the part of the ruthless ignoramuses should be curbed at all events." /Rock, 1919/

"Eia mai na puu o ka Moku o Kama ponoi iho, Puu Kukui Wailuku, Puu Nianiau Makawao, Puu Ouli Nuu, Puu Olai Makena, Puu o Kali Keokea, aia mahea iho o Puu Koae? [*Here are the Island of Kama's very own hills, Pu'u Kukui Wailuku, Pu'uni'ani'au Makawao, Pu'u 'Ōuli Nu'u, Pu'u Ōla'i Mākena, Pu'u o Kali Keōkea; where is Pu'u Koa'e?*]" /Ka Hoku o Hawaii, Buke 40, Helu 10, 4 Iulai 1945/

12 West Maui

Superimposed name of foreign origin for Maui Komohana and Pū'ali Komohana. *See also*: Maui Komohana & Puali Komohana.

13 West Maui Mountains

Superimposed name of foreign origin for 'E'eka, 'E'eke, and Mauna Kahālāwai. *See also*: Eeka, Eeke, & Mauna Kahalawai.

REGIONAL VOCABULARY PREFERENCES OF MAUI KOMOHANA

Place names not only transmit information of the cultural and historical heritage of a place, but they may also provide insight on the regional vocabulary preferences favored by the people of that place.

Following the renaissance and resurgence of the Hawaiian language, efforts began by which to teach and spread the Hawaiian language through formal standardized systems. These systems have resulted in the successful revitalization of a language once considered to be on the brink of extinction. Understandably, distinct regional varieties of language, pronunciation, and preferences in vocabulary are often not prioritized or thoroughly addressed in these efforts. As such, regional varieties of the Hawaiian language have become increasingly rare amongst the generations of students whose Hawaiian-language speaking abilities did not stem directly from mānaleo transmission.

The following is a brief listing of place names compiled through this project, which provides a glimpse into some of the regional vocabulary preferences of Maui Komohana.

14 *ehu* ("ke ehu" vs. "ka 'ehu")
Kēhu
Ke-ehu

Literally, the sea spray.

_____

Famed surf area in the ahupuaʻa of Wailuku.

This name provides attestation for the usage of the article "ke" before the word "ehu," along with evidence of a regional preference for "ehu" versus "ʻehu."

However, "ka ʻehu" is also attested in the same region:

Kaehu
Kaʻehu
Ka-ʻehu

Literally, the spray (of the sea).

_____

Name listed as a shoreline region of the ahupuaʻa of Waiehu, kalana of Waiehu. Perhaps short for "Kaʻehu a ka Mōʻī." *See also*: Kaehu a ka Moi (*"Wailuku Moku"*).

Variants: Kaehu Beach, Kaehu Bay, Kaʻehu Bay.

15 *emi* ("ka 'emi" vs. "ke emi")
Kaemi
Ka-'emi

"*Lit.*, the ebbing." /PNOH/

An islet in the ahupua'a of Makaliua (1), kalana of Kahakuloa.

This name provides attestation for the usage of the article "ka" before the word "emi." Although both "ka" and "ke" are acceptable, "ke" has become more common in modern times. As pointed out by the Hawaiian language editor of this book, F. Ka'iuokalani Damas, the article "ka" may also indicate the presence of a preceding 'okina ('emi).

16 *kauila / kauwila* ("kauila/kauwila" vs. "o'a")
Kauila / Kauwila

Literally, Colubrina oppositifolia (endemic tree), or *Alphitonia ponderosa* (endemic tree).

This word is present in the place names:

Kauila (Honolua & Hononana, Kā'anapali); Kauwila (Waiehu, Wailuku); Kapahukauwila (Waihe'e, Wailuku); and Pahukauila (Mailepai, Kā'anapali).

In these place names, it is not entirely clear whether or not "kauila/kauwila" refers to the tree, to lightning (*ka uila*), or to the *kauila* ceremony. However, the two forms containing the word "pahu (stake/pole)" may lend more clarity in discerning the intention of the name.

An entry in *Hawaiian Dictionary* reads: "o'a n. . . . 3. Maui name for kauila (*Colubrina oppositifolia*), a tree."

As such, the *kauila/kauwila* mentioned in the place names listed above may refer to the *Alphitonia ponderosa* variety of *kauila/kauwila*.

For perspective, there is also the place name "Keo'a (Ke-o'a)" found in the ahupua'a of Honokeana (Kā'anapali). However, due to lack of context, it is uncertain whether or not "o'a" means "rafter," "fish gill," "eel mouth," or the tree "*Colubrina oppositifolia*."

17 *kuhe* ("kuhe" vs. "'ōkuhe")
Punauekuhe
Pūnauekuhe
Pūnaue-kuhe

Literally, to divide shares of *kuhe* goby fish.

'Ili in the ahupua'a of Kahakuloa, kalana of Kahakuloa.

This name provides attestation for the usage of "kuhe" instead of "'ōkuhe" for the endemic *Eleotris sandwicensis* (goby fish).

18 *limalau* ("limalau" vs. "laulima")

Limalau

"lima.lau same as laulima, but some persons limit limalau cooperation to canoe and house building." /HD/

——————

Gulch in the ahupuaʻa of Honokōwai that joins Pālaha Gulch.

This name provides attestation for the usage of "limalau," although the context is not ascertainable.

19 *mākila* ("mākila" vs. "mānai")

Makila

Mākila

"mā.kila. nvt. Maui name for mānai, needle; to string, as leis." /HD/

——————

Ahupuaʻa in the kalana of Lahaina. Also, a shoreline point now known as "Puamana Beach," a reservoir, and a ditch in the same vicinity.

This name provides evidence for the assertion in *Hawaiian Dictionary* that "mākila" is a term used at least in the moku of Lahaina in Maui Komohana.

20 *māniania* ("māniania" vs. "mānienie")

Maniania

Māniania

Literally, "redup. of mania 1. nvi. Shuddering sensation as on looking down a great height, or hearing a saw filed; dizziness; dizzy; to shudder; to be contracted." /HD, 238/

——————

ʻIlikū in the ahupuaʻa of Wailuku.

This name provides attestation for the usage for the term "māniania" instead of "mānienie" to refer to the "shuddering sensation as on looking down a great height." Although "Manienie" was found as a rare variant for this place name, "Maniania" was much more common amongst Hawaiian language and English resources. This term is also common amongst kūpuna of the region to this day.

The shortened form, "mania," is also present in place names from other parts of Maui. For this reason, the place name of Mānienie (Honokōhau, Kāʻanapali) may most likely refer to either the *mānienie* grasses, or to mean "bare, barren."

21 *pohale* ("pohale" vs. "poale")
Pohale

"PO-HA-LE v. *See* POALE, h inserted. To be very full of waves; to be open on top, as a rough sea" /Andrews/, and "Deep, open, as a hole or sore...." /HD/

A fishing ground in the ahupua'a of Kahana.

This name provides attestation for the usage of "pohale" instead of "poale."

22 *nu'ukole* ("nu'ukole" vs. "'alamo'o," "hi'ukole," "hi'u'ula")
Waianuukole
Waianu'ukole
Wai-a-nu'ukole

Literally, water of the *nu'ukole* goby fish.

Dry stream bed in the ahupua'a of Polanui, kalana of Lahaina.

This name provides attestation for the usage of "nu'ukole" for the *Len tipes concolor* species of goby fish instead of the terms "'alamo'o," "hi'ukole," or "hi'u'ula" used elsewhere.

23 *nuku* ("nuku" vs. "waha")
Kanukuokeana
Ka-nuku-o-ke-ana

Literally, the entrance of the cave.

'Ili in the ahupua'a of Waiokila, kalana of Kahakuloa.

This name provides attestation for the usage of "nuku" instead of "waha" for the "mouth/ entrance" of caves.

24 *piele* ("piele" vs. "kālepa")
Kahakapiele
Ka-haka-piele

Literally, the peddler's rack.

'Ili in the ahupua'a of Ahikuli, kalana of Waiehu.

This name provides attestation for the usage of "piele" instead of "kālepa" in reference to peddling and trading.

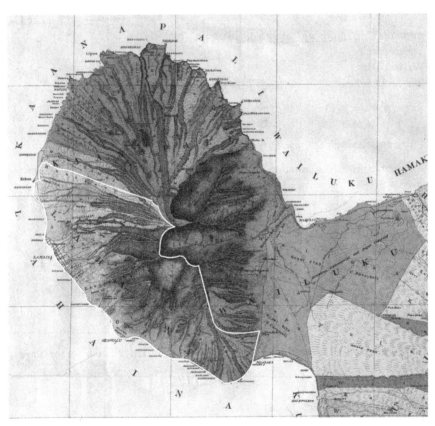

Map of Lahaina Moku

CHAPTER 2

LAHAINA MOKU

Wahī 'ahu'ula 'o Lahaina—
Kau welowelo lā i nā pali,
Papa 'uo nōweo kini kohu—
Kumu hu'a pa'a pono lā i kai.

The district of Lahaina is swathed in a feathered cape—
Draped fluttering along the cliffs,
Fine-looking panel of bright feather clusters—
Firmly secured hem falling along the shoreline.

na Cody Pueo Pata[1]

1 Aaka

'A'aka

"'a'aka. 1. vs. Surly, cranky, roiled, complaining, irritable, peevish, bad tempered, cantankerous, cross; severe, as labor. . . 2. vs. Dry, as coral of the reef at low tide; parched, wrinkled, dry and thirsty; peeling off, as the tough skin of such fish as the humuhumu after it has been in the fire; to crackle, burst, as a ripe melon. 3. n. Rocky undersea cavern (PH 219, Malo 26). 4. n. Wood of the naio, bastard sandalwood." /HD/

"Ancient surfing area, Lahaina, Maui." /PNOH/

"A ua hai maikai mai la ka nalu o na kulana heenalu, oia hoi o Uo, ka nalu kaulana i ka haihaimaka o Aaka a me Hauola, aia laua ma kela a me keia aoao o Keawaiki. . . . [*And the wave for surfing broke finely, it was 'Uo, 'A'aka and Hauola are the surfs famous for breaking roughly; they are there on either side of Keawaiki. . . .*]" /Ke Au Okoa, Buke 7, Helu 28, 26 'Okakopa 1871/

---

1. A description of the appearance of the Moku of Lahaina comparing the shape of the district with that of a regal 'ahu'ula.

17

2 Aalaloloa
'A'alaloloa
'A'ala-loloa

Literally, very fragrant.

Ridge, cliff, and trail that joins the windward and leeward sides of the ahupua'a of Ukumehame. Also, "'A'ala Loloa. n. Wind name." /HD/

"He wahine ui io maoli no keia. Aohe lua e loaa ai kona ui ma Maui a puni, koe wale o Waialohiikalauakolea, ke aliiwahine i hanaiia iluna o ka piko o ke kuahiwi o Haleakala. O keia kaikamahine hoi o Lihau, oia ke kaikamahine a Pa'upa'u ame Aalaloloa, he mau alii nui no na kuahiwi o Maui komohana; a he mau kupua nohoi laua ma kekahi ano. A he ohana lakou mailoko mai o Lihau-ula, kekahi hoahanau o Wakea. He mau keiki keia na Kahikoluamea (k) ame Kupulanakehau (w). A mamuli o Lihau ula ka hoahanau o Wakea i heaia ai keia kaikamahine o Lihau. [*This was truly an exceedingly beautiful woman. Her beauty was unmatched around Maui, except for that of Wai'alohiikalau'ākōlea, the princess who was raised upon the peak of the mountain of Haleakalā. As for this girl Līhau, she was the daughter of Pa'upa'u and 'A'alaloloa, chiefs of the mountains of Maui Komohana; and these two were also demigods of sorts. And they were all family from within the line of Līhau'ula, a sibling of Wākea. They were children of Kahikoluamea (m) and Kupulanakēhau (f). It was after Līhau'ula, the sibling of Wākea, that this girl was called Līhau.*]" /*Ka Na'i Aupuni*, Buke 3, Helu 115, 10 Iune 1907/

Variants: Pali 'A'alalolaua [*sic*], Kealaloloa [*sic*] Ridge.

3 Ahikuli
Ahi-kuli

Literally, noisy fire.

'Ili in the ahupua'a of Māla, kalana of Lahaina.

4 Aimakalepo
'Aimakalepo
'Ai-ma-ka-lepo

Literally, eating on the dirt.

Pond found just inland of the shore in the ahupua'a of Moali'i, kalana of Lahaina.

Variant: Loko Aimakalepo.

5 Akau
'Ākau

Literally, right (side), north.

_____

'Ili in the ahupua'a of Kōpili, kalana of Lahaina.

6 Aki
'Aki

" 'aki. 1. nvt. To take a nip and let go, snap; to nibble, as fish; to bite off the bark of sugar cane to heal, as a wound; to scar over; sharp recurring pain, as in head or stomach...2. n. Height, tip, top (preceded by ke)...3. n. Pillow. 4. n. Block on which a canoe is placed on the shore...5. vs. Filled, as a canoe with waves. 6. Same as 'aki'aki 2, a rush." /HD/

_____

Ahupua'a in the kalana of Lahaina.

Variants: Akinui, Aki 2, Aki Uuku.

7 Akiaiole
See Akiakaiole.

8 Akiaole
See Akiakaiole.

9 Akiakaiole
'Akiaka'iole
'Aki-a-ka-'iole

Literally, nibbling of the rat.

_____

'Ili in the ahupua'a of 'Aki, kalana of Lahaina.

Variants: Akiaole, Akiaiole.

10 Akinui
See 'Aki.

11 Aki Uuku
See 'Aki.

12 Alamihi
'Alamihi

" 'ala.mihi. n. A common black crab (*Metopograpsus thukuhar*)." /HD/

Ahupua'a near the area of Māla, kalana of Lahaina.

Formerly site of pond, Loko 'Alamihi, famed for mullet.

Variant: Alanuhi.

13 Alanuikikeekee a Maui
Alanuikīke'eke'e a Māui
Alanui-kīke'eke'e a Māui

Literally, zigzagging road of Māui.

An ancient trail in the ahupua'a of Hanaka'ō'ō, kalana of Lahaina, found just inland of Pu'u Keka'a (Kā'anapali), that is attributed to the demigod Māui.

"An ancient trail connecting Keka'a Point and Ka-hakuloa, West Maui; only the two ends are visible." /Place Names (ULUK)/

14 Alio
'Ālī'ō
'Ā-lī'ō

Pronunciation and meaning undetermined, perhaps: "ā- + li'o—'Alio (ā'-li-o'): to scream...." /Parker/

'Ili in the ahupua'a of Kaua'ula, kalana of Lahaina.

15 Anapenape
'Ānapenape

Word unattested in the dictionaries, perhaps: 'ānapenape ('ā- + napenape), to flutter rapidly.

'Ili in the ahupua'a of Pāhoa, kalana of Lahaina.

16 Anapuka
Ana-puka

Literally, tunnel.

Cave located just mauka of Pu'u Lāina, ahupua'a of Wahikuli, kalana of Lahaina.

17 Anehe
See Kai o Anehe.

18 Anehenehe
'Ānehenehe

"ā.nehe.nehe Redup. of ānehe"; "ā.nehe. vi. To come upon quietly, move stealthily, poise" /HD/; "A-NE-HE v. To be on the alert; ready for a start, as a cat for a mouse; as a bird to fly. 2. To be ready to seize upon a person or thing when circumstances require." /Andrews/

[NOTE: In online database searches, "ka anehenehe" returned more hits than "ke anehenehe." As such, it is likely that "anehenehe" is represented as " 'ānehenehe" in native speech.]

———————

Shoreline point in the ahupua'a of Ukumehame. 'Ānehenehe is contemporarily called by the superimposed name of foreign origin "McGregor Point," and is the site of the McGregor Point Lighthouse.

19 Anu
See Pu'u Anu.

20 Apaa
'Āpa'a

Literally, dry/arid area.

———————

'Ili in the ahupua'a of Kaua'ula, kalana of Lahaina.

21 Apahua
'Āpahua

Pronunciation and meaning undetermined, perhaps: 'āpahua ('āpahu + -a), cut/chopped squarely off.

———————

Heiau in the ahupua'a of Ku'ia, kalana of Lahaina, said to have been constructed by Hua-nui-kālailai (a.k.a. Hua-nui-i-ka-lā-la'ila'i).

———————

" 'Apahua. Wainee, Lahaina. Credited to Hua-nui, about 50 years later than [Waiie]; fragments of foundation only remain (Thrum). 'Walker Site 8. Cane fields above Wainee. Totally destroyed.' (Sterling)" /Place Names (ULUK)/

22 Apuakaio
'Apuakaiao

Pronunciation and meaning undetermined, perhaps: 'Apu-a-kaiao, medicine or *'awa* taken at dawn, or, coconut shell cup belonging to Kaiao.

Lo'i in the area of Pā Pelekāne, in the ahupua'a of Pa'ūnā'ū, kalana of Lahaina.

Variants: Apukaiao, Kapukaiao.

23 Auau
'Au'au

Literally, to bathe.

Channel between Maui and Lāna'i.

24 Aupokopoko
'Aupokopoko
'Au-pokopoko

Literally, short stalk/shaft/handle.

Ahupua'a in the kalana of Lahaina.

25 Auwaiawao
'Auwaiawao
'Auwai-a-Wao

Literally, Wao's ditch.

A ditch, and the flatland area through which it runs, in the ahupua'a of Kelawea, in the kalana of Lahaina.

"No ka nui o ka ai. Ua nui ka ai ma keia kula, ua ai a ukauka na waha o makou. Eia na inoa o na papaaina o makou, o Pohakunui, no ke ku ana o kekahi pohaku nui i kahi a makou i mahiai ai, oia ka mea i kapaia'i ka inoa oia papaaina. O Auwaiawao ka inoa o kekahi papaaina, no ka pili no o ko makou auwai, me ko Awao, oia ka mea i kapaia'i ka inoa oia papaaina. O Kapauma ka inoa o kekahi papaaina, no ke kukulu ia ana o kekahi pauma wai mamua malaila, oia ka mea i kapaia'i ka inoa oia papaaina. O Kumuwi ka inoa o kekahi papaaina, no ka ulu ana o kekahi kumu wi malaila, oia ka mea i kapaia'i ka inoa oia papaaina, pela i kapaia'i ka inoa pakahi e makou no. [*Regarding the amount of poi. There was a lot of poi at this school; we ate until our mouths smacked noisily. Here are the names of our dining tables: Pōhakunui, because of a large stone standing at the place where we farmed, that's why the table was named that way. 'Auwaiawao is the name of another dining table, because of how our ditch was close to that of Awao, that's how that table was named. Kapauma is the name of another dining table, because a water pump was constructed there before, that's how that table was named. Kumuwī is the name of another table, because a wī (tamarind tree) grew there, that's how that table was named; that's how each name was given by us.*]" /*Ka Nupepa Kuokoa*, Buke 11, Helu 41, 12 'Okakopa 1872/

Variant: Auwaiowao.

26 Auwaimalino

'Auwaimalino

'Auwai-malino

Literally, calm canal/ditch.

'Ili in the ahupua'a of Kelawea, kalana of Lahaina.

27 Auwaiowao

See Auwaiawao.

28 Awalau

'Awalau

'Awa-lau

" 'awa lau. n. A young kava plant (root, stem, and leaves) used as an offering to the gods." /HD/

'Ili in the ahupua'a of Moali'i, in the kalana of Lahaina.

29 Awalua

Awa-lua

Literally, double harbor.

Shoreline region in the ahupua'a of Launiupoko.

30 Aweoweoluna

'Āweoweoluna

'Āweoweo-luna

Literally, upper 'āweoweo (" 'ā.weo.weo. n. 1. Various Hawaiian species of *Priacanthus*, red fishes, sometimes called bigeye . . . 2. A variety of sugar cane named for the fish. 3. Same as 'āheahea [*Chenopodium oahuense*]. 4. A seaweed." /HD/)

'Ilikū in the ahupua'a of Ukumehame.

Variant: Auweoweoluna.

31 **Ball Mountain**
See Paupau.

32 **Banyan Tree Park**

Also known as Lahaina Banyan Court Park, and Lahaina Courthouse Square. *See also*: Papu o Lahaina.

33 **Belekane, Beretane, Beretania**
See Pa Pelekane.

34 **Breakwalls**
See Keawaiki, Uo, & Aaka.

35 **Crater**
See Puulaina.

36 **Crater Camp**
See Puʻulāina.

37 **Eleluli**
ʻEleluli
ʻEle-luli

Meaning and pronunciation undetermined, perhaps short for: ʻeleʻele luli, swaying ʻeleʻele taro; or, a colloquial elision of: ʻale luli—swaying ripples.

———————

ʻIli in the ahupuaʻa of Kaulalo, in the kalana of Lahaina.

38 **Haai**
Hāʻai
Hā-ʻai

"Haai (hă-aʻi): edible taro stalks." /Parker/

———————

ʻIli in in the ahupuaʻa of Ukumehame.

39 **Hahakea**
Hāhākea
Hāhā-kea

"Perhaps *lit.*, white stalk." /PNOH/

———————

Ahupuaʻa and gulch in the kalana of Lahaina.

40 Halaaniani

Hala-aniani

Literally, waving pandanus.

A ditch perhaps once found in an area north of the present Lahainaluna Road.

41 Halakaa

Halaka'a

Hala-ka'a

"Probably *lit.*, rolling pandanus." /PNOH/

Ahupua'a in the kalana of Lahaina. Once site of the heiau Halekumukalani.

Variant: Halekaa.

42 Hale Aloha

Literally, Mercy House.

Structure built over the years of 1855–1858, becoming the first stone church built in the Waine'e area in the kalana of Lahaina.

"Rich in History, within a short distance of Lahaina's center, are to be found such points of interest as Hale Aloha, the first stone church built in Lahaina, and reputed to be the first stone church built in the Territory." /Ashdown, *The Honolulu Advertiser*, 1 March 1959/

43 Halehuki

Hale-huki

Literally, hoisted house.

Iron-roofed building built for the ali'i just makai of Mōkuhinia, in the ahupua'a of Waine'e, in the kalana of Lahaina. Alternative name for Halepiula.

Variants: Halehuku [*sic*], Halepiula, Halipiula, Palace.

44 Halekaa

See Halakaa.

45 Halekamani
Hale-kamani

Literally, kamani-tree house.

———————

Lot in Lua'ehu, just makai of the pond of Ho'olili, where once stood the royal pili grass house of Nāhi'ena'ena, and where she erected the first tomb for her mother, Keōpūolani.

Variant: Pa Hale Kamani (*literally*, kamani tree house lot).

46 Halekumukalani
Hale-kumu-ka-lani

Literally, house of the establishment of the heavens.

———————

Small sacrificial heiau once found in the 'ili of Pūehuehunui, ahupua'a of Halaka'a, kalana of Lahaina.

Variant: Hale-kumu-lani.

47 Hale-kumu-lani
See Halekumukalani.

48 Halelua
Hale-lua

Literally, pit house.

———————

Surf site in an unknown area of the Lahaina region.

49 Hale Mahina

Literally, Moon House.

———————

A name of unknown origin, and which appears to be a fairly recent coinage, for Nā Mauna o 'E'eka (the mountain range of Maui Komohana), or for Pu'uwaiohina, the back ridge of Kaua'ula Valley.

50 Haleokane
Haleokāne
Hale-o-Kāne

Literally, house of Kāne.

———————

'Ili in the ahupua'a of Kaua'ula, kalana of Lahaina.

51 Halepai
Halepa'i
Hale-pa'i

Literally, printing building.

Site of the first printing press in Hawai'i, installed in 1833 on the grounds of the Lahainaluna High School, registered (Hawaii Site No. 50-03-1596) with the National Register of Historic Places in 1976.

Variants: Hale Pai, Halepai Palapala.

52 Halepai Palapala
See Halepai.

53 Halepiula
Hale-piula

Literally, corrugated iron (roofed) house.

Corrugated iron-roofed building built for the ali'i just makai of Mōkuhinia, in the ahupua'a of Waine'e, in the kalana of Lahaina. Alternative name for Halehuki.

Variants: Halehuki, Palace.

54 Halepohaku
Halepōhaku
Hale-pōhaku

Literally, stone house.

Mountain peak (3,786 feet) between the valleys of Olowalu and Ukumehame.

55 Haleu
Hāleu

Literally, to wipe (as with toilet paper).

Ahupua'a in the kalana of Lahaina, just north of Wai'anae.

56 Halipiula
See Halepiula.

57 Halona
Hālona

"Stream inland of Lahaina, Maui, mentioned in the Lahaina Luna [*sic*] song 'Alma Mater,' and in the Lahaina song 'Hālona' (Elbert and Mahoe 40)...*Lit., peering place.*" /PNOH/

Stream and gulch in the ahupua'a of Pana'ewa, kalana of Lahaina.

58 Halulukoakoa
Haluluko'ako'a
Halulu-ko'ako'a

Literally, roar of the coral.

Heiau in the ahupua'a of Wahikuli, kalana of Lahaina.

59 Hanaia
Hānaia

Pronunciation and meaning undetermined, perhaps: hānaia—adopted, fed.

'Ili in the ahupua'a of Kaua'ula, kalana of Lahaina.

60 Hanakaoo
Hanaka'ō'ō
Hana-ka-'ō'ō

"*Lit., the digging stick bay.*" /PNOH/

However, a different meaning can be found in this paraphrasing of a mo'olelo told to the author by Maui kupuna, Diane Amadeo: When Pele first came to Maui, she began to dig. The place where she dug was "Hanaka'ō'ō (The Digging Stick Works)." Because of the noise, part of the area was called "Wahikuli (Noisy Place)." The hill on which she first lived was called "Lāina (Day of Prying).

[NOTE: Of the many bays in Maui Komohana, none begin with the title "hana-."]

Ahupua'a and beach park in the kalana of Lahaina.

61 Hanakapuaa
See Hanauakapuaa.

28

62 Hanauakapuaa

Hānauakapua'a

Hānau-a-ka-pua'a

Literally, offspring of the pig.

Ahupua'a in the kalana of Lahaina.

Variant: Hanakapuaa.

63 Hanaula

Hana'ula

Hana-'ula

"*Lit.*, red bay." /PNOH/

However, judging by the attributes of this peak, well detached from the sea, another interpretation of the name could be: hana 'ula—red notch.

[NOTE: Of the many bays in Maui Komohana, none begin with the title "hana-."]

Peak (4,616 feet) between the valleys of Ukumehame and Waikapū.

Also, name of a gulch in the ahupua'a of Ukumehame, found between the gulches of Makaiwa and Pāpalaua.

64 Hana'ulaiki

Hana-'ula-iki

Literally, lesser Hana'ula (hana 'ula—red notch).

Peak (2,956 feet) in the ahupua'a of Ukumehame, above Hana'ula Gulch.

From a mo'olelo told to the author by Maui kupuna, Diane Amadeo, regarding the gulch and shoreline of Pāpalaua: Pāpalaua was a violent mo'o from Moloka'i. As Hi'iakaikapoliopele journeyed toward Kaua'i on her quest to find Lohi'au, Pāpalaua—a female mo'o in this telling—swam forth to challenge her. The mo'o told Hi'iaka that she would soon be stomping on her head—a most heinous offense! Hi'iaka tried several times to dissuade Pāpalaua, but a fight eventually ensued in which Pāpalaua was slain just off the shore of Ukumehame. Hi'iaka cast the lifeless Pāpalaua up onto the land where her body formed the large mountainous mass below Hana'ulaiki, her tail descends down Pu'u Kauoha, and her head is buried under the sand at Pāpalaua Beach—where it would be trampled upon by beachgoers for eternity. The gulch of Makaiwa/Makiwa is formed between her tail and her body.

65 Harbor Left/Right

See Keawaiki.

29

66 Haui
See Kai o Haui.

67 Hauola
Hau-ola

"*Lit.*, dew [of] life." /PNOH/

_____

"Ancient surfing area, Lahaina, Maui (Finney and Houston 28); an off-shore stone here is believed to have been a woman who was fleeing from her enemies when the gods turned her into a stone." /PNOH/

68 Hawaiikekee
Hawaii'keke'e
Hawai'i-keke'e

Meaning undetermined, perhaps: distorted Hawai'i.

_____

'Ili in the ahupua'a of Olowalu.

69 Hawaii Route 30
See Honoapiilani Highway.

70 Hekili
Literally, thunder.

_____

Shoreline point in the ahupua'a of Olowalu.

Variants: Hekili Point, L. Hekili, Lae o Hekili.

71 Helu
"*Lit.*, scratch or count." /PNOH/

_____

Peak (4,685 feet) between the valleys of Kaua'ula and Launiupoko, moku of Lahaina.

72 Hema
Literally, south, left, or Hema (proper name).

_____

'Ili in the ahupua'a of Kōpili, kalana of Lahaina.

73 Hikii
Hīki'i

Literally, to bind.

Heiau in the ahupua'a of Ukumehame.

74 Hipa
See Pu'u Hipa.

75 Hokuula
Hōkū'ula
Hōkū-'ula

"Hō.kū-'ula n. A star, perhaps Mars, but see Auhaele *Lit.*, red star." /HD/

Large, conspicuous hill (2,524 feet) in the valley of Ukumehame.

76 Holanui
See Polanui.

77 Holili
See Hoolili.

78 Hona
See Puu Hona.

79 Honoapiilani
Honoapi'ilani
Hono-a-Pi'ilani

Literally, Bay(s) of Pi'ilani; *figuratively*, the islands joined [hono] by Pi'ilani.

"... ua waiho kapalua wale iho no o Lahaina i ka lai, ma kona hoopuni ia ana e na moku-puni, nolaila mai kekahi inoa ona, oia hoi na Honoapiilani, a me he mea la, ekolu inoa o keia kulanakauhale, he oiaio no, ekolu wale inoa, o Lele kona inoa kahiko, o Lahaina, he inoa hou ia, a o na Honoapiilani, he inoa mua no ia. [... *Lahaina in the calm is bordered on two sides as it is surrounded by the islands; that's where one of its names comes from, Nāhonoapi'ilani, and it's as if this town has three names; it's true, only three names, Lele is its ancient name, Lahaina is a new name, and Nāhonoapi'ilani is a former name.*]" /*Ke Au Okoa*, Buke 7, Helu 28, 26 'Okakopa 1871/

"Lahaina is said by early native writers to have had two other names in ancient times, it being first known as Honoapiilani. Subsequently this was changed to Lele, and in later times to Lahaina—as known to this day." /SOM 70/

Variants: Nā Hono a['o] Pi'ilani.

80 Honoapiilani Highway
Honoapi'ilani
Hono-a-Pi'ilani

Literally, Bay(s) of Pi'ilani.

Hawai'i Route 30, which extends south from the town of Wailuku [Wailuku] toward Mā'alaea, turns west into the moku of Lahaina, and continues north through to the moku of Kā'anapali, terminating in the ahupua'a of Honokōhau.

81 Hono o na Moku
Hono o nā Moku

Literally, Bay of Islands.

A poetic name for the seas found between the islands of Maui, Lāna'i and Moloka'i.

Variant: Hawaii Route 30.

82 Hoolili
Ho'olili
Ho'o-lili

"ho'o.lili, holili Rippled surface of the sea, as caused by fish; undulation or vibration of light in the hot sun; to ripple, vibrate, undulate; to close or blink the eyes in bright glare. Var. of ha'alili." /HD/

Pond in the ahupua'a of Puakō, kalana of Lahaina.

Variant: Holili.

83 Hoomanamana
Ho'omanamana
Ho'o-manamana

"ho'o.mana.mana. vs. Superstitious. See manamana.; mana.mana. 1. Redup. of mana 1. ho'o.mana.mana To impart mana, as to idols or objects; to deify; superstitious." /HD/

House lot in the ahupua'a of Kelawea, kalana of Lahaina.

84 Huemiemi

See Kuemiemi.

85 Iki

"iki nvs. Small, little, slightly; a little, trifle; not at all (with a negative)." /HD/

———

'Ili in the ahupua'a of Wai'anae, kalana of Lahaina.

86 Ilikahi
'Ilikahi
'Ili-kahi

Meaning undetermined, perhaps: 'ili kahi—singular 'ili (land unit), or, leather shaving strap.

———

An ahupua'a in the kalana of Lahaina.

87 Kaakau
Ka'ākau
Ka-'ākau

Literally, the right (side), the north.

———

'Ili in the ahupua'a of Polanui, kalana of Lahaina.

88 Kaalaino
Kā'ala'ino
Kā'ala-'ino

Pronunciation and meaning undetermined, perhaps: kā'ala 'ino—spoiled limpet.

———

Gulch between the gulches of Makahuna and Kamanawai in the ahupua'a of Ukumehame.
[NOTE: On the 1838 Kalama map, the area where Kā'ala'ino is found is labeled "L. Opihi ('Opihi Point)."]
Variant: Kaalaina.

89 Kaalo
Kā'alo

"kā.'alo. vt. To pass by, go by." /HD/

———

'Ili in the ahupua'a of Pūehuehunui, kalana of Lahaina.

90 Kaaula
See Keaaula.

91 Kahala
Kahala / Kāhala
Ka-hala / Kāhala

Pronunciation and meaning undetermined, perhaps: ka hala, the pandanus tree, or the offense; or, "kāhala, vs. Ripe, said of a gourd with stem beginning to wither." /HD/

—

Area mentioned in moʻolelo within the context of the kalana of Lahaina, below the hill of Paʻupaʻu.

—

"O keia kanaka, ua moe ia Kapulani a hanau mai o Ihiihi, ka mea nona keia inoa Paʻupaʻu. No ka luhi o na makua a me na kahu i ke kii pinepine i ka wai ilalo o Kahala i wai auau no ua keiki nei, ua kaniuhu na makua a olelo iho: 'He nui ka paʻu ma keia hana, a he uuku ka pomaikai.' Nolaila kapa laua i kahi i noho ai o ka laua keiki la o Paʻupaʻu. [*This man, he lay with Kapulani and begat ʻIhiʻihi, the one to whom belongs this name of Paʻupaʻu. Due to the weariness of the parents and guardians in constantly fetching water from below Kahala as bathing water for this child, the parents bemoaned, saying, 'There is much tedium in this work, yet the blessings are few.' So they named the place where their child lived Paʻupaʻu.*]" /Fornander V5/

92 Kahau
Kahau
Ka-hau

Meaning undetermined, perhaps: ka hau—the dew, the hau tree, the Hau breeze, the strike/hit, or, the sacrifice.

—

ʻIli in the ahupuaʻa of Polanui, kalana of Lahaina.

93 Kahea
Kāhea / Kāheʻa

Pronunciation and meaning undetermined, perhaps: "kā.hea nvt. To call, cry out, invoke, greet, name; recital of the first lines of a stanza by the dancer as a cue to the chanter; to recite the kāhea; to give a military command; to summon; a call, alarm…" /HD/; or, "kā.heʻa nvs. Red stains or streaks, as at dawn; bloody." /HD/

—

Ravine in the ahupuaʻa of Launiupoko.

—

"...oiai e lawai'a ana makou i kahi ahiahi ma Puhiaama he Ko-a mamali Oio ia, ke ike ala oe e Mr. Lunahooponopono, he wahi Ko-a lawai'a ia mawaho o kela lae aa o Launiupo [*sic*], mahope mai o kahi puali o Kahea, kahi no au e holoholo mau ai i ke a'o kula olelo Beritania [*sic*] i ko Olowalu kamalii.... [...*while we were fishing one evening at Puhi'a'ama, it is a fishing ground for young 'ō'io, you know it Mr. Editor, it is a fishing Shrine beyond that rough point of Launiupoko, after a certain ravine called Kāhea, the place where you would always travel to teach Olowalu's children at the English language school....*]" / *Ka Nupepa Kuokoa,* Buke 40, Helu 18, 2 Mei 1902/

94 Kaheawa

Kaheawa / Kahe'awa
Kahe-awa / Kahe-'awa

Pronunciation and meaning undetermined, perhaps: kahe awa—flows to the cove (of Keanapa'akai?), or, school of awa fish; kahe 'awa—flow of/caused by the 'Awa rain; or, an elision of: kāhe'e 'awa—to pour 'awa (in relation to Kāne and Kanaloa who dwelt on the nearby Hana'ula in the story of Kūapī'ei).

'Ili in the ahupua'a of Ukumehame. Location of the Kaheawa Wind Power wind farm.

95 Kahili

Kāhili

"kā.hili 1. nvt. Feather standard, symbolic of royalty; segment of a rainbow standing like a shaft (also a sign of royalty); to brush, sweep, switch." /HD/

Cliff at the head of Kaua'ula Valley, kalana of Lahaina.

96 Kahinahina

Ka-hinahina

Literally, the hinahina: "hinahina 1. n. The silversword (*Argyroxiphium sandwicense*)...3. n. Native heliotrope (*Heliotropium anomalum* var. *argenteum*), a low, spreading beach plant, with narrow, clustered, silvery leaves and small, white, fragrant flowers. As designated by the Territorial legislature in 1923, it represents Ka-ho'olawe in the leis of the islands; it is used for tea and medicine...4. n. Native geraniums (*Geranium cuneatum* var. *tridens* and other native silvery geraniums), shrubs or small trees of the high mountains, with ovate, toothed leaves and red or white flowers...5. n. Native artemisia (*Artemisia australis*). See 'āhinahina 3. 6. vs. Gray, grayish. 7. n. A variety of sugar cane, gray-green with a rosy flush, the whole covered with a wax bloom; pith dark brown..." /HD

'Ili in the ahupua'a of Kaua'ula, kalana of Lahaina.

97 Kahoma
Ka-homa

"*Lit.*, the thin one." /PNOH/

Valley, stream, and gulch in the ahupuaʻa of Paʻūnāʻū, kalana of Lahaina.

98 Kahoolewa
Kahoʻolewa
Ka-hoʻo-lewa

Literally, the hoʻolewa: "Hoolewa 1. To cause to swing; to vibrate; to float in the air. 2. To lift up and carry, as between two persons; to carry in a manele or palanquin. 3. To carry a corpse in a funeral procession. 4. To cause a swinging or rotary motion, as in certain forms of dancing." /Parker/

Ridge along the upper part of the ahupuaʻa of Panaʻewa and Paʻūnāʻū which separates that area of the kalana of Lahaina from the back of ʻĪao Valley [Wailuku].

99 Kahua
Kahua / Ka-hua

Meaning undetermined, perhaps: kahua—site; or ka hua—"*Lit.*, the fruit." /PNOH/

ʻIli in the kalana of Lahaina.

100 Kahuaiki
Ka-hua-iki

Literally, lesser Kahua (*see* Kahua).

ʻIli in the kalana of Lahaina.

101 Kailiili
Kaʻiliʻili
Ka-ʻiliʻili

Literally, the pebble.

Shoreline area along Mōpua, ahupuaʻa of Olowalu.

102 Kainehe
Kai-nehe

Literally, rustling sea.

Ahupuaʻa in the kalana of Lahaina.

103 Kai o Anehe
Kai o ʻĀnehe

Literally, sea of ʻĀnehe ("ā.nehe. vi. To come upon quietly, move stealthily, poise" /HD/).

[NOTE: In online database searches, "ka anehe" returned more hits than "ke anehe." As such, it is likely that "anehe" is represented as " ʻānehe" in native speech.]

"Kai-o-Anehe, sea from Maalaea to Keoneoio, between Kahoolawe and Molokini." /SOM (Maui) 11/

See also: Anehenehe.

104 Kai o Haui

Literally, sea of Haui:

"haui A word known only in the chant called Haui ka lani ...; according to Andrews...an ancient, poetical name for hāʻule which he translates 'fallen' but more probably hau, to strike + -i, transitivizer. A more accurate translation of the chant's title is "the chief is struck down.";...A less plausible interpretation is hau i ka lani, offer to the royal chief." /HD/; "Haui (haʻ-uʼi), n. 1. A mythological character conspicuous in Hawaiian tradition. Haui was said to be the first of Hawaii's aliis, or chiefs, and a demigod: O Haui ka lani, he alii kiekie, Haui is the lani (highest), a distinguished chief, He kumu alii, he kumu akua. Begetter of chiefs, origin of the gods. 2. The title of a chief, as a noble, a descendant of kings." /Parker/

"Kai-o-Haui, sea from Lahaina to Maalaea." /SOM 5/

105 Kaiwaloa
See Kawaialoa.

106 Kaiwihole
Ka-iwi-hole

Literally, the stripped bones.

_____

'Ili in the ahupua'a of Pana'ewa, kalana of Lahaina.

[NOTE: Found as "Kaiwiholi" in /Place Names (ULUK)/.]

Variant: Kaiwiholi.

107 Kaiwiholi
See Kaiwihole.

108 Kalanipapa
Ka-lani-papa

Literally, the chief of *papa* rank.

_____

Unidentified area in the ahupua'a of Ukumehame.

109 Kalawea
See Kelawea.

110 Kalehua
Ka-lehua

"*Lit.,* the expert." /PNOH/, or, the *lehua* blossom.

_____

"Ka-lehua...Ancient surfing area, Lahaina, West Maui...." /PNOH/

Perhaps also the same as Leilehua. *See also*: Leilehua.

111 Kalimaohe
Kalima'ohe
Ka-lima-'ohe

Meaning undetermined, perhaps: ka lima 'ohe—the bamboo hand/arm, or, the bunch of five bamboos; may also refer to the 'ohe tree.

_____

Ahupua'a in the kalana of Lahaina.

112 Kalolo

Kalolo / Kalōlō
Ka-lolo / Ka-lōlō

Pronunciation and meaning undetermined, perhaps: ka lolo—the "lolo 1. n. Brains, bone marrow...2. nvs. Religious ceremony at which the brain of the sacrificed animal was eaten (such ceremonies occurred at a canoe launching, start of journey, completion of instruction); to have completed the lolo ceremony, hence expert, skilled...3. n. Pithy, white sponge in a sprouting coconut. Also iho. 4. n. Long slender pole placed above the second ridgepole of a house, functioning as a batten for the attachment of additional layers of thatch. 5. n. First brew made from ti root. 6. Short for hīnālea 'akilolo, a fish...7. Same as holowa'a, sheath covering coconut flowers." /HD/; or, ka lōlō—the crazy." /HD/

Pond found just inland of the shore in the ahupua'a of Pākalā, kalana of Lahaina.

113 Kalolopahu

Ka-lolo-pahū

Literally, the exploding brains.

The name of the 1789 massacre that happened off the shore of Olowalu. Enraged at the death of one of his watchmen and the appropriation of one of his small boats in Mākena, Captain Simon Metcalf pursued those who he accused as the perpetrators to Olowalu in his vessel, the *Eleanora*. Upon return of some of the watchman's remains, as well as the keel of the boat, Captain Metcalf lured the villagers of Olowalu toward the *Eleanora* and opened fire with his cannons, slaughtering over one hundred villagers.

Variant: Olowalu Massacre.

114 Kaluaaha

Kalua'aha
Ka-lua-'aha

In defining another region of the same name, "Ka-lua-'aha...*Lit.*, the gathering pit." /PNOH/

'Ili in the ahupua'a of Olowalu.

Variants: Kaluaaho, Kaluaana, Kaluaha.

115 Kaluaaho

See Kaluaaha.

116 Kaluaana
See Kaluaaha.

117 Kaluaha
See Kaluaaha.

118 Kaluaehu
See Luaehu.

119 Kaluakanaka
Kāluakanaka / Kaluakanaka
Kālua-kanaka / Ka-lua-kanaka

Pronunciation and meaning undetermined, perhaps: kālua kanaka—to bake a human; or, ka lua kanaka—the human grave.

———————

'Ili in the ahupua'a of Olowalu.

120 Kalualepo
Ka-lua-lepo

Literally, the dirt pit.

———————

Ahupua'a in the kalana of Lahaina.

121 Kaluaokiha
Ka-lua-o-Kiha

Literally, the pit of Kiha [wahine].

———————

'Ili and pond in the ahupua'a of Waine'e, kalana of Lahaina.

122 Kamaalaea
See Maalaea.

123 Kamaiki
Kama-iki

Literally, small person/child.

———————

Shoreline point along the ahupua'a of Mākila, kalana of Lahaina. Also known by the superimposed name of foreign origin "Pools."

Variant: Pools.

124 Kamakalaukalo

See Makalaukalo.

125 Kamanawai

Ka-manawai

Literally, the stream branch.

———

Gulch, stream, and small bay just northwest of Manawainui Gulch in the ahupuaʻa of Ukumehame.

126 Kamani

"kamani 1. n. A large tree (*Calophyllum inophyllum*) . . . 2. vt. Smooth, shiny, polished, as of kamani wood." /HD/

———

Ahupuaʻa in the kalana of Lahaina.

Also, an ʻili (Kamani 1–3) in the ahupuaʻa of Olowalu.

127 Kamaohi

"*Lit.*, young child." /PNOH/

———

Gulch, stream, and small cove in the ahupuaʻa of Ukumehame.

128 Kamehameha Iki

"Park: Kamehameha Iki. Park, Lahaina, Maui. Small beach park at 525 Front Street, with a canoe repair and storage building. A detrital sand beach that terminates at Lahaina Small Boat Harbor fronts the park. *Lit.,* small Kamehameha." /HPN/

129 Kamohomoho

Literally, Kamohomoho (proper name).

———

A large heiau once found on Paʻupaʻu, in the kalana of Lahaina.

130 Kanaha
Kanahā
Ka-nahā

Literally, the shattering.

‘Ili in the ahupua‘a of ‘Akinui, kalana of Lahaina.

Also, a valley and stream in the kalana of Lahaina.

131 Kapaahu
Kapa‘ahu
Kapa-‘ahu

Literally, tapa worn as a garment.

‘Ili in the ahupua‘a of Moali‘i, kalana of Lahaina.

132 Kapahumanamana
Ka-pahu-manamana

Literally, the point where many paths converge.

‘Ili in the ahupua‘a of Pa‘ūnā‘ū, kalana of Lahaina. Also, site of the old market in Lahaina.

Variant: Pahu-manamana.

133 Kapaulu
Kapā‘ulu
Ka-pā-‘ulu

Pronunciation and meaning undetermined, perhaps: ka pā ‘ulu—the breadfruit fence/yard/enclosure.

Unidentified upland area in the vicinity the ahupua‘a of Kelawea and Pa‘ūnā‘ū, kalana of Lahaina. [NOTE: Records of heiau listed in “Kapaulu” place the ‘ili in either Kelawea or Pa‘ūnā‘ū.]

134 Kapauma
Ka-pauma

Literally, the pump.

Plot of land on an island in Kahoma stream on the grounds of Lahainaluna High School, in the ahupuaʻa of Kūholilea, kalana of Lahaina.

———————

"No ka nui o ka ai. Ua nui ka ai ma keia kula, ua ai a ukauka na waha o makou. Eia na inoa o na papaaina o makou, o Pohakunui, no ke ku ana o kekahi pohaku nui i kahi a makou i mahiai ai, oia ka mea i kapaiaʻi ka inoa oia papaaina. O Auwaiawao ka inoa o kekahi papaaina, no ka pili no o ko makou auwai, me ko Awao, oia ka mea i kapaiaʻi ka inoa oia papaaina. O Kapauma ka inoa o kekahi papaaina, no ke kukulu ia ana o kekahi pauma wai mamua malaila, oia ka mea i kapaiaʻi ka inoa oia papaaina. O Kumuwi ka inoa o kekahi papaaina, no ka ulu ana o kekahi kumu wi malaila, oia ka mea i kapaiaʻi ka inoa oia papaaina, pela i kapaiaʻi ka inoa pakahi e makou no. [*Regarding the amount of poi. There was a lot of poi at this school; we ate until our mouths smacked noisily. Here are the names of our dining tables: Pōhakunui, because of a large stone standing at the place where we farmed, that's why the table was named that way. ʻAuwaiawao is the name of another dining table, because of how our ditch was close to that of Awao, that's how that table was named. Kapauma is the name of another dining table, because a water pump was constructed there before, that's how that table was named. Kumuwī is the name of another table, because a tamarind tree grew there, that's how that table was named; that's how each name was given by us.*]" /*Ka Nupepa Kuokoa*, Buke 11, Helu 41, 12 ʻOkakopa 1872/

135 Kapewakua
Ka-pewa-kua

Meaning undetermined, perhaps: ka pewa kua—hewn clump of trees.

———————

Ahupuaʻa in the kalana of Lahaina.

Variant: Pawakua.

136 Kapoli
Ka-poli

Literally, the bosom/breast/depression [indentation].

———————

Spring in the ahupuaʻa of Ukumehame, found above Māʻalaea. Also, the area along the boundary between the moku of Lahaina and the ahupuaʻa of Waikapū in the moku of Wailuku. Currently, the name of a beach park in the Māʻalaea area.

———————

"Kapoli. Beach park, Māʻalaea, Maui. Unimproved park on the low cliffs southwest of Māʻalaea Small Boat Harbor. *Lit.*, the bosom. Kapoli is the name of a former spring in the area." /HPN/

137 Kapoulu
Kapō'ulu
Ka-pō'ulu

Literally, the *pō'ulu* ("pō.'ulu. n. 1. Bark of tender breadfruit shoots, as used for less fine tapa. 2. Euphemism for pōule ['pō.ule n. Male flower of the breadfruit.'].") /HD/

'Ili and water source in the ahupua'a of Ko'okā, kalana of Lahaina. In the "Kuaialii" narrative found serially in the newspaper *Kuokoa Home Rula* of 1912, Kapō'ulu is the brother-in-law of Mōkuhinia.

"...akahi no o Mokuhinia a hoomanao ae i ke aloha no kona kaikunane, na makaainana ame ka aina, aka, aole hoi e hiki ke paleia ae i kela mau olelo hoohaahaa a kona kaikoeke (Kapoulu) ana i lohe pono aku ai.... [... *Mōkuhinia just recalled her affection for her brother, the commoners and the land, but the humbling words that she heard from her brother-in-law (Kapō'ulu) could not be avoided....*]" /*Kuokoa Home Rula*, Buke 10, Helu 48, 28 Nowemapa 1912/

138 Kapuali
Kapū'ali
Ka-pū'ali

Literally, the *pū'ali* ("pū.'ali. 1. n. Warrior, soldier, so called because Hawaiian fighters tied (pū'ali) their malos at the waist so that no flap would dangle for a foe to seize; army, host, multitude... 2. nvt. To gird tightly about the waist, as of malo-clad warriors, or as corseted women; compressed, constricted in the middle; grooved, notched; irregularly shaped, as taro; notch; tight belt... 6. n. Irregularly shaped ravine. 7. n. A vague term for an adopted man or boy who had no servants." /HD/)

Shoreline area between Kūlanaokala'i and Nālimawai in the ahupua'a of Launiupoko.

139 Kapualiilii
Kapuali'ili'i
Ka-pua-li'ili'i

Literally, the small fry/spawn, or, the small flower.

A former canoe-landing beach along 'Ūhā'īlio in the ahupua'a of Halaka'a.

140 Kapukaiao
See Apuakaiao.

141 Kapunakea
Ka-puna-kea

"*Lit.*, the clear spring or the white coral." /PNOH/

Ahupua'a in the kalana of Lahaina.

142 Kau

Meaning undetermined, perhaps: "kau 1. vt. To place, put, hang, suspend, affix, gird on; to set, settle, perch, alight, rest, pose; to enact, impose, or pass, as a law; to levy, as a tax; to ride on or mount, as on a horse or in a car; to board, mount, get in or on; to rise up, appear, as the moon; to place in sacrifice, as a pig; to come to rest, as the setting sun; to arrive, come to pass; to hang up, as a telephone receiver...2. n. Period of time, lifetime; any season, especially summer; session of a legislature; term, semester; time of late night before dawn...3. nvt. A sacred chant, as Hi'iaka's chants of affectionate greeting to persons, hills, and landmarks; a chant of sacrifice to a deity; to chant thus...4. n. Wooden handle, as on stone chisels; perch; pole raised longitudinally over a canoe in stormy weather, on which mats were placed for protection. 5. nvi. A method of feeding children or high-born persons as a special honor; the recipient held back his head and opened his mouth; the morsel of poi was dropped into his mouth; much enjoyed by children as a game...6. n. Center tapa under which the stone was hidden in the game of pūhenehene...10. (Cap.) Name of a star in the northern sky that served as guide to mariners. 11. (Cap.) The Milky Way." /HD/

'Ili in the ahupua'a of Moali'i, kalana of Lahaina.

143 Kauakahikaula
Kauakahikāula
Kauakahi-kāula

Pronunciation and meaning undetermined, perhaps: Kauakahi kāula—Kauakahi the prophet/seer.

'Ili in the ahupua'a of Moali'i, kalana of Lahaina.

144 Kauaula
Kaua'ula
Ka-ua-'ula

Literally, the red rain.

Ahupua'a and famed wind in the kalana of Lahaina.

"No ka hoolua makani kauaula, / Nana i ku kehu a ula ke kai, / Ula maka lehua ke kai ula i ka lepo, / I ke hu [*sic*] lepo i ka lepo a makani .... [*For the boost of the Kaua'ula wind, / The one that causes the ocean spray to stand and the sea to become red, / The sea reddened with dirt is red like the* lehua *blossoms, / Stirring and raising the wind's dust....*]" /*Ka Elele, Buke 1, Helu 11, 26 Aukake 1845*/

"Hanaio ka makani kauaula.—I keia pule i aui ae nei. Ua hoomaka ka pa ana o ka makani mai ka Poakahi a i ka Poalima e hapai ana i na huna lepo i ka lewa. Pouli ka la nalowale na moku, me he uahi la o na hale mahu. Ula pu ka moana, ua huna ia o Kahoolawe, Lanai, Molokai, e ka ula o ka lepo, piha pu na hale. [*The Kaua'ula wind was unrelenting.—This past week. The wind began blowing from Monday to Friday and it was raising the dust particles into the atmosphere. The sun was obscured and the islands disappeared, like from the smoke of the factories. The ocean was completely red, Kaho'olawe, Lāna'i, (and) Moloka'i were hidden by the redness of the dirt, the houses were completely filled with it.*] /*Ka Nupepa Kuokoa, Buke 5, Helu 1, 6 Ianuali 1866*/

145 Kauheana
Kau-heana

Literally, set the human sacrifice slain in battle.

The breadfruit tree, found on the former property of David Malo in the ahupua'a of Pākalā, kalana of Lahaina, upon which the first victim slain in a battle was laid.

146 Kaukahoku
Kau-ka-hōkū

Literally, the star rises/appears.

A taro patch in the ahupua'a of Kelawea, kalana of Lahaina.

147 Kaukaiweli
See Kaukaweli.

148 Kaukaweli
Kau-ka-weli

Literally, filled with fear.

Name of the kukui grove on the campus of the Lahainaluna Seminary. "Ka malu kukui o Kaukaweli" is an epithet for the Lahainaluna Seminary.

Variant: Kaukaiweli.

149 Kaulalo
Kau-lalo

Literally, set below.

Ahupua'a in the kalana of Lahaina.

150 Kaulu
Ka'ulu

Ka-'ulu

Literally, the breadfruit.

'Ili in the ahupua'a of Ukumehame.

151 Kaunukukahi
Kaunukūkahi

Ka-unu-kū-kahi

Literally, the altar that stands alone.

'Ili in the ahupua'a of Olowalu.

152 Kauohiokalani
Ka-uohi-o-ka-lani

Pronunciation and meaning undetermined, perhaps a misspelling of: Ka wohi o ka lani—The wohi-ranked chief of the heavens.

'Ili in the ahupua'a of Kaua'ula, kalana of Lahaina.

153 Kawaialoa
Ka-wai-a-Loa

Literally, the waters of Loa.

Heiau in the ahupua'a of Olowalu.

Perhaps related to the 'ili in Olowalu called Wailoa.

Variants: Kaiwaloa, Kawai'āloa, Kawailoa, Wailoa.

154 Kawailoa
See Kawaialoa.

155 Keaaula
Keaʻaʻula
Ke-aʻa-ʻula

Literally, the red rootlet.

———

ʻIli in the ahupuaʻa of Moaliʻi, kalana of Lahaina.

Variant: Kaaula.

156 Keahua
Keāhua
Ke-āhua

Literally, the mound/heap.

———

ʻIli in the valley of Kahoma, kalana of Lahaina.

157 Keahuakamalii
Keahuakamaliʻi
Ke-ahu-a-kamaliʻi

Literally, the children's mound/cairn.

———

Point along the boundary between the ahupuaʻa of Olowalu and the ahupuaʻa of Kauaʻula in the kalana of Lahaina.

———

"Course 8 of the Kauaula/Olowalu boundary runs along the narrow ridge between Olowalu Valley and Kauaula Valley to Keahuakamalii, then along the ridge between Wailuku Valley and Kauaula Valley. Elevation 5200 ft." /Place Names (ULUK)/

158 Keahuiki
Ke-ahu-iki

Literally, the small altar/cairn.

———

Point in the ahupuaʻa of Launiupoko.

159 Kealaloloa
Ke-ala-loloa

Literally, the very long path.

———

The name found on modern maps for the prominent ridge that forms on the east side of Manawainui Gulch, ahupuaʻa of Ukumehame. *See also*: Aalaloloa.

Variants: Keaalaloloa, Aalaloloa.

160 Kealii
Kealiʻi
Ke-aliʻi

Literally, the chief.

Gulch that adjoins the gulch of Hāhākea in the upper part of the ahupuaʻa of ʻAki, kalana of Lahaina.

161 Keana
Ke-ana

Literally, the cave.

ʻIli in the ahupuaʻa of Polanui, kalana of Lahaina.

162 Keanapaakai
Keanapaʻakai
Ke-ana-paʻakai

Literally, the salt cave.

Cove, which historically served as a port, along the shoreline below ʻAʻalaloloa Ridge, just to the west of ʻĀnehenehe in the ahupuaʻa of Ukumehame. The port has more recently been called by the superimposed name of foreign origin "McGregor's Landing."

Variant: McGregor's Landing.

163 Keawaiki
Ke-awa-iki

Literally, the small cove/port.

ʻIli, shoreline, wharf, and harbor (Lahaina Small Boat Harbor) in the ahupuaʻa of Waiʻanae, kalana of Lahaina. Also, site of the oldest (1840) lighthouse now found on any Pacific coast in the United States.

164 **Keawanui**
Ke-awa-nui

Literally, the large port/harbor.

_____

Site of the current Māʻalaea Harbor.

165 **Keawawa**
Keawāwa
Ke-awāwa

Literally, the valley/gulch/ravine.

_____

Site of the Kokoonāmoku battle at the mouth of Hāhākea Stream in the kalana of Lahaina.

Variant: Keawaawa.

166 **Keekeehia**
Keʻekeʻehia

Literally, trodden upon.

_____

The peak to the south of the cliff of Kāhili, kalana of Lahaina.

167 **Keekeenui**
Keʻekeʻenui
Keʻekeʻe-nui

Literally, big bend.

_____

ʻIli in the ahupuaʻa of Ukumehame.

Variants: Kekenui, Keekenui.

168 **Keekenui**
See Keekeenui.

169 **Kekenui**
See Keekeenui.

170 **Kelauea**
See Kelawea.

171 Kelawea

Pronunciation and meaning undetermined, perhaps an elided version of: kele ʻāweʻa— (red) streaked mud.

Large and prominent ahupuaʻa in the kalana of Lahaina.

" ʻO ka ʻāina kalo ma kahawai o Kanahā, ʻo ka palena ma kai. Mai ka ʻāina kalo o Kelawea e ʻoki ana i ka loʻi ʻo Kaukahōkū a holo pololei i Kumuʻula a iho i kahawai, a piʻi e ʻoki ana i ka ʻāina ʻo Hoʻolulu, a piʻi i ka pali, ʻo ia ka palena ma kai. ʻO ka palena ma uka, ʻo ka lae pōhaku ma uka o kahi o Rev. L. ʻAnerū, a iho pololei i lalo o kahawai, a holo pololei aku a piʻi i ka pali. ʻO nā wahi mahi kalo a pau ma luna o Makailiʻi a pili i Kukuikapu. [*The taro lands along the stream of Kanahā, that was the makai boundary. From the taro lands of Kelawea cutting across the taro patch called Kaukahōkū and running straight toward Kumuʻula and descending to the stream, and climbing and cutting the land of Hoʻolulu, ascending the cliff, that is the makai boundary. The mauka boundary was the boulder above Rev. L. Andrews' place and descends straight down to the stream, and runs straight up the cliff. All of the places to farm taro upon Makaʻiliʻi and up to Kukuikapu.*]" /Ke Aupuni Mōʻī/

Variants: Kalawea, Kelauea.

172 Keonepohuehue
Keonepōhuehue
Ke-one-pōhuehue

Literally, the beach morning-glory sand/beach.

Shoreline area in the ahupuaʻa of Olowalu.

173 Keonepoko
Ke-one-poko

Literally, the short sand/beach.

Shoreline area west of Māla, kalana of Lahaina.

174 Kiholaa

Pronunciation and meaning undetermined, perhaps a colloquial elision of: kī hoʻolaʻa— tī leaf used in blessing.

An ʻili listed in the ahupuaʻa of Moaliʻi, kalana of Lahaina.

175 Kilea
Kīlea

"*Lit.*, small but conspicuous hill." /PNOH/

Famed hill in the ahupuaʻa of Olowalu, just north of the Kawaialoa heiau. The north side of the hill features impressive panels of pre-contact and contemporary petroglyphs. On the northwest side can be found the "Olowalu Bluff Shelter (Bishop Museum Site M-4)." Graves have also been recorded on the summit of this hill.

"Ma ia po no ua hala aku la ua kamaeu nei mauka, a ua hele pololei aku oia a hiki i ka hale o na makua ponoi o Lihau e noho mai ana me na manao o ka pihoihoi no keia owela o ke ahi ma ke kai a ia Makanikeoe i hiki aku ai malaila ua loli ae la kona mau helehelena e like me ka ui nohea oia aina Lihau a oia ka kona makuakane Puukilea i pane ae ai i kana wahine Punahoa Auhea oe e kuu wahine? [*That night this mischievous one disappeared inland, and he went directly to the house of Līhau's own parents who were sitting there wondering about the glow of fire upon the ocean. As Makanikeoe arrived, his features changed to match that of the youthful beauty of that land, Līhau, and that is how her father Puʻukīlea responded to his wife Punahoa. Say, my wife?*]" /*Ka Leo o ka Lahui*, Buke 2, Helu 942, 16 Mei 1894/

Variants: Puu Kilea, Puukilea.

176 Kilolani
Kilo-lani

"kilo lani n.v. Soothsayer who predicts the future by observing the sky; to do so; astronomer, astronomy, astrologer." /HD/

Ahupuaʻa in the kalana of Lahaina.

177 Kiolani
Kiʻolani
Kiʻo-lani

Pronunciation and meaning undetermined, perhaps: kiʻo lani—royal pond.

ʻIli in the ahupuaʻa of Paʻūnāʻū, kalana of Lahaina.

178 Keoihuihu
Keōihuihu / Ke'ōihuihu
Ke-ō-ihuihu / Ke-'ō-ihuihu

Pronunciation and meaning undetermined, perhaps: ke ō ihuihu—the scornful reply; or, ke 'ō ihuihu—the scornful greeting.

The point where the streams of Kahoma and Kanahā meet, in the ahupua'a of Pa'ūnā'ū.

179 Koai
Kō'ai

"kō.'ai. vt. To stir with a circular motion of the hand; to wind around, creep around, as a vine; to gird around, as a pā'ū sarong; to brace with a paddle." /HD/

Peak (2,585 feet) in the ahupua'a of Ukumehame, found on a ridge that is shaded on the north by 'Ula'ula Peak (3,078 feet).

180 Koheeleele
Kohe'ele'ele
Kohe-'ele'ele

Meaning undetermined, perhaps: black *kohe* ("kohe. n. 1. Mortise; crease, as in the center of the crown of a hat; groove in wood; corner in a pandanus mat; fork at the lower ends of house rafters...2. Vagina. 3. Inside barb of a fishhook." /HD/)

A pond once found just inland of the shore in the ahupua'a of Pu'unoa, kalana of Lahaina.

181 Kokonamoku
See Kokoonamoku.

182 Kokoonamoku
Kokoonāmoku / Kōko'onāmoku
Koko-o-nā-moku / Kōko'o-nā-moku

Pronunciation and meaning undetermined, perhaps: koko o nā moku—blood of the islands, and, perhaps *figuratively*, blood relatives of the islands; or, kōko'o nā moku—partnership of the islands.

Seaside area along the northwestern side of the kalana of Lahaina.

Variant: Kokonamoku.

183 Kooka
Koʻokā

"koʻo.kā. 1. vt. To lambaste, buffet, hit … 2. n. A variety of sweet potato." /HD/

Ahupuaʻa in the kalana of Lahaina.

184 Kopili
Kōpili

"kō.pili. 1. n. Thin, transparent tapa made of mulberry bark. 2. Small white tapa placed over images and altars during religious services; the ceremony; to perform the ceremony. Also kōpilo nui. 3. Birthday gift to a child. (AP)" /HD/

Ahupuaʻa in the kalana of Lahaina.

Variants: Kopili Hema, Kopili Akau; Kopele.

185 Kuekue
Kuekue / Kuʻekuʻe / Kūʻēkūʻē

Pronunciation and meaning undetermined, perhaps: "kue.kue. nvt. Sound of tapping, tap, as of a mallet on a tapa anvil; to tap-tap." /HD/; "kuʻe.kuʻe. n. Elbow, wristbone, joint, knuckle." /HD/; or, "kūʻē.kūʻē. Same as kūʻēʻē. – 1. Redup. of kūʻē; disagreement, dissension, opposition, quarrel, bickering, animosity; to quarrel, bicker, disagree." /HD/

ʻIli in the ahupuaʻa of Olowalu.

186 Kuemiemi
Kūemiemi

This term is unattatested in the dictionaries, however, it is most likely a reduplication of: "kuemi vi. To step back; to walk backward, as from the presence of a chief; to retreat; to shrink back, recoil, flinch, withdraw." /HD/

ʻIli in the ahupuaʻa of Kauaʻula, kalana of Lahaina.

Variant: Huemiemi.

187 Kuholilea
Kūholilea
Kū-holilea

Pronunciation and meaning undetermined, perhaps: kū holilea—standing sallow.

––––––––––

Ahupua'a in the kalana of Lahaina.

Variant: Kuholileanui.

188 Kuhua

Literally, to thicken, to become pasty.

––––––––––

Ahupua'a in the kalana of Lahaina.

189 Kuia
Ku'ia

Literally, obstructed, hindered.

––––––––––

Ahupua'a in the kalana of Lahaina.

190 Kukuikapu
Kukui-kapu

Literally, sacred/tabooed candlenut tree.

––––––––––

'Ili in the ahupua'a of Kelawea, kalana of Lahaina.

––––––––––

"Now site of Kelawea Mauka Subdivision." /Place Names (ULUK)/

191 Kulahuhu
Kulahūhū
Kula-hūhū

Pronunciation and meaning undetermined, perhaps: overflowing container, or, overflowing flat land.

––––––––––

Perhaps an 'ili in the ahupua'a of Hāleu, kalana of Lahaina.

––––––––––

"Not named in the Māhele Book or Indices. RPG 482 to John Young Kanehoa, 4.47 acres. Perhaps only an 'ili of Haleu." /Ulukau, Inoa 'Āina Hawai'i/

192 Kulanaokalai
Kūlanaokala'i
Kūlana-o-ka-la'i

Literally, site of serenity.

Shoreline area in the ahupua'a of Launiupoko.

193 Kuliole
Kuli'ole
Kuli-'ole

Meaning undetermined, perhaps: not noisy, not deaf, or, not disobedient.

A ridge between the valleys of Kanahā and Kahoma, near the border of the Lahaina-luna Seminary.

194 Kumuula
Kumu'ula
Kumu-'ula

Literally, red stump.

Land found along the boundary of Lahainaluna.

"He gave, under protest of the natives who owned the land, the taro land by the stream of Kanaha on the side toward the sea to the taro land of Kelawea cutting the water taro patches of Kaukahoku, running straight down to Kumu'ula and down to the stream and rising and cutting the land of Ho'olulu and ascending to the *pali*." /SOM 57/

195 Kumuwi
Kumuwī
Kumu-wī

Literally, tamarind tree.

Plot of land along the Kahoma Stream on the grounds of Lahainaluna High School, in the ahupua'a of Kūholilea, kalana of Lahaina.

"No ka nui o ka ai. Ua nui ka ai ma keia kula, ua ai a ukauka na waha o makou. Eia na inoa o na papaaina o makou, o Pohakunui, no ke ku ana o kekahi pohaku nui i kahi a makou i mahiai ai, oia ka mea i kapaia'i ka inoa oia papaaina. O Auwaiawao ka inoa o kekahi papaaina, no ka pili no o ko makou auwai, me ko Awao, oia ka mea i kapaia'i ka inoa oia papaaina. O Kapauma ka inoa o kekahi papaaina, no ke kukulu ia ana o kekahi pauma wai mamua malaila, oia ka mea i kapaia'i ka inoa oia papaaina. O Kumuwi ka inoa o kekahi papaaina, no ka ulu ana o kekahi kumu wi malaila, oia ka mea i kapaia'i ka inoa oia papaaina, pela i kapaia'i ka inoa pakahi e makou no. [*Regarding the amount of poi. There was a lot of poi at this school; we ate until our mouths smacked noisily. Here are the names of our dining tables: Pōhakunui, because of a large stone standing at the place where we farmed, that's why the table was named that way. 'Auwaiawao is the name of another dining table, because of how our ditch was close to that of Awao, that's how that table was named. Kapauma is the name of another dining table, because a water pump was constructed there, that's how that table was named. Kumuwī is the name of another table, because a tamarind tree grew there, that's how that table was named; that's how each name was given by us.*]" /*Ka Nupepa Kuokoa*, Buke 11, Helu 41, 12 'Okakopa 1872/

196 Kunamoe
Kuna-moe

Literally, sleeping fresh-water eel.

'Ili in the ahupua'a of Kaua'ula, kalana of Lahaina.

197 Lae o Hekili
See Hekili.

198 Lae o Opihi
See Opihi.

199 Lahaina
Lahaina / Lāhainā
Lahaina / Lā-hainā

Pronunciation and meaning undetermined, perhaps: "lahaina n. 1. A variety of sugar cane, usually free tasseling, heavy stooling, and with rather semierect to recumbent growth; large, long heavy tops...2. A variety of sweet potato...3. Poising; leaping." /HD/; or, lā hainā—merciless sun.

The name of one of three moku of Maui Komohana. Lahaina is also the name of the kalana found in the moku of Lahaina. From 1820 to 1845, Lahaina was the capital of the Hawaiian Kingdom.

Although scholars provide evidence that an older pronunciation for Lahaina was "Lāhainā," most modern-day scholars choose the spelling that reflects modern-day pronunciation, "Lahaina." Even in the vast majority of her works, native Hawaiian speaker and renowned scholar Mary Kawena Pukui chose to represent this place name without diacritical markings, as have other contemporary scholars. This is likewise reflected in the pronunciations of residents, kūpuna, and in recordings of mānaleo.

"...ua waiho kapalua wale iho no o Lahaina i ka lai, ma kona hoopuni ia ana e na moku-puni, nolaila mai kekahi inoa ona, oia hoi na Honoapiilani, a me he mea la, ekolu inoa o keia kulanakauhale, he oiaio no, ekolu wale inoa, o Lele kona inoa kahiko, o Lahaina, he inoa hou ia, a o na Honoapiilani, he inoa mua no ia. [... *Lahaina in the calm is bordered on two sides as it is surrounded by the islands; that's where one of its names comes from, Nāhonoapiʻilani, and it's as if this town has three names, it's true, only three names; Lele is its ancient name, Lahaina is a new name, and Nāhonoapiʻilani is a former name.*]" /*Ke Au Okoa*, Buke 7, Helu 28, 26 ʻOkakopa 1871/

Variants: Lāhainā, Lāhaina, Raheina.

200 Lahaina Fort
See Pāpū o Lahaina.

201 Lahainakai
Lahaina-kai
See Lahainalalo.

202 Lahainalalo
Lahaina-lalo

Literally, Lower Lahaina.

The term "Lahainalalo" refers to the ʻili and ahupuaʻa of what is currently considered the "Lahaina Town" area nearest to, and including, the coast.

"Eia kekahi; aia ma ka aoao komohana o keia puu [Paʻupaʻu] ke kupapau o kekahi kanaka kaulana a me ka naauao, oia hoi o Davida Malo. Eia kekahi wahi olelo kaulana ana: ʻIna i noho kakou, a make au, mai kanu oukou iaʻu ma Lahaina lalo nei, e lawe oukou iaʻu a kanu maluna pono o Paʻupaʻu, no ka mea he poe imi aina ka haole,ʻ a ua ko no kana olelo i wanana ai. [*Also, there on the west side of this hill (Paʻupaʻu) is the grave of a certain famous and educated person; he is David Malo. Here is something famous that he said: 'If we all live, and I die, don't bury me here in Lahainalalo; take me and bury me directly on top of Paʻupaʻu, because the haole (foreigners) are land-seeking people,' and the words he prophesied were fulfilled.*]" /Fornander, V, 521/

Variant: Lahainakai.

203 Lahainaluna
Lahaina-luna

Literally, Upper Lahaina.

The term "Lahainaluna" refers to the region beginning around the area of Kukuikapu in the ahupuaʻa of Kelawea and Paʻūnāʻū, above the main part of "Lahaina Town," up to, and including, the lands of Lahainaluna High School.

204 Lahainaluna High School

The current public high school for the moku of Lahaina and Kāʻanapali located in the region known as Lahainaluna, ahupuaʻa of Lahaina. Also, the only public boarding school in Hawaiʻi. This school was originally founded in 1831 as Lahainaluna Seminary, a Protestant teacher-training school.

205 Lahaina Pali Trail
See Aalaloloa.

206 Lahainawaena
Lahaina-waena

Literally, Central Lahaina.

This term has been historically used in two different manners. Firstly, in the Māhele documents that detail Miriam Kekāuluohi's transfer of land to Rev. Lorrin Andrews for his house site [L.C.A. 77], his property was said to have been in Lahainawaena. The boulder just mauka of his lot, in Kukuikapu, was one of the boundaries for the lands of the Lahainaluna Seminary. This suggests that the term "Lahainawaena" was once applied to the region's vertical position between Lahainalalo (Lower Lahaina) and Lahainaluna (Upper Lahaina) during this time period.

In an 1841 newspaper article, the term "Lahainawaena" was used in conjuction with "Lahaina Hema (South Lahaina)" and "Lahaina Akau (North Lahaina)," suggesting a lateral positioning of these areas' delineations.

Finally, in an 1869 news article, "Lahainawaena" is mentioned along with "Lahainaluna" and "Lahainakai (Seaside Lahaina)." In this same article, the area of Waineʻe is found in Lahainawaena, whereas Waineʻe was recorded in an 1860 article as being in Lahainalalo.

207 Laina
See Puu Laina.

208 Lainapokii
Lāinapōkiʻi

Lāina-pōkiʻi

Literally, Lāina, the younger sibling.

———————

ʻIli in the ahupuaʻa of Kūholilea, kalana of Lahaina.

The ahupuaʻa of Kūholilea, in which Lāinapōkiʻi is found, runs along the southern base of Puʻu Lāina. *See also*: Puu Laina.

209 Laiolele
Laʻiolele

Laʻi-o-Lele

Literally, calm of Lele.

———————

Term condensed into a single name that refers to the area of Lele/Lahaina in the kalana of Lahaina.

210 Lapakea
Lapa-kea

Literally, white ridge/slope.

———————

Ahupuaʻa in the kalana of Lahaina.

211 Launiupoko
Lau-niu-poko

Literally, short-fronded coconut (trees).

———————

Ahupuaʻa, valley, and stream in the moku of Lahaina. The valley is found beneath the peaks of Keʻekeʻehia on the north and Līhau on the south.

Variant: Olauniupoko.

212 Leilehua
Lei-lehua

Literally, *lehua* flower garland.

———————

Seaside area mentioned in the context of the kalana of Lahaina. Perhaps an alternative name for the surf of Kalehua. *See also*: Kalehua.

———————

"Kuu papa i ka ua Paupili, / Kuu papa i ka ua o Kanaha, / Kuu papa i ke kai nehe o Hauola; / Kuu papa i ke kai nehe o Uo, / Kuu papa i ke kai nehe o Leilehua; / Kuu papa i ke kai nehe o Makila.... [*My dad amidst the Paʻūpili rain, / My dad amidst the rain of Kanahā, / My dad amidst the rustling sea of Hauola; / My dad amidst the rustling sea of ʻUo, / My dad amidst the rustling sea of Leilehua; / My dad amidst the rustling sea of Mākila....*]" /*Ka Nupepa Kuokoa*, Buke 57, Helu 52, 26 Kekemapa 1919/

213 Lele

"lele. 1. nvi. To fly, jump, leap, hop, skip, swing, bounce, burst forth; to sail through the air, as a meteor; to rush out, as to attack; to get out of, as from a car; to dismount, as from a horse; to land, disembark, as from a canoe; to undertake; to move, as stars in the sky; to move, as in checkers; a jump, leap, attack...." /HD/

Former name for the area of Lahainalalo in the kalana of Lahaina.

"...ua waiho kapalua wale iho no o Lahaina i ka lai, ma kona hoopuni ia ana e na moku-puni, nolaila mai kekahi inoa ona, oia hoi na Honoapiilani, a me he mea la, ekolu inoa o keia kulanakauhale, he oiaio no, ekolu wale inoa, o Lele kona inoa kahiko, o Lahaina, he inoa hou ia, a o na Honoapiilani, he inoa mua no ia. [*...Lahaina in the calm is bordered on two sides as it is surrounded by the islands; that's where one of its names comes from, Nāhonoapiʻilani, and it's as if this town has three names, it's true, only three names; Lele is its ancient name, Lahaina is a new name, and Nāhonoapiʻilani is a former name.*]" /*Ke Au Okoa*, Buke 7, Helu 28, 26 ʻOkakopa 1871/

"Old name for the Lahaina district, so-called because of the short stay of chiefs there...." /Place Names (ULUK)/

214 Lelekahauli
Lele-ka-hauli

"Lele ka hauli, greatly shocked, astonished, moved, startled, frightened." /HD/

Area mentioned in the context of the Lahainaluna region in the kalana of Lahaina.

"Kuu wahine mai ke kula wela o Puopelu, / Mai ka piina ikiiki o Lelekahauli, / Hoomaha aku i ka olu o ke kukui o Kaukaweli, / Huli nana i ka hono o na Moku.... [*My wife from the hot plains of Pūʻōpelu, / From the stifling incline of Lelekahauli, / Resting in the pleasantness of the kukui grove of Kaukaweli, / Turn and look upon the bay of Islands....*]" /*Ka Nupepa Kuokoa*, Buke 14, Helu 18, 1 Mei 1875/

215 Liha

Meaning undetermined, perhaps: "liha. 1. n. Nit, louse egg. Also lia. 2. Same as liliha; dreadful, fearful." /HD/

———————

Peak below Līhau, found between the valleys of Launiupoko and Olowalu.

216 Lihau
Līhau

"lī.hau. 1. nvi. Gentle cool rain that was considered lucky for fishermen (UL 241); moist and fresh, as plants in the dew or rain; cool, fresh, as dew-laden air . . . 2. n. A variety of sweet potato (no data)." /HD/

———————

Storied mountain and peak (4,193 feet) between the valleys of Launiupoko and Olowalu.

"Ma ia po no ua hala aku la ua kamaeu nei mauka, a ua hele pololei aku oia a hiki i ka hale o na makua ponoi o Lihau e noho mai ana me na manao o ka pihoihoi no keia owela o ke ahi ma ke kai a ia Makanikeoe i hiki aku ai malaila ua loli ae la kona mau helehelena e like me ka ui nohea oia aina Lihau a oia ka kona makuakane Puukilea i pane ae ai i kana wahine Punahoa Auhea oe e kuu wahine? [*That night this mischievous one disappeared inland, and he went directly to the house of Līhau's own parents, who were sitting there wondering about the glow of fire upon the ocean. As Makanikeoe arrived, his features changed to match that of the youthful beauty of that land, Līhau, and that is how her father Pu'ukīlea responded to his wife Punahoa. Say, my wife?*]" /Ka Leo o ka Lahui, Buke 2, Helu 942, 16 Mei 1894/

"He wahine ui io maoli no keia. Aohe lua e loaa ai kona ui ma Maui a puni, koe wale o Waialohiikalauakolea, ke aliiwahine i hanaiia iluna o ka piko o ke kuahiwi o Haleakala. O keia kaikamahine hoi o Lihau, oia ke kaikamahine a Pa'upa'u ame Aalaloloa, he mau alii nui no na kuahiwi o Maui komohana; a he mau kupua nohoi laua ma kekahi ano. A he ohana lakou mailoko mai o Lihau-ula, kekahi hoahanau o Wakea. He mau keiki keia na Kahikoluamea (k) ame Kupulanakehau (w). A mamuli o Lihau ula ka hoahanau o Wakea i heaia ai keia kaikamahine o Lihau. [*This was truly an exceedingly beautiful woman. Her beauty was unmatched around Maui, except for that of Wai'alohii-kalau'ākōlea, the princess who was raised upon the peak of the mountain of Haleakalā. As for this girl Līhau, she was the daughter of Pa'upa'u and 'A'alaloloa, chiefs of the mountains of Maui Komohana; and these two were also demigods of sorts. And they were all family from within the line of Līhau'ula, a sibling of Wākea. They were children of Kahikoluamea (m) and Kupulanakēhau (f). It was after Līhau'ula, the sibling of Wākea, that this girl was called Līhau.*]" /Ka Na'i Aupuni, Buke 3, Helu 115, 10 Iune 1907/

Variant: Lihauwaiekeekeikalani.

217 Lihauwaiekeekeikalani
Līhauwai'eke'ekeikalani
Līhau-wai-'eke'eke-i-ka-lani

Literally, Līhau of the waters that recede into the heavens.

A name for Līhau, the mountain and peak (4,193 feet) between the valleys of Launiu-poko and Olowalu. *See also*: Līhau.

Regarding Lahaina: "Kona Mau Hiohiona: Ua paku ia mai oia e ka lalani mauna o Lihauwaiekeekeikalani, ka mauna nona na lehua kaulana e lei ia'i e na kamalii o kakou iloko o kona mau la, a i hoopuniia mai hoi e na mokupuni eha.... [*Its Attributes: It is partitioned by the mountain line of Līhauwai'eke'ekeikalani, the mountain to which belongs the famed lehua worn as garlands by our children during its days, and surrounded by the four islands....*]" /*Ke Au Okoa*, Buke 7, Helu 28, 26 'Okakopa 1871/

218 Loinui
Lo'inui
Lo'i-nui

Literally, large wetland taro patch.

Ahupua'a in the kalana of Lahaina.

219 Loko Alamihi
Loko 'Alamihi

Literally, 'Alamihi (ahupua'a) Pond.

Pond once found in the ahupua'a of 'Alamihi, kalana of Lahaina. *See also*: Alamihi.

220 Loko o Nalehu
See Nalehu.

221 Luaehu
Lua'ehu
Lua-'ehu

Literally, pit of the red-haired [mo'o].

Also: "lua.'ehu vs. Many and colorful." /HD

'Ili, pond, houselot, and site of a meeting house in the ahupua'a of Puakō, kalana of Lahaina.

"He kulanakauhale kahiko o Lahaina. I ka wa e ku mau ana na moku okohola, ua kaulana kela kulanakauhale no ka noho ana o ka Moi Kauikeaouli malaila. A malaila no hoi i hoomaka mua ai ke kumukanawai a me ke kau kanawai ana no Hawaii nei, a ua kapaia na 'kanawai o Luaehu.' [*Lahaina is an old town. During the times when the whaling ships would dock, that town was famous as the residence of King Kauikeaouli there. And it was there that the first laws and legislation began for Hawai'i, and they were called the 'laws of Lua'ehu.'*]" / *Ka Lahui Hawaii*, Buke 3, Helu 41, 11 'Okakopa 1877/

Variant: Kalua'ehu.

222 Luakoi
Luako'i
Lua-ko'i

Literally, adze quarry/pit.

———

Ridge and peak (3,000 feet) between the valleys of Launiupoko and Kaua'ula.

223 Luakona
Luakona / Luākona
Lua-kona / Lua-(a)-kona

Pronunciation and meaning undetermined, perhaps: lua kona—pit on the leeward side; or, lua a Kona—Kona's pit.

———

Heiau once found near the 'ili of Kapā'ulu in the ahupua'a of Kelawea, kalana of Lahaina, said to have been constructed by Hua-a-pohukaina/Hua-a-kapua'i-manakū.

224 Luau
Lū'au
See Pu'u Lū'au.

225 Maalaea
Mā'alaea
Mā-'alaea

Literally, origin of ocherous earth.

———

Bay along the southeast border of the moku of Lahaina, formerly known as Keawanui, which contains the waters of Kai o 'Ānehe.

A story of this region's creation was shared with the author by Maui kupuna Diane Amadeo. It is herein paraphrased: When Pele fled from the Lahaina side after a fight with Nāmakaokaha'i, she created Haleakalā for her family and herself. The favorite food of Pele and her sisters is pē'ū [ceremonially prepared lū'au leaves cooked with salt]. But, on this side of the island, their followers had no salt with which to prepare it. So, Pele created Māʻalaea—then called Kamāʻalaea—she took some salt [of her tears, in one version, and some that she had kept since Kauaʻi in another] and created Keālia Pond. The lūʻau for their pēʻū was grown on Puʻu Lūʻau, above Māʻalaea.

"Māʻalaea 1. Bay, beach, Māʻalaea, Maui. Māʻalaea Bay is an important part of the Hawaiian Islands Humpback Whale National Marine Sanctuary. Although humpbacks are seen throughout the islands, they concentrate in the waters between the four islands of Maui County, where they calve, nurse, and mate. Māʻalaea Beach is a narrow calcareous sand beach approximately 3 miles long and backed by low dunes at the head of the bay. The northeast end of the beach is also known as Sugar Beach. 2. Small boat harbor, Māʻalaea, Maui. Constructed in 1952. Facilities include eighty-nine berth/moorings, a ramp, a drydock, and a vessel washdown area. 3. Surf site, Māʻalaea, Maui. On the northeast side of the entrance channel to the small boat harbor. The steep, hollow, plunging waves here form one of the longest and fastest rides in Hawaiʻi and possibly in the world. *Surfer Magazine* (established in 1960) has rated it as one of the ten best waves in the world and the fastest-breaking right in the world. Also known as Māʻalaea Pipeline, Pipeline. 4. U.S. Coast Guard station. On the shore of the small boat harbor... *Lit.*, ocherous earth beginnings. Māʻalaea is a contracted form of Makaʻalaea." /HPN/

Variants: Kamaalaea, Keawanui.

226 Māʻalaea Small Boat Harbor

A small harbor found at Keawanui, on the border of the moku of Lahaina and the moku of Wailuku.

"Located on the west coast of Maui, approximately 16 miles southeast of Lahaina; 89 berths/moorings, 1 ramp, loading dock, drydock, fuel delivered by truck, vessel washdown, restrooms and shower, restaurant and boat club, U.S. Coast Guard Station, harbor office." /DLNR/

227 Mahanaluanui, Puu
Puʻu Māhanaluanui
Puʻu Māhana-lua-nui

"*Lit.*, large twin hills." /PNOH/

Large hill (129 feet) in the ahupuaʻa of Launiupoko, also known as "Launiupoko Hill."

Variant: Launiupoko Hill.

228 Maihikuli

See Wahikuli.

229 Makahuna

Maka-huna

"*Lit.*, hidden point or hidden eyes." /PNOH/

___

Shoreline area between Ōpūnahā and Kāʻalaʻino in the ahupuaʻa of Ukumehame.

230 Makailii

Mākailiʻi / Makaʻiliʻi
Mākai-liʻi / Makaʻi-liʻi

Pronunciation and meaning undetermined. Because of the implications that "liʻi" refers to small in size, as opposed to "iki," referring to diminuitive in status and/or stature, then perhaps: mākai liʻi—small needle; or, mākaʻi liʻi—small guard/spy.

[NOTE: Because no other references have been found to date for this place name, perhaps it is a misspelling of "Makaliʻi." In the orignal 1869 article in *Ke Au Okoa*, the name is split, without hyphenation, along two lines: at the end of the first line, "Maka," and at the beginning of the next line, "ilii." Also, according to the Andrews dictionary, "makaʻi s. a person that owns no land; o ka mea aina ole, he *makaʻi* ka inoa."]

___

Land found within the bounds of Lahainaluna, kalana of Lahaina.

___

"'O ka ʻāina kalo ma kahawai o Kanahā, ʻo ka palena ma kai. Mai ka ʻāina kalo o Kelawea e ʻoki ana i ka loʻi ʻo Kaukahōkū a holo pololei i Kumuʻula a iho i kahawai, a piʻi e ʻoki ana i ka ʻāina ʻo Hoʻolulu, a piʻi i ka pali, ʻo ia ka palena ma kai. ʻO ka palena ma uka, ʻo ka lae pōhaku ma uka o kahi o Rev. L. ʻAnerū, a iho pololei i lalo o kahawai, a holo pololei aku a piʻi i ka pali. ʻO nā wahi mahi kalo a pau ma luna o Makailiʻi a pili i Kukuikapu. [*The taro lands along the stream of Kanahā, that was the makai boundary. From the taro lands of Kelawea cutting across the taro patch called Kaukahōkū and running straight toward Kumuʻula and descending to the stream, and climbing and cutting the land of Hoʻolulu, ascending the cliff, that is the makai boundary. The mauka boundary was the boulder above Rev. L. Andrews' place and descends straight down to the stream, and runs straight up the cliff. All of the places to farm taro upon Makaʻiliʻi and up to Kukuikapu.*] /Ke Aupuni Mōʻī/

231 Makaiwa

"maka.iwa n. 1. Mother-of-pearl eyes, as in an image, especially of the god Lono. 2. (Cap.) Nine guiding stars...." /HD/

___

Shoreline area below Keawāwa in the kalana of Lahaina.

Also, the gulch to the east of Puʻu Kauoha, in the ahupuaʻa of Ukumehame, along with the shoreline region below it.

From a moʻolelo told to the author by Maui kupuna, Diane Amadeo, regarding the gulch and shoreline of Pāpalaua: Pāpalaua was a violent moʻo from Molokaʻi. As Hiʻiakaikapoliopele journeyed toward Kauaʻi on her quest to find Lohiʻau, Pāpalaua—a female moʻo in this telling—swam forth to challenge her. The moʻo told Hiʻiaka that she would soon be stomping on her head—a most heinous offense! Hiʻiaka tried several times to dissuade Pāpalaua, but a fight eventually ensued in which Pāpalaua was slain just off the shore of Ukumehame. Hiʻiaka cast the lifeless Pāpalaua up onto the land where her body formed the large mountainous mass below Hanaʻulaiki; her tail descends down Puʻu Kauoha, and her head is buried under the sand at Pāpalaua Beach—where it would be trampled upon by beachgoers for eternity. The gulch of Makaiwa/Makiwa is formed between her tail and her body.

Variant: Makiwa.

232 Makalaukalo
Maka-lau-kalo

Literally, bud of the taro leaf.

———

ʻIli in the ahupuaʻa of Hānauakapuaʻa, kalana of Lahaina.

Variant: Kamakalaukalo.

233 Makenewa
Make-newa

Literally, death by a *newa* (war club).

———

ʻIli in the ahupuaʻa of Ukumehame.

234 Makila
Mākila

"mā.kila. nvt. Maui name for mānai, needle; to string, as leis." /HD/

———

Ahupuaʻa in the kalana of Lahaina. Also, a reservoir, and a ditch, and a shoreline point now known as "Puamana Beach."

235 Makiwa
See Makaiwa.

236 Māla

Literally, garden.

———————

Ahupuaʻa and former port in the kalana of Lahaina.

———————

"Māla. 1. Offshore mooring, Lahaina, Maui. State mooring site off the former wharf. 2. Ramp, Lahaina, Maui. On the west side of the former wharf. Facilities include two ramps, a pier, two docks, and a vessel washdown area. 3. Wharf, Lahaina, Maui. Dedicated on April 5, 1922, by Governor Wallace R. Farrington, the wharf was built specifically to accommodate interisland steamers instead of having them anchor offshore in the Lahaina Roadstead. However, after strong currents and heavy surf damaged several steamers, they reverted to anchoring offshore and the wharf was never used again as a major interisland passenger and cargo terminal. Smaller boats continued to use it until 1950. *Lit.,* garden." /HPN/

"Māla Wharf. Dive site, surf site, Lahaina, Maui. The dive site is off the ruins of Māla Wharf. The surf site is a long left on the east side of the ruins." /HPN/

237 Malalowaiaole
Malalowaiaʻole
Ma-lalo-wai-a-ʻOle

Pronunciation and meaning undetermined, perhaps: ma lalo wai a ʻOle—under-waters of ʻOle.

———————

Gulch to the west of Kealaloa Ridge, which opens to the east of ʻĀnehenehe in the ahupuaʻa of Ukumehame.

238 Malu Ulu o Lele
MaluʻUlu o Lele

Literally, breadfruit tree grove of Lele.

———————

Epithet for Lele, an older name for what is now part of the kalana of Lahaina.

Also, the name of the park now overlaid upon the pond of Mōkuhinia, and island of Mokuʻula.

239 Manawainui
Mana-wai-nui

Literally, large stream branch.

———————

The largest gulch along the cliffs of ʻAʻalaloloa on the southern side of the ahupuaʻa of Ukumehame.

Variant: Manowainui.

240 Manawaipueo
Mana-wai-pueo

Literally, owl stream branch.

Gulch at the western base of "the Pali," ahupuaʻa of Ukumehame. Also, the western end of the ʻAʻalaloloa trail.

241 Manoa
Mānoa

"mā.noa. 1. nvs. Thick, solid, vast; depth, thickness." /HD/

ʻIli in the ahupuaʻa of Kauaʻula, kalana of Lahaina.

242 Manowainui
See Manawainui.

243 Manuohule
Manuʻōhūle
Manu-ʻōhūle

"Probably *lit.,* bird [of the] meeting point of receding and incoming waves." /PNOH/

Shoreline point and area found between the points of Papawai and ʻĀnehenehe, in the ahupuaʻa of Ukumehame.

"Manuʻōhule. Dive site, Lahaina Pali, Maui. Also known as Wash Rock. *Lit.,* bird [of the] whitewash." /HPN/

Variant: Wash Rock.

244 Maomao
Maʻomaʻo

"maʻo.maʻo. 1. nvs. Green, greenness. ʻAno maʻomaʻo, somewhat green, greenish. hoʻo. maʻo.maʻo To paint green, make green. 2. n. A green tapa, as of māmaki bark." /HD/

ʻIli in the ahupuaʻa of Ukumehame.

245 Maria Lanakila

Historic Catholic church in the ahupua'a of 'Ilikahi, kalana of Lahaina.

"The Lahaina church was dedicated in 1858. *Lit.,* Mary [Our Lady of] Victory." /PNOH/

246 Maunaanu
Mauna-anu

Literally, Cold Mountain.

Region mentioned in mele in the context of the kalana of Lahaina.

"A luna oe o Paupau—la, / Nana i ka nani o Lele—la, / I ka holu a ka lau o ka Ulu—la, / Ke nape mai la i ka makani—la, / O ka liu la nopu i ke Kula—la, / I ka uka o Mauna-hoomaha—la, / Na pua rose o Maunaanu—la, / Ua pulu ia i ke kehau—la.... [*You are upon Pa'upa'u—la, / Look upon the beauty of Lele—la, / Upon the swaying of the Bread-fruit leaves—la, / Swaying there in the wind—la, / The mirage of heat upon the Plains—la, / In the uplands of Maunaho'omaha—la, / Are the rose blossoms of Maunaanu—la, / Dampened by the cool mist—la....*]" /Ka Nupepa Kuokoa, Buke 1, Helu 28, 7 Iune 1862/

"Aloha Lahaina i ka malu o ka ulu, / Aloha wale ka ua Paupili o Lele, / Lele ke aloha mokumokuahua i ka manao / I manao aku au he hoa no'u o Maunaanu, / Anu maeele i ka ua a ke kiowao.... [*Greetings to Lahaina in the shade of the breadfruit, / Fond memories of the Pa'ūpili rain of Lele, / Grief-filled pity leaps within the mind / I believed Maunaanu was a companion of mine, / Chilled numb in the rain brought by the misty mountain shower....*]" /Ka Lahui Hawaii, Buke 3, Helu 39, 27 Kepakemapa 1877/

247 Maunahoomaha
Maunaho'omaha
Mauna-ho'omaha

Literally, rest mountain.

Mountain region adjacent to the gulch of Kahoma (perhaps in the ahupua'a of Hāhākea) in the kalana of Lahaina. The English-language coinage for this mountain is "Mount Retreat." It is yet unclear whether "Maunaho'omaha" is a name of ancient origin.

"I ko laua noho a kane a wahine ana, hanau mai la ka laua keiki, he keiki kane, oia ka mea nona ka moolelo a kakou e kamailio nei. Aka, i kekahi manawa, loaa iho la ka hihia ia Eeke, no ka mea, ua ike aku la o Eeke i ka wahine maikai o Puuwaiohina, no Kauaula ia, a ua hana laua i ka hewa. No ia mea, manao iho la o Lihau e umi i ke keiki, a hele pu aku no hoi i ke kalohe; a noia mea, hoopaapaa ae la laua. Lawe ae la o Eeke i ke keiki na kona makuahine e hanai, oia hoi o Maunahoomaha. Ma ia hope iho hookapu mai la ko lakou akua, o Hinaikauluau, aole e noho pu laua, aole hoi e launa aku me kekahi mea e; aka he anahulu mahope iho o keia olelo, haule hou iho la o Eeke i ka hewa, me Puuwaiohina, oia kela mea mua i hai ia ae nei, a o ko Lihau muli iho nohoi ia. No ia mea, hoopai mai la ua akua nei o lakou, a hoolilo ia o Eeke i mauna, a o Puuwaiohina hoi i kualapa, oia no kela kualapa i Kauaula e ku mai la. A aia ma ka welau o ua pali la malalo iho, he puka; ina e kani ana ua puka nei, oia iho la ka wa e pa ai ke kauaula, aole o kana mai. Mahope iho oia manawa, kupu mai ke aloha ia Lihau no ka laua kamalei; nonoi mai la ia ia Maunahoomaha, e ike mai i kana keiki. He mea oluolu ia i kona makuahonowai, a ike ia i kana keiki, alaila, oluolu kona manao. [*As they ['E'eke and Līhau] lived together as husband and wife, their child was born, a boy; he [Lāina] is the one for whom the tale about which we are talking belongs. But at a certain time, 'E'eke became entangled in scandal, because 'E'eke saw the beautiful woman named Pu'uwaiohina; she was from Kaua'ula, and they perpetrated a sin. For this reason, Līhau thought to strangle the child, and go about in adultery as well; and for this reason, the two of them argued. 'E'eke took the child to be raised by his mother; she was Maunaho'omaha. Right after that their god, Hinaikauluau, placed restrictions upon them: the two of them were not to live together, and they were not to fornicate with anyone else; but ten days after this proclamation, 'E'eke fell again into sin, with Pu'uwaiohina; she's the one told of above, and she was indeed Līhau's younger sister. For this reason, their god punished them, and 'E'eke was changed into a mountain, and Pu'uwaiohina into a ridge; that's the ridge standing there at Kaua'ula. And there, right below the tip of this ridge, is a hole; if that hole is issuing forth a sound, that is the time when the Kaua'ula wind will blow, without limit. Right after this time, fondness welled up within Līhau for their beloved child; she requested of Maunaho'omaha to see her child. This was agreeable to her mother-in-law, and she saw her child; then, her mind was contented.*]" /Fornander, 5/

"Several accidents have occurred lately on the new flume being constructed by the Pioneer Mill Co. in the Kahoma gulch near Mount Retreat, due, it would seem to carelessness on the part of the victims themselves." /*The Maui News*, May 3, 1902/

Variants: Mauna Ho'omaha, Mount Retreat.

248 Maunaihi
Mauna'ihi
Mauna-'ihi

Literally, sacred mountain.

———

Area mentioned in the context of Lahainaluna in the kalana of Lahaina.

———

"Aia o Lahainaluna maluna o kahi kiekie, aia pono ma ke alo o Paupau, o ke kahawai o Kanaha ma kona aoao akau, o ke kula o Kuia ma ka hema, a ke huli pono la kona alo i ka malu ulu o Lele, ke kilohi la i ka hono o na moku, o ka mea a ke keiki Lahainaluna e aloha ai ke puka aku oia mai laila aku, o ke kiowai o Auwaiawao, a me ka piina o Maunaihi, me ka ihona o Kanaha, o ka ohu o Kahili a me na kukui o Kau-kaweli.... [*Lahainaluna is up in an elevated place, directly across from Pa'upa'u; the stream of Kanahā is on its north side, the plains of Ku'ia are on the south, and it directly faces the sheltered breadfruit groves of Lele, gazing upon the bay of the islands; the thing that the Lahainaluna lad recalls fondly when he graduates from there is the pond of 'Auwaiawao, the ascent of Mauna'ihi, and the descent of Kanahā, the mists of Kāhili and the* kukui *of Kaukaweli....*]" /*Ke Au Okoa,* Buke 3, Helu 6, 30 Mei 1867/

249 Maunakui

Maunakui / Māunakui
Mau-na-kui / Māuna-kui

Pronunciation and meaning undetermined, perhaps: mau na kui—snagged by a nail; or, māuna kui—excess/wasted nails, or, injury caused by a nail.

Lot in the ahupua'a of Puakō, kalana of Lahaina.

"...e kali ana no ka lele mai o na puhi ohe o Honolulu mai, ua ku mai lakou ia kaka-hiaka, ma ka moku *Kilauea,* a i ko lakou pae ana mai, hoonohoia'e la lakou mamua o ka Aha, a puhi ae la i ke mele, a kai malie aku la ka Aha holookoa a komo ma ka pa i kapaia o 'Maunakui,' a hookuuia ae la ka Aha ia kakahiaka. [... *waiting for the band members from Honolulu to get off the ship, they arrived that morning, on the ship Kīlauea, and when they landed, they were set up in front of the party, and they played songs, and then the whole party slowly made its way and entered the yard called 'Māunakui,' and the party was dismissed that morning.*]" /*Ka Nupepa Kuokoa,* Buke 2, Helu 35, 29 Aukake 1863/

250 McGregor's Landing

See Keanapaakai.

251 McGregor Point

Superimposed name of foreign origin for the point of 'Ānehenehe, in the ahupua'a of Ukumehame. The historic landing was found in the cove of Keanapa'akai. *See also*: Anehenehe.

"McGregor. Landing, point, point light, Mā'alaea, Maui. Landing for interisland steamers that was discovered at the foot of the sea cliffs to the southwest of Mā'alaea Bay by Captain Daniel McGregor (1857–1887). A wharf constructed at the landing was eventually dismantled. The ruins of the landing below the Federal Aviation Agency blockhouse include only a few concrete foundations and a cleat embedded in the rock. McGregor Point Light was established in 1906 to replace the discontinued Mā'alaea Bay Light. The 20-foot concrete pyramidal tower is on a site 48 feet above sea level." /HPN/

252 Miana
Mīana

"mī.ana. n. Place for urinating (formerly certain places outdoors were set aside for this purpose); urinal." /HD/

'Ili in the ahupua'a of Kūholilea, kalana of Lahaina.

253 Moalii
Moali'i
Moa-li'i

Literally, small chicken.

Prominent ahupua'a in the kalana of Lahaina.

254 Moanui
Moa-nui

Literally, big chicken.

Ahupua'a in the kalana of Lahaina.

255 Mokahi
Mōkahi
Mō-kahi

Meaning undetermined, perhaps: mō- + kahi—single mo'o (land unit).

'Ili in the ahupua'a of Moali'i, kalana of Lahaina.

256 Mokuhinia
Mōkuhinia / Mokuhinia

Pronunciation and meaning undetermined, perhaps a colloquially elided version of: mo'o kuhinia—satiated lizard, or, fat *mo'o* land, or moku kuhinia—satiated islet; or, "mokuhinia" may be an unattested word related to "kuhinia—rich, fat," as in: "Ahe; o oe ka paha o Leinaala, ka mea nana i kaihi [*sic*] mai i kela hua ai mokuhinia i ka piko o ke Kihapai pua o Elenale, ka mea hoi a ke kupua Mariorodo i palama loa ai. [*So; perhaps you are Leinā'ala, the one who snatched that sweet-tasting fruit on the border of Elenale's flower garden, the one that the demigod Mariorodo was protecting.*]" /*Ko Hawaii Pae Aina*, Buke 10, Helu 13, 26 Malaki 1887/

'Ili loko in the ahupua'a of Waine'e, kalana of Lahaina. Now, the site of Malu 'Ulu o Lele Park. The name "Mōkuhinia" is part of the full name for the pond's famed mo'o, Kihawahine Mōkuhinia Kalama'ula Kalā'aiheana. "Mōkuhinia" is also a character in the "Kuaialii" narrative found serially in the newspaper *Kuokoa Home rula* of 1912.

"Lohe aku la o Mokuhinia ko laila wahine u'i i ka pae ana aku o keia poe kaikama-hine malihini [Lu'ukia mā] ilaila, ua koi mai la oia a hookipa aku la ia lakou nei, a o ko laila oi nohoi ia iloko oia mau la, a o Paupili kona kaikunane, a o laua iho la nohoi na'lii ai-aina oia wahi. [*Mōkuhinia, that region's beauty, heard about these newcomer girls (Lu'ukia and her companions) landing there; she insisted on hosting them, and the best that could be offered in those days was provided to them. Pa'ūpili was her brother, and they two were indeed the ruling chiefs of that region.*]" /*Kuokoa Home Rula*, Buke 10, Helu 38, 19 Kepakemapa 1912/

257 Mokumana
Moku-mana

Literally, stream branch severance/break.

Gulch that ends in the same cove as Ōpūnahā, in the ahupua'a of Ukumehame.

258 Mokuula
Moku'ula
Moku-'ula

Literally, red island, or, sacred island.

The small islet once found with in the pond of Mōkuhinia, ahupua'a of Waine'e, kalana of Lahaina.

"...the tomb of the chiefess Nahienaena which stood in the [Mōkuhinia] pond on the east bank, was Mokuula, a little rock island." /Place Names (ULUK)/

259 Molakia

Literally, set twising and turning.

'Ili in the ahupua'a of Ko'okā, kalana of Lahaina.

260 Mooahia
Moʻoahia
Moʻo-ahia

Pronunciation and meaning undetermined, perhaps: ridge faded in color; or, an elided version of: moʻo wāhia—cleaved ridge.

Ridge, along with Kuliʻole, between the gulches of Kanahā and Kahoma, kalana of Lahaina.

261 Mopua
Mōpua

"*Lit.*, melodious (said to be the name of a legendary character)." /PNOH/

ʻIli along the shoreline in the ahupuaʻa of Olowalu.

262 Mount Ball
See Paupau.

263 Muliwaikane
Muliwaikāne
Muliwai-kāne

Literally, male river/river mouth.

An ʻauwai in the valley of Kauaʻula, kalana of Lahaina.

264 Nakalepo
Naka-lepo

Literally, crack in the soil.

Ahupuaʻa in the kalana of Lahaina.

265 Nalehu, Loko o
Nālehu, Loko o
Loko o Nālehu

Literally, ponds of Nālehu.

A series of inshore ponds in the ahupuaʻa of Waineʻe and Waiokama, kalana of Lahaina, which were once owned by Nālehu. On maps, these ponds are simply called "Loko o Nalehu."

266 **Nalimawai**
Nālimawai
Nā-lima-wai

"*Lit.*, the five waters." /PNOH/

Shoreline area and bay between Kapūʻali and Launiupoko point in the ahupuaʻa of Launiupoko.

Variant: Nalima Wai.

267 **Nalowale**

"nalo.wale. vs. Lost, gone, forgotten, vanished, missing, hidden, extinct, disappeared (especially if unaccountably so)." /HD/

Name given to a small heiau in the vicinity of the Kawaialoa heiau in the ahupuaʻa of Olowalu, the name of which has been lost (nalowale).

268 **Ohia**
ʻŌhiʻa

"ʻō.hi.ʻa. 1. n. Two kinds of trees: see *ʻōhiʻa ʻai* and *ʻōhiʻa lehua*…3. n. A native variety of sugar cane…4. n. A variety of taro. 5. n. A red birthmark…vs. Tabooed, as food patches during famine, so-called because people did not eat from their taro patches, but from upland ʻōhiʻa ʻai, ti, and sweet potatoes." /HD/

ʻIli in the ahupuaʻa of ʻAkinui, kalana of Lahaina.

Also, an ʻili in the ahupuaʻa of Ukumehame.

Variants (in Ukumehame): ʻŌhiʻanui, ʻŌhiʻaiki.

269 **Olauniupoko**
See Launiupoko.

270 **Old Lady's**
See Pāpalaua.

271 **Olowalu**

"olo.walu…1. nvi. Joint action; simultaneous sounds; din of many voices, sounds, as of horns or roosters; to rush or attack in concert; a group, as of hills (olowalu puʻu)…2. n. Storehouse, as for chief's property. *Rare.*" /HD/

Valley, stream, peninsula, ahupuaʻa, and sugar plantation in the moku of Lahaina, situated between the ahupuaʻa of Ukumehame and Launiupoko. The site of the former Olowalu Mill of the Olowalu Company and the Olowalu Landing.

272 Olowalu Gap

No Hawaiian name yet recovered.

Low spot on the ridge between the valleys of Olowalu and ʻĪao (Wailuku).

273 Olowalu Lanakila (Hawaiian) Church
Lanakila

Literally, victorious.

Historic church and cemetery founded in 1835 by E. Spaulding in the Mōpua vicinity of the ahupuaʻa of Olowalu. The church burned down around 1930. /Olowalu Lanakila Hawaiian Church/

Variant: Olowalu Lanakila Hawaiian Church.

274 Olowalu Massacre
See Kalolopahu.

275 Olualu
See Olowalu.

276 Onehali
One-hali

Literally, carried sand.

Area mentioned in mele in the context of the ahupuaʻa of Launiupoko.

"Kuu makuakane mai ke one loa la e Onehali, / Mai ka la haoa kunono la e Kulanaokalai, / E makahehi ana i na lehua o Lihau.... [*My father from the long beach of Onehali, / From the bright scorching sun of Kūlanaokalaʻi, / Admiring the lehua of Lihau....*]" /*Ka Nupepa Kuokoa*, Buke 3, Helu 22, 28 Mei 1864/

277 Opaeula
'Ōpae'ula
'Ōpae-'ula

Literally, red shrimp.

Ahupua'a in the kalana of Lahaina.

278 Opihi
'Opihi

"'opihi. n. 1. Limpets…3. Design for tapa and mats consisting of small triangles, probably named for the limpet." /HD/

Seaside point along coastline of Ukumehame. Perhaps the entire peninsula forming the southeast border of the ahupua'a of Ukumehame.

Variant: Lae o Opihi.

279 Opunaha
Ōpūnahā / 'Ōpūnahā
Ōpū-nahā / 'Ōpū-nahā

Pronunciation and meaning undetermined, perhaps: ōpū nahā—"*Lit.*, broken cluster." /PNOH/; or, 'ōpū nahā—split belly.

Gulch that ends in the same cove as Mokumana, in the ahupua'a of Ukumehame.

280 Paeohi
Pae'ohi
Pae-'ohi

Pronunciation and meaning undetermined, perhaps: pae 'ohi—bank (of taro patch) upon which to harvest.

Ahupua'a in the kalana of Lahaina.

Variant: Paiohi.

281 Pa Hale Kamani
See Halekamani.

282 Pahalona
Pāhālona
Pā-hālona

Literally, plot/point from which to peer.

The plain between the gulches of Kahoma and Kanahā, kalana of Lahaina.

283 Pahe'e

"pahe'e 1. vi. Slippery, smooth, as a surface; soft, satiny; to slide, slip, skid; sliding, slipping...2. n. Cleared area, bare dirt. 3. n. Spear throwing...4. n. Shallow hole or grave, as for flexed burial. 5. Same as pāhe'ehe'e, seaweed." /HD/

Fishing area in the ahupua'a of Launiupoko.

284 Pahoa
Pāhoa

"pā.hoa. n. Short dagger; sharp stone, especially as used for a weapon;...taboo sign...Kūkulu i ka pāhoa, to set up a taboo sign." /HD/

Ahupua'a in the kalana of Lahaina.

285 Pahumanamana
See Kapahumanamana.

286 Paiula
Pa'i'ula

"pa'i.'ula. 1. n. Tapa made by beating red rags or tapa pieces to form a mixture of white and red (as outer or kilohana sheet for bedcovers)...2. Calabash receptacle for sarongs." /HD/

'Ili in the ahupua'a of 'Ilikahi, kalana of Lahaina.

287 Pakala
Pākala / Pākalā
Pākala / Pā-kala / Pā-ka-lā

Pronunciation and meaning undetermined, perhaps: "pā.kala. 1. n. Young of the kala, a fish. 2. vs. Rough, as skin of kala, a fish" /HD/; "pā kala a releasing enclosure. Land section, Lahaina, Maui." /Parker/, pā kala—parcel of *kala* sweet potatoes, or rough fence; or, pā ka lā—the sun shines.

[NOTE: "Pākalā" reflects the pronunciation of a Hawaiian family that lives in this ahupuaʻa.]

_____

Ahupuaʻa in the kalana of Lahaina.

288 Pali
See ʻAʻalaloloa.

289 Panaewa
Panaʻewa

Although the meaning of the name is undetermined, perhaps: "to shoot crookedly. Land section, Lahaina, Maui." /Parker/

_____

Ahupuaʻa found between the streams of Kahoma and Kanahā in the kalana of Lahaina. Part of Lahainaluna High School is found in this ahupuaʻa.

290 Papalaau
See Papalaua.

291 Papalau
See Papalaua.

292 Papalaua
Pāpalaua
Pāpala-ua

Literally, rainy fog.

_____

ʻIli in the ahuuaʻa of Ukumehame.

The beach park along this shoreline is also known by the superimposed name of foreign origin "Old Lady's."

From a moʻolelo told to the author by Maui kupuna, Diane Amadeo, regarding the gulch and shoreline of Pāpalaua: Pāpalaua was a violent moʻo from Molokaʻi. As Hiʻiakaikapoliopele journeyed toward Kauaʻi on her quest to find Lohiʻau, Pāpalaua—a female moʻo in this telling—swam forth to challenge her. The moʻo told Hiʻiaka that she would soon be stomping on her head—a most heinous offense! Hiʻiaka tried several times to dissuade Pāpalaua, but a fight eventually ensued in which Pāpalaua was slain just off the shore of Ukumehame. Hiʻiaka cast the lifeless Pāpalaua up onto the land, where her body formed the large mountainous mass below Hanaʻulaiki—her tail descends down Puʻu Kauoha, and her head is buried under the sand at Pāpalaua Beach, where it would be trampled upon by beachgoers for eternity. The gulch of Makaiwa/ Makiwa is formed between her tail and her body.

"Coastal area and gulch, Māʻalaea qd., Maui. Valley and falls, Hālawa qd., Molokaʻi; a variant name is Pāpala. Because of the lack of sunshine here there was the saying *Pupuhi kukui o Pāpala-ua, he ʻino*, light the lights of Pāpala-ua, the weather is bad (said of any gloomy place where lights were lit in the daytime). (Summers 172–173.) *Lit.*, rain fog." /PNOH/

Variants: Papalau, Papalaau.

293 Papawai
Papa-wai

"*Lit.*, water stratum." /PNOH/

Point along the coast in the ahupuaʻa of Ukumehame. Location of the Papawai Scenic Lookout.

"Papawai... Dive site, Papawai, Maui. Off Papawai Point at Lahaina Pali. *Lit.*, water stratum." /HPN/

294 Pa Pelekane
Pā Pelekāne

Literally, British lot/enclosure/fence.

ʻIli in the ahupuaʻa of Paʻūnāʻū, kalana of Lahaina.

Variants: Belekane, Beretane, Beretania, Pelekane.

295 Papiha Cemetery
Pāpīhā
Pā-pīhā

Literally, driftwood lot.

Cemetery listed as a border of ʻAlamihi Loko in the ahupuaʻa of Māla, kalana of Lahaina.

296 Papu o Lahaina
Pāpū o Lahaina

Literally, Fort of Lahaina.

Fort of Lahaina, the partial restoration of which is found on the grounds of the Lahaina Courthouse in the ahupuaʻa of Waiʻanae, kalana of Lahaina. It is generally agreed upon as having been constructed under the supervision of Hoapili, beginning in 1831.

297 Pauma

See Kapauma.

298 Paumauma

See Paumaumau.

299 Paumaumau

Paumaumau / Pa'umaumau / Pa'ūmaumau
Pau-maumau / Pa'u-maumau / Pa'ū-maumau

Pronunciation and meaning undetermined, perhaps: pau maumau—forever done; pa'u maumau—continued tedium; or, pa'ū maumau—continuously damp.

———————

'Ili in Olowalu.

Variant: Paumauma.

300 Paunau

Pa'ūnā'ū
Pa'ū-nā'ū

Literally, nā'ū *plant dampness.*

———————

Prominent ahupua'a in the kalana of Lahaina.

This spelling stems from conversations the author had with Maui kupuna Diane Amadeo, whose grandfather was from the ahupua'a of Kaua'ula, kalana of Lahaina. Her pronunciation of this place name, and her explanation: "Makes the nā'ū damp, like that rain, Pa'ūpili." To date, the only other form available, beyond the colloquial "Paunau," comes from the "Māhele 'Āina Index" database for Kahalelole: "Honolulu 27 Oct 1852. Helu 6389 Kahalelole... Pauna'u Lahaina." /Place Names (ULUK)/

[NOTE: In the Parker dictionary, the name of this ahupua'a is featured as: "Paunau (păŭ-nă'ū): all masticated Land section. Lahaina, Maui," and in *Place Names of Hawaii* as: "Pau-nau. Land division, Lahaina qd., Maui. *Lit.*, completely chewed up."]

Variants: Paunau, Paunaunui, Paunauiki.

301 Paupau

Pa'upa'u

"pa'u.pa'u. nvs. Drudgery, slaving; tedious and laborious work, toil; toilsome." /HD/

———————

Prominent upland hill (2,248 feet) in the ahupua'a of Ku'ia, kalana of Lahaina. Pa'upa'u is the site of famed Hawaiian historian Davida Malo's grave, the heiau built by Kamo-

homoho, and currently features a large "L" for Lahainaluna High School. The superimposed names of foreign origin for this hill include Mount Ball and Ball Mountain.

"O keia kanaka, ua moe ia Kapulani a hanau mai o Ihiihi, ka mea nona keia inoa
Pa'upa'u. No ka luhi o na makua a me na kahu i ke kii pinepine i ka wai ilalo o Kahala
i wai auau no ua keiki nei, ua kaniuhu na makua a olelo iho: 'He nui ka pa'u ma keia
hana, a he uuku ka pomaikai.' Nolaila kapa laua i kahi i noho ai o ka laua keiki la o
Pa'upa'u. [*This man, he lay with Kapulani and begat 'Ihi'ihi, the one to whom belongs this
name of Pa'upa'u. Due to the weariness of the parents and guardians in constantly fetching
water from below Kahala as bathing water for this child, the parents bemoaned, saying,
'There is much tedium in this work, yet the blessings are few.' So they named the place where
their child lived Pa'upa'u.*]" /Fornander V5, 520/

"He wahine ui io maoli no keia. Aohe lua e loaa ai kona ui ma Maui a puni, koe wale
o Waialohiikalauakolea, ke aliiwahine i hanaiia iluna o ka piko o ke kuahiwi o Haleakala. O keia kaikamahine hoi o Lihau, oia ke kaikamahine a Pa'upa'u ame Aalaloloa, he
mau alii nui no na kuahiwi o Maui komohana; a he mau kupua nohoi laua ma kekahi
ano. A he ohana lakou mailoko mai o Lihau-ula, kekahi hoahanau o Wakea. He mau
keiki keia na Kahikoluamea (k) ame Kupulanakehau (w). A mamuli o Lihau ula ka
hoahanau o Wakea i heaia ai keia kaikamahine o Lihau. [*This was truly an exceedingly
beautiful woman. Her beauty was unmatched around Maui, except for that of Wai'alohii-
kalau'ākōlea, the princess who was raised upon the peak of the mountain of Haleakalā. As
for this girl Līhau, she was the daughter of Pa'upa'u and 'A'alaloloa, chiefs of the mountains
of Maui Komohana; and these two were also demigods of sorts. And they were all family
from within the line of Līhau'ula, a sibling of Wākea. They were children of Kahikoluamea
(m) and Kupulanakēhau (f). It was after Līhau'ula, the sibling of Wākea, that this girl was
called Līhau.*]" /*Ka Na'i Aupuni*, Buke 3, Helu 115, 10 Iune 1907/

Variants: Ball Mountain, Mount Ball.

302 Pawakua
See Kapewakua.

303 Pelekane
See Pā Pelekāne.

304 Piilani Auwai
Pi'ilani 'Auwai

Literally, Pi'ilani Ditch.

An 'auwai in the ahupua'a of Kaua'ula, kalana of Lahaina.

305 Pioneer Mill Company

Historic sugar mill in the town of Lahaina, moku of Lahaina.

306 Pohakea
Pōhākea
Pōhā-kea

Literally, white stone.

Gulch on the east-northeast side of Kealaloloa Ridge, which forms the border between the ahupuaʻa of Ukumehame and the ahupuaʻa of Waikapū in the moku of Wailuku.

307 Pohakuloa
Pōhakuloa
Pōhaku-loa

Literally, long stone.

An upland place to the west of Manawainui Gulch, inland of Kāʻalaʻino and Kamanawai, in the ahupuaʻa of Ukumehame.

308 Pohakunui
Pōhakunui
Pōhaku-nui

Literally, large stone, boulder.

Plot of land along the Kahoma stream on the grounds of Lahainaluna High School, in the ahupuaʻa of Kūholilea, kalana of Lahaina.

"No ka nui o ka ai. Ua nui ka ai ma keia kula, ua ai a ukauka na waha o makou. Eia na inoa o na papaaina o makou, o Pohakunui, no ke ku ana o kekahi pohaku nui i kahi a makou i mahiai ai, oia ka mea i kapaiaʻi ka inoa oia papaaina. O Auwaiawao ka inoa o kekahi papaaina, no ka pili no o ko makou auwai, me ko Awao, oia ka mea i kapaiaʻi ka inoa oia papaaina. O Kapauma ka inoa o kekahi papaaina, no ke kukulu ia ana o kekahi pauma wai mamua malaila, oia ka mea i kapaiaʻi ka inoa oia papaaina. O Kumuwi ka inoa o kekahi papaaina, no ka ulu ana o kekahi kumu wi malaila, oia ka mea i kapaiaʻi ka inoa oia papaaina, pela i kapaiaʻi ka inoa pakahi e makou no. [*Regarding the amount of poi. There was a lot of poi at this school; we ate until our mouths smacked noisily. Here are the names of our dining tables: Pōhakunui, because of a large stone standing at the place where we farmed, that's why the table was named that way. ʻAuwaiawao is the name of another dining table; because of how our ditch was close to that of Awao, that's how that table was named. Kapauma is the name of another dining table; because a water pump was constructed there before, that's how that table was named. Kumuwī is the name of another table; because a tamarind tree grew there, that's how that table was named—that's how each name was given by us.*]" /*Ka Nupepa Kuokoa*, Buke 11, Helu 41, 12 ʻOkakopa 1872/

309 Pohaku o Wahikuli
Pōhaku o Wahikuli

Literally, stone of Wahikuli.

Point along the shore from which ascends the boundary between the ahupuaʻa of Wahikuli, kalana of Lahaina, and the moku of Kāʻanapali.

310 Polaiki
Pola-iki

Literally, Lesser Pola—"pola. n. 1. Flap, as of a loincloth or sarong; tail of a kite...2. Platform or high seat between the canoes of a double canoe. (PH XI.) 3. Blossoms and sheath of a banana. 4. Rare. var. of kākala, spines on fish." /HD/

Ahupuaʻa in the kalana of Lahaina.

311 Polanui
Pola-nui

Literally, Greater Pola—"pola. n. 1. Flap, as of a loincloth or sarong; tail of a kite...2. Platform or high seat between the canoes of a double canoe. (PH XI.) 3. Blossoms and sheath of a banana. 4. Rare. var. of kākala, spines on fish." /HD/

Large ahupuaʻa in the kalana of Lahaina.

312 Polapola

"pola.pola. 1. nvi. Recovered from sickness; well, after sickness; to get well, convalesce; filling out, as after loss of weight; sprouting, as a bud...2. *(Cap.)* nvs. Tahiti, Borabora; Tahitian...3. Same as hēʻī, the Tahitian banana. 4. Redup. of pola 1; flapping...5. *(Cap.)* n. Star name, paired with the star Melemele." /HD/

Ahupuaʻa in the kalana of Lahaina.

313 Pools

Superimposed term of foreign origin for the shoreline point of Kamaiki in the ahupua'a of Mākila, kalana of Lahaina. *See also*: Kamaiki.

"Pools. Surf site, Lahaina, Maui. Off the community center swimming pool in the Puamana subdivision." /HPN/

Variant: Kamaiki.

314 Pua'a

"pua'a. n. 1. Pig, hog, swine, pork...2. Formerly a general name for introduced quadrupeds...3. Banks of fog or clouds, often as gathered over a mountain summit, a sign of rain and believed to be the cloud forms of Kama-pua'a..." /HD/

Ahupua'a in the kalana of Lahaina.

Variants: Puaanui, Puaaiki.

315 Puaaloa
Pua'aloa
Pua'a-loa

Literally, long *pua'a* ("pua'a. n. 1. Pig, hog, swine, pork...2. Formerly a general name for introduced quadrupeds...3. Banks of fog or clouds, often as gathered over a mountain summit, a sign of rain and believed to be the cloud forms of Kama-pua'a...." /HD/)

'Ilikū in the ahupua'a of Ukumehame.

316 Puahoowali
See Pu'uho'owali.

317 Puako
Puakō
Pua-kō

Literally, sugar cane tassel/blossom.

Ahupua'a in the kalana of Lahaina. Also, an inland pond in the same ahupua'a.

318 Puamana
Puamana
Pua-mana

Meaning undetermined, perhaps: branched flower.

'Ili in the ahupua'a of Ko'okā, kalana of Lahaina.

Also, the name of the renowned home of the Farden Family in the same area.

"Puamana. 1. Beach park, Lahaina, Maui. Puamana was the family home of Annie Kahalepouli Shaw Farden and Charles Kekua Farden. Their large two-story home, built in 1915, was located on Front Street. When the Fardens purchased the half-acre lot, it was already named Puamana. They agreed to keep the name for their home, translating it to mean the home that holds its members close. Puamana is probably best known to Hawai'i's residents through the song of the same name. Irmgard Farden Aluli, one of the twelve Farden children, composed it in 1935. Puamana Beach Park and Puamana subdivision adjacent to the park took their name from the Farden's family home. Also known as Mākila. 2. Surf site, Lahaina, Maui. Off the beach park." /HPN/

319 Puehuehu
Pūehuehu

"pū.ehu.ehu Redup. of puehu 1–3; tousled; flaky." /HD/; and, "puehu. 1. vs. Scattered, dispersed, routed, gone, tousled; fine, crumbling; every which way, as hair in the wind...2. vi. Peeling, as sunburn. 3. nvi. Remainder, remnant; to remain." /HD/

Large ahupua'a in the kalana of Lahaina.

Also, Pūehuehunui and Pūehuehuiki.

Variants: Puehuehunui, Puehuehuiki.

320 Puhako
Pūhākō
Pū-hā-kō

Pronunciation and meaning undetermined, perhaps: pū hā kō—clump of sugar cane stalks.

Obscure 'ili listed in the "Indices of Awards" as being located in the ahupua'a of Puakō, kalana of Lahaina.

321 Puhiaama

Puhi'a'ama

Puhi-'a'ama

Meaning undetermined, perhaps: puhi 'a'ama—to blow bits of 'a'ama crab (as chum), to bake 'a'ama crab, or, to bake an " 'a'ama" variety of eel.

Shoreline fishing shrine in the ahupua'a of Launiupoko.

"...oiai e lawai'a ana makou i kahi ahiahi ma Puhiaama he Ko-a mamali Oio ia, ke ike ala oe e Mr. Lunahooponopono, he wahi Ko-a lawai'a ia mawaho o kela lae aa o Lau-niupo [*sic*], mahope mai o kahi puali o Kahea, kahi no au e holoholo mau ai i ke a'o kula olelo Beritania [*sic*] i ko Olowalu kamalii.... [... *while we were fishing one evening at Puhi'a'ama, it is a fishing ground for young 'ō'io, you know it, Mr. Editor; it is a fishing Shrine beyond that rough point of Launiupoko, after a certain ravine called Kāhea, the place where you would always travel to teach Olowalu's children at the English language school....*]" /*Ka Nupepa Kuokoa*, Buke 40, Helu 18, 2 Mei 1902/

322 Pukalale

Puka-lale

Meaning undetermined, perhaps: puka lale—to come out in a hurry.

'Ili in the ahupua'a of Pua'a, kalana of Lahaina.

323 Punahoa

Puna-hoa

Literally, companion spring.

Shoreline and spring near the mouth of Olowalu Stream in the ahupua'a of Olowalu.

"Ma ia po no ua hala aku la ua kamaeu nei mauka, a ua hele pololei aku oia a hiki i ka hale o na makua ponoi o Lihau e noho mai ana me na manao o ka pihoihoi no keia owela o ke ahi ma ke kai a ia Makanikeoe i hiki aku ai malaila ua loli ae la kona mau helehelena e like me ka ui nohea oia aina Lihau a oia ka kona makuakane Puukilea i pane ae ai i kana wahine Punahoa Auhea oe e kuu wahine? [*That night this mischievous one disappeared inland, and he went directly to the house of Lihau's own parents, who were sitting there wondering about the glow of fire upon the ocean. As Makanikeoe arrived, his features changed to match that of the youthful beauty of that land, Lihau, and that is how her father Pu'ukīlea responded to his wife Punahoa. Say, my wife?*]" /*Ka Leo o ka Lahui*, Buke 2, Helu 942, 16 Mei 1894/

324 Punawai

Pūnāwai

"pū.nā.wai. n. Water spring." /HD/

'Ili in the ahupua'a of Moali'i, kalana of Lahaina.

325 Puopelu

Pū'ōpelu

Pū-'ōpelu

Literally, 'ōpelu hill ("'ō.pelu n. 1. Mackerel scad (*Decapterus pinnulatus* and *D. maruadsi*); an 'aumakua for some people... 2. A variety of taro. 3. *Lobelia hypoleuca*, a plant named for the supposed resemblance of its leaf to the fish of the same name." /HD/)

The name of the plain upon which the grounds of Lahainaluna are located.

326 Puou

Pū'ou

Meaning undetermined, perhaps: Sharply protruding hill.

Ahupua'a in the kalana of Lahaina.

327 Puu Anu

Pu'u Anu

Literally, cool hill.

Prominent hill (3,041 feet) in the ahupua'a of Ukumehame, situated just within the shared border between the moku of Lahaina and the moku of Wailuku.

Variant: Puuanu.

328 Puuhale

Pu'uhale

Pu'u-hale

Literally, house hill.

A luakini temple, assumed to be in Lahaina, mentioned in the mo'olelo of 'Ele'io as having been used by Kaululā'au. Positive identification and location have yet to be confirmed.

"A certain chief of Maui named Ohoohukulani rebelled. He was put to death by Kaulula'au [then] taken to the heiau of Pu'uhale [in Lahaina] and offered as a sacrifice…"
/Place Names (ULUK)/

329 Puuheehee
Pu'uhe'ehe'e
Pu'u-he'ehe'e

Literally, sliding hill.

———————

Name of the sea-side branch of Pu'u Lāina in the ahupua'a of Wahikuli, kalana of Lahaina.

330 Puu Hipa
Pu'u Hipa

Literally, Hipa hill: "Hipa is said to have been a mythological character." /PNOH/ Perhaps related to: Hipakāne—Aries.

———————

Prominent hill (1,002 feet) in the ahupua'a of Launiupoko, found above Pu'u Māhanaluanui.

Variant: Puuhipa.

331 Puu Hona
Pu'u Hona

Literally, Hona hill: "… probably named for a native tree." /PNOH/

[NOTE: Although a definition of this hill's name has historically been posited, the definition in the "Hawaiian Dictionary" for "hona," as a plant, is "Same as hōpue, a tree." "Hōpue" is further defined as, "A native tree, endemic to Kaua'i (*Urera sandvicensis* var. *kauaiensis*), in the nettle family, with broad-ovate, long-stemmed leaves, and red, clustered, male flowers. Also hona, ōpuhe." As such, the description of an ōpuhe-like plant in such a dry, windblown region seems unlikely. Perhaps the "hona" in this place name, found at the bottom of the trail, is a colloquially elided form for "ihona—descent, slope," as such: Pu'u Ihona.]

———————

Hill in the ahupua'a of Ukumehame, found on the "Wailuku" side of the trailhead for the Lahaina Pali Trail.

Variant: Puuhona.

332 Puuhoowali

Puʻuhoʻowali

Puʻu-hoʻowali

Literally, broken ground hill.

Ahupuaʻa in the kalana of Lahaina.

Variant: Puahoowali.

333 Puuhulilole

Puʻuhulilole

Puʻu-huli-lole

Meaning undetermined, perhaps: puʻu huli lole—searching for clothes hill, or, peeled taro-top hill.

An ʻauwai in the valley of Kauaʻula, kalana of Lahaina.

334 Puuiki

Puʻuiki

Puʻu-iki

Literally, small hill.

Ahupuaʻa in the kalana of Lahaina.

Variant: Puʻu Iki.

335 Puu Kauoha

Puʻu Kauoha

Literally, decree hill.

Hill (1,100 feet) in the ahupuaʻa of Ukumehame, situated in between the valley of Ukumehame and the gulch of Makaiwa.

From a moʻolelo told to the author by Maui kupuna Diane Amadeo regarding the gulch and shoreline of Pāpalaua: Pāpalaua was a violent moʻo from Molokaʻi. As Hiʻiakaika-poliopele journeyed toward Kauaʻi on her quest to find Lohiʻau, Pāpalaua—a female moʻo in this telling—swam forth to challenge her. The moʻo told Hiʻiaka that she would soon be stomping on her head—a most heinous offense! Hiʻiaka tried several times to dissuade Pāpalaua, but a fight eventually ensued in which Pāpalaua was slain just off the shore of Ukumehame. Hiʻiaka cast the lifeless Pāpalaua up onto the land where her body formed the large mountainous mass below Hanaʻulaiki; her tail descends down

Puʻu Kauoha, and her head is buried under the sand at Pāpalaua Beach, where it would be trampled upon by beachgoers for eternity. The gulch of Makaiwa/Makiwa is formed between her tail and her body.

336 Puuki
Puʻukī
Puʻu-kī

Literally, ti plant hill, or, pile of ti leaves.

Ahupuaʻa in the kalana of Lahaina.

337 Puukilea / Puu Kilea
See Kīlea.

338 Puʻukoliʻi
Puʻu-koliʻi

Literally, koliʻi shrub hill.

Hill, camp, reservoir, and residential area in the ahupuaʻa of Hanakaʻōʻō, kalana of Lahaina.

339 Puukoleaohilo
Puʻukōleaohilo
Puʻu-kōlea-o-Hilo

Literally, plover of Hilo hill.

ʻIli in the ahupuaʻa of Olowalu.

Variants: Puukoliolio, Puukoliohilo, Puukoleohilo.

340 Puukoleohilo
See Puukoleaohilo.

341 Puukoliohilo
See Puukoleaohilo.

342 Puukoliolio
See Puukoleaohilo.

343 Puu Laina
Pu'u Lāina
Pu'u Lā-ina

Literally, day-of-prying hill.

———

Prominent hill (650 feet) in the ahupua'a of Wahikuli, kalana of Lahaina.

———

"Moolelo no Puulaina... I ko laua noho a kane a wahine ana, hanau mai la ka laua keiki, he keiki kane, oia ka mea nona ka moolelo a kakou e kamailio nei. Aka, i kekahi manawa, loaa iho la ka hihia ia Eeke, no ka mea, ua ike aku la o Eeke i ka wahine maikai o Puuwaiohina, no Kauaula ia, a ua hana laua i ka hewa. No ia mea, manao iho la o Lihau e umi i ke keiki, a hele pu aku no hoi i ke kalohe; a noia mea, hoopaapaa ae la laua. Lawe ae la o Eeke i ke keiki na kona makuahine e hanai, oia hoi o Maunahoomaha. Ma ia hope iho hookapu mai la ko lakou akua, o Hinaikauluau, aole e noho pu laua, aole hoi e launa aku me kekahi mea e; aka he anahulu mahope iho o keia olelo, haule hou iho la o Eeke i ka hewa, me Puuwaiohina, oia kela mea mua i hai ia ae nei, a o ko Lihau muli iho nohoi ia. No ia mea, hoopai mai la ua akua nei o lakou, a hoolilo ia o Eeke i mauna, a o Puuwaiohina hoi i kualapa, oia no kela kualapa i Kauaula e ku mai la. A aia ma ka welau o ua pali la malalo iho, he puka; ina e kani ana ua puka nei, oia iho la ka wa e pa ai ke kauaula, aole o kana mai. Mahope iho oia manawa, kupu mai ke aloha ia Lihau no ka laua kamalei; nonoi mai la ia ia Maunahoomaha, e ike mai i kana keiki. He mea oluolu ia i kona makuahonowai, a ike ia i kana keiki, alaila, oluolu kona manao. [*Story regarding Pu'u Lāina... As they ('E'eke and Līhau) lived together as husband and wife, their child (Lāina) was born, a boy; he is the one for whom the tale about which we are talking belongs. But, at a certain time, 'E'eke became entangled in scandal, because 'E'eke saw the beautiful woman named Pu'uwaiohina; she was from Kaua'ula, and they perpetrated a sin. For this reason, Līhau thought to strangle the child, and go about in adultery as well; and for this reason, the two of them argued. 'E'eke took the child to be raised by his mother; she was Maunaho'omaha. Right after that their god, Hinaikauluau, placed restrictions upon them: the two of them were not to live together, and they were not to fornicate with anyone else; but ten days after this proclamation, 'E'eke fell again into sin with Pu'uwaiohina: she's the one told of above, and she was indeed Līhau's younger sister. For this reason, their god punished them, and 'E'eke was changed into a mountain, and Pu'uwaiohina into a ridge—that's the ridge standing there at Kaua'ula. And there, right below the tip of this ridge, is a hole; if that hole is issuing forth a sound, that is the time when the Kaua'ula wind will blow, without limit. Right after this time, fondness welled up within Līhau for their beloved child; she requested of Maunaho'omaha to see her child. This was agreeable to her mother-in-law, and she saw her child; then, her mind was contented.*]" /Fornander, V, 535/

Variant: Puulaina.

344 Puu Luau

Pu'u Lū'au

"*Lit.*, taro tops hill." /PNOH/

_____

Prominent upland hill (2,336 feet) found on the west side of Manawainui Gulch, ahupua'a of Ukumehame.

A story relating to Pu'u Lū'au, shared with the author by Maui kupuna Diane Amadeo, is herein paraphrased: When Pele fled from the Lahaina side, after a fight with Nāmaka-okaha'i, she created Haleakalā for her family and her. The favorite food of Pele and her sisters is pē'ū [ceremonially prepared lū'au leaves cooked with salt]. But, on this side of the island, their followers had no salt with which to prepare it. So, Pele created Mā'alaea—then called Kamā'alaea—and then took some salt [of her tears, in one version; and, some that she had kept since Kaua'i in another] and created Keālia Pond. The lū'au for their pē'ū was grown on Pu'u Lū'au, above Mā'alaea.

345 Puu Moe

Pu'u Moe

"*Lit.*, sleeping hill or prostrate hill." /PNOH/

_____

Prominent upland hill (2,433 feet) found to the east of Manawainui Gulch, higher up on the ridge above Pu'u Hona, in the ahupua'a of Ukumehame.

346 Puunau

Pu'unā'ū

Pu'u-nā'ū

Pronunciation and meaning undetermined, perhaps: pu'u nā'ū—*nā'ū* (variety of sweet potato; native gardenia) hill.

_____

Ahupua'a in the kalana of Lahaina.

[NOTE: Puunau is not synonymous with the ahupua'a of "Pa'ūnā'ū."]

Variants: Puunauiki, Puunau 2.

347 Puunoa

Pu'unoa

Pu'u-noa

Literally, hill freed of taboo.

_____

Ahupua'a in the kalana of Lahaina.

Variants: Punoa, Puunoa Hema, Puunoa Akahi, Puunoa 1, 2, 3.

348 **Puuokapolei**
Pu'uokapolei
Pu'u-o-Kapolei

Literally, Kapolei's hill.

Unidentified region in the ahupua'a of Olowalu.

"Maanei e hookomo ana makou i kekahi mahele pili i ka moolelo o Kamehameha mahope iho o keia kaua ana i 'Kakanilua'. A ua loaa mai keia mahele mai kekahi mea paanaau moolelo Hawaii mai he alii hanau no hoi ia no ka aina. He eha la mahope iho o ke kaua o Kakanilua, ua loaa i na 'lii o Hawaii na hookipa oluolu ia ana e ka Moi Kahekili o Maui. Ua olelo mai la o Kahekili i ua poe alii la o Hawaii e ka'ulua iki lakou no Maui a e hoomaha hoi. O ka aina a Kahekili i haawi mai ai ia lakou i wahi no lakou e noho ai, oia o Puuokapolei ma Olowalu. O ko lakou kalana ia a hoea i Lahaina. [*Here we will put in a section about the history of Kamehameha just after battling at 'Kakanilua.' This section was gotten from a Hawaiian oral history keeper, one born as a chief from the land. Four days after the battle of Kakanilua, the chiefs of Hawai'i received pleasant invitations by King Kahekili of Maui. Kahekili said to these chiefs of Hawai'i to stay a bit on Maui and to rest. The land that Kahekili gave to them as a place for them to stay, it was Pu'uokapolei at Olowalu. It was to be their district all the way to Lahaina.*] /Ka Na'i Aupuni*, Buke 1, Helu 21, 20 Kekemapa 1905/

"O na alii aimoku koikoi i komo pu ma keia manewanewa no ka make ana o Kalaniopuu, a poe kumakena hoi nona, oia no o Keawemauhili, alii aimoku o Hilo; Kanekoa, o Hamakua; Keeaumokupapaiaheahe o Kealia, Kona Hema, Hawaii, na mahoe kapu a Keawe-Poepoe o Kamanawa a me Kameeiamoku; na keiki ponoi no hoi a Kalaniopuu, Keoua Kuaahuula a me Keouapaale o Kau; Kawelaokalani k. o Kahaluu; Pualinui o Puuokapolei, Olowalu, Maui; Kaleipa'ihala o Kailua, Kona Akau a me na wahine a Kalaniopuu a me na alii aialo nohoi. [*The prominent district ('aimoku) chiefs that joined in the dramatic displays of grief because of the death of Kalani'ōpu'u, and the people who joined in wailing for him, were Keawemauhili, district chief of Hilo; Kānekoa, of Hāmākua; Ke'e'aumokupapāpaiaheahe of Keālia, Kona Hema, Hawai'i, the sacred twins of Keawepoepoe, Kamanawa and Kame'eiamoku; the actual children of Kalani'ōpu'u, Keōuakua'ahu'ula* and Keōuapā'ale** of Ka'ū; Kawelaokalani (male) of Kahalu'u; Pū'ali-nui of Pu'uokapolei, Olowalu, Maui; Kaleipa'ihala of Kailua, Kona 'Ākau and the wives of Kalani'ōpu'u as well as the attendant chiefs.*] /Ka Na'i Aupuni*, Buke 1, Helu 38, 10 Ianuali 1906/

* Keōuakua'ahu'ula, same as Keōuakū'ahu'ula

** Keōuapā'ale, perhaps same as Keōuape'e'ale

"Ka waiho no a ke kula, / Ka moe a Kamaomao, / Ahu kupanaha ia Puuokapolei.... [*The sprawl of the plains, / The lay of Kama'oma'o, / A mass of wonder to Pu'uokapolei....*]" /Ka Nupepa Kuokoa*, Buke 34, Helu 16, 20 'Apelila 1895/

349 Puu Papai
Pu'u Papa'i / Pu'u Pāpa'i

Pronunciation and meaning undetermined, perhaps: pu'u papa'i—temporary hut hill; or, pu'u pāpa'i—*pāpa'i* crab hill.

An 'auwai and area in the valley of Kaua'ula, kalana of Lahaina. Also, a point along the boundary between the ahupua'a of Launiupoko and the ahupua'a of Polanui in the kalana of Lahaina.

"Course 1 of the Launiupoko/Polanui boundary runs 'along boundary line between this land and Polanui to stake in Puupapai...' Elevation about 485 ft." /Place Names (ULUK)/

Variant: Puupapai.

350 Puupiha
Pu'upīhā
Pu'u-pīhā

Literally, driftwood hill.

'Ili and shoreline point in the ahupua'a of Pu'unoa, kalana of Lahaina. This point has more recently been named "Pu'unoa Point." Site of the Puupiha Cemetery.

Variants: Puupiha, Pu'upiha, Pu'u Piha, Puunoa, Puu Noa.

351 Puu Ulaula
Pu'u 'Ula'ula

Literally, red hill.

Point (3,058 feet) along Kaluako'i Ridge found along the boundary between the ahupua'a of Launiupoko and the ahupua'a of Kaua'ula in the kalana of Lahaina.

"Course 4 of the Launiupoko/Kauaula boundary runs 'up Luakoi ridge to angle of ridge (Puuulaula)' called 'Luakoi' (q.v.) on USGS; elevation 2800 ft." /Place Names (ULUK)/

Variant: Ulaula.

352 Puuwaiohina
Pu'uwaiohina
Pu'uwai-o-Hina

Literally, Hina's heart.

The name for the ridge at the back of Kaua'ula Valley, kalana of Lahaina.

"I ko laua noho a kane a wahine ana, hanau mai la ka laua keiki, he keiki kane, oia ka mea nona ka moolelo a kakou e kamailio nei. Aka, i kekahi manawa, loaa iho la ka hihia ia Eeke, no ka mea, ua ike aku la o Eeke i ka wahine maikai o Puuwaiohina, no Kauaula ia, a ua hana laua i ka hewa. No ia mea, manao iho la o Lihau e umi i ke keiki, a hele pu aku no hoi i ke kalohe; a noia mea, hoopaapaa ae la laua. Lawe ae la o Eeke i ke keiki na kona makuahine e hanai, oia hoi o Maunahoomaha. Ma ia hope iho hookapu mai la ko lakou akua, o Hinaikauluau, aole e noho pu laua, aole hoi e launa aku me kekahi mea e; aka he anahulu mahope iho o keia olelo, haule hou iho la o Eeke i ka hewa, me Puuwaiohina, oia kela mea mua i hai ia ae nei, a o ko Lihau muli iho nohoi ia. No ia mea, hoopai mai la ua akua nei o lakou, a hoolilo ia o Eeke i mauna, a o Puuwaiohina hoi i kualapa, oia no kela kualapa i Kauaula e ku mai la. A aia ma ka welau o ua pali la malalo iho, he puka; ina e kani ana ua puka nei, oia iho la ka wa e pa ai ke kauaula, aole o kana mai. Mahope iho oia manawa, kupu mai ke aloha ia Lihau no ka laua kamalei; nonoi mai la ia ia Maunahoomaha, e ike mai i kana keiki. He mea oluolu ia i kona makuahonowai, a ike ia i kana keiki, alaila, oluolu kona manao. [*As they ('E'eke and Līhau) lived together as husband and wife, their child was born, a boy; he (Lāina) is the one for whom the tale about which we are talking belongs. But at a certain time, 'E'eke became entangled in scandal, because 'E'eke saw the beautiful woman named Pu'uwaiohina; she was from Kaua'ula, and they perpetrated a sin. For this reason, Līhau thought to strangle the child, and go about in adultery as well; and for this reason, the two of them argued. 'E'eke took the child to be raised by his mother; she was Maunaho'omaha. Right after that their god, Hinaikauluau, placed restrictions upon them: the two of them were not to live together, and they were not to fornicate with anyone else; but ten days after this proclamation, 'E'eke fell again into sin with Pu'uwaiohina: she's the one told of above, and she was indeed Līhau's younger sister. For this reason, their god punished them, and 'E'eke was changed into a mountain, and Pu'uwaiohina into a ridge—that's the ridge standing there at Kaua'ula. And there, right below the tip of this ridge, is a hole; if that hole is issuing forth a sound, that is the time when the Kaua'ula wind will blow, without limit. Right after this time, fondness welled up within Līhau for their beloved child; she requested of Maunaho'omaha to see her child. This was agreeable to her mother-in-law, and she saw her child; then, her mind was contented.*]" /Fornander, V, 535/

353 Raheina
See Lahaina.

354 Scenic Lookout
See Papawai.

355 Shark Pit
See ʻŪhāʻīlio.

356 Uhailio
ʻŪhāʻīlio
ʻŪhā-ʻīlio

Literally, hindquarter/thigh of a dog.

Shoreline, surf, and cove in the ahupuaʻa of Halakaʻa, kalana of Lahaina.

The surf site has more recently been called by the superimposed name of foreign origin "Shark Pit."

"He lua uluulu, aia makai pono ae o ka Pa o ka Mea Hanohano F. W. Beckley. O Uhailio ka inoa, he ano Ana maoli no keia lua, a he wahi moe ia no na mano Lalakea. [*There is a sea cavern; it's there right off the shore of the lot of the Honorable F. W. Beckley. The name is ʻŪhāʻīlio, and this cavern is a true cave, and it's a sleeping place for the Whitetip Reef Sharks.*]" /*Ka Nupepa Kuokoa*, Buke 40, Helu 18, 2 Mei 1902/

"Shark Pit . . . Surf site, Lahaina, Maui. Off Puamana subdivision. Shark sightings are common here." /HPN/

Variant: Shark Pit.

357 Uhao

Meaning undetermined: "uhao. 1. same as hao 3, 4" /HD/; "hao. 3. nvt. To scoop, dish, or pick up; to grasp, gouge, pillage, plunder, loot; robber. 4. vt. To come with force, as wind or rain; to do with force and energy. . . ." /HD/

Ahupuaʻa in the kalana of Lahaina.

358 Ukumehame
Uku-mehame

Literally, "to pay with mehame wood." /PNOH/

In size, the largest ahupuaʻa in the moku of Lahaina.

359 Ulaula

See Puu Ulaula.

360 Umulau

Umu-lau

Literally, leaf oven.

_____

The name of a large flat stone found somewhere above the ʻAʻalaloloa trail, ahupuaʻa of Ukumehame.

_____

"Olelo aku la o Kihapiilani i kana wahine, mai hele aku kaua ma kahi o ka poe lawaia, e ike mai auanei ia kaua, nolaila, he pono e hele loa ae kaua ma ke alialia; ae mai la ka wahine a o ko laua nei hele aku la no ia a hiki ia Palaau, ike aku la laua nei i na kukuna o ka la e halaoa mai ana maluna o ke kuahiwi of Haleakala, au aku la laua nei a pii ana i na pali o Aalaloloa, hele aku la a hiki i ke kahawai o Manawainui, pii ma kela aoao o ua kahawai nei, hoomau aku la ka hele ana a hala mai la he mau wahi alu, a kiei ana ma kela aoao e nana iho ai ia Kapoli a me Kamaalaea, ma laila laua nei i hoomaha iho ai, huli aku la nana i ka waiho mai o ke kula o Kamaomao, o ka moe kokolo mai a ka uwahi o Kula i ka lawe a ke ahe kehau, aia ma keia wahi a laua e hoomaha nei, aia malaila kekahi pohaku nui palahalaha o Umulau ka inoa, aia keia pohaku mauka o ke alanui. [*Kihāpiʻilani said to his wife, "Let's not go where the people fishing are; they may see us, so, it's best that we go further inland along the salt bed." His wife consented and the two of them went until Palaau (Pāpalaua), they saw the rays of the sun projecting above the mountain of Haleakalā, they swam out and ascended the cliffs of ʻAʻalaloloa, they went until the stream of Manawainui, they climbed that side of the stream, they continued until they passed a few small gulches, and they were gazing down that side looking out at Kapoli and Kamāʻalaea, it was there that they rested; they turned and looked at the sprawl of the plains of Kamaʻomaʻo, at how the wisps of Kula's mists crept along while being carried by the Kēhau breeze—there at this place where they were resting, there was the large flat stone by the name of Umulau; that stone is on the upper side of the road."*] /Ka Nupepa Kuokoa, Buke 23, Helu 6, 9 Pepeluali 1884./

Variants: (from the same story): Ululau, Unula, Unuula.

361 Unahi

Literally, fish scale.

_____

A fishing ground of the ahupuaʻa of Olowalu.

362 Unahiole
Unahiʻole
Unahi-ʻole

Literally, scale-less (of fish).

———————————

Inland pond once found near the mouth of Kahoma Stream in the ahupuaʻa of Moaliʻi, kalana of Lahaina.

363 Uo
ʻUo

"ʻuo, ʻuwo 1. nvt. A group of feathers tied together in a small bunch, to be made into a feather lei or cloak; to tie thus; to tie into a lei; to string on a needle; to splice, interweave, as strands of a rope; seizing turns in lashing." /HD/

———————————

"ʻUo. Ancient surfing area, Lahaina qd., Maui. (Finney and Houston 28.)" /PNOH/

364 Uwai
Uwai / Ūwai
Uwai / Ū-wai

Pronunciation and meaning undetermined, perhaps: "uwai. vt. To move, as an object; to push aside; to move from place to place, as a tethered animal; sliding, as a door; opening and shutting; to be dislocated, as a joint..." /HD/; or, ū wai—water moisture.

———————————

ʻIli in the ahupuaʻa of Ukumehame.

365 Wahikuli
Wahi-kuli

Literally, noisy place.

———————————

Ahupuaʻa in the kalana of Lahaina.

Mentioned in a paraphrasing of a moʻolelo told to the author by Maui kupuna Diane Amadeo: When Pele first came to Maui, she began to dig. The place where she dug was "Hanakaʻōʻō (The Digging Stick Works)." Because of the noise, part of the area was called "Wahikuli (Noisy Place)." The hill on which she first lived was called "Lāina (Day of Prying)."

Variant: Maihikuli.

366 Wahine Pee
Wahine Peʻe

Literally, hiding woman.

_____

The traditional name for what has recently been called Kāʻanapali Beach, in the ahupuaʻa of Hanakaʻōʻō, kalana of Lahaina.

367 Waianae
Waiʻanae
Wai-ʻanae

Literally, mullet water.

_____

Ahupuaʻa in the kalana of Lahaina.

Variant: Waianaenui, Waianaeiki.

368 Waianiokole
See Waianuukole.

369 Waianukole
See Waianuukole.

370 Waianukoli
See Waianuukole.

371 Waianuukole
Waianuʻukole
Wai-a-nuʻukole

Literally, water of the *nuʻukole* goby fish.

_____

Stream bed and area in the ahupuaʻa of Polanui, kalana of Lahaina.

"Hoomau mai no nae keia ['Eleʻio] i ka holo a hala o Ukumehame, hiki keia i Olowalu, a hala Olowalu, hiki keia i Awalua, a hala o Awalua, hiki keia i Kulanaokalai, a hala o Kulanaokalai, hiki keia i Launiupoko, a hala o Launiupoko, hiki keia i Waianuukole, ia ia nei nae i Waianuukole, hookokoke loa ae la o Aahualii ma hope o ia nei. [*He ('Eleʻio) continued running until he passed Ukumehame, came and passed Olowalu, came and passed Awalua, came and passed Kūlanaokalaʻi, came and passed Launiupoko, got to Waianuʻukole, and while he was at Waianuʻukole, ʻAʻahualiʻi came up very close behind him.*]" /*Ka Nupepa Kuokoa*, Buke 2, Helu 36, 5 Kepakemapa 1863/

Variants: Wainukole, Waianukoli, Waianiokole.

372 Waiie
Wai‘ie
Wai-‘ie

Meaning undetermined, perhaps: wai ‘ie—wicker fish-trap water, or, ‘ie vine water.

Heiau once found near Kapā‘ulu in the vicinity of the ahupua‘a most likely in the ahupua‘a of Pa‘ūnā‘ū, kalana of Lahaina.

"Waiie Heiau, Walker Site 9 Location: Kapaulu district south of Lahainaluna Road in cane. Totally destroyed." /Walker, SOM 65/

373 Waiieiki
Wai‘ieiki
Wai-‘ie-iki

Literally, lesser Wai‘ie (meaning of "wai ‘ie" undetermined, perhaps: wai ‘ie—wicker fish-trap water, or, ‘ie vine water.)

‘Ili in the ahupua‘a of Akinui, kalana of Lahaina.

374 Waikapu
Wai-kapu

Literally, sacred/forbidden/tabooed water.

‘Ili in the ahupua‘a of Mākila, kalana of Lahaina.

375 Waikeekeehi
Waike‘eke‘ehi
Wai-ke‘eke‘ehi

Literally, tread water.

Point along the boundary between the ahupua‘a of Kaua‘ula in the kalana of Lahaina, and the moku of Wailuku. *See also*: Keekeehia.

"A place on the ridge between Wailuku Valley and Kauaula Valley." /Place Names (ULUK)/

[NOTE: Spelled "Waikekeehi" in /Place Names (ULUK)/.]

376 Waikekeehi
See Waikeekeehi.

377 Wailehua
Wai-lehua

Literally, lehua blossom nectar.

The name of the shoreline point of the ahupuaʻa of Mākila, as well as the name of a prominent heiau once found in the same ahupuaʻa, kalana of Lahaina.

378 Wailoa
Wai-loa

"Wai-loa. n. Name of a star near the Pleiades, said to be a member of the group called Kaulua. It is also said to be a name of an ancient chief. *Lit.*, long stream." /PNOH/

ʻIli in the ahupuaʻa of Olowalu. Perhaps related to Kawaialoa.

379 Waimana
Wai-mana

Literally, branched stream/watercourse.

An ʻauwai in the valley of Kauaʻula, kalana of Lahaina.

380 Wainala
See Wainalo.

381 Wainalo
Wai-nalo

Literally, disappearing water.

Short gulch adjoining Hāhākea Stream found on the ridge separating the gulches of Hāhākea and Kaliʻi, in the ahupuaʻa of Hāhākea, kalana of Lahaina.

Variant: Wainala.

382 Wainee
Wai-neʻe

"*Lit.*, moving water." /PNOH/

Ahupuaʻa in the kalana of Lahaina.

Variant: Waineenui.

383 Waiokama
Wai-o-Kama

Literally, waters of Kama.

Ahupuaʻa in the kalana of Lahaina.

384 Waiola Church
Wai-ola

Literally, life-giving waters.

Historic church, originally called "Ebenezer Church," then "Wainee Church," in the ahupuaʻa of Waineʻe, kalana of Lahaina. On the church grounds is located the Waineʻe Cemetery, the first Christian graveyard in Hawaiʻi, in which many prominent aliʻi, Hawaiians, and missionaries are buried.

385 Waiolimu
Wai-o-limu

Literally, algae water.

Stream and gulch in the ahupuaʻa of Polaiki, kalana of Lahaina.

386 Waipaahao
Waipaʻahao
Wai-paʻahao

Literally, *paʻahao* storage ("paʻa.hao. n. Proceeds [as pigs, sweet potatoes or taro] paid to holders of land on which tenants worked; penalty for failure to pay was imprisonment. Cf. *lā paʻahao, loʻi paʻahao*." /HD/)

ʻIli in the ahupuaʻa of Kauaʻula, kalana of Lahaina.

387 Wanapa
Wānapa
Wā-napa

Pronunciation and meaning undetermined, perhaps: wā napa—period of procrastinations; or, a colloquial elision of: wai ʻanapa—sparkling water.

ʻIli in the ahupuaʻa of Kauaʻula, kalana of Lahaina.

388 Wash Rock
See Manuohule.

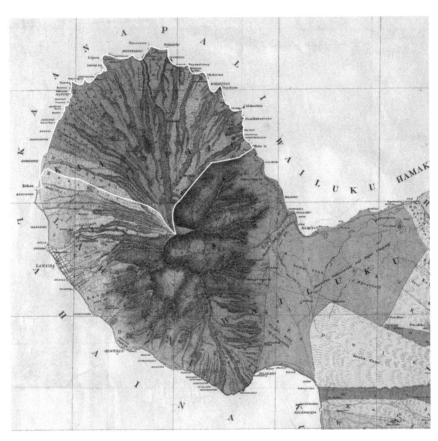

Map of Kāʻanapali Moku

CHAPTER 3

KĀʻANAPALI MOKU

Peʻa lau peʻahi ʻo Kāʻanapali—
Kaʻapeha mahola i ka paʻihi,
Kōaniani papaiāulu i ke konini—
Hoʻolalelale i ka neʻe Uluau.

The borders of the district of Kāʻanapali are like the blade of a fan—
Opening to spread out smoothly with esteem,
Drawing and stirring a breeze as it waves—
Hastening the pass of the Uluau.

na Cody Pueo Pata[1]

1 Aawaiki
ʻAʻawaiki
ʻAʻawa-iki

Literally, lesser ʻAʻawa ("ʻaʻawa 1. n. Wrasse fishes, Hawaiian hogfish [*Bodianus bilunulatus*], considered ʻaumākua by some." /HD/)

Islet between Lahoʻole and Hulu Islet, ahupuaʻa of Kukuipuka, kalana of Kahakuloa.

2 Aawanui
ʻAʻawanui
ʻAʻawa-nui

Literally, greater ʻAʻawa ("ʻaʻawa 1. n. Wrasse fishes, Hawaiian hogfish [*Bodianus bilunulatus*], considered ʻaumākua by some." /HD/)

Islet between Lahoʻole and Hulu Islet, ahupuaʻa of Kukuipuka, kalana of Kahakuloa.

---

1. A description of the moku of Kāʻanapali likening the shape of the district with that of a peʻahi.

3 Ahoa
Ahoa / ʻĀhoa

Pronunciation and meaning undetermined, perhaps: ahoa—breathed; ʻā- + -hoa—indifferent, defiant, harsh, or, friendly; or, an elision of: aʻa hoa—friendly hospitality.

Ahupuaʻa consisting of at least eight ʻili, kalana of Kahakuloa.

Variant: Ahoaiki.

4 Ahoaiki
See Ahoa.

5 Ahuakolea
Ahuakōlea

Ahu-a-kōlea

Literally, mound of the *kōlea* bird.

Shoreline point along the ahupuaʻa of Honokahua.

6 Aikahi
ʻAikahi

ʻAi-kahi

Literally, eat scrapings (as from the side of the poi bowl; thus, *figuratively*, to consume entirely).

ʻIli in the ahupuaʻa of Nāpili.

7 Aimaia
ʻAimaiʻa

ʻAi-maiʻa

Literally, to eat bananas.

Site featuring a fishing shrine in the ahupuaʻa of Honolua. Also called Pūhalakau.

"Location: Makai to Honolua Park along shore. Description: Heiau for Kuula. Level space showing some paving with small stones. Modern stone walls and houses built on the site obliterating its outlines. Remarks: Fisherman's koʻa formerly on beach has washed away. Informant, Kepuhi Keahi at Honolua." /Walker, SOM 28/

8 Aipohopoho

ʻAipohopoho / ʻAipohōpohō
ʻAi-pohopoho / ʻAi-pohōpohō

Pronunciation and meaning undetermined, perhaps: ʻai pohopoho—kneaded poi; or, ʻai pohōpohō—vegetable food grown in a marshy area, or, food gone to total waste (a metaphor used in traditional agricultural prayers to imply an abundant excess of crop yields).

———

ʻIli in the ahupuaʻa of Honokōwai.

Variants: Aipokopooo, Aipopo, Aipopoo

9 Aipopo

See Aipohopoho.

10 Aipopoo

See Aipohopoho.

11 Aipuaa

ʻAipuaʻa
ʻAi-puaʻa

Literally, to eat pork, or, to eat like a pig.

———

ʻIli in the ahupuaʻa of Māhinahina.

12 Akaluaiki

ʻĀkaluaiki
ʻĀ-ka-lua-iki

Pronunciation and meaning undetermined, perhaps: ʻā ka lua iki—lesser the-pit/oven-burns.

———

Shoreline area just to the east of Waiakeakua Gulch in the ahupuaʻa of Honokōhau. *See also*: Akaluanui.

Variant: Akhluaiki.

13 Akaluanui

ʻĀkaluanui
ʻĀ-ka-lua-nui

Pronunciation and meaning undetermined, perhaps: ʻā ka lua nui—greater the-pit/ oven-burns.

———

Shoreline area just to the west of Waiakeakua Gulch in the ahupuaʻa of Honokōhau. *See also*: Akaluaiki.

14 Akhluaiki
See Akaluaiki.

15 Alaapapa
ʻĀlaʻapapa / Alaʻāpapa
ʻĀlaʻapapa / Ala-ʻāpapa

Pronunciation and meaning undetermined, perhaps: " ʻā.laʻa.papa 1. v. To tell publicly, as of the past 2. n. Type of ancient dramatic hula... 3. n. Long cloud formation" /HD/; or, ala ʻāpapa—path along the flat/stratum.

———

Flatland area mentioned in mele in the context of the ahupuaʻa of Pōʻelua, kalana of Kahakuloa.

———

"Mai ka ihona la e Keanaakaluahine, / Mai ka piina la i Awalua, / Mai ke kahawai la e Poelua, / Elua no kaua i ke kula o Alaapapa, / Oia kula mehameha kanaka ole.... [*From the descent of Keanaakaluahine, / From the ascent at Awalua, / From the stream of Pōʻelua, / We two upon the flatlands of ʻĀlaʻapapa, / That lonely unpopulated plain....*]." /*Ko Hawaii Pae Aina*, Buke 2, Helu 14, 5 ʻApelila 1879/

Variant: Alapapa.

16 Alaelae
ʻĀlaelae

Literally, many shoreline points.

———

Shoreline area along the ahupuaʻa of Honolua.

17 Alaeloa
ʻAlaeloa
ʻAlae-loa

"*Lit.*, distant mudhen." /PNOH/

———

Ahupuaʻa containing 12 ʻili in the moku of Kāʻanapali.

Also, a seaside area in the ahupuaʻa of ʻAlaeloa.

———

[NOTE: Not included in the Māhele databases amongst the 12 ʻili is the ʻili of Kalaekole.] "3801 Lupea Kanapali [*sic*] Ian 19. 1848... Ke hoopii aku nei au ia oukou no koʻu kuleana aina, aia iloko o Alaeloa ke ahupuaa he ili aina o ka inoa o Kalaekole.... [*3801 Lupea Kāʻanapali Jan 19, 1848... I am petitioning you all regarding my property; it is within the ahupuaʻa of ʻAlaeloa, it's an ʻili of land by the name of Kalaekole....]"* /Native Register (KPA)/

Variants: Alaeloa 1, 2; Alaeloanui, Alaeloaiki.

18 Alapapa
See Alaapapa.

19 Aliʻi Kahekili Nui ʻAhumanu Beach Park

County beach park in the ahupuaʻa of Honokōwai.

Variant: Kahekili Beach Park.

20 Amalu
ʻĀmalu
ʻĀ-malu

Pronunciation and meaning undetermined, perhaps: ʻā- + malu—protected.

———————

Tributary joining with that of Kapaloa to the southwest to form Honokōwai Stream.

21 Anakaluahine
Anākaluahine
Ana-(a)-ka-luahine

Literally, cave of the old woman.

———————

Gulch and stream opening into Keawalua Bay, ahupuaʻa of Honokōhau.

Variant: Keanaakaluahine.

22 Anakaualehu
Ana-(a)-ka-Ualehu

Literally, cave of the Ualehu (rain).

———————

Shoreline area along the ahupuaʻa of Honokahua.

Variant: Wanakaluaehu.

23 Analoa
Ana-loa

Literally, long cave.

_____

'Ili in the ahupua'a of Honokōwai.

Variant: Wanaloa.

24 Anamoo
Anamo'o
Ana-mo'o

Literally, *mo'o* (lizard, water spirit) cave.

_____

'Ili in the ahupua'a of Honokahua.

25 Apakawaha
'Apakawaha
'Apa-ka-waha

Meaning undetermined, perhaps: the speaker delays.

_____

'Ili in the ahupua'a of Honokeana.

26 Apopo
'Apōpō / 'Āpōpō

Literally, tomorrow.

_____

'Ili in the ahupua'a of Honokōhau.

Variant: Opopo.

27 Auwailimunui
'Ili in the ahupua'a of Waikapū (Wailuku), wrongly labeled as being in the ahupua'a of Honokōwai.

28 Auwaipaki
'Auwaipakī
'Auwai-pakī

Literally, spattering ditch.

_____

Cliff found between Waiheʻe (Wailuku) and the ahupuaʻa of Kahakuloa in the kalana of Kahakuloa.

Variant: Kaauwaipaki.

29 Awalua
See Keawalua.

30 Black Rock

Superimposed name of foreign origin for Kaleinākaʻuhane. *See also*: Kaleinakauhane.

31 Camp Maluhia

Maluhia, *literally,* serenity.

Extensive camp facility managed by the Aloha Council of the Boy Scouts of America found in the ahupuaʻa of Kukuipuka, kalana of Kahakuloa.

32 D.T. Fleming's Beach County Park

Superimposed name of foreign origin for the beach of Honokahua (bay). *See also*: Honokahua.

33 Eke
ʻEke

"ʻeke 1. n. Sack, pocket, bag, basket; bag-shaped fish net; scrotum. 2. vi. To cringe, shrink from, draw away from, flinch, wince; to become smaller, shrink." /HD/

Name of the famed conspicuous crater (4,449 feet) at the head of the kalana of Kahakuloa, and which is on the border between the kalana of Kahakuloa and the ahupuaʻa of Honokōhau.

[NOTE: Toward the very end of the 1800s and into the 1900s, the term "Mauna Eeke" began to become synonymous with ʻEke.]

"No ke Kalana o Kahakuloa a me Kona mau Hiohiona. Aia no keia Kalana ma ke komohana akau o na Waieha, a o kekahi hapa ia e ka apana o Lahaina, he aina alopali keia i pakuku ia e na pali kona mau aoao a hamama i mai, e huli aku ana ke alo o keia wahi aina kahawai i ka Hikina Akau, a he ake [sic] iki makai o ka nuku muliwai e pili ala me ke kai, o ko laila poe ka ike pono i ke kai o Hoomanunu, a ike no hoi i ka moku holo ae ma ka moana, a o ka poe ma uka aku, aole lakou e ike mai i ke kai, ua alai ia e kekahi wahi lapa e ku kalali ana mawaena o ke kahawai, o Lapaiki ka inoa, a o Haleino mauka iho. Aia ma ka lae kahakai ma ka hikina iho, e ku ana kona puu kaulana o ʻPuukoae papa i ka makaniʻ ʻKuinalehua o Kaukini.' A o ka mauna o Eke ma ke komohana, nolaila ka oleloia ana e ka poe haku mele kahiko, 'Hana ekeeke i ka ipu a ka makani.' Hiolo lua i ka pali o Leinaha. [*Regarding the District of Kahakuloa and Its Features. This district is northwest of the Waiʻehā region, and it's a portion of the precinct of Lahaina; this is a land in the face of the cliffs with its sides screened in by steep precipices and wide open along the sea, the front of this place of many streams and gulches faces Northeast, and the entrance of the rivermouth widens a little as it joins with the sea; the people there can view the sea of Hoʻomanunu, and they can see the ships traveling on the ocean, and the people inland, they cannot see the sea, the view is obscured by a small ridge standing proudly in the middle of the valley, Lapaiki is its name, and Haleʻino is just inland of that. There at the seaside point just to the east, its famous hill stands 'Puʻukoaʻe ever brushed against by the wind' 'Stringing Lehua of Kaukini.' And the mountain of ʻEke is to the west, from which comes mention by the composers of old, 'Forming a holder for the gourd of winds.' Tumbling incessantly down the cliffs of Leinahā.*] " / Ka Nupepa Kuokoa, Buke 14, Helu 33, 14 ʻAukake 1875/

"DIMENSIONS OF IAO VALLEY, MAUI. Length (from Wailuku), about 5 miles. Width of valley, 2 miles. Depth, near head, 4,000 feet. Elevation of Puu Kukui, above head of Valley, 5,788 feet. Elevation of Crater of Eke, above Waihee Valley, 4,500 feet." /Thrum, 1912/

"The finest of our Lobelias is *Lobelia gloria-montis*, a truly royal and superb plant. It occurs on the summit of Puukukui on West Maui, also on Mauna Eeke of the same range." /Rock, 1919/

"Pocket. Crater, West Maui. Elevation, 4,500 feet." /Thrum in Parker 1922, 628/

Variants: Puu Eke, Eke Crater, Mauna Eke.

34 Eke Crater
See Eke.

35 Elekii
See Kaelekii.

36 Elekini
ʻElekini
ʻEle-kini

Meaning undetermined, perhaps: ʻele kini—multitudinous (from "E-LE An intensive added to many words; very; much; greatly, &c." /Andrews/, with kini "1. num. Multitude, many; forty thousand." /HD/)

ʻIli in the ahupuaʻa of Honokōhau.

37 Eliwahine
ʻEliwahine
ʻEli-wahine

Meaning undetermined, perhaps: to dig like a woman.

———————

ʻIli in the ahupuaʻa of Kahakuloa, kalana of Kahakuloa.

38 Fleming's Beach

Superimposed name of foreign origin for Kapalua Beach. *See also*: Kapalua.

39 Haawekaula
Hāʻawekaula
Hāʻawe-kaula

Literally, to carry/pack rope.

———————

Shoreline area along the ahupuaʻa of Honokahua.

40 Haelaau
Haelāʻau
Hae-lāʻau

Meaning undetermined, perhaps: tearing caused by the forest thicket, or, ferocity of the club, or, ferocity of the club stroke.

———————

Historic cabin along Kaulalewalewa Ridge, ahupuaʻa of Māhinahina.

Variants: Kaulalewelewe House, Haelaau House, Hailaau.

41 Haena
Hāʻena

"hā.ʻena 1. nvs. Red-hot, burning, red. Hāʻena nā ihu, a red nose (with blood). 2. *(Cap.)* Place names on Hawaiʻi, Kauaʻi, and Oʻahu 3. Same as hāʻeʻena … 4. n. Kind of tapa wrapped about images." /HD/

———————

ʻIli in the ahupuaʻa of Honokōwai.

Variants: Haenaiki, Haenanui.

42 Haenaiki
See Haena.

43 Haenanui
See Haena.

44 Hailaau
See Haelaau.

45 Hainau
Haʻinau

"haʻi.nau vt. to bend the head forward." /HD/

ʻIli in the ahupuaʻa of Kahakuloa, kalana of Kahakuloa.

Variant: Heinau.

46 Hakuhee
Hakuheʻe
Haku-heʻe

"Probably *lit.*, fleeing lord." /PNOH/

Prominent seaside point (257 feet) in the ahupuaʻa of Makaliua 1, found below Puʻu Ōlaʻi, in the kalana of Kahakuloa.

47 Hale
Literally, house.

ʻIli in the ahupuaʻa of Makaliua 2, kalana of Kahakuloa.

48 Haleino
Haleʻino
Hale-ʻino

Meaning undetermined, perhaps: inhospitable house, or, wicked host.

An area mentioned as being inland of Lapaiki Ridge in the valley and ahupuaʻa of Kahakuloa, kalana of Kahakuloa.

"No ke Kalana o Kahakuloa a me Kona mau Hiohiona. Aia no keia Kalana ma ke komohana akau o na Waieha, a o kekahi hapa ia o ka apana o Lahaina, he aina alopali keia i pakuku ia e na pali kona mau aoao a hamama ma kai, e huli aku ana ke alo o keia wahi aina kahawai i ka Hikina Akau, a he ake iki makai o ka nuku muliwai e pili ala me ke kai, o ko laila poe ka ike pono i ke kai o Hoomanunu, a ike no hoi i ka moku holo ae ma ka moana, a o ka poe ma uka aku, aole lakou e ike mai i ke kai, ua alai ia e kekahi wahi lapa e ku kalali ana mawaena o ke kahawai, o Lapaiki ka inoa, a o Haleino mauka iho. Aia ma ka lae kahakai ma ka hikina iho, e ku ana kona puu kaulana o ʻPuukoae papa i ka makani' 'Kuinalehua o Kaukini.' A o ka mauna o Eke ma ke komohana, nolaila ka oleloia ana e ka poe haku mele kahiko, 'Hana ekeeke i ka ipu a ka makani.' Hiolo lua i ka pali o Leinaha. [*Regarding the District of Kahakuloa and Its Features. This district is northwest of the Waiʻehā region, and it's a portion of the precinct of Lahaina; this is a land in the face of the cliffs with its sides screened in by steep precipices and wide open along the sea, the front of this place of many streams and gulches faces Northeast, and the entrance of the rivermouth desires to join with the sea; the people there can view the sea of Hoʻoma-nunu, and they can see the ships traveling on the ocean, and the people inland, they cannot see the sea, the view is obscured by a small ridge standing proudly in the middle of the valley, Lapaiki is its name, and Haleʻino is just inland of that. There at the seaside point just to the east, its famous hill stands ʻPuʻukoaʻe ever brushed against by the wind' 'Stringing Lehua of Kaukini.' And the mountain of ʻEke is to the west, from which comes mention by the composers of old, 'Forming pockets for the gourd of winds.' Tumbling incessantly down the cliffs of Leinahā.*] ” / *Ka Nupepa Kuokoa*, Buke 14, Helu 33, 14 ʻAukake 1875/

49 Halelani
Hale-lani

Literally, royal house.

———

ʻIli in the ahupuaʻa of Mailepai.

50 Haleokane
Haleokāne
Hale-o-Kāne

Literally, House of Kāne.

———

ʻIli in the ahupuaʻa of Kahakuloa, kalana of Kahakuloa.

51 Hanaloa
See Kahanaloa.

52 Hanonana
See Hononana.

53 Haohao
Haohao / Haʻohaʻo

Pronunciation and meaning undetermined, perhaps: haohao—to scoop/gouge, or, to plunder/loot; or, haʻohaʻo—to wonder.

_____

ʻIli in the ahupuaʻa of Honokahua.

54 Haua

Literally, whipped or smitten.

_____

ʻIli in the ahupuaʻa of Honokōhau.

Also, ʻili (Haua 1, 2) in the ahupuaʻa of Mailepai.

55 Haukoe
Hau-koe

Pronunciation and meaning undetermined, perhaps: hau koe—*hau* branch stripped of bark, mother-of-pearl shell used to scrape bark, or, "remaining dew" /Parker/; or, to wield the stick beset with hooks to impale fish.

_____

Seaside point in the ahupuaʻa of ʻAlaeloa.

56 Haukoi
Haukoʻi
Hau-koʻi

Literally, adze strike, or hau branch used for adze hafts.

_____

ʻIli in the ahupuaʻa of Honokeana.

57 Haunaa
See Puu Haunaka.

58 Haunaku

Literally, to root, wallow.

_____

ʻIli in the ahupuaʻa of Honokahua.

59 Hawaii Route 30
See Honoapiilani Highway.

60 Hawaii Route 340
See Kahekili Highway.

61 Hawea
Hāwea

A proper name, "perhaps named for the famous drum brought by Laʻa-mai-Kahiki from Kahiki." /PNOH/

___

Seaside point between the ahupuaʻa of Nāpili and Honokahua.

62 Hawea Point Light
Hāwea Point Light

The minor-light beacon upon Hāwea Point.

___

"Hawea Point Light originally consisted of an acetylene lens lantern mounted atop a sixteen-foot pyramidal skeleton tower. First established in 1911 or 1912, the light is now a metal pole flanked by diamond-shaped daymarkers and topped by a flashing, solar-power light." /lighthousefriends.com/

Variant: Kapalua Lighthouse.

63 Heakalani
He-aka-lani / Hea-ka-lani

Meaning undetermined, perhaps: he aka lani—"a heavenly shadow" /PNOH/; or, hea ka lani—the sky/chief calls.

___

Heiau in the ahupuaʻa of Honokōhau. Perhaps the same as, or associated with, the heiau called ʻIliʻilikea.

___

"On the west side of Punaha Gulch, elevation 160 ft. Same as Iliilikea?" /Place Names (ULUK)/

64 Heinau
See Hainau.

65 Hihiho

Pronunciation and meaning undetermined, perhaps the proper name of a person, or a misinterpretation of "hihio" or "hihiʻo."

___

A heiau in the ahupuaʻa of Kahana.

66 Hikiapo
Hiki-ʻapo / Hiki-apo

Pronunciation and meaning undetermined, perhaps: hiki ʻapo—to fetch and grasp, to carry back and forth by grasping; or, hiki apo—to carry back and forth in embrace.

ʻIli in the ahupuaʻa of Honolua.

67 Hinapikao
Hinapīkaʻo

Hina-pīkaʻo

Meaning undetermined, perhaps: an unattested proper name of a goddess, Hina pīkaʻo—old-parched Hina; or, hina pīkaʻo—to topple over parched.

ʻIli in the ahupuaʻa of Kahana 1.

68 Hoaka

"hoaka 1. n. Crescent; arch, as over door of ancient house; crescent-shaped design at base of temple drum; crest, as on a helmet. 2. *(Cap.)* n. Second day of the month . . . 3. nvi. Brightness; shining, glittering, splendid; to glitter, shine, flash as lightning, become daylight; to flame . . . 4. v. To cast a shadow; to brandish, as a spear (2 Sam. 23.18), to drive away, ward off, frighten . . . 5. vt. To open, as the mouth . . . 6. n. Spirit, apparition, ghost . . . 7. n. Disease of the abdomen, perhaps appendicitis, rupture (followed by a qualifier)." /HD/

ʻIli in the ahupuaʻa of Kahana 3.

69 Hokolo
Hōkolo

Pronunciation and meaning undetermined, perhaps an elided form of: "hoʻo.kolo To cause to creep, crawl; to follow a trail, track, clue; to trace to a source." /HD/

Inland point along Kaulalewalewa Ridge from which the ahupuaʻa of Honokahua begins.

70 Hokuanui
Hokua-nui

Literally, tip of a great wave.

Shoreline point on the south side of Kapalua Bay in the ahupuaʻa of Nāpili.

71 Hono-
See Nā Hono a Piʻilani.

72 Honoapiilani Highway
Honoapiʻilani
Hono-a-Piʻilani

Literally, Bay(s) of Piʻilani.

Hawaiʻi Route 30, which extends south from the town of Wailuku toward Māʻalaea, turns west into the moku of Lahaina, and continues north through to the moku of Kāʻanapali, terminating in the ahupuaʻa of Honokōhau.

73 Honokahau
See Honokohau.

74 Honokawai
See Honokowai.

75 Honokahua
Hono-kahua

"*Lit.*, sites bay." /PNOH/

One of the six "hono-" ahupuaʻa in the moku of Kāʻanapali.

Also, the bay of the ahupuaʻa of Honokahua.

"Retained by Kale Davis at the Māhele, LCAw 8522-B:1, 2650 acres. No kuleana are listed in Indices of Awards or shown on Tax Maps. Identified in IDLM 397 as an ahupuaʻa containing 39 ili: Anamoo, Haohao, Haunaku, Iole, Kahanaha, Kahanaloa (3), Kalana, Kaluakanaka, Kanuku, Kaonahi, Kaohe, Kapili, Kaulu (2), Mahoe, Mokupea (2), Moomuku, Naio, Ohia, Opukaha (2), Paehala (2), Paina (2), Pakala (3), Paliuli, Paopao, Pehukanukunuku, Pohakuloa, Poopueo, Puulu (2), Wahalau." /Place Names (ULUK)/

"[Earl Ray Kukahiko]: When we were born had mid-wifes. Name came out Kapalua @ Ritz-Carlton given by Mr. Fleming. Before, it was called Honokohua [*sic*]. There was a scout camp there. Many people who have moved off Maui that lived @ Honokohua ask about Kapalua when they return or visit and are surprised to find the name change from Honokohua to Kapalua. Our house was the last house @ the corner with the coconut trees that my dad planted next to the store." /Tauʻa, 2005/

Variant: Honokohua.

76 Honokeana
Hono-ke-ana

"*Lit.*, the cave bay." /PNOH/

One of the six "hono-" ahupuaʻa with sixteen ʻili in the moku of Kāʻanapali.

Also, the gulch and bay of Honokeana.

"Retained by Konia at the Māhele, LCAw 5524:2, 603 acres. Also LCAw 3687 to Malo, 3925-K to Miki, 3925-L to Ili, 3925-O to Kekaa, 4240 to Kau, 4740 to Manuwai. Identified in IDLM 397 as an ahupuaʻa containing 16 ili in Honokeana 1 and 2: Apakawaha, Haukoi, Kahuki (2), Kaluanui, Kalelo, Kaluaoopu, Kaolapalapa, Kaukeke, Keoa, Kiiakapapa, Lapamuku, Naio (2), Ouolii, Pohakuloa." /Place Names (ULUK)/

Variants: Honokeana 1, 2.

77 Honokohau
Honokōhau
Hono-kō-hau

"*Lit.*, bay drawing dew." /PNOH/

One of the six "hono-" ahupuaʻa with thirty-nine ʻili in the moku of Kāʻanapali.

Also, the bay of the ahupuaʻa of Honokōhau.

"Retained by Kekuaiwa at the Māhele, LCAw 7714-B:8, 6680 acres. Also LCAw 74-B to C. Cockett, 25.25 acres. In addition are 94 kuleana in 39 named ili." /Place Names (ULUK)/

Variant: Honokahau.

78 Honokōhau Falls
The tallest waterfall (1,119 ft) on Maui found at the head of the Honokōhau River/Stream, in the ahupuaʻa of Honokōhau.

79 Honokohua
See Honokahua.

80 Honokowai
Honokōwai

Hono-kō-wai

"*Lit.*, bay drawing water." /PNOH/

_____

One of the six "hono-" ahupuaʻa in the moku of Kāʻanapali.

Variant: Honokawai.

81 Honokōwai Beach Park

County beach park in the ʻili of Moʻomuku, ahupuaʻa of Honokōwai.

82 Honolua
Hono-lua

"*Lit.*, two harbors. /PNOH/

_____

One of the six "hono-" ahupuaʻa in the moku of Kāʻanapali. Also, a bay of this ahupuaʻa.

83 Hononana
Hono-nana

"*Lit.*, animated [as of life or or activity] bay." /PNOH/

_____

An ahupuaʻa containing seven ʻili in the kalana of Kahakuloa, and included as one of the six "hono-" ahupuaʻa in the moku of Kāʻanapali.

_____

"Not named in the Mahele Book. Hononana ahupuaʻa may be defined as the land between Mokolea Point and Papanalahoa Point, drained by Hononana stream, Papanahoa stream and Alapapa stream. Identified in IDLM 397 as an ahupuaʻa containing 7 ili: Kapuna (2), Kauila, Keahupuaa, Koaeloa, Kulanaumeume, Waihapapa. Claim no. 6147-I by Puana is ʻin the ahupuaa of Hononanaʻ. Misspelt ʻHanonanaʻ in Award Book and Indices, ʻHonananaʻ on USGS quad. Hononana is one of the six bays comprising ʻNa Hono-a-Piilaniʻ of legend and song." /Place Names (ULUK)/

84 Hono o na Moku
Hono o nā Moku

Literally, Bay of Islands.

_____

A poetic name for the seas and channels found between the islands of Maui, Lānaʻi and Molokaʻi.

85 Honuaula

Honua-ʻula

"*Lit.*, red land." /PNOH/

Heiau in the ahupuaʻa of Honolua.

"Honuaula Heiau, Walker Site 18. Honolua Gulch just east of bend in road. Remains of old stone platforms and walls. Measures 29 ft. on south, 46 on west, 20 on north, 54 on east." /Place Names (ULUK)/

86 Hoomanunu

Hoʻomanunu

Meaning undetermined, perhaps: "To break out, as with a skin eruption." /HD/, to cause tremors (as an earthquake), or, to cause numbness.

The sea that fronts the ahupuaʻa and valley of Kahakuloa in the kalana of Kahakuloa.

"No ke Kalana o Kahakuloa a me Kona mau Hiohiona. Aia no keia Kalana ma ke komohana akau o na Waieha, a o kekahi hapa ia o ka apana o Lahaina, he aina alopali keia i pakuku ia e na pali kona mau aoao a hamama ma kai, e huli aku ana ke alo o keia wahi aina kahawai i ka Hikina Akau, a he ake [*sic*] iki makai o ka nuku muliwai e pili ala me ke kai, o ko laila poe ka ike pono i ke kai o Hoomanunu, a ike no hoi i ka moku holo ae ma ka moana, a o ka poe ma uka aku, aole lakou e ike mai i ke kai, ua alai ia e kekahi wahi lapa e ku kalali ana mawaena o ke kahawai, o Lapaiki ka inoa, a o Haleino mauka iho. Aia ma ka lae kahakai ma ka hikina iho, e ku ana kona puu kaulana o ʻPuukoae papa i ka makani' ʻKuinalehua o Kaukini.' A o ka mauna o Eke ma ke komohana, nolaila ka oleloia ana e ka poe haku mele kahiko, ʻHana ekeeke i ka ipu a ka makani.' Hiolo lua i ka pali o Leinaha. [*Regarding the District of Kahakuloa and Its Features. This district is northwest of the Waiʻehā region, and it's a portion of the precinct of Lahaina; this is a land in the face of the cliffs with its sides screened in by steep precipices and wide open along the sea, the front of this place of many streams and gulches faces Northeast, and the entrance of the rivermouth widens a little as it joins with the sea; the people there can view the sea of Hoʻomanunu, and they can see the ships traveling on the ocean, and the people inland, they cannot see the sea; the view is obscured by a small ridge standing proudly in the middle of the valley, Lapaiki is its name, and Haleʻino is just inland of that. There at the seaside point just to the east, its famous hill stands ʻPuʻukoaʻe ever brushed against by the wind' ʻStringing Lehua of Kaukini.' And the mountain of ʻEke is to the west, from which comes mention by the composers of old, ʻForming a holder for the gourd of winds.' Tumbling incessantly down the cliffs of Leinahā.*]" /Ka Nupepa Kuokoa, Buke 14, Helu 33, 14 ʻAukake 1875/

87 Huakukui
Hua-kukui

Literally, fruit and nut of the *kukui* tree.

ʻIli in the ahupuaʻa of Honokōhau.

88 Hulu

"hulu 1. n. Feather, quill, plumage...5. n. Hackle; fishhook with barb on the outside...7. n. Muscle attaching a bivalve to rocks...10. Same as hulu ʻīlio 1, nahawele 2, pūhuluhulu 2, a seaweed." /HD/

Islet and bird sanctuary off the coast of the ahupuaʻa of Kukuipuka, kalana of Kahakuloa.

89 Hunonaaahu
Hūnōnaaʻahu
Hūnōna-a-ʻAhu

Literally, ʻAhu's son/daughter-in-law.

Shoreline area along Kulaokaʻea, ahupuaʻa of Honolua.

90 Ihukoko
Ihu-koko

Literally, bloody nose.

Shoreline area along the ahupuaʻa of Honokahua.

91 Iliilikea
ʻIliʻilikea
ʻIliʻili-kea

Literally, white pebbles.

Heiau in the ahupuaʻa of Honokōhau. Perhaps the same as, or associated with, the heiau called Heakalani.

Regarding Heakalani: "On the west side of Punaha Gulch, elevation 160 ft. Same as Iliilikea?" /Place Names (ULUK)/

92 Ilikikoo
ʻIlikīkoʻo
ʻIli-kīkoʻo

Meaning undetermined, perhaps: elongated ʻili land unit.

———————

ʻIli in the ahupuaʻa of Honokōwai.

Variants: Uilikiko, Ulukikoo.

93 Iole
ʻIole

Literally, rat.

———————

ʻIli in the ahupuaʻa of Honokahua.

94 Iuao
ʻIuao / ʻĪʻuao
ʻIu-ao / ʻĪ-ʻuao

Pronunciation and meaning undetermined, perhaps: ʻiu ao—cloud loftiness; or, ʻī ʻuao—address of the peacemaker.

———————

Shoreline area along the ahupuaʻa of Nāpili.

95 Kaainaiki
Kaʻāinaiki
Ka-ʻāina-iki

Literally, the lesser land.

———————

ʻIli in the ahupuaʻa of Honokōwai.

96 Kaainanui
Kaʻāinanui
Ka-ʻāina-nui

Literally, the main land.

———————

Gulch and ʻili in the ahupuaʻa of Honokōwai.

97 Kaaio
See Kaalo.

98 Kaakua
Kaʻakua

"kaʻa.kua nvi. Violent dizziness; to lie down or lean back in pain, to roll over backwards." /HD/

ʻIli in the ahupuaʻa of Waiokila, kalana of Kahakuloa.

99 Kaalo
Kāʻalo

Literally, to pass by.

Shoreline point along the ahupuaʻa of ʻAlaeloa.

Variant: Kaaio.

00 Kaanapali
Kāʻanapali
Kāʻana-pali

Meaning undetermined, perhaps: to divide a cliff, or, to share a cliff; or, "*Lit.*, Kāʻana cliff." /PNOH/

[NOTE: The spelling "Kāʻanapali" has become widespread. It is herein employed out of respect to scholars of repute who use this spelling; however, it does not reflect the pronunciation of kūpuna and kamaʻāina of the region.]

One of the three moku of West Maui.

"One of twelve ancient districts on Maui, reduced to four in 1859. Kāʻanapali contained the ahupuaʻa from Kahakuloa to Honokōwai, but in 1909 Kahakuloa was taken from Kāʻanapali and added to the new Wailuku district. Kāʻanapali and Lahaina were merged to form the present Lahaina District." /Place Names (ULUK)/

[NOTE: In stories shared with the author by the late Maui kupuna Diane Amadeo, the district of Kāʻanapali was named as such because the majority of its lands share (kaʻana) the cliff-like (pali) ridgeline of Kahoʻolewa as a common boundary.]

01 Kaanapali Church
See Lahuiokalani Kaanapali Church.

02 Kaanapali Pohaku
See Pohaku o Kaanapali.

103 Kaape

Kaʻape

Ka-ʻape

Literally, the ʻape plant.

ʻIli in the ahupuaʻa of Kahana 1.

104 Kaauwaipaki

See Auwaipaki.

105 Kaawaiki

Kaʻawaiki

Ka-ʻawa-iki

Literally, the small ʻawa plant.

Gulch in the ahupuaʻa of Honokōwai that joins Māhinahina Gulch.

106 Kaea

Kaea / Kaʻea / Kaʻeʻa

Kaea / Ka-ʻea / Ka-ʻeʻa / Kaʻeʻa

Pronunciation and meaning undetermined, perhaps: kaea—"Cessation or lack of appetite or desire" /HD/; ka ʻea—the hawksbill turtle, or, the spray; or, ka ʻeʻa—the spray, or, the "fish similar to ʻaʻawa, but with dark flesh" /HD/; or kaʻeʻa—"Expert, hero, fighter." /HD/

ʻIli in the ahupuaʻa of Honolua.

107 Kaehaiko

See Kaihukiako.

108 Kaehakiko

See Kaihukiako.

109 Kaekaha

Kaʻēkaha

Ka-ʻēkaha

Meaning undetermined, perhaps: the ʻēkaha—"ʻē.kaha n. 1. The bird's-nest fern (*Asplenium nidus*)...2. A moss growing on rotted trees...3. Same as ʻēkaha *kū moana* [n. "Black coral" (*Antipathes grandis*), used medicinally.]" /HD/

Large seaside stone and shoreline point found along the boundary separating the ahupuaʻa of Nāpili and Honokahua.

10 Kaelekii
Kaʻelekiʻi
Ka-ʻele-kiʻi

"*Lit.*, the image blackness." /PNOH/

Seaside point in between the ahupuaʻa of Honokeana and Nāpili.

Variant: Elekii.

11 Kaelepuni
Kaʻelepuni / Kāʻelepuni
Ka-ʻele-puni / Kā-ʻele-puni

Pronunciation and meaning undetermined, perhaps: ka ʻele puni—the dark overgrown spring that is surrounded; or, kāʻele puni—surrounding darkness.

ʻIli in the ahupuaʻa of Honokōwai.

12 Kaemi
Ka-ʻemi

"*Lit.*, the ebbing." /PNOH/

An islet in the ahupuaʻa of Makaliua 1, kalana of Kahakuloa.

13 Kaeo
See Puu Kaeo.

14 Kahakahalani
Kahakaha-lani

Meaning undetermined, perhaps: striped heavens, or, royal procession.

Area, perhaps a cliff, mentioned in mele in the context of the kalana of Kahakuloa.

"Nana iho ia Puukoae au ike kai, / Au halaoa i ke kai o Kulaloa, / Loa na lima o ka ale o Makawela, / Aloha wale ka pali o Kahakahalani, / Ka hilinai e ka pali o Mana, / Ke kauna pali o Kaimalolo.... [*Look down at Puʻu Koaʻe jutting out into the sea, / Projecting out into the sea of Kulaloa, / The reach of the waves of Makawela is long, / Fond memories for the cliff of Kahakahalani, / The confidant of the cliff of Mānā, / The resting place upon the cliff of Kaimalolo....*]" /Ke Au Okoa, Buke 2, Helu 33, 3 Kekemapa 1866/

115 Kahakapuaa
Kahakapuaʻa
Ka-haka-puaʻa / Kaha-ka-puaʻa / Kaha-(a)-ka-puaʻa

Meaning undetermined, perhaps: ka haka puaʻa—the pork rack; kaha ka puaʻa—the pig passes by; or, kaha a ka puaʻa—the mark made by the pig.

ʻIli in the ahupuaʻa of Kahana (3).

116 Kahakuloa
Ka-haku-loa

"*Lit.*, the tall lord." /PNOH/

The sole kalana, containing nine ahupuaʻa, in the moku of Kāʻanapali. Also, an ahupuaʻa in the same kalana.

"The ahupuaʻa of Kahakuloa, in the kalana of Kahakuloa, may be defined as the land drained by the Kahakuloa Stream, and lying between the lands of Kapaloa and Moomuku." /Place Names (ULUK)/

"Returned by Lunalilo at the Māhele, retained by Crown. In the Māhele Book, page 24, Kahakuloa is identified as an ahupuaʻa in the kalana (district) of Kaanapali, but on page 210 it is classified as a kalana, i.e., it contains ahupuaʻa. See Poelua, Hononana, Ahoa, Moomuku, Kahakuloa, Kapaloa, Makaliua, Waiokila, Kukuipuka. Except for Kukuipuka, none has had its boundaries surveyed. As a kalana it extends from Honokohau to Waihee. Kahakuloa was an ahupuaʻa as well, encompassing Kahakuloa Valley and its tributaries. In 1909 the legislature took the kalana of Kahakuloa from Lahaina District and gave it to Wailuku District." /Place Names (ULUK)/

"No ke Kalana o Kahakuloa a me Kona mau Hiohiona. Aia no keia Kalana ma ke komohana akau o na Waieha, a o kekahi hapa ia o ka apana o Lahaina, he aina alopali keia i pakuku ia e na pali kona mau aoao a hamama i kai, e huli aku ana ke alo o keia wahi aina kahawai i ka Hikina Akau, a he ake [*sic*] iki makai o ka nuku muliwai e pili ala me ke kai, o ko laila poe ka ike pono i ke kai o Hoomanunu, a ike no hoi i ka moku holo ae ma ka moana, a o ka poe ma uka aku, aole lakou e ike mai i ke kai, ua alai ia e kekahi wahi lapa e ku kalali ana mawaena o ke kahawai, o Lapaiki ka inoa, a o Haleino mauka iho. Aia ma ka lae kahakai ma ka hikina iho, e ku ana kona puu kaulana o ʻPuukoae papa i ka makani' ʻKuinalehua o Kaukini.' A o ka mauna o Eke ma ke komohana, nolaila ka oleloia ana e ka poe haku mele kahiko, 'Hana ekeeke i ka ipu a ka makani.' Hiolo lua i ka pali o Leinaha. [*Regarding the District of Kahakuloa and Its Features. This district is northwest of the Waiʻehā region, and it's a portion of the precinct of Lahaina, this is a land in the face of the cliffs with its sides screened in by steep precipices and wide open along the sea, the front of this place of many streams and gulches faces Northeast, and the entrance of the rivermouth widens a little as it joins with the sea; the people there can view the sea of*

Hoʻomanunu, and they can see the ships traveling on the ocean, and the people inland, they cannot see the sea; the view is obscured by a small ridge standing proudly in the middle of the valley, Lapaiki is its name, and Haleʻino is just inland of that. There at the seaside point just to the east, its famous hill stands ʻPuʻukoaʻe ever brushed against by the wind' ʻStringing Lehua of Kaukini.' And the mountain of ʻEke is to the west, from which comes mention by the composers of old, ʻForming a holder for the gourd of winds.' Tumbling incessantly down the cliffs of Leinahā.]" /*Ka Nupepa Kuokoa*, Buke 14, Helu 33, 14 ʻAukake 1875/

17 Kahakuloa Game Management Area

A 1.92-square-mile reserve managed by the Division of Forestry and Wildlife of the State of Hawaiʻiʻs Department of Land and Natural Resources in the vicinity of the ahupuaʻa of Pōʻelua, kalana of Kahakuloa.

18 Kahakuloa Head
See Puu Koae.

19 Kahakuloa Homesteads

"The Kahakuloa Homesteads include Crown lands in Kukuipuka, Waiokila, Makaliua, Kapaloa." /Place Names (ULUK)/

20 Kahalamanu
Kahalamanu / Kāhalamanu
Ka-hala-manu / Kāhala-manu

Pronunciation and meaning undetermined, perhaps: ka hala manu—the bird departure; or, kāhala manu—acrid tasting saltiness.

———————

Shoreline point along the ʻili of Punalau, ahupuaʻa of Honokōhau.

21 Kahalua
Kahalua / Kahālua
Kaha-lua / Ka-hālua

Pronunciation and meaning undetermined, perhaps: kaha lua—two stretches of land; or, ka hālua—the furrow, the pits, or, the ambush.

———————

ʻIli in the ahupuaʻa of Mailepai.

Also, perhaps a misrepresentation of the "Kapalua" areas in the ahupuaʻa of Nāpili and Honokahua in some documents.

122 Kahana

"*Lit.*, the cutting." /PNOH/

Ahupuaʻa containing eighteen ʻili, stream, shoreline point, and heiau in the moku of Kāʻanapali.

Variant: Kahuna.

123 Kahanaha
Kahanahā / Kahānaha / Kahānahā
Kaha-nahā / Ka-hā-naha / Ka-hā-nahā

Pronunciation and meaning undetermined, perhaps: kaha nahā—cracked dry place; ka hā naha—the curved stalk; or, ka hā nahā—the broken ditch.

ʻIli in the ahupuaʻa of Honokahua.

124 Kahanahana
Kāhanahana / Kahanahana
Kāhanahana / Ka-hanahana

Pronunciation and meaning undetermined, perhaps: kāhanahana—"n. Clearing, as in a forest…" /HD/; or, "n. Cutting, drawing of a line; turning point" /HD/; or, ka hanahana—the heat or vehemence, or, the stink/souring.

ʻIli in the ahupuaʻa of Kahakuloa, kalana of Kahakuloa.

Variant: Kuhanahana.

125 Kahanaiki
Kahana-iki

Literally, lesser Kahana.

Gulch in the ahupuaʻa of Kahana.

126 Kahanaiole
Kahanaʻiole / Kahānaiʻole
Kahana-ʻiole / Ka-hānai-ʻole

Pronunciation and meaning undetermined, perhaps: kahana ʻiole—rat Kahana, or, the scratch mark made by a rat; or, ka hānai ʻole—the one unadopted, or, the one unfed.

Ahupuaʻa in the moku of Kāʻanapali famed for salt patches. [NOTE: This ahupuaʻa is found in a record of the Māhele database as paired with Kahananui.]

27 Kahanalo

Kaha-nalo

Literally, hidden place.

'Ili in the ahupua'a of Honokahua.

28 Kahanaloa

Ka-hana-loa

Meaning undetermined, perhaps: the long valley.

Upland gulch that adjoins Mokupe'a Gulch in the ahupua'a of Honokahua.

Variant: Hanaloa.

29 Kahananui

Kahana-nui

Literally, greater Kahana.

Ahupua'a in the moku of Kā'anapali. Also, a gulch in the ahupua'a of Kahana.

Variant: Kahana.

30 Kahao

Ka-hao

Meaning undetermined, perhaps: the hao ("hao 1. n. Iron, general name for metal tools, a bit; brand, as on a horse. 2. n. All native species of a genus of small trees [*Rauvolfia*] related to the maile and the hōlei...3. nvt. To scoop, dish, or pick up; to grasp, gouge, pillage, plunder, loot; robber...4. vt. To come with force, as wind or rain; to do with force and energy...5. Same as mai'a 'oa, a variety of banana. 6. n. Horn, as of a goat." /HD/)

'Ili in the ahupua'a of Nāpili.

31 Kahau

Kahau / Kāhau / Kāha'u

Ka-hau / Kāhau / Kāha'u

Pronunciation and meaning undetermined, perhaps: ka hau—the *hau* tree, the strike, the offering, or, the *Hau* breeze; kāhau—to hurl *hau* wood spears; or, kāha'u—to abate (as a storm or sickness).

'Ili in the ahupua'a of Waiokila, kalana of Kahakuloa.

132 Kahauiki
Ka-hau-iki

Meaning undetermined, perhaps: Kahau-iki—lesser Kahau; or, ka hau iki—the small *hau* tree.

ʻIli and gulch in the ahupuaʻa of Honolua. Also, a shoreline in the same area.

133 Kahauloa
Ka-hau-loa

Literally, the long *hau* tree/branch.

ʻIli in the ahupuaʻa of Nāpili.

134 Kahekili Beach Park
See Aliʻi Kahekili Nui ʻAhumanu Beach Park.

135 Kahekili Highway

Hawaiʻi Route 340, which begins in the town of Wailuku (Wailuku), heads north into the moku of Kāʻanapali, and continues until it terminates in the ahupuaʻa of Honokōhau.

Named for the famed Maui chief Kahekilinuiʻahumanu.

Variant: Hawaii Route 340.

136 Kahikinui
Kahiki-nui

Literally, great Kahiki.

ʻIli in the ahupuaʻa of Honolua.

137 Kahiku
See Makahiku.

138 Kahilianapa
See Puu Kahulianapa.

139 Kahina
Kāhina

Literally, to knock over.

ʻIli in the ahupuaʻa of Māhinahina.

40 Kaholua
Kahōlua
Ka-hōlua

Literally, the sled, or, the sled course.

ʻIli in the ahupuaʻa of Nāpili.

41 Kahoolewa
Kahoʻolewa
Ka-hoʻo-lewa

Literally, the hoʻolewa: "Hoolewa 1. To cause to swing; to vibrate; to float in the air. 2. To lift up and carry, as between two persons; to carry in a manele or palanquin. 3. To carry a corpse in a funeral procession. 4. To cause a swinging or rotary motion, as in certain forms of dancing." /Parker/

Ridge forming the uppermost boundary for most of the moku of Kāʻanapali, with the exception of the kalana of Kahakuloa.

42 Kahoomano
Kahoʻomano
Ka-hoʻomano

Literally, the persistence (in action).

ʻIli in the ahupuaʻa of ʻAlaeloa.

43 Kahooulu
Kahoʻoulu
Ka-hoʻoulu

Literally, to cause to grow.

Shoreline point along Kulaokaʻea, ahupuaʻa of Honolua.

44 Kahuki
Kahuki / Ka-huki

Meaning undetermined, perhaps: kahuki—"vs. Rotten, as a banana stump; overripe, as banana fruit with juice dripping and black skin, as used in medicine" /HD/; or, ka huki—the pulling, or, the convulsion.

ʻIli in the ahupuaʻa of Honokeana.

145 Kahuku
Ka-huku

Literally, the protuberance.

'Ili in the ahupua'a of Waiokila 2, kalana of Kahakuloa.

146 Kahulianapa
Kāhuli'anapa
Kāhuli-'anapa

Literally, gleaming-*kāhuli*-shell hill.

Hill (547 feet) and seaside point to the southeast of Pu'u Koa'e in ahupua'a of Kapaloa, kalana of Kahakuloa.

Variant: Lae Kahilianapa.

147 Kahuna
See Kahana.

148 Kaia
See Kalaeokaia.

149 Kaieie
Ka'ie'ie
Ka-'ie'ie

Literally, the 'ie'ie plant, or, the 'ie'ie taro.

'Ili in the ahupua'a of Nāpili.

150 Kaihukiako
Ka'ihukiako / Ka'ihuki'ako
Ka'i-huki-ako / Ka'i-huki-'ako

Pronunciation and meaning undetermined, perhaps: ka'i huki ako—to proceed along pulling thatch; or, ka'i huki 'ako—pulling-tugging-plucking.

Upland point (1,845 feet) along the boundary between the ahupua'a of Honokōhau and the kalana of Kahakuloa.

Variants: Kaehaiko, Kaehakiko.

51 Kaikaina

Literally, younger sibling (of the same gender).

Hill (305 feet) to the north of Puʻu Hāunakā in the kalana of Kahakuloa.

52 Kaimalolo
Kai-malolo

Literally, low-tide sea.

Area mentioned in mele in the context of the kalana of Kahakuloa.

"Nana iho ia Puukoae au ike kai, / Au halaoa i ke kai o Kulaloa, / Loa na lima o ka ale o Makawela, / Aloha wale ka pali o Kahakahalani, / Ka hilinai e ka pali o Mana, / Ke kauna pali o Kaimalolo.... [*Look down at Puʻu Koaʻe jutting out into the sea, / Projecting out into the sea of Kulaloa, / The reach of the waves of Makawela is long, / Fond memories for the cliff of Kahakahalani, / The confidant of the cliff of Mānā, / The resting place on the cliff of Kaimalolo....*]" /*Ke Au Okoa*, Buke 2, Helu 33, 3 Kekemapa 1866/

53 Kaimooalii
See Kamoouli & Keamoalii.

54 Kainui
Kai-nui

Literally, high tide.

ʻIli in the ahupuaʻa of Waiokila, kalana of Kahakuloa.

55 Kaioo
Kaioʻo
Kai-oʻo

"*Lit.*, strong sea." /HD/

Beach that begins on the north side of Puʻu Kekaʻa (Lahaina) and extends toward Honokōwai Point. The Aliʻi Kahekili Nui ʻAhumanu Beach Park is located along this beach.

56 Kakapa

"kakapa Redup. of kapa, edge, border." /HD/

ʻIli in the ahupuaʻa of Kahakuloa, kalana of Kahakuloa.

157 Kalaeiliili
Kalaeʻiliʻili
Ka-lae-ʻiliʻili

Literally, the pebble point.

Shoreline point along the ahupuaʻa of Kahana.

158 Kalaekole
Ka-lae-kole

Meaning undetermined, perhaps: the *kole* fish (sea)point, or, the raw forehead.

ʻIli in the ahupuaʻa of ʻAlaeloa. [NOTE: Not included in the Māhele databases amongst the 12 ʻili of Honokeana is the ʻili of Kalaekole.]

"3801 Lupea Kanapali [*sic*] Ian 19. 1848 ... Ke hoopii aku nei au ia oukou no koʻu kuleana aina, aia iloko o Alaeloa ke ahupuaa he ili aina o ka inoa o Kalaekole.... [*3801 Lupea Kāʻanapali Jan 19, 1848 ... I am petitioning you all regarding my property; it is within ʻAlaeloa the ahupuaʻa an ʻili of land by the name of Kalaekole....*]" /Native Register (KPA)/

159 Kalaeokaea
Kalaeokaʻea
Ka-lae-o-ka-ʻea

Meaning undetermined, perhaps: the point of the spray, or, the point of the hawksbill turtle.

Shoreline point in the ahupuaʻa of Kahana.

160 Kalaeokaia
Kalaeokaiʻa
Ka-lae-o-ka-iʻa

Literally, the (shoreline) point of the fish.

Shoreline point and fishing ground between the two ahupuaʻa of Mailepai and Kahana.

Interview between Larry Kimura and John Nākoa, Ka Leo Hawaiʻi radio program. Orthography reflects pronunciation of speaker.

JOHN NĀKOA: A iā mākou o Maui, mai Kahana, nui kēia mea kuʻuna. Nui. Ma Pohale, ʻekolu ma leila. Ma Kapua, Kapua, aia ma leila ʻehā, ma leila. Kapua ma nuna, aia ʻelua ma leila. A ma Kapua, aia ma leila nō ʻelua, ma Kapua. Nē ʻoe hele ma Kapalua, ō nui hewahewa ma leila, Hāwea mā. Kēia mea kuʻuna. Nui ka iʻa!... / LARRY KIMURA: Pehea? He inoa nō ke kuʻuna? / JK: ʻAe, he inoa nō. Ke kuʻuna nui ʻo Pohale...aia i Honokōwai...Kēia poʻe kuʻuna e walaʻau nei iā ʻoe, he inoa wale nō lākou, but, poina wau kekahi poʻe kuʻuna. Poina. But, kēia poʻe kuʻuna nui, ʻo ia kaʻu mea e walaʻau nei, kuʻuna nui ʻo Pohale. Nui kēlā kuʻuna. ʻUmi kapuaʻi ka hohonu...Nui nā kuʻuna. Kalaeokaiʻa, aia ma leila kekahi poʻe kuʻuna, ʻo ia nō ka inoa. / LK: ʻO wai? / JN: Kalaeokaiʻa...Kalaeokaiʻa, Kalaeʻiliʻili...aia ma leila. Ā, Kapua. Kapua, aia nō ma leila kekahi kuʻuna. Ā, me ka hapanui, kala mai iaʻu, poina loa. [*JOHN NĀKOA: And to us from Maui, from Kahana, there are a lot of these* kuʻuna *(net setting places). So many. At Pohale, there are three there. At Kapua, Kapua, there are four there. Upper Kapua, there are two there. And at Kapua, there are two there, at Kapua. If you go to Kapalua, oh so many there, Hāwea and places like that. These* kuʻuna. *Plenty of fish!...* | *LARRY KIMURA: So how is it? Are the* kuʻuna *formally named?* | *JK: Yes, they're formally named. Pohale is a big* kuʻuna...*it's at Honokōwai...These* kuʻuna *that I'm talking with you about, they are all formally named, but I forget some* kuʻuna. *I forget. But, these main* kuʻuna, *those are what I'm talking with you about, the big* kuʻuna *of Pohale. That's a big* kuʻuna. *Ten feet deep...There are a lot of* kuʻuna. *Kalaeokaiʻa, there are some* kuʻuna *there, that's the name.* | *LK: What was the name?* | *JN: Kalaeokaiʻa...Kalaeokaiʻa, Kalaeʻiliʻili...there are some there. Ah, Kapua. Kapua, there is a* kuʻuna *there. Uh, but the majority, so sorry, I have completely forgotten.*]. /"Ka Leo Hawaiʻi" 378/

Variant: Mailepai Point.

61 Kalaepiha
Kalaepīhā
Ka-lae-pīhā

Literally, the flotsam point.

———————

Shoreline point and area along the ahupuaʻa of Honolua.

62 Kalaepohaku
Kalaepōhaku
Ka-lae-pōhaku

Literally, the boulder point.

———————

Shoreline point along the ahupuaʻa of Honokahua.

163 Kalakahi
Kalakahi / Kalākahi
Kala-kahi / Ka-lā-kahi

Pronunciation and meaning undetermined, perhaps: kala kahi—single crag; or, ka lā kahi—the single day/sun.

Point along Kaulalewalewa Ridge along the boundary between the two ahupuaʻa of Kahana and Honokahua.

"A peak between Kaulalewalewa and Puu Hokolo on the Honokahua/Kahana boundary." /Place Names (ULUK)/

Variant: Puu Kalakahi.

164 Kalana
Kalana / Kālana
Kalana / Kālana / Ka-lana

Pronunciation and meaning undetermined, perhaps: kalana—*kalana* land unit, or, forgiveness; kālana—to strain/sieve; or, ka lana—the buoyancy.

ʻIli in the ahupuaʻa of Honokahua.

165 Kalanikawai
See Kalaniwai.

166 Kalaniwai
Ka-lani-wai

Literally, the heavens flowing with water.

A broad plateau in the kalana of Kahakuloa that overlooks the valley of Waiheʻe (Wailuku).

"Ascending southwest, out of this crater, I crossed over a broad plateau, well named from its abundance of water, Kalaniwai, on which were many more such pits. I estimated that there were over seventy on the whole mountain. Above this plateau I came to another crater, of which I wish especially to speak. This crater, called Eke, is about the size and depth of Punchbowl crater, stretching from near the Waihee to the Honokahau Valley, forming the terminal point of valleys for seven or eight miles of the coast, and the resevoir, I was told, of the greater part of the streams of the Waihee, Kahakuloa, and Honokahau Valleys." /Alexander, 1874/

67 Kalalalaolao
See Kula o Kalaulaolao.

68 Kalama
Ka-lama

Meaning undetermined, perhaps: the *lama* tree, or, the torch.

'Ili in the ahupua'a of Nāpili.

Variants: Kalama 1, 2.

69 Kalaoa
Ka-laoa

Literally, the choking (as on a bone).

An 'ili in the ahupua'a of Waiokila, kalana of Kahakuloa. Also, an alternative name for Waiola'i Gulch in the same ahupua'a and kalana.

70 Kalauhulu
Ka-lauhulu

Literally, the dried banana leaf.

'Ili in the ahupua'a of Pō'elua, kalana of Kahakuloa.

71 Kalaulaolao
See Kula o Kalaulaolao.

72 Kalaulaula
Kalaulaulā
Ka-lau-laulā

Literally, the wide *lau* dragnet.

Shoreline area along the ahupua'a of Honokōhau.

73 Kaleinaakauhane
Kaleinaaka'uhane
Ka-leina-a-ka-'uhane

Literally, the leaping point of the spirit.

Name of the shoreline point of Puʻu Kekaʻa in the ahupuaʻa of Honokōwai.

———————

Regarding *leina a ka ʻuhane* in general: "*Leina*, a place to leap from, is often used as a short form of leina-a-ke-akua or *leina-a-ke-ʻuhane* [*sic*], the place from which spirits leaped into eternity or *Pō*. It was thought the spirit of man took this leap after death. Certain cliffs or precipices on each island were believed to be the leina from which spirits plunged into the ocean, symbolizing *Pō*." /Pukui, et al., 1979/

Variant: Black Rock, Leinakauhane.

174 Kalelo
Ka-lelo

Meaning undetermined, perhaps: the tongue, or, the reddish-yellow color; or, a representation of: ka niu lelo—the *lelo* coconut.

———————

ʻIli in the ahupuaʻa of Honokeana.

175 Kalena
Kalena / Ka-lena

Meaning undetermined, perhaps: kalena—taut; or, ka lena—the turmeric, or, the lazy one.

———————

ʻIli in the ahupuaʻa of ʻAlaeloa.

176 Kalila
Kalīlā / Kālīlā
Ka-līlā / Kā-līlā

Pronunciation and meaning undetermined, perhaps: ka līlā—the spindly (plant); or, kā lilā—the spindly sweet potato vine.

———————

ʻIli in the ahupuaʻa of Honolua.

177 Kalokoloko
Ka-lokoloko

Literally, the area of small puddles/pools.

———————

Shoreline area along the ahupuaʻa of Honokahua.

78 Kaluailio
Kaluaʻīlio / Kāluaʻīlio
Ka-lua-ʻīlio / Kālua-ʻīlio

Pronunciation and meaning undetermined, perhaps: ka lua ʻīlio—the dog pit/grave; or, kālua ʻīlio—to bake dogs.

ʻIli in the ahupuaʻa of Kahana 1.

79 Kaluakanaka
Kaluakanaka / Kāluakanaka
Ka-lua-kanaka / Kālua-kanaka

Pronunciation and meaning undetermined, perhaps: ka lua kanaka—the human pit/grave; or, kālua kanaka—to bake humans.

ʻIli in the ahupuaʻa of Honokahua.

80 Kaluaniha
See Kaluanui.

81 Kaluaniho
See Kaluanui.

82 Kaluanui
Ka-lua-nui

Literally, the large pit.

ʻIli and stream in the ʻili of Kahauiki, ahupuaʻa of Honolua.

Also, an ʻili in the ahupuaʻa of Honokeana.

Variants: Kaluaniha, Kaluaniho.

83 Kaluaomano
Ka-lua-o-Mano

Literally, the pit of Mano.

ʻIli in the ahupuaʻa of ʻAlaeloa.

184 **Kaluaoopu**
Kaluaʻoʻopu
Ka-lua-ʻoʻopu

Literally, the ʻoʻopu fish pit/cave.

———————

ʻIli in the ahupuaʻa of Honokeana.

185 **Kamane**
Kamanē
Kama-nē

Meaning undetermined, perhaps: murmuring cavern, or, murmuring child.

———————

Shoreline area along Kulaokaʻea, ahupuaʻa of Honolua.

186 **Kamani**

Literally, kamani tree.

———————

The name for ʻili found in the ahupuaʻa of ʻAlaeloa, Honokōhau; and in the ahupuaʻa of Kahakuloa, kalana of Kahakuloa.

Variant: Kamani 1.

187 **Kamoa**
Ka-moa

Literally, the chicken.

———————

ʻIli in the ahupuaʻa of Makaliua 1, kalana of Kahakuloa.

188 **Kamoouli**
Kamoʻouli
Ka-moʻo-uli

Meaning undetermined, perhaps: the dark ridge, or, the dark supernatural lizard, or, the dark raised path.

———————

ʻIli in the ahupuaʻa of Honokōhau.

Variants: Kaimoouli, Kuimooalii, Moouli.

89 Kanaele

Kanaele / Kanāʻele

Ka-naele / Ka-nāʻele

Pronunciation and meaning undetermined, perhaps: ka naele—the bog, or, the crevice; or, ka nāʻele—the weedy undergrowth.

———————

ʻIli in the ahupuaʻa of ʻĀhoa, kalana of Kahakuloa.

Also, ʻili in the ahupuaʻa of Mailepai.

90 Kananau

Ka-nanau

Meaning undetermined, perhaps: the unsociable, or, the chewing.

———————

Gulch near the ʻili of Waihale, ahupuaʻa of Honokōwai.

91 Kanea

Literally, loss of appetite.

———————

ʻIli in the ahupuaʻa of Waiokila, kalana of Kahakuloa.

92 Kaneauau

Kāneʻauʻau

Kāne-ʻauʻau

Literally, swimming man, or swimming Kāne (deity).

———————

ʻIli in the ahupuaʻa of Honokōwai.

93 Kanehalaoa

Kānehalaʻoʻa

Kāne-halaʻoʻa

Meaning undetermined, perhaps: Kāne (deity) who appears dimly, or, Kāne (deity) who protrudes/extends.

———————

Fishing shrine in the kalana of Kahakuloa.

194 Kaneloa

Kāneloa

Kāne-loa

"*Lit.*, tall Kāne." /PNOH/

ʻIli in the ahupuaʻa of Honokōhau.

195 Kaneneilio

Kanēnēʻīlio

Ka-nēnē-ʻīlio

Literally, the whimpering of a dog.

ʻIli in the ahupuaʻa of Honokōhau.

196 Kaneola

Kāneola

Kāne-ola

Literally, life-granting Kāne (deity).

Heiau in the ahupuaʻa of Kahakuloa, kalana of Kahakuloa.

"Kaneola Heiau, Walker Site 22. West side of Kahakuloa Valley just mauka to school. A good sized heiau with a right-angle outline." /Place Names (ULUK)/

197 Kanoa

Kānoa

"kā.noa n. Bowl, as for kava; hollow of land, pit (rare); circular." /HD/

Ridge along the border between the kalana of Kahakuloa and the ahupuaʻa of Waiheʻe (Wailuku).

198 Kanounou

Ka-nounou

Literally, the buffeting.

Shoreline point on the northeast side of Honokōhau Bay.

Variant: Lae Kunonou.

99 Kanuku
Ka-nuku

Meaning undetermined, perhaps: the *nuku* ("nuku 1. n. Beak, snout, tip, end; spout, beak of a pitcher; mouth or entrance, as of a harbor, river, or mountain pass or gap … 2. nvs. Scolding, raving, ranting, grumbling; to nag … 3. n. Series of hooks attached to a line (Malo 79); first coconut husk attached to an ʻahi fishline, the others being poli (bosom), and manamana (fingers). Ka nuku o ka puaʻa, poetic name for deep-sea ulua fishing line; lit., the pig snout." /Place Names (ULUK)/

ʻIli in the ahupuaʻa of Honokahua.

---

00 Kanukuokeana
Ka-nuku-o-ke-ana

Literally, the entrance of the cave.

ʻIli in the ahupuaʻa of Waiokila, kalana of Kahakuloa.

---

01 Kaohe
Kaʻohe
Ka-ʻohe

Literally, the bamboo.

The name of ʻili in the ahupuaʻa of Nāpili, Honokahua, Honokōhau, Honolua, and an ʻili in the ahupuaʻa of Pōʻelua, kalana of Kahakuloa.

---

02 Kaolanakaloa
See Kaulanakaloa.

---

03 Kaolapalapa
Kaʻōlapalapa
Ka-ʻōlapalapa

Meaning undetermined, perhaps: the ʻōlapalapa tree, or, the flaring.

ʻIli in the ahupuaʻa of Honokeana.

204 Kaolina
Kaʻolina
Ka-ʻolina

Literally, the merrymaking.

Inland ridge along the boundary of the ahupuaʻa of Honokahua and Honolua.

205 Kaonahi
See Kaunahi.

206 Kaopala
Kaʻōpala
Ka-ʻōpala

Literally, the rubbish.

Gulch, stream, and possibly an ʻili in the ahupuaʻa of ʻAlaeloa that eventually forms the bay of the ahupuaʻa of Mailepai.

207 Kaopilopilo
Kaʻōpilopilo
Ka-ʻōpilopilo

Literally, the marshy odor of stagnant water.

ʻIli in the ahupuaʻa of Kahakuloa, kalana of Kahakuloa. *See also*: Kawaiopilopilo and Opilopilo.

208 Kapa
Kapa / Kapā
Kapa / Ka-pā

Pronunciation and meaning undetermined, perhaps: kapa—border, or, tapa cloth; or, ka pā—the wall/fence, or, the yard/lot.

The mouth of Waiʻololī gulch in the ahupuaʻa of Kukuipuka, kalana of Kahakuloa.

209 Kapaaukini
Kapaʻaukini
Kapaʻau-kini

Meaning undetermined, perhaps: raised place on a heiau where the multitudes of akua dwell.

ʻIli in the ahupuaʻa of Honokōhau.

Variants: Kapakini, Kapaakini, Kapaaukini 1 & 2, Paaukini.

10 Kapaeulua
Ka-pae-ulua

Literally, the grounding place of the *ulua* fish.

Shoreline area along Kulaokaʻea, ahupuaʻa of Honolua.

11 Kapahaoholo
Kapāhaʻoholo
Ka-pāhaʻo-holo

Literally, the desire to travel.

Shoreline area along the ahupuaʻa of Honolua.

12 Kapalaalaea
Kapalaʻalaea
Ka-pala-ʻalaea

Literally, the smudge of ocherous earth.

ʻIli in the ahupuaʻa of Honokōhau.

13 Kapalalau
See Kapolalau.

14 Kapaloa
Kapaloa / Kapāloa
Kapa-loa / Ka-pā-loa

Pronunciation and meaning undetermined, perhaps: kapa loa—long boundary; or, ka pā loa—the long enclosure/fence.

Southern tributary of what eventually becomes the Honokōwai Stream.

Also, perhaps an ʻili in the ahupuaʻa of Kahakuloa, kalana of Kahakuloa.

"Not named in the Māhele Book. Kapaloa may be defined as the land between Makaliua ahupuaʻa and Kahakuloa ahupuaʻa, drained by the Waipili and Malalokai streams. The evidence for its status as an ahupuaʻa, rather than an ʻili of the ahupuaʻa of Kahakuloa, is slight. No ʻili have been found within Kapaloa. LCAw 6146-F to Lima: "Apana 2. Aina kalo, ili o Kapaloa...1.0 eka." Also LCAw 6145-X to Kalaiku/Kaleiku, 6147-B to Kaopunaanaa, 6147-E to Kapapuluole, 6147-M to Kapuahi, 6148-P to Nahoa." /Place Names (ULUK)/

215 Kapalua

Kapa-lua

Literally, two borders.

ʻIli, beach, and bay between the long, extended points of Hokuanui and Kuʻunaakaʻiole in the ahupuaʻa of Nāpili. Also, the name of the point on the north side of Kapalua Bay.

"[Earl Ray Kukahiko]: When we were born had mid-wifes. Name came out Kapalua @ Ritz-Carlton given by Mr. Fleming. Before, it was called Honokohua [*sic*]. There was a scout camp there. Many people who have moved off Maui that lived @ Honokohua ask about Kapalua when they return or visit and are surprised to find the name change from Honokohua to Kapalua. Our house was the last house @ the corner with the coconut trees that my dad planted next to the store." /Tauʻa, 2005/

Variants: Kahalua, Kapalua Beach, Fleming's Beach.

216 Kapalua Lighthouse

See Hawea Point Light.

217 Kapalua West Maui Airport

Small airport for commuter, air taxi, and commercial propeller aircraft in the ahupuaʻa of Māhinahina (1 & 2).

"Hawaiian Airlines developed and constructed Kapalua Airport for less than $9 million after the private Kaanapali Airstrip was closed. The airport opened on March 1, 1987. The airport is located in West Maui, approximately .03 miles above Honoapiilani Highway on 57 acres of land." /Hawaii Aviation, 2021/

218 Kapaukua

Ka-paukua

Literally, the one that has been segmented or sectioned off.

ʻIli in the ahupuaʻa of Honokōhau.

19 Kapelekai
Kapelekāī
Ka-pele-kāī

Pronunciation and meaning undetermined, perhaps: the pounded *kāī* taro.

ʻIli in the ahupuaʻa of Waiokila, kalana of Kahakuloa.

20 Kapili
Ka-pili / Kāpili

Pronunciation and meaning undetermined, perhaps: ka pili—the relationship/union, or, the wager; or, kāpili—the mend.

ʻIli in the ahupuaʻa of Honokōwai.

21 Kapohale
See Pohale.

22 Kapolalau
Kapolalau / Kapōlalau / Kapōlālau
Ka-pola-lau / Ka-pō-lalau / Ka-pō-lālau

Pronunciation and meaning undetermined, perhaps: ka pola lau—the loincloth flap made of leaves; or, ka pō lalau—the night of wandering; or, ka pō lālau—the night of seizing.

ʻIli in the ahupuaʻa of Kahakuloa, kalana of Kahakuloa.

Variants: Kapalalau, Kapulalau.

23 Kapua
Ka-pua

Meaning undetermined, perhaps: the blossom, or, the spawn/fry (young fish).

ʻIli and shoreline area in the ahupuaʻa of Nāpili.

Interview between Larry Kimura and John Nākoa, Ka Leo Hawaiʻi radio program. Orthography reflects pronunciation of speaker.

"JOHN NĀKOA: A iā mākou o Maui, mai Kahana, nui kēia mea kuʻuna. Nui. Ma Pohale, ʻekolu ma leila. Ma Kapua, Kapua, aia ma leila ʻehā, ma leila. Kapua ma nuna, aia ʻelua ma leila. A ma Kapua, aia ma leila nō ʻelua, ma Kapua. Nē ʻoe hele ma Kapalua, ō nui hewahewa ma leila, Hāwea mā. Kēia mea kuʻuna. Nui ka iʻa!... /

LARRY KIMURA: Pehea? He inoa nō ke kuʻuna? / JK: ʻAe, he inoa nō. Ke kuʻuna nui ʻo Pohale...aia i Honokōwai...Kēia poʻe kuʻuna e walaʻau nei iā ʻoe, he inoa wale nō lākou, but, poina wau kekahi poʻe kuʻuna. Poina. But, kēia poʻe kuʻuna nui, ʻo ia kaʻu mea e walaʻau nei, kuʻuna nui ʻo Pohale. Nui kēlā kuʻuna. ʻUmi kapuaʻi ka hohonu...Nui nā kuʻuna. Kalaeokaiʻa, aia ma leila kekahi poʻe kuʻuna, ʻo ia nō ka inoa. / LK: ʻO wai? / JN: Kalaeokaiʻa...Kaleokaiʻa, Kalaeʻiliʻili...aia ma leila. Ā, Kapua. Kapua, aia nō ma leila kekahi kuʻuna. Ā, me ka hapanui, kala mai iaʻu, poina loa. [*JOHN NĀKOA: And to us from Maui, from Kahana, there are a lot of these kuʻuna (net setting places). So many. At Pohale, there are three there. At Kapua, Kapua, there are four there. Upper Kapua, there are two there. And at Kapua, there are two there, at Kapua. If you go to Kapalua, oh so many there, Hāwea and places like that. These kuʻuna. Plenty of fish!... | LARRY KIMURA: So how is it? Are the kuʻuna formally named? | JK: Yes, they're formally named. Pohale is a big kuʻuna...it's at Honokōwai...These kuʻuna that I'm talking with you about, they are all formally named, but I forget some kuʻuna. I forget. But these main kuʻuna, those are what I'm talking with you about, the big kuʻuna of Pohale. That's a big kuʻuna. Ten feet deep...There are a lot of kuʻuna. Kalaeokaiʻa, there are some kuʻuna there, that's the name. | LK: What was the name? | JN: Kalaeokaiʻa...Kalaeokaiʻa, Kalaeʻiliʻili...there are some there. Ah, Kapua. Kapua, there is a kuʻuna there. Uh, but the majority, so sorry, I have completely forgotten.*]" /"Ka Leo Hawaiʻi" 378/

224 Kapuaa
Kapuaʻa
Ka-puaʻa

Literally, the pig.

ʻIli in the ahupuaʻa of ʻAlaeloa.

225 Kapuaikahi
Kapuaʻikahi
Kapuaʻi-kahi

Literally, single footprint.

ʻIli in the ahupuaʻa of ʻĀhoa, kalana of Kahakuloa.

226 Kapuakea
Ka-pua-kea

Literally, the white flower.

ʻIli in the ahupuaʻa of Honokōhau.

27 Kapulehu
Kapūlehu
Ka-pūlehu / Kapūlehu

Literally, either: ka pūlehu—the broiling; or, Kapūlehu (name of a star).

Famed cliff in the region of Makamakaʻole, kalana of Kahakuloa.

Variant: Pulehu.

28 Kapuna
Ka-puna

Literally, the (water) spring.

A spring found along the border between the two ahupuaʻa of Kukuipuka and Kahakuloa, both in the kalana of Kahakuloa.

Also, the name of ʻili in the ahupuaʻa Kahana 1, ʻAlaeloa (nui), and in the ahupuaʻa of Hononana, kalana of Kahakuloa.

29 Kapunakea Preserve
Ka-punakea

Literally, the white rainbow.

Nature preserve in the ahupuaʻa of Honokōwai, moku of Kāʻanapali, managed by the Nature Conservancy.

"Kapunakea Preserve was established in 1992 through a perpetual conservation easement with Pioneer Mill Company, Limited. The current landowner is Kāʻanapali Land Management Corp., successor in interest to Pioneer Mill Company, Limited. The conservation easement seeks to preserve and protect the natural, ecological and wildlife features of the property. Kapunakea Preserve is 1,264 acres. The preserve's upper elevations are recognized as among the highest quality native areas in the state. Kapunakea Preserve is adjacent to two other natural areas that are actively managed: Puʻu Kukui Watershed Preserve (which is privately owned and part of the NAP program) and the Honokōwai section of the state West Maui Natural Area Reserve (NAR). The WMMWP is mandated to conserve and protect important forest lands of West Maui, which include Kapunakea Preserve, Puʻu Kukui and the West Maui NARs. These managed native forests and natural areas comprise more than 13,000 acres of contiguous, managed watershed. Kapunakea Preserve is an integrtal part of a contiguous, managed watershed, serving as the primary source of freshwater for area residents, farms and businesses and providing essential habitat for a number of rare, native, and endangered species." /The Nature Conservancy—Hawaiʻi Operating Unit/

230 Kauhihonohono
Ka-uhi-honohono

Literally, the covering of *honohono* (hono.hono 1. n. Short for honohono kukui [the basket grass (*Oplismenus hirtellus*)] ... 2. n. The wandering Jew or dayflower (*Commelina diffusa*). /HD/)

ʻIli in the ahupuaʻa of Honolua.

231 Kauhilua
Ka-uhi-lua

Literally, the pit covering.

ʻIli in the ahupuaʻa of Māhinahina.

232 Kauhipilo
Ka-uhi-pilo

Literally, the covering of *pilo* (pilo 2. n. Some species of native shrubs, in the coffee family (*Hedyotis* [Kadual]) ... 3. n. All Hawaiian species of *Coprosma* ... 4. Same as maiapilo (*Capparis sandwichiana*). /HD/)

ʻIli in the ahupuaʻa of Honolua.

233 Kauhipueo
Ka-uhi-pueo

Literally, the owl engulfment.

Shoreline area along Kulaokaʻea, ahupuaʻa of Honolua.

234 Kauila
Kauila / Ka-uila

Meaning undetermined, perhaps: *kauila* eel, hard reddish basalt stone, *kauila* tree, or, heiau consecrating ceremony; or, ka uila—the lightning.

Shoreline area along Kulaokaʻea, ahupuaʻa of Honolua.

Also, an ʻili in the ahupuaʻa of Hononana, kalana of Kahakuloa.

35 Kaukeke
Ka'ukeke / Ka'ūkēkē
Ka-'ukeke / Ka-'ūkēkē

Pronunciation and meaning undetermined, perhaps: ka 'ukeke—the 'ukeke bird, or, the quivering; or, ka 'ūkēkē—the musical bow (instrument).

'Ili in the ahupua'a of Honokeana.

36 Kaukini
Kau-kini

"*Lit.*, placing multitude." /HD/

Prominent ridge along the northeast side of Kahakuloa Valley, ahupua'a of Kahakuloa, kalana of Kahakuloa.

Also, an 'ili in the ahupua'a of Māhinahina.

37 Kaulalewalewa
Kaula-lewalewa

Literally, dangling rope.

Prominent ridge between the two ahupua'a of Kahana and Honokahua.

"The Honokahua boundary runs up 'the ridge of hills called Kaulalewalewa...to the mountain peak called Kalakahi, being bounded by the land called Kahana...' Misspelt 'Kaulalewelewe' on USGS. El. 2980 ft." /Place Names (ULUK)/

Variant: Kaulalewelewe.

38 Kaulalewelewe
See Kaulalewalewa.

39 Kaulanakaloa
Kaulanakāloa
Kaulana-kāloa

Meaning undetermined, perhaps: setting place of the oval platter, or, position of the Kāloa moons.

'Ili in the ahupua'a of Honokōhau. Also, the southern tributary/gulch to Honokōhau Stream.

Variants: Kaolanakaloa, Kaulanakoloa.

240 Kaulanakoloa
See Kaulanakaloa.

241 Kaulu
Kaulu / Kaʻulu
Ka-ulu / Ka-ʻulu

Pronunciation undetermined, perhaps: ka ulu—the growth; or, ka ʻulu—the breadfruit.

———————

The name of ʻili found in four ahupuaʻa: ʻĀhoa, Kahakuloa, Makaliua 2, and Kukui-puka, all in the kalana of Kahakuloa.

Also, ʻili in the ahupuaʻa of Mailepai and Honokahua.

242 Kaulukanu
Kaʻulukanu
Ka-ʻulu-kanu

Literally, the planted breadfruit.

———————

ʻIli in the ahupuaʻa of Honolua.

243 Kaulunai
See Kaulunui.

244 Kaulunui
Kaʻulunui
Ka-ʻulu-nui

Literally, the large breadfruit.

———————

ʻIli in the ahupuaʻa of Waiokila, kalana of Kahakuloa.

Variant: Kaulunai.

245 Kaumuokama
Ka-umu-o-Kama

Literally, the oven of Kama.

———————

ʻIli in the ahupuaʻa of Mailepai.

46 Kaunahi
Ka-unahi

Literally, the fish scale.

_____

ʻIli in the ahupuaʻa of Honokahua.

Variant: Kaonahi.

47 Kaunuwahine
Kaunu-wahine / Ka-unu-wahine

Meaning undetermined, perhaps: kaunu wahine—female obsession; or, ka unu wahine—woman's altar.

_____

ʻIli in the ahupuaʻa of Kukuipuka, kalana of Kahakuloa.

48 Kauwahine
Kau-wahine

Literally, mounted [by the] woman.

_____

Small islet off the ahupuaʻa of Honolua.

49 Kawaihae
Ka-wai-hae

Literally, the water of fury.

_____

ʻIli in the ahupuaʻa of Moʻomuku, kalana of Kahakuloa.

50 Kawaiopilopilo
Kawaiʻōpilopilo
Ka-wai-ʻōpilopilo

Literally, the stagnant-smelling water.

_____

ʻIli in the ahupuaʻa of Kahakuloa, kalana of Kahakuloa. *See also*: Kaopilopilo and Opilopilo.

51 Kawaipeke
Ka-wai-peke

Literally, the dwarf's water.

_____

Shoreline area along the ahupuaʻa of Honokōhau.

252 Kawelokio
Kawelokiʻo
Kawelo-kiʻo

Meaning undetermined, perhaps: *kawelo* sweet potato that has sprouted rootlets; or, Kawelo (the) pond.

———

ʻIli in the ahupuaʻa of Makaliua 2, kalana of Kahakuloa.

253 Keahau
See Keaahau.

254 Keaahau
Keaʻahau
Ke-aʻa-hau

Literally, the *hau* tree root.

———

ʻIli in the ahupuaʻa of Honokōhau.

Variant: Keahau.

255 Keaakukui
Keaʻakukui
Ke-aʻa-kukui

Literally, the *kukui* tree root.

———

ʻIli in the ahupuaʻa of Kahana 1.

256 Keahialoa
Keahialoa / Keahiʻāloa
Ke-ahi-a-Loa / Ke-ahi-ʻā-loa

Pronunciation and meaning undetermined, perhaps: ke ahi a Loa—the fire made by Loa; or, ke ahi ʻā loa—the long burning fire.

———

Heiau, perhaps in the ʻili of ʻEliwahine, ahupuaʻa of Kahakuloa, kalana of Kahakuloa.

———

"Keahialoa (?) Heiau, Walker Site 24 / Location: East side of Kahakuloa stream just south of trail. Description: The old heiau site forms the foundation of Mrs. Kauhaahaa's house. Just back of the house is a large rock known as Pohaku-o-Kane, but its connection to the heiau could not be determined." /SOM 46/

57 Keahikano
Ke-ahi-ka-nō

Pronunciation and meaning undetermined, perhaps an elided form of: ke ahi i ka nō—the fire in the seepage pit; or, a misrepresentation of: keʻehi i ka nō—treading in the seepage.

———————

A collapsed crater (3,003 feet) found toward the east side of the head of Kahakuloa Valley, kalana of Kahakuloa.

Also, a hill (2,013 feet) toward the upper reaches of Pōhakupule Gulch in the ahupuaʻa of Honolua.

———————

"1. The newly discovered Crater of Maui. (From a letter of T. M. Alexander to the editor of the Hawaiian Gazette, dated Dec. 3, 1873.)—In surveying the district of Kahakuloa on West Maui, I recently discovered volcanic phenomena, quite remarkable for any of our islands except Hawaii. I ascended the mountain two miles west of Waihee, along the sharp crest of the western ridge of Makamaole [*sic*] Valley. At about half way to the summit, I found a crater the size and depth of that of Diamond Head, called Keahikano. The sides within and without were covered with the usual vegetation of our mountains, mantled over all the trunks and branches with thick elegant mosses, and interspersed with a few palm trees. The bottom of the crater and the greater part of the mountain above to the summit were overspread with a thick spongy moss, so saturated with moisture that every tread of the foot would press out a pint of water. Little pools of water ten or fifteen feet in breadth were also very numerous over this place and the upper portion of the mountain." / *The American Journal of Science*, Volume 107, 1874/

[NOTE: On modern maps, there are two inland points in the moku of Kāʻanapali named either "Keahikauo" or "Keahikano." *See also*: Keahikauo.]

Variant: Keahikauo.

58 Keahikauo
Keahikauō
Ke-ahi-kauō

Pronunciation and meaning undetermined, perhaps: the hauled fire; or, a misrepresentation of: keʻehi kauō—feet braced while being dragged.

———————

A hill (2,013 feet) toward the upper reaches of Pōhakupule Gulch in the ahupuaʻa of Honolua.

[NOTE: On modern maps, there are two inland points in the moku of Kāʻanapali named either "Keahikauo" or "Keahikano." *See also*: Keahikano.]

Variant: Keahikano.

259 Keahinaluahine

Keahināluāhine

Ke-ahi-(a)-nā-luāhine

Literally, the fire of the old women.

———————

Gulch that joins Makamakaʻole in the ahupuaʻa of Kukuipuka, kalana of Kahakuloa.

260 Keahua

Keʻāhua

Ke-ʻāhua

Literally, the knoll.

———————

ʻIli lele in the ahupuaʻa of Honokōhau.

Variants: Keahua 1, Keahua 2.

261 Keahupuaa

Keahupuaʻa

Ke-ahu-puaʻa

Literally, the pig cairn.

———————

ʻIli in the ahupuaʻa of Hononana, kalana of Kahakuloa.

262 Kealakahakaha

Ke-ala-kahakaha

Literally, the road that switches back and forth.

———————

An area of old trail in the kalana of Kahakuloa said to have been created by the demigod Māui.

———————

"Ua olelo ia o Maui a Kalana kekahi alii kahiko loa i hana i na alanui i ka wa he iwakalua a keu keneturia mamua, aka, ma kona ano moolelo, ua hanaia na alanui a pololei loa. Ua maa na kanaka i ka hele ma ka pololei o ke alanui, aka, i ke alualu ana o kekahi poe e pepehi ia Maui, ua hele kikeekee oia i ke alanui, a ua kapaia o ʻke alanui kikeekee a Maui,' aia ma Waikane me Waiahole ma Koolaupoko i Oahu, aia ma Kekaa i Lahaina me Kaanapali, a ma Kealakahakaha i Kahakuloa no Maui. [*It is said that Māui of Kalana was a very ancient chief who made the roads during a period some twenty-plus centuries ago, but in versions of his tales, the roads were made very straight. The people were used to traveling along the straight nature of the roads, but when some people chased Māui to kill him, he went zigzaggedly on the road, and they were called 'the crooked road of Māui'; they are found at Waikāne and Waiāhole in Koʻolaupoko on Oʻahu, they are there at Kekaʻa in Lahaina and Kāʻanapali, and at Kealakahakaha in Kahakuloa from Maui.*]" /*Ke Au Okoa,* Buke 5, Helu 26, 14 ʻOkakopa 1869/

63 Ke Alanui Kikeekee a Maui
Ke Alanui Kīkeʻekeʻe a Māui

Literally, the crooked road of Māui.

The name of two sections of road storied to have been made crooked by the demigod Māui: one found near Kekaʻa, in the ahupuaʻa of Honokōwai, and the other in the area of Kealakahakaha, kalana of Kahakuloa.

"Ua olelo ia o Maui a Kalana kekahi alii kahiko loa i hana i na alanui i ka wa he iwakalua a keu keneturia mamua, aka, ma kona ano moolelo, ua hanaia na alanui a pololei loa. Ua maa na kanaka i ka hele ma ka pololei o ke alanui, aka, i ke alualu ana o kekahi poe e pepehi ia Maui, ua hele kikeekee oia i ke alanui, a ua kapaia o ʻke alanui kikeekee a Maui,' aia ma Waikane me Waiahole ma Koolaupoko i Oahu, aia ma Kekaa i Lahaina me Kaanapali, a ma Kealakahakaha i Kahakuloa no Maui. [*It is said that Māui of Kalana was a very ancient chief who made the roads during a period some twenty-plus centuries ago, but in versions of his tales, the roads were made very straight. The people were used to traveling along the straight nature of the roads, but when some people chased Māui to kill him, he went zigzaggedly on the road, and they were called 'the crooked road of Māui'; they are found at Waikāne and Waiāhole in Koʻolaupoko on Oʻahu, they are there at Kekaʻa in Lahaina and Kāʻanapali, and at Kealakahakaha in Kahakuloa from Maui.*] /*Ke Au Okoa,* Buke 5, Helu 26, 14 ʻOkakopa 1869/

64 Keamoalii
Keamoaliʻi
Ke-amo-aliʻi

Literally, the chiefly burden.

ʻIli in the ahupuaʻa of Honokōhau.

Variants: Kaimooalii, Kuimooalii.

65 Keana
Ke-ana

Literally, the cave.

ʻIli in the ahupuaʻa of Pōʻelua, kalana of Kahakuloa.

266 Keanaakaluahine
See Anakaluahine.

267 Keanae
Keʻanae
Ke-ʻanae

"*Lit.*, the mullet." /HD/

ʻIli in the ahupuaʻa of Kahakuloa, kalana of Kahakuloa.

268 Keauhou
Ke-au-hou

Meaning undetermined, perhaps: the new flow (of stream water).

ʻIli lele in the ahupuaʻa of Honokōhau.

Also, an ʻili in the ahupuaʻa of Nāpili.

269 Keaukaia
Keaukaiʻa
Ke-au-(a)-ka-iʻa

Literally, the current of the fish.

Shoreline area along Kulaokaʻea, ahupuaʻa of Honolua.

270 Keawalua
Ke-awa-lua

"*Lit.*, the double channel." /PNOH/

Bay on the east side of the ahupuaʻa of Honokōhau.

Variant: Awalua.

271 Keikapalani
See Keikipalani.

72 Keikipalani
Keiki-palani

Meaning undetermined, perhaps: detested child, rancid-smelling child, or, shoot of the *palani* sweet potato.

Ridge toward the northwest end of the kalana of Kahakuloa.

Variant: Keikapalani.

73 Kekaa
Keka'a
Ke-ka'a

"*Lit.*, the rumble (such sounds are said to be heard during storms)." /PNOH/

Prominent storied hill in the ahupuaʻa of Honokōwai. Also called "Kekahi."

"Ke-kaʻa Black rock and area, site of Sheraton-Maui Hotel, Kāʻana-pali, West Maui. A man, Moemoe, insulted the demigod Māui; after lassoing the sun, Māui chased and killed Moemoe, who turned into this rock... *Lit.*, the rumble (such sounds are said to be heard during storms)." /PNOH/

Variant: Kekahi, Puukekaa, Puu Kekaa.

74 Kekaalaau
Keka'alā'au
Ke-ka'a-lā'au

"*Lit.*, the twirling warclub." /PNOH/

An inland hill above the ahupuaʻa of Māhinahina.

75 Keoa
Keo'a
Ke-o'a

Meaning undetermined, perhaps: the oʻa ("oʻa n. 1. House rafter; timbers in the side of a ship; sides of a rock wall... 2. Gill of a fish; mouth of an eel. 3. Maui name for kauila (*Colubrina oppositifolia*), a tree." /HD/

ʻIli in the ahupuaʻa of Honokeana.

276 **Keonehelelee**
See Keonehelelei.

277 **Keonehelelei**
Keonehelele'i
Ke-one-helele'i

Literally, the crumbling sand.

———————

Region along the northside of Kulaokaʻea, ahupuaʻa of Honolua.

Variant: Keonehelelee.

278 **Keonenui**
Ke-one-nui

Literally, the big beach.

———————

Shoreline area in the ahupuaʻa of ʻAlaeloa.

279 **Keonohuli**
Ke-ono-huli

Meaning undetermined, perhaps: the sixth taro top, or, the turning *ono* fish.

———————

ʻIli in the ahupuaʻa of ʻAlaeloa.

280 **Kepuhi**
Ke-puhi

Literally, the blowhole.

———————

Shoreline area along the ahupuaʻa of Honokōhau.

281 **Kihapiilani Trail**
Kihāpiʻilani
Kiha-a-Piʻilani

Remnant of the circuitous road, originally commissioned by the chief Kihāpiʻilani, which formerly encircled the island of Maui.

———————

"The north end of West Maui also is traversed by a paved trail. Sections of it can be seen from Honolua to Honokohau and Kahakuloa. It is paved with beach rocks and has a width of four to six feet. Disregarding elevations and depressions it takes the shortest route between two points that is possible for foot travel. This trail is also spoken of as the Kihapiilani Trail." /SOM 1/

82 Kiiakapapa
Kiʻiakapapa / Kiʻiakāpapa
Kiʻi-a-Kapapa / Kiʻi-a-kāpapa

Pronunciation and meaning undetermined, perhaps: kiʻi a Kapapa—the statue made by Kapapa, or, to try to accomplish in unison.

———

ʻIli in the ahupuaʻa of Honokeana.

83 Kikalahai
Kīkalahaʻi
Kīkala-haʻi

Literally, snapped canoe stern.

———

Shoreline area along the ahupuaʻa of Honokōhau.

84 Kiki
Kiki / Kikī / Kīkī

Pronunciation and meaning undetermined, perhaps: kiki—"2. vt. To sting, as a bee; to peck, leap at, as a hen...3. Same as ʻukīkiki, a fish" /HD/; kikī—1. vi. To flow swiftly, spout; to spurt, as water from a hose...; to eject, as octopus ink; to do swiftly" /HD/; or, kīkī—4. n. A bird resembling the plover. 5. n. Name given a shellfish...6. n. A seaweed." /HD/

———

Shoreline area along Kulaokaʻea, ahupuaʻa of Honolua.

85 Kikikihale
Kikiki-hale

Literally, stifling heat within a house.

———

ʻIli in the ahupuaʻa of Māhinahina.

286 Kiowaiokihawahine
Kiʻowaiokihawahine
Kiʻo-wai-o-Kihawahine

Literally, Kihawahine's pool.

Highland lake (5,020 feet) found along the boundary between the two ahupuaʻa of Honokahua and Honokōhau. [NOTE: This name may be a new coinage.] Also called by the superimposed name of foreign origin, "Violet Lake."

Variant: Violet Lake.

287 Kipapa
Kīpapa

Literally, paved, level terrace.

ʻIli in the ahupuaʻa of Honokōwai.

288 Kipu
Kīpū

Literally, to hold back.

ʻIli in the ahupuaʻa of Makaliua 1, kalana of Kahakuloa.

289 Kiula
See Niuula.

290 Koaeloa
Koaʻeloa
Koaʻe-loa

Meaning undetermined, perhaps: long tropic bird, long *koaʻe* banana/taro/sweet potato, or, long *koaʻe* snapper.

ʻIli in the ahupuaʻa of Hononana, kalana of Kahakuloa.

291 Kolekole

Literally, rawness.

ʻIli in the ahupuaʻa of Kahana 1.

92 Kou

Literally, kou tree.

———————————

Land parcel, perhaps moʻo, in the ʻili of Waihale, ahupuaʻa of Honokōwai.

93 Kuaaimano
Kuaʻaimanō
Kua-ʻai-manō

Pronunciation and meaning undetermined, perhaps: god that eats sharks, or, god that eats like a shark.

———————————

ʻIli in the ahupuaʻa of Māhinahina.

94 Kuakepa
Kua-kepa

Literally, to chop/hew obliquely.

———————————

Unidentified ʻili in the ahupuaʻa of Honolua.

95 Kuamopua
See Kuamoopua.

96 Kuamoopua
Kuamoʻopua
Kuamoʻo-pua

Literally, flower path.

———————————

ʻIli in the ahupuaʻa of Honokeana.

97 Kue
Kue / Kuʻe / Kūʻē

Pronunciation and meaning undetermined, perhaps: "kue 1. interj. Call to attract ʻuaʻu, petrel birds, believed in imitation of their sound. 2. n. Fishhook with point of hook curved inward almost to the shaft, used for large fish" /HD/; "kuʻe 1. vi. To push with the elbows, to elbow; to move back and forth, as a piston or as the action of the tide…2. vs. Deformed, malformed" /HD/; or, "kū.ʻē nvt. To oppose, resist, protest; opposite, versus, adverse, contrary, antagonistic, unwilling; objection. *Lit.*, stand different. " /HD/

———————————

ʻIli in the ahupuaʻa of Nāpili.

298 Kuewa

Kuewa

Literally, exile, vagabond.

———————

ʻIli in the ahupuaʻa of Kahakuloa, kalana of Kahakuloa. Also, the name of a heiau in the same vicinity.

———————

"LCAw 6147-I to Hoewaa: "Kalo & kula, ili o Kuewaa [*sic*, Kuewa]...1.13 eka." Also LCAw 6623 to Naone. Written 'Kuewa' in FT and NT for both claims. Misspelt 'Kuewaa' in Indices and Award Books." /Place Names (ULUK)/

"The true place name of the kuleana awarded to Naone and now owned by my family is unclear. On survey maps of 1896 and in the Buke Mahele, the place name is recorded as Kuewaa. However, in Walker's manuscript, Kuewa is the name given to a heiau on the said land. My family pronounces this place name as Kuewa. However, it is possible that over the years, the last 'a' has been omitted in speech as a shortened version of Kuewaa." /(footnote pp 31–32) Oliveira, 1999/

Variant: Kuewaa.

299 Kuewaa

See Kuewa.

300 Kuhaa

Kūhaʻa

Kū-haʻa

Literally, low-standing.

———————

ʻIli in the ahupuaʻa of ʻĀhoa, kalana of Kahakuloa.

301 Kuhakea

Kuha-kea

Pronunciation and meaning undetermined, perhaps: "kuha-kea...white spittle." / Place Names (ULUK)/

———————

ʻIli in the ahupuaʻa of Makaliua 1, kalana of Kahakuloa.

302 Kuhanahana

See Kahanahana.

03 **Kuhuwa**
Kūhuwā
Kū-huwā

Pronunciation and meaning undetermined, perhaps: kū huwā—standing jealously.

Gulch in the ʻili of Kapili, ahupuaʻa of Honokōwai.

04 **Kuimooalii**
See Keamoalii.

05 **Kukaeaoa**
Kūkaeʻaoa
Kūkae-ʻaoa

Pronunciation and meaning undetermined, perhaps: barker's (dog) excrement, or, a term for a mushroom or growth/substance (kūkae) associated with, or that smells like, sandalwood (ʻaoa).

ʻIli in the ahupuaʻa of Waiokila, kalana of Kahakuloa.

06 **Kukaekanu**
See Kukuikanu.

07 **Kukaenui**
Kūkaenui / Kūkaʻenui
Kūkae-nui / Kū-kaʻe-nui

Pronunciation and meaning undetermined, perhaps: kūkae nui—large dung; or, kū kaʻe nui—stand on the great border.

Shoreline point along Kulaokaʻea, ahupuaʻa of Honolua.

08 **Kukaua**
Kūkaua
Kū-kaua

Literally, war Kū (deity).

ʻIli in the ahupuaʻa of Mailepai.

309 Kukuikanu
Kukui-kanu

Literally, candlenut tree that has been planted.

_____

'Ili in the ahupua'a of Honolua.

Also, an 'ili in the ahupua'a of Kahana (3).

Variant: Kukaekanu.

310 Kukuikapu
See Kukuipuka.

311 Kukuimamalu
Kukuimāmalu
Kukui-māmalu

Literally, *kukui* tree/grove that provides good shelter/shade.

_____

'Ili in the ahupua'a of Makaliua 1, kalana of Kahakuloa.

312 Kukuiolono
Kukui-o-Lono

Meaning undetermined, perhaps: *kukui* tree of Lono, or, torch of Lono.

_____

'Ili in the ahupua'a of Kahana 3.

313 Kukuipuka
Kukui-puka

Meaning undetermined, perhaps: perforated *kukui* nut, torch at the door, or, *kukui* tree grove through which one emerges.

_____

Ahupua'a in the kalana of Kahakuloa, deemed a pu'uhonua during the reign of Kamehameha I. Listed as an 'ili in some documents.

_____

"Identified in IDLM 397 as an ahupua'a containing 11 ili in Kukuipuka 1 and 2: Kaulu, Kaunuwahine, Luapuaa, Makahuna, Namahana, Opuupuu, Paehala, Pakolo, Palau, Peekoa, Waiololi. Sometimes written 'Kukuikapu.' Kukuipuka was made a pu'uhonua land by Kamehameha I." /Place Names (ULUK)/

Variants: Kukuikapu, Kukuipuka 1, 2.

14 Kukuokaawe
Kūkūoka'awe
Kūkū-o-ka-'awe

Pronunciation and meaning undetermined, perhaps: stand/pedestal of the pack/bundle.

———————

'Ili in the ahupua'a of Nāpili.

15 Kulaloa
Kula-loa

Literally, long plain.

———————

Area mentioned in mele in the context of Pu'u Koa'e in the ahupua'a of Kahakuloa, kalana o Kahakuloa.

"Nana iho ia Puukoae au ike kai, / Au halaoa i ke kai o Kulaloa, / Loa na lima o ka ale o Makawela, / Aloha wale ka pali o Kahakahalani, / Ka hilinai e ka pali o Mana, / Ke kauna pali o Kaimalolo. . . . [*Look down at Pu'u Koa'e jutting out into the sea, / Projecting out into the sea of Kulaloa, / The reach of the waves of Makawela is long, / Fond memories for the cliff of Kahakahalani, / The confidant of the cliff of Mānā, / The resting place on the cliff of Kaimalolo. . . .*]" /*Ke Au Okoa*, Buke 2, Helu 33, 3 Kekemapa 1866/

16 Kulanaumeume
Kulana'ume'ume
Kulana-'ume'ume

Literally, unsteadied while struggling.

———————

'Ili in the ahupua'a of Hononana, kalana of Kahakuloa.

17 Kulaokaea
Kulaoka'ea / Kulaoka'ea / Kulaoka'e'a
Kula-o-ka-'ea / Kula-o-Ka'ea / Kula-o-ka-'e'a / Kula-o-Ka'e'a

Pronunciation and meaning undetermined, perhaps: kula o Ka'ea—plain of Ka'ea (proper name); kula o ka 'ea—plain of dust/spray; or, kula o ka 'e'a—plain of the dust/spray; or, kula o Ka'e'a—plain of Ka'e'a (proper name).

———————

Prominent seaside plateau to the northeast of Honolua Bay, ahupua'a of Honolua.

18 Kulaokalalaoloa
See Kula o Kalaulaolao.

319 Kula o Kalaulaolao
Kula o Kalaulaʻolaʻo
Kula o Ka-lau-la-ʻolaʻo

Literally, field/plain of leaves used for kindling or mulch.

Prominent plateau to the east of Honokōhau Valley, ahupuaʻa of Honokōhau.

Variants: Kalaulaolao, Kulaokalalaolao, Kulaokalalaoloa.

320 Kumukahi
Kumu-kahi

Literally, first origin, or, single tree trunk.

Mountainous piece of land and gulch in the ʻili of Waihale, ahupuaʻa of Honokōwai.

Also, an ʻili in the ahupuaʻa of Kahana 3.

321 Kumukea
Kūmūkea
Kūmū-kea

Literally, kūmū kea taro.

ʻIli in the ahupuaʻa of Honokōhau.

322 Kupaa
Kūpaʻa

Literally, steadfast.

Gulch in the ʻili of Kukuipuka, kalana of Kahakuloa, just north of the boundary between the moku of Kāʻanapali and the moku of Wailuku.

323 Kupoupou
Kūpoupou

Literally, to stagger.

ʻIli in the ahupuaʻa of Kahana 1.

24 Kuulu
Kūʻulu / Kuʻulū
Kū-ʻulu / Kuʻu-lū

Pronunciation and meaning undetermined, perhaps: Kū ʻulu—Kū (deity) of the bread-fruit; or, kuʻu lū—release scattering.

ʻIli in the ahupuaʻa of Makaliua, kalana of Kahakuloa.

25 Kuunaakaiole
Kuʻunaakaʻiole
Kuʻuna-a-ka-ʻiole

Literally, net-fishing place of the rat.

Shoreline area along the ahupuaʻa of Nāpili.

26 Laa
Laʻa

Literally, consecrated.

Shoreline area along the ahupuaʻa of Honokahua.

27 Laau
Lāʻau

Literally, plant.

ʻIli in the ahupuaʻa of Honokōwai.

28 Lae Kahilianapa
See Kahulianapa.

29 Lae Kunonou
See Kanounou.

30 Laeokama
Lae-o-Kama

Literally, shoreline point of Kama.

Shoreline point in the ahupuaʻa of Māhinahina.

331 Lahoole
Lahoʻole
Laho-ʻole

Literally, without a scrotum.

Shoreline area along the mouth of Makamakaʻole Gulch/Stream, in the kalana of Kahakuloa.

332 Lahuiokalani Kaanapali Congregational Church
Lāhuiokalani
Lāhui-o-ka-lani

Literally, nation of Heaven.

Church near Honokōwai Point in the ahupuaʻa of Honokōwai. Also called Kaanapali Church.

Variant: Kaanapali Church.

333 Lainaha
See Leinaha.

334 Lamahihi
Lama-hihi

Literally, creeping *lama* tree.

ʻIli in the ahupuaʻa of ʻĀhoa, kalana of Kahakuloa.

335 Lanihili
See Lanilili.

336 Lanilili
Lanilili / Lanilīlī
Lani-lili / Lani-līlī

Meaning undetermined, perhaps: lani lili—jealous/anguished chief; or, lani līlī—trembling/chilled chief.

Inland hill (2,563 feet) along the boundary between the two moku of Kāʻanapali and Wailuku in the kalana of Kahakuloa.

Variant: Lanihili.

37 Lanipanoa
Lanipanoa / Lanipānoa
Lani-panoa / Lani-pānoa

Pronunciation and meaning undetermined, perhaps: lani panoa—desolate sky; or, lani pānoa—easily approached chief.

___

ʻIli in the ahupuaʻa of Kahakuloa, kalana of Kahakuloa.

38 Lapaiki
Lapa-iki

Literally, small ridge.

___

Ridge toward the mouth of the valley and ahupuaʻa of Kahakuloa, kalana of Kahakuloa.

___

"No ke Kalana o Kahakuloa a me Kona mau Hiohiona. Aia no keia Kalana ma ke komohana akau o na Waieha, a o kekahi hapa ia o ka apana o Lahaina, he aina alopali keia i pakuku ia e na pali kona mau aoao a hamama ma kai, e huli aku ana ke alo o keia wahi aina kahawai i ka Hikina Akau, a he ake [*sic*] iki makai o ka nuku muliwai e pili ala me ke kai, o ko laila poe ka ike pono i ke kai o Hoomanunu, a ike no hoi i ka moku holo ae ma ka moana, a o ka poe ma uka aku, aole lakou e ike mai i ke kai, ua alai ia e kekahi wahi lapa e ku kalali ana mawaena o ke kahawai, o Lapaiki ka inoa, a o Haleino mauka iho. Aia ma ka lae kahakai ma ka hikina iho, e ku ana kona puu kaulana o ʻPuukoae papa i ka makani 'Kuinalehua o Kaukini.' A o ka mauna o Eke ma ke komohana, nolaila ka oleloia ana e ka poe haku mele kahiko, 'Hana ekeeke i ka ipu a ka makani.' Hiolo lua i ka pali o Leinaha. [*Regarding the District of Kahakuloa and Its Features. This district is northwest of the Waiʻehā region, and it's a portion of the precinct of Lahaina; this is a land in the face of the cliffs with its sides screened in by steep precipices and wide open along the sea; the front of this place of many streams and gulches faces Northeast, and the entrance of the rivermouth widens a little as it joins with the sea; the people there can view the sea of Hoʻomanunu, and they can see the ships traveling on the ocean, and the people inland, they cannot see the sea: the view is obscured by a small ridge standing proudly in the middle of the valley. Lapaiki is its name, and Haleʻino is just inland of that. There at the seaside point just to the east, its famous hill stands 'Puʻukoaʻe ever brushed against by the wind' 'Stringing Lehua of Kaukini.' And the mountain of ʻEke is to the west, from which comes mention by the composers of old, 'Forming a holder for the gourd of winds.' Tumbling incessantly down the cliffs of Leinahā.*]" /*Ka Nupepa Kuokoa*, Buke 14, Helu 33, 14 ʻAukake 1875/

339 Lapamuku

Lapa-muku

Literally, shortened ridge.

_____

'Ili in the ahupua'a of Honokeana.

340 Leinaha

Leinahā

Lei-nahā

Pronunciation and meaning undetermined, perhaps: lei nahā—to toss and smash to bits.

_____

'Ili in the ahupua'a of Waiokila, kalana of Kahakuloa.

Variant: Lainaha.

341 Leinakauhane

See Kaleinaakauhane.

342 Lelepaua

Lele-paua

Meaning undetermined, perhaps: *lele* altar made of *paua* shells.

_____

'Ili in the ahupua'a of Makaliua 2, kalana of Kahakuloa.

343 Likipu

Likipū

Liki-pū

Literally, completely tightened.

_____

'Ili in the ahupua'a of Kahana(nui).

344 Limalau

"lima.lau same as laulima [*Literally*, cooperation], but some persons limit limalau cooperation to canoe and house building." /HD/

_____

Gulch in the ahupua'a of Honokōwai that joins Pālaha Gulch.

45 Lipoa

Līpoa

Literally, līpoa seaweed.

Shoreline point off of Kulaokaʻea, ahupuaʻa of Honolua.

46 Loainalu

See Wainalo.

47 Loinui

Loʻinui

Loʻi-nui

Literally, main taro patch.

Inland ʻili in the ahupuaʻa of Honokōwai.

"Survey of No. 2, Loinui in Honokowai Valley. Kalo land mauka loa . . . 2 acres of kalo ground. Note: This Loinui is said to contain all the S. pali of Honokowai Valley, extending to the head of the mountain joining Waihee, and also all of Honokowai river from its source to its mouth. This could not be conveniently measured." /Place Names (ULUK)/

48 Luapuaa

Luapuaʻa

Lua-puaʻa

Literally, pig pit.

ʻIli in the ahupuaʻa of Kukuipuka, kalana of Kahakuloa.

49 Luapuna Bay

Lua-puna

Literally, pond pit.

An alternative name found for Oneloa Bay, in the ahupuaʻa of Honokahua. Perhaps related to the Mākāluapuna Point along this bay's northeast border.

Variant: Makaluapuna, Oneloa.

50 Maele

See Maile.

351 Maepono
Mae-pono

Literally, thoroughly wilted.

ʻIli in the ahupuaʻa of Honokōhau.

Variants: Naipono, Maipono.

352 Mahana
Mahana / Māhana

Pronunciation and meaning undetermined, perhaps: mahana—warm; or, māhana—twins, or, Castor or Pollux.

Ridge and trail (Mahana Ridge Trail) in the ahupuaʻa of Honokahua.

Also, an ʻili in the ahupuaʻa of Nāpili.

353 Mahele
Māhele

Literally, division (of land).

ʻIli in the ahupuaʻa of Pōʻelua, kalana of Kahakuloa.

354 Mahinahina
Māhinahina

Literally, pale moonlight.

Ahupuaʻa said to contain seven ʻili in the moku of Kāʻanapali. Also the name of a shoreline point in the same ahupuaʻa.

"Returned by Konia at the Māhele, retained by aupuni. Mahinahina 1,2,3 were among the lands set aside by the Legislature in 1850 for the support of the public schools; sold together with Kahana 1 and 2 to Dwight Baldwin et al. as RPG 1166. Mahinahina 4 was awarded to Charles Cockett, LCAw 75, 149 acres. Also in Mahinahina 4 are LCAw 4239 to Kaukau, 4248 to Kekalohe, 6539 to Hoonoho. Identified in IDLM 397 as an ahupuaʻa containing 7 ili in Mahinahina 1, 2, 3 and 4: Aipuaa, Kahina, Kauhilua, Kaukini, Kikikihale, Kuaaimano, Paupolo." /Place Names (ULUK)/

Variants: Mahinahina 1, 2, 3, 4.

55 Mahinahina Camp
Māhinahina Camp

Plantation camp found inland of the Kapalua-West Maui Airport.

56 Mahinanui
Mahina-nui

Literally, large moon.

Islet southeast of Puʻu Koaʻa in the kalana of Kahakuloa.

57 Mahoe
Māhoe

Meaning undetermined, perhaps: "mā.hoe n. 1. Twins. 2. Two native trees (*Alectryon macrococcum* and *A. mahoe*), related to the soapberry and the litchi; they have compound leaves and globose, brown, twinned or single fruits. (Neal 531.) Also ʻalaʻala hua. 3. *(Cap.)* Names of months and stars. See Māhoe Hope, Māhoe Mua, and Māhana 2." /HD/

ʻIli in the ahupuaʻa of Honokahua.

58 Mailapa
Maʻilapa
Maʻi-lapa

Pronunciation and meaning undetermined, perhaps: sickness that causes swelling, or, swollen genitals.

ʻIli in the ahupuaʻa of Honokōhau.

59 Maile

Literally, *maile* plant.

ʻIli in the ahupuaʻa of Honokōwai.

Variant: Maele.

360 Mailepai
Mailepai / Mailepaʻi
Maile-pai / Maile-paʻi

Pronunciation and meaning undetermined, perhaps: maile pai—*maile* vines used to make the *pai* shrimp trap, or, raised *maile* stick (used in birdcatching); or, maile paʻi—stripped *maile* vine/plant.

[NOTE: "Mailepai" is the pronunciation favored by the Hawaiian families of this area.]

Ahupuaʻa with 14 ʻili, gulch, and intermittent stream in the moku of Kāʻanapali.

Variants: Mailapa, Mailepai.

361 Mailepai Point
See Kalaeokaia.

362 Maipono
See Maepono.

363 Maiu
Māʻiu

Pronunciation and meaning undetermined, perhaps: mā- + ʻiu—in the state of consecration; or, lofty eyes.

Heiau in the ahupuaʻa of Honokōhau.

"Maiu Heiau, Walker Site 20. East side of Honokohau Valley on cliff 200 ft. above sea level. A large heiau for human sacrifice... rectangular... about 96 × 200 ft." /Place Names (ULUK)/

364 Makaa
Mākaʻa

"mā.ka.ʻa 1. nvs. Clear and open, as a view; a clearing. 2. n. A faint green striped mutant of the sweet potato." /HD/

ʻIli in the ahupuaʻa of Honokōwai.

365 Makahiki
See Makahiku.

66 Makahiku

Meaning undetermined, perhaps: seven eyes, or, seven buds.

———

ʻIli in the ahupuaʻa of Honokōwai.

Variants: Kahiku, Makahiki.

67 Makahuna
Maka-huna

Literally, hidden eyes/face.

———

ʻIli in the ahupuaʻa of Kukuipuka, kalana of Kahakuloa.

68 Makalina
See Makaliua.

69 Makaliua
Maka-liua

Literally, dizzying/fascinating sight.

———

Ahupuaʻa containg 12 ʻili in the kalana of Kahakuloa.

———

"Not named in the Māhele Book. Identified in IDLM 397 as an ahupuaʻa containing 12 ili in Waaiokila 1 and 2: Hale, Kamoa, Kaulu, Kawelokio, Kipu, Kukuimamalu, Lelepaua, Noni, Omaolehulehu, Pauhulu, Pueno, Waialae. LCAw 6148-O to Kamalalawalu: ʻIli o Waialae, ahupuaa o Makalina [*sic*, Makaliua] 1, Kahakuloa...2.3 eka.' TMK 3101:7. LCAw 9639-B to Kumaiepaa: 'Maloko o ke ahupuaa o Kahakuloa, Maui. Ap. 1. Ili o Makaliua 1...0.62 eka.' TMK 3101:10. LCAw 6148-B to Nahalea: 'Makaliua, Kahakuloa, Maui. Kalo a me kula...3.20 eka.' TMK 3101:9. Also LCAw 6740 to Luwale in Kaliua (q.v.). Misspelt 'Makalina' in Indices." /Place Names (ULUK)/

70 Makaluapuna
Mākāluapuna
Mākālua-puna

Meaning undetermined, perhaps: hole dug for planting (taro) in coral, or, hole dug for planting (taro) near a spring.

———

Seaside point on the east side of Oneloa Bay, in the ahupuaʻa of Honokahua.

Variants: Luapuna, Oneloa.

371 Makamakaole
Makamakaʻole
Makamaka-ʻole

Literally, friendless.

Gulch and stream in the ahupuaʻa of Kukuipuka, kalana of Kahakuloa.

372 Makaoioi
Makaʻoiʻoi
Maka-ʻoiʻoi

Literally, penetrating eyes.

The name of David Thomas Fleming's home, which later became the Pineapple Hill Restaurant in the ahupuaʻa of Honokahua.

373 Makaulii
Makauliʻi

"makau.liʻi vs. 1. Saving, economical, thrifty, provident; miserly, avaricious, eager to own . . . 2. Broad-backed, thick-shelled, of a turtle." /HD/

ʻIli in the ahupuaʻa of Mailepai.

374 Makawela
Literally, "n. Type of stone from which weights for cowry octopus lures were made." /HD/

Area mentioned in mele in the context of the kalana of Kahakuloa.

"Nana iho ia Puukoae au ike kai, / Au halaoa i ke kai o Kulaloa, / Loa na lima o ka ale o Makawela, / Aloha wale ka pali o Kahakahalani, / Ka hilinai e ka pali o Mana, / Ke kauna pali o Kaimalolo. . . . [*Look down at Puʻu Koaʻe jutting out into the sea, / Projecting out into the sea of Kulaloa, / The reach of the waves of Makawela is long, / Fond memories for the cliff of Kahakahalani, / The confidant of the cliff of Mānā, / The resting place on the cliff of Kaimalolo. . . .*]" /Ke Au Okoa, Buke 2, Helu 33, 3 Kekemapa 1866/

375 Makuleia
See Mokuleia.

76 Malalokai
Ma-lalo-kai

Literally, sea down below.

_____

Gulch and stream in the ahupuaʻa of Kapaloa, kalana of Kahakuloa. The upper reach of this stream is called Waipili.

Variant: Walpili.

77 Malama
Malama / Mālama

Pronunciation and meaning undetermined, perhaps: malama—light, or, moon; or, mālama—care.

_____

Cliff in the Makamakaʻole region, ahupuaʻa of Kukuipuka, kalana of Kahakuloa.

78 Malili
Mālili

"mā.lili 1. vs. Blighted, blasted, withered, stunted, as fruits... 2. Rare. var. of maʻalili, cooled, calmed." /HD/

_____

ʻIli in the ahupuaʻa of Honolua.

79 Malo
Malo / Malō / Mālō

Pronunciation and meaning undetermined, perhaps: malo—loincloth; malō—dry; or, mālō—taut.

_____

Hill found upon Kulaokaʻea in the ahupuaʻa of Honolua.

80 Malu

Literally, shaded/protected.

_____

ʻIli in the ahupuaʻa of Kahakuloa, kalana of Kahakuloa.

81 Maluaka
Malu-aka

Literally, shaded by the shadow.

_____

ʻIli in the ahupuaʻa of Honokōhau.

382 Maluhia

See Camp Maluhia.

383 Mana

Literally, stream branch.

The name of the lower reach of Wailena Gulch in the ahupuaʻa of Makaliua 1, kalana of Kahakuloa.

384 Manaaiole

Māna'ai'ole
Māna-'ai-'ole

Literally, uneaten chewed mass.

Shoreline area between the ahupuaʻa of ʻAlaeloa and Honokeana.

385 Manawaikaha

Mana-wai-kaha

Literally, dry stream branch.

Gulch in the ahupuaʻa of Honolua, and which joins the Honolua Stream gulch.

386 Manawaikalupe

Manawaikalupe
Mana-wai-(a)-Kalupe

Literally, Kalupe's stream branch; or, perhaps a misrepresentation of: māno wai (a) Kalupe—Kalupe's water diversion.

ʻIli in the ahupuaʻa of ʻAlaeloa.

Variant: Waikalupe.

387 Manienie

Mānienie

"mā.nie.nie 1. n. Bermuda grass (*Cynodon dactylon*), a fine-leafed, cosmopolitan grass, much used for lawns in Hawaiʻi . . . 2. Short for mānienie ʻakiʻaki [a grass]. 3. vs. Bare, barren." /HD/

Gulch in the ahupuaʻa of Honokōhau, located inland of Kulaokalaulaʻolaʻo, and which joins Anākaluahine Gulch.

88 Manokiei
Manōkiʻei
Manō-kiʻei

Literally, slyly peeping shark.

———————

Shoreline area along Pōhakupule Gulch in the ahupuaʻa of Honokōhau.

89 Maopo
See Maupo.

90 Mauakini
See Maunakini.

91 Maumea
Mau-mea

Meaning undetermined, perhaps: snags things.

———————

Shoreline area along Kulaokaʻea, ahupuaʻa of Honolua.

92 Mauna Eeke
See Eke.

93 Maunakini
Mauna-kini

"*Lit.*, many mountains." /PNOH/

———————

Famed, prominent hill (1,437 feet) in the ahupuaʻa of Kahakuloa, kalana of Kahakuloa, located on a ridge that separates the valleys of Kahakuloa and Waihali.

Variant: Mauakini.

94 Maunalei Arboretum

(Maunalei—garland mountain)

Arboretum created by D.T. Fleming, which is the end point of the Mahana Ridge Trail between the two ahupuaʻa of Honokahua and Honolua.

395 Maunaohuohu

Maunaʻohuʻohu

Mauna-ʻohuʻohu

Literally, misty mountain.

_____

Area mentioned in mele in the context of the ahupuaʻa of Kukuipuka, kalana of Kahakuloa.

_____

"Kuu wahine mai ke kula la e Maunaohuohu, / Mai ke kahawai la e Makamakaole, / Mai ka piina la e Kukuipuka.... [*My beloved wife from the plains of Maunaʻohuʻohu, / From the stream of Makamakaʻole, / From the ascent of Kukuipuka....*]" /*Ko Hawaii Pae Aina*, Buke 2, Helu 14, 5 ʻApelila 1879/

396 Maupo

Maupō

Mau-pō

Literally, grounded/stuck (as a canoe) in the night.

_____

ʻIli in the ahupuaʻa of ʻĀhoa, kalana of Kahakuloa.

Variant: Maopo.

397 Miloiki

Milo-iki

Meaning undetermined, perhaps: small *milo* tree, or, slight whirling [of the sea].

_____

Shoreline area along Kulaokaʻea, ahupuaʻa of Honolua.

398 Moho

"moho 1. n. Candidate, as in politics; representative selected to participate in a race, wrestling, or betting contest, champion. 2. n. Hawaiian rail (*Pennula sandwichensis*), an extinct flightless bird...3. vi. To unfold, of leaves, especially upper leaf of a plant, as sugar cane, taro." /HD/

_____

Shoreline point in the ahupuaʻa of Makaliua 2, found near the opening of Waiolaʻi Gulch in the kalana of Kahakuloa.

399 Mokeehia

Mōkeʻehia

Mō-keʻehia

"*Lit.*, trodden island (*mō-* is short for *moku*)." /PNOH/

Islet and bird sanctuary in the ahupuaʻa of Makaliua 1, found just off of Hakuheʻe Point, kalana of Kahakuloa.

00 Mokolea
Mōkōlea
Mō-kōlea

Literally, kōlea (bird) island.

Seaside point along the eastern boundary of the ahupuaʻa of Hononana, kalana of Kahakuloa.

"Mōkōlea 2. Dive site, point, Kahakuloa, Maui. At Mōkōlea Point north of Kahakuloa." /PNOH/

01 Mokuleia
Mokuleʻia / Mokulēʻia

Pronunciation and meaning undetermined, perhaps: mokuleʻia—amberjack fish; or, moku lēʻia—district of abundance.

One of the two bays in the ahupuaʻa of Honolua, found between the points of ʻĀlaelae and Kalaepīhā. Also, the gulch that feeds this bay.

Variant: Makuleia.

02 Mokupea
Mokupeʻa
Moku-peʻa

Meaning undetermined, perhaps: division of a boundary, or, sail broken in two, or, "cross district." /PNOH/

ʻIli, gulch, and intermittent stream in the ahupuaʻa of Honokahua.

03 Momole o Kekaa
Momole o Kekaʻa

Literally, the smooth, rounded surface of Kekaʻa (hill).

A poetic reference for Kekaʻa.

"Ua hoohana ia iho nei na alanui o Kaanapali mai ka Momole o Kekaa a ka pali o Kapu-lehu, no kela haawina dala \$1,500 no ka hoohana ia ana. Ma kela hana ana ua nui ka pilikia o na pali i hana ia iho nei, ma keia ua ana a ua lilo keia mau alanui i mea ino no ka nui o ka wai e hele ana i na pali. [*The roads of Kāʻanapali, from the Smooth Rounded Surface of Kekaʻa to the cliff of Kapūlehu, were just used, due to the \$1,500 grant for their use. In using them, there were many problems with the steep banks that were just made; in the rain, these roads became bad because of the amount of water moving down the banks.*]" /*Ka Nupepa Kuokoa*, Buke 33, Helu 49, 8 Kekemapa 1894/

Variant: Kekaa.

404 Moomaka
Moʻomaka
Moʻo-maka

Meaning undetermined, perhaps: *maka* (sweet potato variety) strip of land.

ʻIli in the ahupuaʻa of Honolua.

405 Moomuku
Moʻomuku
Moʻo-muku

Meaning undetermined, perhaps: shortened *moʻo* land unit, or, cut-off ridge.

ʻIlikū in the ahupuaʻa of Honokōwai.

ʻIli in the ahupuaʻa of Mailepai and Honokahua.

Also, an ahupuaʻa in the kalana of Kahakuloa.

"Not named in the Māhele Book, Award Books or Indices. The ahupuaʻa of Moomuku may be defined as the land drained by the Waihali Stream and its tributaries, and lying between Kahakuloa ahupuaʻa and Ahoa ahupuaʻa. The evidence for its status as an ahupuaʻa, rather than an ʻili of the ahupuaʻa of Kahakuloa, is slight. As shown on Tax Map 3-1-02, Moomuku encompasses several kuleana along Waihali Stream, in the ʻili of Kawaihae." /Place Names (ULUK)/

406 Na Hono a Piilani
Nā Hono a Piʻilani

Literally, the bays of Piʻilani.

" 'Six West Maui bays whose names begin with Hono- (bay) and the islands seen from them (Kahoʻolawe, Lānaʻi, Molokaʻi) were ruled by Piʻilani and are famous in song; the six bays are [in geographical order: Honokowai, Honokeana, Honokahua, Honolua, Honokōhau, Hononana].' The bays are named from their adjoining ahupua'a; all are in the ancient district of Kaanapali." /Place Names (ULUK)/

Variants: Honoapiilani, Hono a Piilani, Na Hono ao Piilani.

07 Naio

Meaning undetermined, perhaps: "1. Pinworm, as in the rectum; white specks in feces; larvae, as of mosquitos; worm in dung or in taro... 2. Inferior taro left in the field after the crop is removed. 3. The bastard sandal-wood (*Myoporum sandwicense*)... 4. Name of a seaweed." /HD/

'Ili in the ahupua'a of Honokeana, Honokahua, and also in the ahupua'a of Waiokila 2, kalana of Kahakuloa.

08 Naioio
See Waioio.

09 Naipono
See Maepono.

10 Nakalalua
Nākalalua
Nā-kala-lua

Literally, the two sharp points.

Upland point at the head of the ahupua'a of Honokahua.

11 Nakalele
Nākālele
Nā-kālele

"*Lit.*, the leaning." /PNOH/

Prominent seaside point in the ahupua'a of Honokōhau. Site of a popular blowhole and lighthouse.

12 Nākālele Lighthouse

Beacon located near Nākālele Point in the ahupua'a of Honokōhau.

"Minor light of Maui—Nakalele Lighthouse In 1908, the Lighthouse Board selected 'the most northerly point of the westerly part' of Maui, known as Nakalele Point, for the erection of a forty-foot wooden mast atop which a temporary light could be displayed. By 1910, a keeper's dwelling had been constructed on the point and a boxlike platform was built on its roof for displaying a fixed-white light. John M. Hanuna was keeper of the Nakalele Point Light from 1910 to 1915, when John K. Mahoe took over responsibility for the light. Luther K. Kalama was appointed keeper in 1917, and he served until the light was automated in 1922. The characteristic of the light was changed to flashing white upon automation. Head Keepers: George N. Kanaulalena (1908–1909), John H. Kanekoa (1909), John M. Hanuna (1909–1915), John K. Mahoe (1915–1916), Luther K. Kalama (1917–1923)." /lighthousefriends.com/

413 Nalaalono
Nālaʻālono
Nā-laʻa-(a)-Lono

Literally, the consecrations of Lono.

Shoreline area along the ahupuaʻa of Honokahua.

414 Nalowale

Literally, vanished.

Heiau in the ahupuaʻa of Hononana, kalana of Kahakuloa.

Also, a heiau in the ahupuaʻa of ʻAlaeloa.

"Heiau at Hononana, Walker Site 21. Hononana Gulch near the shore. A walled heiau of pentagonal shape 150 feet long and 85 feet at the widest part...The walls are 6 feet thick and 8 high." /Place Names (ULUK)/

"Heiau, Walker Site 15. On bluff at south side of rocky cove between Alaeloa and Papuaa Points. Small rectangular enclosure measuring 50 × 66 ft." /Place Names (ULUK)/

415 Namahana
Nāmāhana
Nā-māhana

Literally, the twins.

ʻIli in the ahupuaʻa of Kukuipuka, kalana of Kahakuloa.

16 Namalu
Nāmalu
Nā-malu

Literally, the shelters.

Small bay directly south of Hāwea Point in the ahupua'a of Honokahua.

17 Nanahu
Nanahu / Nānahu

Pronunciation and meaning undetermined, perhaps: nanahu—chomping; or, nānahu—charcoal.

Shoreline area along the ahupua'a of Honokahua.

18 Na Pali Po i ka Ohu
Nā Pali Pō i ka 'Ohu

Literally, The Cliffs Dense with Mist.

A poetic epithet for the moku of Kā'anapali.

19 Napili
Nāpili
Nāpili / Nā-pili

Meaning undetermined, perhaps: nāpili—*napili* variety of 'o'opu fish; or, nā pili—the relatives, the *pili* varieties of grasses, or, the wagers.

Ahupua'a with 18 'ili, and bay in the moku of Kā'anapali, now a small town and residential area.

"Napili 1–3 retained by Konia at the Māhele, LCAw 5524:1, 601 acres. Napili 4 returned by Laahili at the Māhele, retained by Crown. Napili 5 returned by Alika Mela at the Māhele, retained by Crown. No kuleana are listed in Indices of Awards or shown on Tax Maps. Identified in IDLM 397 as an ahupua'a containing 18 ili in 4 of the 5 Napili: Aikahi (2), Kahao, Kahauloa, Kaholua, Kaieie, Kalama (2), Kaohe, Kapua, Keauhou, Kue, Kukuokaawe, Mahana, Waiakekua, Waipae (2), Waipueo." /Place Names (ULUK)/

Variants: Napili 1, 2, 3, 4, 5.

20 Naunaunawele
See Naunaunahawele.

421 Naunaunahawele
Naunau-nahawele

Literally, to munch on *nahawele* (a type of shellfish).

───────────

ʻIli in the ahupuaʻa of Honokōwai.

Variant: Naunaunawele.

422 Niholau
Niho-lau

Meaning undetermined, perhaps: young leaf bud emerging from the ground, or, scalloping of leaves.

───────────

ʻIli in the ahupuaʻa of ʻAlaeloa (iki).

423 Niu

Literally, coconut.

───────────

ʻIli in the ahupuaʻa of Waiokila, kalana of Kahakuloa.

424 Niula
See Niuula.

425 Niuula
Niuʻula
Niu-ʻula

Literally, red coconut.

───────────

ʻIli in the ahupuaʻa of Honokōhau.

Variant: Kiula, Niula.

426 Noni

Literally, *noni* tree.

───────────

ʻIli in the ahupuaʻa of Makaliua 1, kalana of Kahakuloa.

27 Nukunukuapuaa

Nukunukuapuaʻa

Nukunuku-a-puaʻa

Literally, snout like a pig.

___

Gulch in the ahupuaʻa of Honokōwai.

28 Ohia

ʻŌhiʻa

" ʻō.hiʻa 1. n. Two kinds of trees: see ʻōhiʻa ʻai and ʻōhiʻa lehua...3. n. A native variety of sugar cane...4. n. A variety of taro. 5. n. A red birthmark, said to be caused by the pregnant mother's longing for mountain apples (ʻohiʻa ʻai) and eating them. 6. vs. Tabooed, as food patches during famine, so-called because people did not eat from their taro patches, but from upland ʻōhiʻa ʻai, ti, and sweet potatoes." /HD/

___

ʻIli in the ahupuaʻa of Honokōwai, Mailepai (Ohia 1, 2), Honokahua, and in the ahupuaʻa of Kahakuloa, kalana of Kahakuloa.

Also, possibly an ʻili lele found in the ahupuaʻa of Kahana 1 & 3.

29 Ohiapoko

ʻŌhiʻapoko

ʻŌhiʻa-poko

Literally, short ʻōhiʻa tree.

___

ʻIli in the ahupuaʻa of Honokōhau.

30 Olohe

ʻŌlohe

" ʻō.lohe 1. vs. Bare, naked, barren; hairless, as a dog; bald; destitute, needy...2. nvs. Skilled, especially in lua fighting...also said of hula experts; skilled fighter...3. vs. Pale...4. vs. Sick, as after childbirth. 5. n. Ghost; image, as in clouds. 6. n. A small salt-water ʻoʻopu, a fish, found with the ʻōhune." /HD/

___

A set of ʻili, found as ʻŌlohe 1 & 2, in the ahupuaʻa of ʻAlaeloa.

Variants: Olohe 1, 2.

431 Omaolehulehu
'Ōma'olehulehu
'Ōma'o-lehulehu

Meaning undetermined, perhaps: multitudes of 'ōma'o birds, or, for the multitudes to come into view.

'Ili in the ahupua'a of Makaliua 1, kalana of Kahakuloa.

432 Oneloa
One-loa

Literally, long beach.

Bay between the seaside points of Hāwea and Mākāluapuna, in the ahupua'a of Honokahua.

433 Onepeha
One-peha

Pronunciation and meaning undetermined, perhaps a variation of: one pehe—unsteady sand; or, a misrepresentation of: one pīhā—sand carried down by floodwaters.

Gulch in the ahupua'a of Honokōwai.

434 Opihi
'Opihi

Literally, limpet.

'Ili in the ahupua'a of Kahana 1.

435 Opilopilo
'Ōpilopilo

Literally, marshy-smelling.

'Ili in the ahupua'a of Kahakuloa, kalana of Kahakuloa. *See also*: Kaopilopilo and Kawaiopilopilo.

436 Opopo
See Apopo.

37 Opukaha

ʻŌpūkaha

ʻŌpū-kaha

Literally, sliced belly.

ʻIli in the ahupuaʻa of Honokahua.

38 Opuupuu

ʻŌpuʻupuʻu

Literally, hilly.

ʻIli in the ahupuaʻa of Kukuipuka, kalana of Kahakuloa.

39 Ouohau

ʻOuohau

ʻOuo-hau

Literally, young *hau* tree.

ʻIli in the ahupuaʻa of ʻAlaeloa.

40 Ouolii

ʻOuoliʻi

ʻOuo-liʻi

Literally, small ʻouo (" ʻouo...nvs. Young animal, plant or person; young woman, pullet, cock, youth.../HD/).

ʻIli in the ahupuaʻa of Honokeana.

41 Owaluhi

ʻOwāluhi

ʻOwā-luhi

Meaning undetermined, perhaps: bereaved due to the loss of a favored attendant or child.

Gulch and intermittent stream near the western boundary of the kalana of Kahakuloa.

442 Paauhulu

Paʻauhulu / Pāʻauhulu
Paʻau-hulu / Pā-ʻau-hulu

Pronunciation and meaning undetermined, perhaps: paʻau hulu—fuzzy banana sheath fibers; or, pā ʻau hulu—pearl-shell lure with feathered shank.

Shoreline area along Honokeana.

443 Paaukini

See Kapaaukini.

444 Paehala

Pae-hala

Literally, pandanus tree grove.

ʻIli in the ahupuaʻa of Honokahua, and the ahupuaʻa of Kukuipuka, kalana of Kahakuloa.

445 Pahahao

See Papahao.

446 Pahala

Pāhala

"pā.hala n. A method of making mulch soil by placing pandanus (hala) branches and leaves in holes in rocky soil containing mulch, and then burning the hala for fertilizer." /HD/

ʻIli in the ahupuaʻa of Honolua.

Variant: Paiala.

447 Pahua

Pahua / Pahuʻa / Pāhuʻa

Pronunciation and meaning undetermined, perhaps: pahua—hurled, or, trampled; pahuʻa—ruined; or, pāhuʻa—a clearing, oasis, clear spot, or opening.

ʻIli in the ahupuaʻa of Honokōhau.

48 Pahuaa
Pahū'aʻā / Pahuʻaʻā
Pahū-ʻaʻā / Pahu-ʻaʻā

Pronunciation and meaning undetermined, perhaps: pahū ʻaʻā—burning explosion; pahu ʻaʻā—burning pahu land region, or, burning stake/post.

———

ʻIli in the ahupuaʻa of Mailepai.

49 Pahukauila
Pahu-kauila

Meaning undetermined, perhaps: *kauila* wood drum, or, *kauila* wood stake/post.

———

Gulch in the ahupuaʻa of Mailepai.

50 Paiala
See Pahala.

51 Pailolo
Pailolo / Pailōlo
Pailolo / Pai-(o)lōlo

Meaning undetermined, perhaps an elided form of: pai olōlo—lifted upon the roiling (waves).

———

The sea channel off the shores of the moku of Kāʻanapali, between Maui and Molokaʻi.

———

"pai.lolo—2. (*Cap.*) Name of channel between Molokaʻi and Maui." /Pukui & Elbert 1986, 303/

52 Paina
Paina / Paʻina / Pāʻina

Pronunciation and meaning undetermined, perhaps: paina—swelling (as waves); paʻina—crackling; or, pāʻina—meal.

———

ʻIli in the ahupuaʻa of Honokahua.

53 Pakahea
See Pakihi.

454 Pakala
Pākala / Pākalā
Pākala / Pā-ka-lā

Pronunciation and meaning undetermined, perhaps: pākala—young *kala* fish, or, rough; or, pā ka lā—the sun shines.

───────────

ʻIli in the ahupuaʻa of Honokahua.

455 Pakao
Pākaʻo

"pā.ka.ʻo similar to pō.ka.ʻo vs. Barren; dry and tasteless, as flavorless meat; naked, destitute. Fig., boring, lacking in humor." /HD/

───────────

Heiau on the east side of the ahupuaʻa of Kahakuloa, kalana of Kahakuloa.

456 Pakei
Pakei / Pākei
Pakei / Pā-kei

Meaning undetermined, perhaps: pā kei—enclosure made of *kei* stone; or, a colloquial pronunciation of pakai—spleen amaranth.

───────────

ʻIli in the ahupuaʻa of Kahana 1.

457 Pakihi
Pākihi
Pā-kihi

Meaning undetermined, perhaps: angled wall, or, lot on which *kihi* sweet potatoes are grown.

───────────

ʻIli and gulch in the ahupuaʻa of Honolua.

Variant: Pakahea.

458 Pakolo
Pākolo

Meaning undetermined, perhaps related to: "pā.kolo.kolo n. Probably a weir (term used in land claims of the 1840s)." /HD/

───────────

ʻIli in the ahupuaʻa of Kukuipuka, kalana of Kahakuloa.

59 Palaala

See Palauhulu.

60 Palaha

Palaha / Pālaha

Pronunciation and meaning undetermined, perhaps: palaha—to stumble; or, pālaha—spread out, wide, broad.

'Ili in the ahupuaʻa of Honokōwai.

61 Palau

Palau / Pālau

Pronunciation and meaning undetermined, perhaps: "palau 1. nvs. Betrothal; betrothed, engaged" /HD/; or, "pā.lau 1. vt. To tell tall tales, exaggerate, talk...2. n. War club; wooden implement with convex cutting edges, for cutting off ends of taro corm for planting (also pālau kōhi); knife. 3. n. Mat, wrapper...4. Short for kōʻelepālau, a pudding of sweet potatoes and coconut cream...5. n. A variety of hīnālea, a fish. 6. n. Maui name for yam. 7. n. A variety of taro." /HD/

'Ili in the ahupuaʻa of Kukuipuka, kalana of Kahakuloa.

62 Palauhulu

Pālauhulu

Pālauhulu / Pā-lauhulu

Meaning undetermined, perhaps: "pā.lau.hulu vt. To take all of a fish catch for a chief instead of dividing it" /HD/; or, pā lauhulu—plate of dried banana leaf.

'Ili in the ahupuaʻa of Makaliua, kalana of Kahakuloa.

Variants: Palaala, Palaula.

63 Palaula

See Palauhulu.

64 Paliuli

Pali-uli

Literally, dark-colored cliff.

'Ili in the ahupuaʻa of Honokahua.

465 Panioi
Pānīoi
Pā-nīoi

Literally, *nīoi* wood fence/enclosure.

———————

ʻIli in the ahupuaʻa of Honokōhau.

466 Paopao

Literally, to gouge/scoop/chisel.

———————

ʻIli in the ahupuaʻa of Honokahua.

467 Papahao
Papa-hao

Meaning undetermined, perhaps: scooped dish, or, iron board.

———————

ʻIli in the ahupuaʻa of Honolua.

Variant: Pahahao.

468 Papanalahoa
Papānālahoa / Papānalahoa
Papāna-(a)la-hoa / Papa(ʻa)-nala-hoa

Pronunciation and meaning undetermined, perhaps: papāna ala hoa—hurrying along the friendly path, or, hurrying along the club-strike road; or, an elision of: papaʻa nala hoa—secured through braiding a lashing.

———————

Seaside point along the western boundary of the kalana of Kahakuloa.

Variant: Papanahoa.

469 Papanahoa
Papa-nahoa

Literally, defiant flats.

———————

Gulch in the ahupuaʻa of Honokōwai.

Also, a misrepresentation of Papanalahoa in the kalana of Kahakuloa in some sources.

70 Papano

Literally, very dark.

Shoreline area along the ahupuaʻa of Honokeana.

71 Papaolena
Papaʻōlena
Papa-ʻōlena

Literally, turmeric flat.

ʻIli in the ahupuaʻa of Honokōwai.

Variant: Papaolina.

72 Papaolina
See Papaolena.

73 Popohaku
See Poopohaku.

74 Papua
Pāpua
Pāpua / Pā-pua

Meaning undetermined, perhaps: pāpua—"To shoot with bow and arrow; archery" /HD/; or, pā pua—flower enclosure.

Gulch that parallels, and then joins, the valley of Honolua in the ahupuaʻa of Honolua.

75 Pauhulu
Pāʻūhulu
Pāʻū-hulu

Pronunciation and meaning undetermined, perhaps: feathers used to form the *pāʻū* bunch used in featherwork; or, a colloquial elision of Pāʻauhulu—mother-of-pearl shell lure with feathered shank.

ʻIli in the ahupuaʻa of Makaliua 2, kalana of Kahakuloa.

76 Paulae
See Paulai.

477 Paulai

Paulāʻī / Pāʻūlāʻī

Paulāʻī / Pāʻū-lāʻī

Pronunciation and meaning undetermined, perhaps: "pau.lā.ʻī vi. To walk over the sea or fire, as a god" /HD/; or, pāʻū lāʻī—ti leaf skirt.

ʻIli in the ahupuaʻa of Kahakuloa, kalana of Kahakuloa.

Variants: Paulae, Puulae.

478 Paulole

See Puuloli.

479 Pauoa

"pau.oa n. A fern (*Dryopteris squamigera*) to 90 cm or more high, the stem clothed with tan scales, the frond triangular to ovate and two or three times pinnate." /HD/

ʻIli in the ahupuaʻa of Honokōhau.

480 Paupolo

Pronunciation and meaning undetermined, perhaps a misrepresentation of: paʻū polu—moist wetness.

ʻIli in the ahupuaʻa of Māhinahina.

481 Pawili

Pāwili

Pā-wili

Meaning undetermined, perhaps: for the wind to blow whirlingly.

Area mentioned in mele in the context of the ahupuaʻa of Kahakuloa, kalana of Kahakuloa.

"Ake ka manao e ike ia Kahakuloa, / Mai ka piina la e Kaukini, / He kini nui ko aloha naʻu e lei nei, / Ua ana au ua luhi i ko aloha, / Pii aku kaua i ke kula la e Pawili, / Hoomaha aku i ka luna e Pohakuloa, / Loa ka helena oia kula ua anu au.... [*The mind desires to see Kahakuloa, / From the ascent of Kaukini, / Greatly multitudinous is your love for me to wear as my garland, / I weighed and I am ladened with your love, / We climbed to the plains of Pāwili, / Rested upon the top of Pōhakuloa, / Travels upon that chilly plain were long....*]" /*Ko Hawaii Pae Aina*, Buke 2, Helu 14, 5 ʻApelila 1879/

32 Peekoa
Peʻekoa
Peʻe-koa

Literally, to hide amongst the koa trees.

ʻIli in the ahupuaʻa of Kukuipuka, kalana of Kahakuloa.

33 Pehukanukunuku
Pehu-ka-nukunuku

Literally, the snout is swollen.

ʻIli in the ahupuaʻa of Honokahua.

34 Piilani
Piʻilani
Piʻi-lani

Literally, heavenly ascencion.

ʻIli in the ahupuaʻa of Kahakuloa, kalana of Kahakuloa.

35 Piliamoo
Piliamoʻo
Pili-a-moʻo

Literally, to cling like a lizard.

ʻIli in the ahupuaʻa of Waiokila, kalana of Kahakuloa.

36 Pineapple Hill

Site of Makaʻoiʻoi, the home of D.T. Fleming, in the ahupuaʻa of Honokahua.

37 Pipipi

"pipipi 1. n. General name for small mollusks, including *Theodoxus neglectus*...2. vs. Small and close together, as stars or pipipi shells; small, squinting, as eyes...." /HD/

Hill (600 feet) found on the border between the ahupuaʻa of Honokōhau and the kalana of Kahakuloa.

488 Poehu
Pōʻehu
Pō-ʻehu

Meaning undetermined, perhaps: densely covered with mist, or, misty night.

———————

ʻIli in the ahupuaʻa of Honokōwai.

489 Poelua
Poelua / Poʻelua / Pōʻelua
Poe-lua / Poʻe-lua / Pō-ʻelua

Pronunciation and meaning undetermined, perhaps: poe lua—*poe* sweet potato grown in a pit; or, poʻe lua—pits; or, *lua* martial artists; or, pō ʻelua—two nights (this may be more likely due to the variant "Polua" [pō lua]).

———————

Gulch, bay, and ahupuaʻa in the kalana of Kahakuloa.

———————

Regarding Pōʻelua: "Returned by K. Kaleoku at the Māhele, retained by Crown. Identified in IDLM 397 as an ahupuaʻa containing 4 ili: Kalauhulu, Kaohe, Keana, Mahele." /Place Names (ULUK)/

Variant: Polua.

490 Pohakea
Pōhākea
Pōhā-kea

Literally, limestone.

———————

ʻIli in the ahupuaʻa of Honokōwai.

491 Pohakiki
Pohākikī
Pohā-kikī

Literally, to burst and spurt.

———————

Name of a piece of land (listed as *kula*) located in the ʻili of Waihale in the ahupuaʻa of Honokōwai.

92 Pohakuiolea
Pōhakuʻiolea
Pōhaku-ʻiolea

Literally, standoffish stone.

"A stone at the shore marking the boundary between Honokohau and Honolua. Written 'Pohakuioleia' in RP 8129." /Place Names (ULUK)/

93 Pohakukani
Pōhakukani
Pōhaku-kani

Literally, reverberating stone.

The storied "Bell Stone" found on the south side of the highway leading west out of Kahakuloa Valley, kalana of Kahakuloa.

94 Pohakuloa
Pōhakuloa
Pōhaku-loa

Literally, long boulder.

Inland site along Kaukini Ridge in the ahupuaʻa of Kahakuloa, kalana of Kahakuloa.

Also, ʻili in the ahupuaʻa of Honokeana and Honokahua.

95 Pohakuoholonae
Pōhakuoholonaʻe
Pōhaku-o-Holonaʻe

Literally, Holonaʻeʻs Stone.

Place mentioned in mele in the context of the ahupuaʻa of Hononana and Kahakuloa in the kalana of Kahakuloa.

"Kuu wahine mai ke kula e Hononana, / Hoomaha aku kaua i ka luna o Pohakuoholonae, / Mai ke kahawai la e Waihali.... [*My wife from the plains of Hononana, / We rested on the top of Pōhakuoholonaʻe, / From the stream of Waihali....*]" /Ko Hawaii Pae Aina, Buke 2, Helu 14, 5 ʻApelila 1879/

496 Pohaku o Kaanapali
Pōhaku o Kāʻanapali

Literally, Boulder of Kāʻanapali.

_____

Storied landmark boulder found along the seaside of the ahupuaʻa of Māhinahina.

_____

"A large but not high rock (pōhaku) near the sea at the border of Māhinahina and Kahana...." /Place Names (ULUK)/

Variants: Kaanapali Pohaku, Pohaku Kaanapali.

497 Pohaku o Kane
Pōhaku o Kāne

Literally, Kāne's stone.

_____

Stone located at a private residence in the ahupuaʻa of Kahakuloa, kalana of Kahakuloa.

498 Pohakuowahineomanua
Pōhakuowahineomanuʻa
Pōhaku-o-Wahineomanuʻa

Literally, Wahineomanuʻa's rock.

_____

Storied boulder inland of Puʻu Kekaʻa, ahupuaʻa of Honokōwai.

499 Pohakupule
Pōhakupule
Pōhaku-pule

Literally, prayer rock.

_____

The name of a boulder and gulch found on the east side of the ahupuaʻa of Honokōhau. The stone is located along the shore to the east of Punalau Point.

500 Pohale

"PO-HA-LE v. See POALE, h inserted. To be very full of waves; to be open on top, as a rough sea" /Andrews/; and "Deep, open, as a hole or sore...." /HD/

_____

A fishing ground in the ahupuaʻa of Kahana.

_____

Interview between Larry Kimura and John Nākoa, Ka Leo Hawaiʻi radio program. Orthography reflects pronunciation of speaker.

"JOHN NĀKOA: A iā mākou o Maui, mai Kahana, nui kēia mea kuʻuna. Nui. Ma Pohale, ʻekolu ma leila. Ma Kapua, Kapua, aia ma leila ʻehā, ma leila. Kapua ma nuna, aia ʻelua ma leila. A ma Kapua, aia ma leila nō ʻelua, ma Kapua. Nē ʻoe hele ma Kapalua, ō nui hewahewa ma leila, Hāwea mā. Kēia mea kuʻuna. Nui ka iʻa!... / LARRY KIMURA: Pehea? He inoa nō ke kuʻuna? / JK: ʻAe, he inoa nō. Ke kuʻuna nui ʻo Pohale...aia i Honokōwai...Kēia poʻe kuʻuna e walaʻau nei iā ʻoe, he inoa wale nō lākou, but, poina wau kekahi poʻe kuʻuna. Poina. But, kēia poʻe kuʻuna nui, ʻo ia kaʻu mea e walaʻau nei, kuʻuna nui ʻo Pohale. Nui kēlā kuʻuna. ʻUmi kapuaʻi ka hohonu...Nui nā kuʻuna. Kalaeokaiʻa, aia ma leila kekahi poʻe kuʻuna, ʻo ia nō ka inoa. / LK: ʻO wai? / JN: Kalaeokaiʻa...Kaleokaiʻa, Kalaeʻiliʻili...aia ma leila. Ā, Kapua. Kapua, aia nō ma leila kekahi kuʻuna. Ā, me ka hapanui, kala mai iaʻu, poina loa. [*JOHN NĀKOA: And to us from Maui, from Kahana, there are a lot of these* kuʻuna *(net setting places). So many. At Pohale, there are three there. At Kapua, Kapua, there are four there. Upper Kapua, there are two there. And at Kapua, there are two there, at Kapua. If you go to Kapalua, oh so many there, Hāwea and places like that. These* kuʻuna. *Plenty of fish!...* | *LARRY KIMURA: So how is it? Are the* kuʻuna *formally named?* | *JK: Yes, they're formally named. Pohale is a big* kuʻuna... *it's at Honokōwai...These* kuʻuna *that I'm talking with you about, they are all formally named, but I forget some* kuʻuna. *I forget. But, these main* kuʻuna, *those are what I'm talking with you about, the big* kuʻuna *of Pohale. That's a big* kuʻuna. *Ten feet deep...There are a lot of* kuʻuna. *Kalaeokaiʻa, there are some* kuʻuna *there, that's the name.* | *LK: What was the name?* | *JN: Kalaeokaiʻa...Kalaeokaiʻa, Kalaeʻiliʻili...there are some there. Ah, Kapua. Kapua, there is a* kuʻuna *there. Uh, but the majority, so sorry, I have completely forgotten.*]" /"Ka Leo Hawaiʻi" 378/

Variant: Kapohale.

01 Pohina
Pōhina

Literally, misty/foggy.

Shoreline area along the ahupuaʻa of Honokahua.

02 Polanui
Pola-nui

Meaning undetermined, perhaps: large banana bloom sheath.

ʻIli in the ahupuaʻa of Waiokila, kalana of Kahakuloa.

03 Polua
See Poelua.

04 Poohumoi
See Poehu.

505 Poopohaku
Poʻopōhaku
Poʻo-pōhaku

Meaning undetermined, perhaps: stone head, or, cavity in a stone.

_____

ʻIli in Honokōwai.

Variant: Popohaku.

506 Poopueo
Poʻopueo
Poʻo-pueo

Literally, owl head.

_____

ʻIli in the ahupuaʻa of Honokahua.

507 Pua Ka Huahua
See Puu Kahuahua.

508 Puakea

"pua.kea 1. nvs. Pale-colored, especially a tint between white and pink, as sunset clouds; the color of a buckskin horse . . . 2. vi. To spread, as a ship's sails or as fog." /HD/

_____

ʻIli in the ahupuaʻa of Honolua.

509 Pua Melia Home
Pua Mēlia Home

Literally, Plumeria Home.

_____

The name of the home of J.S. Kuoha in the ahupuaʻa of Honokōhau.

510 Puawa
Pūʻawa / Pū-ʻawa

Meaning undetermined, perhaps: pūʻawa—"1. n. Young white pandanus leaves that are good for plaiting. 2. nvs. Bitter; bitterness" /HD/; or, pū ʻawa—n. Kava plant or root portion, formerly used as offerings. . . ." /HD/

_____

Inland point along the border between the ahupuaʻa of Honokōhau and the kalana of Kahakuloa.

11 Puekahi
Puʻekahi
Puʻe-kahi

Literally, single sweet potato mound.

ʻIli in the ahupuaʻa of Kahakuloa, kalana of Kahakuloa.

12 Pueno
Pūʻeno
Pū-ʻeno

Pronunuciation and meaning undetermined, perhaps: pū ʻeno—startled wild.

ʻIli in the ahupuaʻa of Makaliua 2, kalana of Kahakuloa.

13 Puhalakau
Pūhalakau
Pū-hala-kau

Literally, pandanus tree that is perched upon.

Site of a kūʻula heiau in the ahupuaʻa of Honolua.

"Puhalakau Heiau, Walker Site 17. Makai to Honolua Park along shore. Heiau for Kuula…Modern stone walls and houses built on the site obliterating its outlines. Fisherman's koʻa formerly on beach has been washed away." /Place Names (ULUK)/

14 Puiwa
Pūʻiwa

Literally, startled.

Shoreline area along Kulaokaʻea, ahupuaʻa of Honolua.

15 Pukaulua
Puka-ulua

Literally, *ulua* fishing hole/opening.

Shoreline area along the ahupuaʻa of Honokeana.

516 Pukukui
Pukukuʻi

Literally, huddled together.

———

ʻIli in the ahupuaʻa of Honokōhau.

517 Pulehu
See Kapulehu.

518 Pulepule

Literally, speckled.

———

Gulch and ʻili in the ahupuaʻa of Kahana 1.

519 Puloi
Pūloʻi
Pū-loʻi

Meaning undetermined, perhaps: spring within the taro patch.

———

ʻIli in the ahupuaʻa of Kahakuloa, kalana of Kahakuloa.

520 Punaha
Punahā / Pūnahā
Puna-hā / Pū-nahā

Pronunciation and meaning undetermined, perhaps: puna hā—spring with/in a ditch; or pū- + nahā—cracked hill.

———

Gulch to the west of the mouth of Honokōhau Valley, ahupuaʻa of Honokōhau.

521 Punaholo
Puna-holo

Literally, flowing spring.

———

Shoreline area along the ahupuaʻa of Nāpili.

22 Punalau
Puna-lau

Literally, many springs.

ʻIli on the western side of the ahupuaʻa of Honokōhau.

23 Punanakuhe
See Punauekuhe.

24 Punauekuhe
Pūnauekuhe

Pūnaue-kuhe

Literally, to divide shares of ʻōkuhe goby fish.

ʻIli in the ahupuaʻa of Kahakuloa, kalana of Kahakuloa.

Variant: Punanakuhe.

25 Puu Eke
See Eke.

26 Puu Haunaka
Puʻu Hāunakā

Puʻu Hāuna-kā

Literally, Striking-blow Hill.

Inland hill (617 feet) on the west side of Hononana Gulch, kalana of Kahakuloa.

Variants: Haunaa, Puuhaunaka, Puu Haunako.

27 Puu Haunako
See Puu Haunaka.

28 Puu Hewale
See Puu Heewale.

29 Puu Heewale
Puʻu Heʻewale

Puʻu Heʻe-wale

Literally, continually dripping/flowing hill.

Inland spring (600 feet) in the ahupuaʻa of ʻAlaeloa.

530 Puu Kaeo
Puʻu Kaʻeo / Puʻu Kāʻeo

Pronunciation and meaning undetermined, perhaps: puʻu kaʻeo—resentful hill, or, *kaʻeo* taro hill; or, puʻu kāʻeo—zealous hill; or, filled/full hill.

Name belonging to two hills, one found in the ahupuaʻa of Honolua (1,683 feet), and one in the ahupuaʻa of Honokōhau (351 feet).

531 Puu Kahuahua
Puʻu Kāhuahua

Literally, site hill.

Unknown site in the ahupuaʻa of Honokahua, listed in "Place Names (ULUK)" as *Pua Ka Huahua*. Based upon other attestations of "Puu Kahuahua" on other islands, instances of usage for the term "kahuahua" in the newspapers, and the location in the ahupuaʻa of Honokahua, the name "Puʻu Kāhuahua" may be more accurate.

"Perhaps an ʻili inland of Hawea Point." /Place Names (ULUK)/

Variant: Pua ka Huahua.

532 Puu Kahulianapa
See Kahulianapa.

533 Puu Kalakahi
See Kalakahi.

534 Puu Kekahi
Puʻu Kekahi
Puʻu Ke-kahi

Literally, the scrape hill.

Alternative, perhaps older, name for Puʻu Kekaʻa in the ahupuaʻa of Honokōwai.

"Kauhi was slain and received burial services at Puʻu Kekahi, now called Puʻu Kekaʻa, or 'Black Rock.' " /SOM (Lahaina) 111/

Variant: Kekaa.

35 Puu Kilea
Puʻu Kīlea

Literally, small-conspicuous-hill hill.

Hill (728 feet) to the west of Pōhakupule Gulch, ahupuaʻa of Honokōhau.

36 Puu Koae
Puʻu Koaʻe

Literally, tropic bird hill.

Prominent seaside head (636 feet) in the ahupua of Kahakuloa, kalana of Kahakuloa.
Variants: Kahakuloa Head, Puukoae, Sugarloaf.

37 Puu Kukae
Puʻu Kūkae

Literally, dung hill.

Hill (1,645 feet) along the boundary between the two ahupuaʻa of Kukuipuka and Kahakuloa in the kalana of Kahakuloa.

38 Puulae
See Paulai.

39 Puulena
Puʻulena
Puʻu-lena

Literally, turmeric hill.

ʻIli in the ahupuaʻa of Honokōwai.

40 Puuloli
Puʻu-loli

Meaning undetermined, perhaps: sea cucumber hill, or, turn-over hill.

ʻIli in the ahupuaʻa of Honokōhau.
Variant: Paulole.

541 **Puulu**
Pūʻulu

Literally, group, crowd.

ʻIli in the ahupuaʻa of Honokahua.

542 **Puu Makawana**
Puʻu Makawana
Puʻu Maka-wana

Meaning undetermined, perhaps: urchin-spine-tip hill, or, ray-of-light-appearance hill.

Seaside point and hill (610 feet) to the south of Hakuheʻe Point in the ahupuaʻa of Makaliua 1, kalana of Kahakuloa.

543 **Puu Makina**
Puʻu Mākīnā

Pronunciation and meaning undetermined, perhaps: blemished-eyes hill.

Hill (1,959 feet) on the ridge between the two ahupuaʻa of Mailepai and ʻAlaeloa.

544 **Puu Nene**
Puʻu Nēnē

Literally, goose hill.

Hill (300 feet) in the ahupuaʻa of ʻAlaeloa. Also, perhaps an ʻili in the same ahupuaʻa.

545 **Puu o Kalauliko**
Puʻu o Kalauliko
Puʻu o Ka-lau-liko

Meaning undetermined, perhaps: Kalauliko's hill, or, hill of the budding leaf.

Hill (560 feet) and cemetery in the ahupuaʻa of ʻAlaeloa.

546 **Puu o Kaopuu**
Puʻu o Kaʻōpuʻu / Puʻu o ka-ʻōpuʻu

Meaning undetermined, perhaps: puʻu o Kaʻōpuʻu—Kaʻōpuʻu's Hill, or, puʻu o ka ʻōpuʻu—the whale-tooth pendant hill, or, the bud hill.

Upland hill (860 feet) in the ahupuaʻa of Honolua.

47 Puu Olai
Puʻu olaʻi / Puʻu ʻŌlaʻi
Puu o-Laʻi / Puʻu Ōlaʻi /

Pronunciation and meaning undetermined, perhaps: puʻu o Laʻi—Laʻiʻs hill; or puʻu ōlaʻi—earthquake hill.

Inland hill (998 feet) in the ahupuaʻa of Makaliua 1, kalana of Kahakuloa. *See also*: Waiolai in the same area.

48 Puu Olelo
Puʻu ʻŌlelo

Literally, conversation hill.

Hill (1,389 feet) in the ahupuaʻa of Kahakuloa.

49 Puweu
Pūweu
Pū-weu

Literally, grass tuft.

Area mentioned in the context of Kāʻanapali.

"E ike auanei na kanaka a pau ma keia Palapala. Ke hookapu a ke papa loa ia aku nei, na aina Kula o Wahikuli; Hahakea, Kapunakea, Maunahoomaha, Puweu, na Pali, a me Mahinahina, ma Kaanapali, mai lawe wale i na mea e ulu ana maluna iho o keia mau aina.... [*All people will know in this document. Forbidden and prohibited are the Plains lands of Wahikuli, Hahakea, Kapunakea, Maunahoomaha, Pueweu, Nāpili, and Māhinahina, in Kāʻanapali, do not simply take the things growing on these lands....*]" / *Ka Nupepa Kuokoa*, Buke 23, Helu 11, 17 Malaki 1883/

50 Sugarloaf
See Puu Koae.

51 Uahaili
Uahaili / ʻUāhāʻili
Ua-haili / ʻUā-hāʻili

Pronunciation and meaning undetermined, perhaps: ua haili—rain that evokes memories; or, ʻuā hāʻili—to cry out suddenly, or to yell while cursing.

ʻIli in the ahupuaʻa of Mailepai.

552 Uau

ʻUaʻu

Literally, dark-rumped petrel.

———

Point (2,068 feet) along the boundary between the ahupuaʻa of Honokōhau and the kalana of Kahakuloa.

———

"Hill between Kaihukiako and Eke on the Honokohau/Kahakuloa boundary. Perhaps the hill on USGS 1956 with elevation 2068 ft." /Place Names (ULUK)/

553 Uhali

Literally, to carry (plural form).

———

ʻIli in the ahupuaʻa of Kahana 1.

554 Uilikiko

See Ilikikoo.

555 Ulukikoo

See Ilikikoo.

556 Umi

ʻUmi

" ʻumi 1. vt. To strangle, choke, suffocate, stifle, throttle, smother, suppress; to repress, as desire...2. num. Ten, tenth." /HD/

———

Hill (440 feet) to the east of ʻAwalau Gulch in the kalana of Kahakuloa.

557 Violet Lake

Superimposed name of foreign origin for the highland lake (5,020 feet) found along the boundary between the two ahupuaʻa of Honokahua and Honokōhau.

Variant: Kiowaiokihawahine.

558 Wahalau

Waha-lau

Meaning undetermined, perhaps: mouth of the *lau* dragnet, or, numerous mouths.

———

ʻIli in the ahupuaʻa of Honokahua.

59 Wahikolokolo
Wahi-kolokolo

Literally, creeping place.

_____

Gulch in the ahupuaʻa of Kahauiki, ahupuaʻa of Honolua.

60 Waiakeakua
Wai-a-ke-akua

Literally, water of/made by/used by the god.

_____

Upland spring to the west of Anākaluahine in the ahupuaʻa of Honokōhau.

Also, an ʻili in the ahupuaʻa of Nāpili.

Variants: Waikeakua, Waiokeakua.

61 Waialae
Waiʻalae
Wai-ʻalae

Literally, mudhen water.

_____

ʻIli in the ahupuaʻa of Makaliua 2, kalana of Kahakuloa.

62 Waiaololi
See Waiololi.

63 Waihale
Wai-hale

Meaning undetermined, perhaps: house water, or, placed within the house.

_____

ʻIli in the ahupuaʻa of Honokōwai.

64 Waihali
Wai-hali

Literally, fetched water.

_____

Gulch and intermittent stream in the ahupuaʻa of Kahakuloa, kalana of Kahakuloa.

565 Waihapapa
Waihāpapa
Wai-hāpapa

Literally, coral-flat water.

———

ʻIli in the ahupuaʻa of Hononana, kalana of Kahakuloa.

566 Waikala
See Waikulu.

567 Waikalae
Wai-(a)-ka-lae

Literally, water of the seaside point/cape.

———

Area near Papānālahoa Point toward the western boundary of the kalana of Kahakuloa.

568 Waikalupe
See Manawaikalupe.

569 Waikeakua
See Waiakeakua.

570 Waikiki
Waikīkī
Wai-kīkī

Literally, spouting water.

———

Gulch in the ahupuaʻa of Honokōwai.

571 Waikulu
Wai-kulu

Literally, dripping water.

———

A pair of ʻili, Waikulu 1 & 2, in the ahupuaʻa of ʻAlaeloa. Also, an upland spring located on the boundary between the ahupuaʻa of ʻAlaeloa and Honokeana.

Variants: Waikala, Waikulu 1, 2.

72 Wailena
Wai-lena

Literally, yellow-hued water.

Gulch and intermittent stream to the east of Kaukini Ridge in the ahupuaʻa of Maka-liua 1, kalana of Kahakuloa.

73 Wainalo
Wai-nalo

Literally, vanishing water.

The name of a house lot in the ʻili of Waihale, ahupuaʻa of Honokōwai.

Variant: Loainalu, Wainalu.

74 Wainalu
See Wainalo.

75 Waioio
Waiʻōʻio
Wai-ʻōʻio

Literally, ʻōʻio fish water.

ʻIli in the ahupuaʻa of Honolua.

76 Waiokeakua
See Waiakeakua.

77 Waiokila
Wai-o-Kila

Literally, Kila's water.

Ahupuaʻa in the kalana of Kahakuloa.

"Returned by Lot Kamehameha at the Māhele, retained by Crown. Shown on Tax Map as Waiokila 1, Waiokila 2 but with no kuleana. Identified in IDLM 397 as an ahupuaʻa containing 16 ili: Kaakua, Kahau, Kahuku (2), Kainui, Kalaoa, Kanea, Kanukuokeana, Kapelekai, Kaulunai, Kukaeaoa, Leinaha, Naio, Niu, Piliamoo, Polanui." /Place Names (ULUK)/

578 Waiolai
Waiolaʻi / Waiōlaʻi
Wai-o-Laʻi / Wai-ōlaʻi

Pronunciation and meaning undetermined, perhaps: wai o Laʻi—Laʻi's water; or, wai ōlaʻi—earthquake water.

———————

Gulch in the ahupuaʻa of Waiokila, kalana of Kahakuloa. This gulch is alternatively called Kalaoa.

Also, the name of a heiau at Maluhia in the ahupuaʻa of Kukuipuka, kalana of Kahakuloa. *See also*: Puu Olai, a hill found in the same vicinity.

Variant: Kalaoa.

579 Waiololi
Waiʻololī
Wai-ʻololī

Literally, narrow water.

———————

ʻIli in the ahupuaʻa of Kukuipuka, kalana of Kahakuloa.

Variant: Waiaololi.

580 Waipae
Wai-pae

Meaning undetermined, perhaps: (fresh) water that grounds driftwood; or, an elided variation of: wai ʻōpae—shrimp water.

———————

ʻIli in the ahupuaʻa of Nāpili.

581 Waipapa
Wai-papa

Literally, freshwater of the shallow reef.

———————

Shoreline area along the ahupuaʻa of Honolua.

582 Waipili
Wai-pili

Literally, clinging water.

———————

Gulch and stream in the ahupuaʻa of Kapaloa, kalana of Kahakuloa. The lower reach of this stream is called Malalokai.

Variant: Malalokai.

83 Waipiliamoo
Waipiliamoʻo
Wai-pili-a-moʻo

Literally, water that clings (to the cliff) like a lizard.

Heiau at the mouth of Makamakaʻole Gulch in the ahupuaʻa of Kukuipuka, kalana of Kahakuloa.

"Waipiliamoo Heiau, Walker Site 26. Mouth of Makamakaole Gulch 50 yds. from the shore. Site largely destroyed...." /Place Names (ULUK)/

84 Waipueo
Wai-pueo

Literally, owl water, or, *pueo* taro water.

ʻIli in the ahupuaʻa of Nāpili.

85 Waiuli
Wai-uli

Literally, dark water.

ʻIli in the ahupuaʻa of Honokōhau. Also, the famed burial pit found above the ahupuaʻa of Honokōhau, Honolua, and Honokahua.

86 Walahaha
Walahāhā
Wala-hāhā

Literally, to fall backwards while feeling about with the hands.

Shoreline area along the ahupuaʻa of Honokahua.

87 Wanaloa
See Analoa.

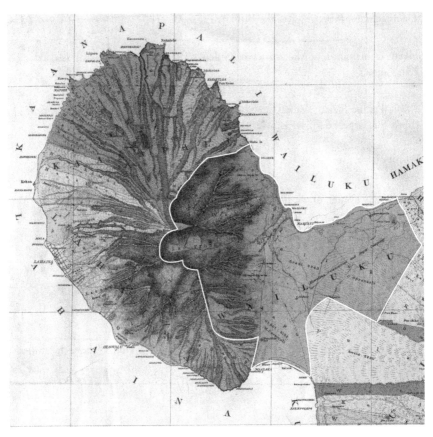

Map of Wailuku Moku

CHAPTER 4

WAILUKU MOKU

Kīpōʻaeʻae kualapa ʻo Wailuku—
Lima kīkoʻo aniani ʻili kai,
ʻOhi hāpuku ahe lau makani,
Apo aloha iā Kamaʻomaʻo.

The district of Wailuku has mountain ridges for its shoulders—
Hands that reach out to caress the surface of the seas,
Gathering up the winds,
Affectionately embracing Kamaʻomaʻo.

na Cody Pueo Pata[1]

1 Aawa
ʻAʻawa

"ʻaʻawa 1. n. Wrasse fishes, Hawaiian hogfish (*Bodianus bilunulatus*), considered ʻaumā-kua by some." /HD/

Famed surf and fishing ground off the shore of the kalana of Waiehu.

2 Ae
Aʻe / ʻAe / ʻAʻe

Pronunciation and meaning undetermined, perhaps: aʻe—northeast tradewind, or *Xylosma hawaiiense* (maua) tree; ʻae—second or third crop of taro, or wauke shoots; or, ʻaʻe—to tread upon.

---

1. A description of the unique geographical layout of the Moku of Wailuku, likening it to a person spreading their arms in embrace.

Steep gulch and small stream tributary of the ʻĪao Stream descending from Kahoʻolewa in ʻĪao Valley, below Puʻu Kāne, in the ahupuaʻa of Wailuku.

Variant: Black Gorge.

3 Ahikuli
Ahi-kuli

Literally, noisy fire.

Ahupuaʻa incorporated into the kalana of Waiehu, and which mostly runs along the North Waiehu Stream. Also, the name of a peak (*perhaps* 1,860 feet) present on the 1887 Monsarrat map, found below the peak of Kalanipuʻu (*perhaps* 2,760 feet) along the boundary between the ahupuaʻa of Waiheʻe and Ahikuli in the kalana of Waiehu.

Ahikuli is one of the ahupuaʻa, along with Hananui, Polipoli, and Kou, that form the region known as "Nāpoko."

Variants: Ahikula, Waikuli.

4 Ahuakokole
Ahu-a-kokole

Literally, mound of stunted growth or stunted taro.

ʻIli in the ahupuaʻa of Wailuku.

Variant: Ahuakokoli.

5 Ahuakokoli
See Ahuakokole.

6 Ahuakolea
Ahuakōlea
Ahu-a-kōlea

Literally, plover's hill.

The name of ʻili in the ahupuaʻa of Waikapū and Waiheʻe.

Variant: Huakolea.

7 Ahuena
Ahu'ena
Ahu-'ena

Literally, red-hot cairn.

'Ili lele in the ahupua'a of Wailuku.

Variant: Ahuna.

8 Ahuka
Ahukā
Ahu-kā

Pronunciation and meaning undetermined, perhaps: mound of sweet potato vines.

'Ili in the ahupua'a of Wailuku.

9 Ahuwahine
Ahuwahine / 'Ahuwahine
Ahu-wahine / 'Ahu-wahine

Meaning and pronunciation undetermined, perhaps: ahu wahine—women's shrine; or 'ahu wahine—woman's garment.

Area in 'Īao Valley, ahupua'a of Wailuku.

"He kula wauke kekahi o'u ma keia aina ke pili aku la ma ka wao makai o ka aina o Kane[,] he kahua hale kekahi o'u maloko o keia aina, o Ahuwahine ka inoa, he kula, ke pili la i ko Kalaeloa aina[.] Na Kailihune. [*A wauke field of mine abutting the forest toward the seaside of the land of Kāne, a house site of mine within this land, 'Ahuwahine by name, a field, near Kalaeloa's land. From Ka'ilihune.*]" /Native Register (KPA)/

"No ka makau o na'lii o hiki mai o Alapai ka Moi o Hawaii no ke kaua, nolaila, waimahoehoe ia iho la o Kekaulike i mama ka lawe ana iuka o Iao, nolaila, hooili hou maluna o ka waa, a holo aku la a pae i Kapoli ma Maalaea, a malaila i lawe ia aku ai a hiki i Puuhele, i Kaluamanu, i Waikapu, i Wahanemaili, i Kaumuilio, i Aoakamanu, i Puuelinapao, i Kaumulanahu i Kapohakoi, i Kalua, i Kekio, i Kamaauwai, i Kahua i Kailipoe, i Kalihi i Kaluaoiki, i Kihahale, kuu i Ahuwahine, waiho i Loiloa, o Kekaulike komo iloko o Kapela. [*Due to the fear of the chiefs that Alapa'i, the King of Hawai'i, would come for war, Kekaulike's bones were stripped of flesh so that they could be expediently taken to the uplands of 'Īao, then placed again upon a canoe that journeyed forth and landed at Kapoli in Mā'alaea; and there they were taken to Pu'uhele, to Kaluamanu, to Waikapū, to Wahanemaili [sic], to Kaumu'ilio, to Aoakamanu [sic], to Pu'u'elinapao, to Kaumulānahu at Kapōhāko'i, to Kalua, to Keki'o, to Kama'auwai, to Kahua at Kā'ilipoe, to Kalihi at*

Kaluaoiki, to Kihahale, to the descent at 'Ahuwahine; deposited at Lo'iloa, Kekaulike was interred within Kapela.]" /*Ka Nupepa Kuokoa*, Buke 5, Helu 43, 27 'Okakopa 1866/

"Mama koleilei i ke hau, Na lehua wai maka noe, / Iluna o Kauweloweloula, / Ke kuia la e Ahuwahine, / He lei no ka makani Kilipoe [*sic*], / Paapono ka lima o Iao i ke koekoe.... [*You delicately wear the dew as your garland, / The misty-eyed lehua, / Above Kauwelowelo'ula, / Being sewn there by 'Ahuwahine, / A garland for the Kilipoe [Kā'ilipoe] wind, / The hand of 'Iao is fixed by the chill....*]" /Hawaiian Historical Society, 2001/

Perhaps related to an unidentified "heiau" in 'Iao. Interview between Larry Kimura and Joseph Kekaua, Ka Leo Hawai'i radio program. Orthography reflects pronunciation of speaker.

"Ka 'ohana ho'i, ma ko'u makuakāne, wehewehe aku au iā 'oukou, mālama ho'i mākou i ka, 'oia ho'i, ka heiau, ka mea…ka'u mea i mālama me ka'u makuakāne…kēia heiau? 'O ka heiau kēia, 'o ka heiau i kāhea 'ia 'o Kealoha. Kealoha, no 'Iao, a ma ka 'ao'ao o ko mākou hale. Aia kēia mau heiau 'elua—heiau wahine, heiau kāne. A ka 'ohana o ka'u makuakāne, 'o ia kāna hana mālama kēia…a na'u i hele waele, kanu nō ho'i nā pua, nā mea like 'ole, kanu i kēlā heiau. A hoihoi ho'i ka'u hana me ka makuakāne i ka heiau no ka mea i leila wau i 'ike ai i nā mea like 'ole…aia nō ke kū nei ma lalo o ke kumu hau. Kēlā manawa a'u i hele ai me nā po'e holoholo, a 'ike wau i kēlā heiau, aia nō ke kū ala ma leila…a, ka pili ho'i o kēia mau heiau i kāhea, i kapa 'ia ai i Kealoha, nānā 'oe 'o ke kāne, like hana 'ia ho'i nā pōhaku like 'ole, a kona home ia. Ka heiau o ka wahine, nānā 'oe i kēlā, nē 'oe a hele a mamao, i 'ole 'umi paha kapua'i mai kēlā heiau mai, nānā aku 'oe i kēlā heiau, kohu mea he wahine e moe maila i loko. 'O ia ke kumu i kapa 'ia ho'i kēlā heiau, wahine. A kapa 'ia ke kāne, nānā 'oukou he kohu mea ke kāne e kū ana. A 'o ia ke kumu i kapa 'ia, wahine me ke kāne. [*The family, on my father's side, I will explain to you all, we cared for, well, the heiau, the one… that I took care of with my father… this heiau? This is the heiau, the heiau called Kealoha. Kealoha, from 'Iao, and on the side of our house. There are these two heiau—female heiau, male heiau. And my father's family, that's what he did, cared for… and I went to weed, plant flowers, all sorts of things, I planted on that heiau. And what I did with my father at that heiau was so interesting, because that's where I saw all sorts of things… it's there standing under the hau tree. That time I went with the visitors, I saw that heiau, it's standing there… and how these heiau are called, named Kealoha, look at the male one, it's like it was made from all sorts of stones, and that's his home. The heiau of the female, look at it, if you go back a ways, maybe ten feet from that heiau, you look at that heiau, it's like it's a woman lying there inside. That's the reason that heiau was named female. And the male was named, you all look, it's as if a male was standing. And that's why it was called female with the male.*]" /Joseph Kekaua, "Ka Leo Hawai'i 212"/

10 Aikanaha
'Aikanahā
'Ai-kanahā

Literally, to consume forty.

'Ili in the ahupua'a of Waikapū.

Variants: Aikanaka, Aukanaha.

11 Aikanaka
See Aikanaha.

12 Aipaako
'Aipa'akō
'Ai-pa'akō

Meaning undetermined, perhaps: to exercise privilege over the dry lowland plain, or, eat fiber of the sugar cane stalk.

The name of Kūihelani's land in the 'ili of Puakō, ahupua'a of Wailuku.

13 Alae
'Alae

Literally, mudhen.

'Ili in the ahupua'a of Waihe'e.

"Still farther up was the Kanoa (bowl for kava, hollow of land, pit) of Kane and Kanaloa—a pot hole about 2' in diameter according to the description on the land of Kaulu. The two gods were accustomed to drink awa at this place. Once they saw down below an Alae at a place now called Alae on that account. One of them threw his arrow (spear?) at it and struck it. The Alae flew against the cliff and where it struck and died is now a hole through which the water now flows." /SOM 29/

14 Alaha
'Ālaha

Pronunciation and meaning undetermined, perhaps: 'ā- + laha—common.

Stone located along the eastern boundary of the ahupua'a of Wailuku.

"I ka wa e noho alii ana o Kanenenuiakawaikalu no Maui (ma Wailuku kona wahi noho mau), e noho ana kekahi kanaka kaulana o ia wahi—o Kapoi me kana wahine—ma Kaimuhee, ma uka ae o na wai elua o Kanaha me Mauoni. He mau loko kaulana ia no Wailuku. I kekahi la, makemake ihola ka wahine a ua Kapoi nei e hele i ke kula i ke poi uhini, a hiki o ia ma ke kula o Papalekailiu. A, ma laila ka hele ana a hiki ma Pohaku o Makaku. A hiki loa aku keia ma nae aku o laila, he pohaku nui i kapa ia kona inoa o Alaha ma ka aoao e pili la me Hamakuapoko. Loaa ihola i ua wahine hele poi uhini nei a Kapoi he punana hua pueo ma ka aoao o ua pohaku nei. Ehiku ka nui o na hua ma ka punana. [*At the time when Kanēnēnuiakawaikalu of Maui was ruling as chief (his permanent residence was at Wailuku), a famed person of that place was living—Kapoi with his wife—at Kaimuheʻe, just inland of the two waters of Kanahā and Mauʻoni. These are famous ponds of Wailuku. One day, the wife of this Kapoi wanted to go to the plains to catch grasshoppers, and she arrived upon the plains of Papalekailiʻu. There she continued on until she reached Pōhaku o Makakū. When she was well beyond the easterly side of that area, there was a large rock called ʻĀlaha on the side bordering Hāmākuapoko. This grasshopper-catching wife of Kapoi found a nest of owl eggs on the side of that rock. There were seven eggs within the nest.*] / Ke Au Okoa, Buke 12, Helu 11, 29 Iune 1871/*

15 Alakaha
Ala-kaha

Literally, passage way.

————————

ʻIli in the ahupuaʻa of Waiehu, kalana of Waiehu.

16 Alapaka
ʻAlāpākā / ʻAlapaka / Alapāka
ʻAlā-pākā / ʻAla-paka / Ala-pāka

Pronunciation and meaning undetermined, perhaps: ʻalā pākā—basalt stone used for sinkers; ʻala paka—scent of tobacco; or, ala pāka—park road.

————————

ʻIli in the ahupuaʻa of Waiehu, kalana of Waiehu.

17 Aliele
See Eleile.

18 Anahi
ʻĀnāhi
ʻĀ-nā-ahi

Pronunciation and meaning undetermined, perhaps: the fires blaze.

————————

Point (*perhaps* 2,470 feet) present on the 1887 Monsarrat map, along ʻŌnihi ridge that runs between the ahupuaʻa of Hananui and Kou, in the kalana of Waiehu.

19 Anehe
See Kai o Anehe.

20 Anukoli
See Nuukole.

21 Aoakamanu
See Awakamanu.

22 Auhaka
'Auhaka
'Au-haka

Meaning undetermined, perhaps: slender-legged, or, shaft used as a perch (as for chickens).

———————

'Ili in the ahupua'a of Wailuku.

23 Aukanaha
See Aikanaha.

24 Auwailumunui / Auwailiumuuuku
See Auwaiolimu.

25 Auwai Ohia
'Auwai 'Ōhi'a

Literally, 'Ōhi'a Ditch.

———————

Water ditch in the 'ili of 'Ōhi'anui, ahupua'a of Waiehu, kalana of Waiehu.

26 Auwaiolimu
'Auwaiolimu
'Auwai-o-limu

Literally, ditch of algae.

———————

'Ili in the ahupua'a of Waikapū.

Variants: Auwailimunui, Auwailimuuuku, Waiolimu.

27 Auwakamanu
See Awakamanu.

28 Awakamanu
Āwākamanu
Āwā-ka-manu

"Awakamanu (ā-wā'-kǎ-mǎ'nu): birds breaking silence." /Parker/

'Ili in the ahupua'a of Waikapū.

Variants: Aoakamanu, Auwakamanu.

29 Awau
See Wawau.

30 Awikiwiki
'Āwikiwiki

" 'ā.wiki.wiki. 1. Redup. of 'āwiki. ['vi. To hurry, be quick, swift.' /HD/] 2. n. A vine (*Canavalia* spp.), native to Hawai'i, related to the maunaloa (*C. cathartica*), but with narrower pods; used for small, temporary fish traps. ... 3. Same as kō'ele'ele, a seaweed." /HD/

'Ili in the ahupua'a of Waikapū.

31 Baldwin Beach Park

Name of the county beach park located along the Kapukaulua region on the eastern end of the ahupua'a and moku of Wailuku.

"Community park between Village 5 and Yung Hee Village in Puunene." /Place Names (ULUK)/

32 Black Gorge
See Ae.

"Black Gorge. Valley, tributary to 'Ī-ao Valley, Wai-luku qd., West Maui." /PNOH/

33 Dream City
See Kaihuwaa.

34 Eleele
See Eleile.

35 Eleile
'Eleile

Pronunciation attested amongst kūpuna, meaning undetermined. Perhaps a colloquial elision of: 'eleī + lei—dark [place] into which something is tossed.

Famed spring, pool, and tributary of the Waiheʻe River in the ahupuaʻa of Waiheʻe.

"An elderly *kamaaina*, William Kahalekai, says there are numerous abandoned terraces at Eleile, far up in the valley beyond the end of the road and above the new reservoir. He says that in ancient times the terraces were more or less continuous in a belt between the sand dunes and the present irrigation ditch." /SOM 13/

"There were two young women, perhaps in very ancient times, who belonged to that cave [at 'Eleile]. Eleile was the younger sister and she was prettier. The older was Wailua. Their work was tapa making in this cave. One night they were washed out by the water because there was a stream along side of the cave. When this happened and it stormed, the water flowed until it reached these women, Eleile and Wailua, and that is why it became the water of Eleile. After this time the people took the umbilical cords to hide in that cave. Those who could hold their breath dived down and hid the piko." /SOM 18/

"'This new [Waihee Canal] has its origin just below the Aliele Falls, two and a half miles up the Waihee Valley, at an elevation of nearly 650 feet...' Also known as Eleele [Falls] (q.v.). Coordinates approximate." /Place Names (ULUK)/

Variants: Aliele, Eleele, Eliile.

36 Eliile
See Eleile.

37 Haaiwo
See Kuaiwa.

38 Haakupu
Haʻakupu

Meaning undetermined, perhaps a colloquial variation of: "hoʻo.kupu. Tribute, tax, ceremonial gift-giving to a chief as a sign of honor and respect; to pay such a tribute." /HD/

Hill (*perhaps* 1,130 feet) found within the east boundary of the 'ili of Loʻinui, ahupuaʻa of Wailuku.

Variant: Hakupu.

39 Haanui
Ha'anui

"ha'a.nui. vt. To boast, brag, exaggerate, gloat." /HD/

———————

'Ili in the ahupua'a of Waikapū.

Variant: Haaua.

40 Haaua
See Haanui.

41 Hakuao
Haku-ao

Meaning undetermined, perhaps: haku ao—dawn creator.

———————

Main branch of the stream that flows past Piliokāka'e in 'Īao Valley, ahupua'a of Wailuku.

42 Halaula
Hala'ula
Hala-'ula

Literally, red (fruited) pandanus.

———————

Large 'ili in the ahupua'a of Wailuku.

Variants: Halaula 1/i/'akahi, 2/ii/'alua/, 3/iii/'akolu.

43 Halawa
Hālawa

"hā.lawa. Same as kālawa 1–3" /HD/; "kā.lawa. 1. n. Curve, as in the road or along a beach. Also hālawa. 2. vi. To go from one side to another . . . 3. n. Intermittent pains in the side of the neck, probably neuritis." /HD/

———————

'Ili in the ahupua'a of Ahikuli, kalana of Waiehu.

Variant: Holawa.

44 Halekii
Halekiʻi
Hale-kiʻi

Literally, image/statue house.

Heiau in the ʻili of Paukūkalo, ahupuaʻa of Wailuku. Also, a fishery in the ahupuaʻa of Wailuku. An alternative name is Kalola. *See also*: Kalola.

"ʻHalekii Heiau, Walker Site 44. N.N.W. [*sic*, N.E.] of Pihana 350 [*sic*, 850] feet on another sand dune. A large heiau of the same type as Pihana... It shows massive wall facings in ruins of four terraces on the south side. Water-worn boulders are used in its construction. It measures 300 × 150 feet.' (Sterling) ʻHalekii, Wailuku, some 300 ft. [*sic*, yards] to the N.E. of Pihana, and about 100 ft. square in size. (Thrum)'" /Place Names (ULUK)/

"Holu pipio ka wai o Paihi i ka makani / Ua ii mau i ka wai o Kaikoo, / I ke ka alele ia e ke one o Halekii, / Puliki ka aweawe hee i Nakohola, / I ke koali hoomoe ia e ke kaahaaha.... [*The waters of Paihi arch rippling in the wind / Ever gathering the water of Kaikoʻo, / As it reels on toward the sands of Halekiʻi, / The octopus tentacles embrace Nākohola, / Amidst the morning glory vines flattened by the Kāʻahaʻaha (wind)....*]" /Ka Nupepa Kuokoa, Buke 7, Helu 40, 3 ʻOkakopa 1868/

45 Halekou
Hale-kou

Literally, kou [tree] house.

ʻIli in the ahupuaʻa of Wailuku.

46 Halelani
Hale-lani

Literally, chiefly/heavenly house.

Name of ʻili found in the two ahupuaʻa of Waiheʻe and Wailuku.

47 Halelau
Hale-lau

Literally, leaf (thatched) house.

ʻIli in the ahupuaʻa of Polipoli, kalana of Waiehu.

48 Halelena
Hale-lena

Literally, yellow/turmeric house.

———————

ʻIlikū in the ahupuaʻa of Ahikuli, kalana of Waiehu.

Variant: Halelenaiki.

49 Halemano
Hale-mano

Literally, many houses.

———————

ʻIli in the ahupuaʻa of Wailuku.

50 Halepahu
Hale-pahu

Meaning undetermined, perhaps: drum house, or, house in the pahu region (below the region termed ʻilima, but above the region termed kula).

———————

ʻIli in the ahupuaʻa of Waiheʻe.

Variant: Kalepahu.

51 Halepaka
Halepāka
Hale-pāka

Literally, park building.

———————

"Halepaka—in Waihee Village at park." /SOM 46/

52 Halepalahalaha
See Haliipalahalaha.

53 Haliaipalala
See Haliipalahalaha.

54 Haliau
See Haliiau.

55 Haliiau
Hāli'iau / Hāli'i'au
Hāli'i-au / Hāli'i-'au

Pronunciation and meaning undetermined, perhaps: hāli'i au—spreading current; or, hāli'i 'au—ground covering made of stems/stalks.

———————

'Ili in the ahupua'a of Wailuku.

Variant: Haliau.

56 Haliipalahalaha
Hāli'ipālahalaha
Hāli'i-pālahalaha

Literally, flat covering/spread.

———————

'Ili in the ahupua'a of Waikapū, the appurtenant fishery for which was Nu'ukole.

Variants: Haliaipalala, Haliipalalii, Halipalahalaha, Halepalahalaha.

57 Haliipalalii
See Haliipalahalaha.

58 Hananui
Hana-nui

Meaning undetermined, perhaps: much/important work, or, large notch.

———————

Ahupua'a incorporated into the kalana of Waiehu. Hananui is one of four ahupua'a, along with Ahikuli, Polipoli, and Kou, that form the region known as "Nāpoko."

Variant: Nananui.

59 Hanohano
See Honuhonu.

60 Happy Valley

Superimposed name of foreign origin for the small town area spread mainly across the 'ili of Mokuhau, Kepūhāke'eo, Puakō, 'Umi'eu, and Wai'au in the ahupua'a of Wailuku.

61 Haunaka
Hau-naka

Meaning undetermined, perhaps: trembling strike, or, trembling *hau* tree. "Haunaka" represents the pronunciation favored by modern day scholars and chanters.

A hallowed area within ʻĪao Valley in the ahupuaʻa of Wailuku.

"Kahaʻi-nui (Kahaʻi the strong) is son of Hema, a chief of East Maui living on the hill Kauiki in Hana district, and of Lua (Ula, Ulu)-mahahoa from Iao valley in Wailuku district. He is born in Iao valley at a place called Ka-halulu-kahi above Loiloa at Haunaka." /Beckwith, 1970/

62 Hawaii Route 30
See Honoapiilani Highway.

63 Hawaii Route 340
See Kahekili Highway.

64 Hei

"hei. 1. nvt. Net, snare, stratagem, ruse; to ensnare, entangle, catch in a net; to festoon with leis . . . 2. nvi. String figure, cat's cradle; to make such . . . 3. n. Motion of hands and fingers, especially of the dying . . . 4. vs. Adept, deft; to absorb, as knowledge or skill . . . 5. Var. of hai, to sacrifice . . . 6. n. Water oozing from a cliff and trickling down." /HD/

Area in ʻĪao Valley, ahupuaʻa of Wailuku.

"Kuu nahele lipo i ka ua, / I poponi i ka luna o Hei, / Mama koleilei i ke hau, / Na lehua wai maka noe, / Iluna o Kauweloweloula, / Ke kuia la e Ahuwahine, / He lei no ka makani Kilipoe [*sic*], Paapono ka lima o Iao i ke koekoe. . . . [*My forest darkened by the rain / That anoints the top of Hei, / You delicately wear the dew as your garland, / The misty-eyed lehua, / Above Kauwelowelo'ula, / Being sewn there by ʻAhuwahine, / A garland for the Kilipoe (Kāʻilipoe) wind, / The hand of ʻIao is affixed by the chill. . . .*]" /Hawaiian Historical Society, 2001/

65 Hihika
Hīhīkā / Hihikā
Hīhīkā / Hihi-kā

Pronunciation and meaning undetermined, perhaps an unattested reduplication of: "hīkā . . . nvi. To stagger, totter, reel; spreading, as vines (Kep. 157); unsteady gait" /HD/; or, hihi kā—creeping of vines.

Shoreline point mentioned in the context of Kaʻākau in the ahupuaʻa of Wailuku.

"Lea kahela i ke one o Malama, / I ka nome ia e ke one o Maluihi, / I ka noke aihaa ia e ke kai o Kehu, / Ahu kapeke lua i ka nalu o Huiha, / I ka pinai mau ia e ka nalu o Kaakau, / Haki nuanua i ka lae o Hihika…. [*Spreading merrily across the sands of Mālama, / Being slowly consumed by the sands of Maluʻihi, / Vigorously persisted upon by the sea of Kēhu, / Laid completely exposed by the waves of Huihā, / Repeatedly encroached upon by the the waves of Kaʻākau, / Which break along the point of Hīhīkā….*]" /*Ka Nupepa Kuokoa*, Buke 7, Helu 40, 3 ʻOkakopa 1868/

In an interview with Kumu Hula Hōkūlani Holt, PhD, the following was shared with the author: "My Aunty Kāhili pointed out to me where Makawela is, which is where the breakwater is now in Kahului, and she had a name for a place that was kind of where she said Y. Hata used to be—right on that corner—and, she called it ʻHihita.' So, I don't know, I've never seen that name anywhere else. But, she called it Hihita." /January 21, 2022/

66 Hiiwela
See Kiiwela.

67 Hoaloha Park
Hoāloha

Literally, friend.

County park along the southern shore of Kahului Harbor in the ahupuaʻa of Wailuku.

Variant: Hoʻaloha Park.

68 Holawa
See Halawa.

69 Holile
See Hoolili.

70 Holili
See Hoolili.

71 Holoikauai
Holoikauaʻi
Holo-i-Kauaʻi

Literally, traveled to Kauaʻi.

ʻIli in the ahupuaʻa of Waiehu, kalana of Waiehu.

72 Holu

"holu. 1. vi. Springy, pliable, resilient, as a mattress; to sway, as palm fronds; to ripple, as waves; to play back and forth; bumpy, as an airplane ride...2. (Cap;) n. Name of a star. 3. (Cap;) n. Name of a fish god." /HD/

'Ili in the ahupua'a of Wailuku.

73 Honoapiilani Highway
Honoapi'ilani
Hono-a-Pi'ilani

Literally, Bay(s) of Pi'ilani Highway.

Hawai'i Route 30, which extends south from the town of Wailuku toward Mā'alaea, turns west into the moku of Lahaina, and continues north through to the moku of Kā'anapali, terminating in the ahupua'a of Honokōhau (Kā'anapali).

74 Honohono
See Honuhonu.

75 Honuakaua
Honua-kaua

Literally, battleground.

'Ili in the ahupua'a of Waihe'e.

Variant: Honukaua.

76 Honuhonu

"honu.honu. 1. nvi. A game in which player and opponent sat with legs crossed and tried to unseat each other; to play this game. 2. nvi. A game in which one boy sat astride the back of another who was down on all fours; to play this game. 3. A tapa pattern said to have its surface raised in ridges like corduroy." /HD/

'Ili lele in the ahupua'a of Waiehu, kalana of Waiehu.

Variants: Hanohanoiki, Hanohanonui, Kanohanoiki, Honohono, Honuhonuiki.

77 Hoolele
See Hoolili.

78 Hoolili
Hoʻolili
Hoʻo-lili

"hoʻo.lili. holili Rippled surface of the sea, as caused by fish; undulation or vibration of light in the hot sun; to ripple, vibrate, undulate; to close or blink the eyes in bright glare. Var. of haʻalili." /HD/

'Ili in the ahupuaʻa of Waiheʻe.

Variants: Hoolile, Hoolele.

79 Hoopahelo
Hoʻopahelo
Hoʻo-pahelo

"Var. of hoʻopakelo" /HD/; "hoʻo.pakelo. caus/sim. of pakelo 1"—"pakelo. 1. vi. To slip out, as an animal from a trap or a fish from the hand; slippery, slick, slipping, sliding; to thrust, as a spear."

'Ili in the ahupuaʻa of Waikapū.

80 Hopoi
Hopoʻi

Literally, to alarm.

A reservoir and former plantation village in the ahupuaʻa of Wailuku.

"Former plantation residential area. Also called 'Hopoi Camp'. Elevation 400 ft." /Place Names (ULUK)/

81 Hopukoa
Hopukoʻa
Hopu-koʻa

Literally, to seize coral.

Fishing ground that accompanied the two 'ili of Loʻiloa and Kuʻunaheana in the ahupuaʻa of Wailuku.

"Macy, George W.... There is a sea belonging to the land of Kunaheana & Loiloa for the purpose of fishing by the name of Hopukea, extent unascertained." /Mahele Awards (KPA)/ *See also*: Hopukoa Nui & Hopukoa Iki.

Variants: Hopukoa Nui, Hopukoa Iki.

82 Hopukoa Nui & Hopukoa Iki
Hopukoʻa Nui & Hopukoʻa Iki
Hopu-koʻa Nui & Hopu-koʻa Iki

Literally, greater to seize coral & lesser to seize coral.

———

Hopukoʻa Nui and Hopukoʻa Iki are the names of two divisions of the Wailuku Fishery. From west to east, the divisions of the fishery are: Kaʻehu a ka Mōʻī, Paukūkalo, Malae-haʻakoa (Malehaakoa on the original map), Kaihuwaʻa, Makawela, Kahului, Puʻuiki, Kaipuʻula, Kanahā, Palaʻeke, Kalua, Kaʻa, Hopukoʻa Nui, Hopukoʻa Iki, Papaʻula, Kapahu, Palaha, Wawaʻu (Kawau on the original map), Kānepaʻina, and Kahue. /H.K.L. & R.L., 1947/ *See also*: Hopukoa.

83 Huakolea
See Ahuakolea.

84 Huiha
Huihā
Hui-hā

Although the name is attested in one other region, the meaning remains undetermined. Perhaps: uniting in fours, mingling stone sinkers, or troughs coming together.

———

Surf mentioned in the context of Kēhu and Kaʻākau in the ahupuaʻa of Wailuku.

———

"Lea kahela i ke one o Malama, / I ka nome ia e ke one o Maluihi, / I ka noke aihaa ia e ke kai o Kehu, / Ahu kapeke lua i ka nalu o Huiha, / I ka pinai mau ia e ka nalu o Kaakau, / Haki nuanua i ka lae o Hihika.... [*Spreading merrily across the sands of Mālama, / Being slowly consumed by the sands of Maluʻihi, / Vigorously persisted upon by the sea of Kēhu, / Laid completely exposed by the waves of Huihā, / Repeatedly encroached upon by the the waves of Kaʻākau, / Which break along the point of Hīhīkā....*]" /Ka Nupepa Kuokoa, Buke 7, Helu 40, 3 ʻOkakopa 1868/

85 Huluhulupueo
Huluhulu-pueo

Literally, owl feathers.

———

Tributary stream of the Waiheʻe River, ahupuaʻa of Waiheʻe.

86 Iao
'Īao / 'Iao
'Ī-ao / 'Iao

Pronunciation and meaning undetermined, perhaps: "*Lit.*, cloud supreme" /PNOH/; 'ī ao—supreme upland region, or, supreme dawn; or, 'Iao—Jupiter.

Valley and stream in the ahupua'a of Wailuku.

An alternative name for the battle of Ka'uwa'upali, which took place between Kamehameha I and Kalanikūpule at what is now Kepaniwai in 'Īao Valley, ahupua'a of Wailuku. "Kepaniwai" is another alternative name for this battle.

Also, an 'ili lele (*see also*: Iao Makai) in the ahupua'a of Wailuku found in the vicinity of Haleki'i.

Variant: Iao makai.

87 Iao Makai
'Īao Makai

Literally, lowland 'Īao.

An 'ili lele ('Īao Makai) in the ahupua'a of Wailuku found in the vicinity of Haleki'i.

88 Iao Maniania Ditch
See Maniania Ditch.

89 Iao Needle
See Kukaemoku, Nanahoa, & Puuokamoa.

90 Iao Stream
'Īao / 'Iao
'Ī-ao / 'Iao

Pronunciation and meaning undetermined, perhaps: "*Lit.*, cloud supreme" /PNOH/; or, 'ī ao—supreme upland region, or, supreme dawn; or 'Iao—Jupiter.

The name of the middle portion of the Wailuku River below the juncture of the Kapela Stream and the Kinihāpai Stream. (*See also*: Wailuku River.)

"Stream begins at the junction of Poonahoahoa and Nakalaloa streams at about 1100 ft. elevation, flows to sea. Sometimes called 'Wailuku River' in descriptions of awards." /Place Names (ULUK)/

"During the four months of Makahiki and harvest season, which began with the rising of Makalii (the Pleiades) in the fall, the populace was allowed to enter 'Iao Valley to enjoy its delicious shrimp, 'o'opu fish, and other delicacies in company with the alii. But the populace traveled the trail up Kini-hapai (Uplifting of the multitude) stream that flows by the base of Ku Ka A'e Moku [*Ku Ka'e Moku*] (now called the Needle) while the alii followed Kapela stream past Ka Pili o Kaka'e." /SOM 100/

91 Imiau

See Umieu.

92 Kaa

Ka'a

"ka'a. 1. vi. To roll, turn, twist, wallow, wind, braid, revolve; to scud or move along, as clouds; to wield, as a club; rolling, twisting, turning, sloping...2. n. Vehicle, carriage, wagon, automobile, car, cart, coach, buggy...3. vi. To go past, pass by, reach; to be in a state of; to be located at; to take effect, as medicine; gone, absent, past, turned over, transferred, delivered...4. vi. To pay; paid...5. vi. To manage, run, be in charge of; given, as work to a person; well versed, skilled (used very broadly to indicate custom, nature, character, habit...). 6. n. Resin...8. n. Pulley. 9. See *hoana ka'a*. 10. n. Tale, legend (now replaced by ka'ao)." /HD/

A shoreline area to the east of Kahului.

Ka'a is also the name of a division of the Wailuku Fishery directly offshore of this region. From west to east, the divisions of the fishery are: Ka'ehu a ka Mō'ī, Paukūkalo, Malaeha'akoa (Malehaakoa on the original map), Kaihuwa'a, Makawela, Kahului, Pu'uiki, Kaipu'ula, Kanahā, Pala'eke, Kalua, Ka'a, Hopuko'a Nui, Hopuko'a Iki, Papa'ula, Kapahu, Palaha, Wawa'u (Kawau on the original map), Kānepa'ina, and Kahue. /H.K.L. & R.L., 1947/

Also, an 'ili mentioned in the ahupua'a of Waikapū (perhaps Ka'a'a).

93 Kaaa

Ka'a'a / Ka'a'ā / Ka'ā'ā / Kāa'a
Ka-'a'a / Ka-'a'ā / Ka-'ā'ā / Kā-a'a

Pronunciation and meaning undetermined, perhaps: ka 'a'a—the valiant; ka 'a'ā—the blaze, or, the *'a'ā* lava; ka 'ā'ā—the stutter(er); or, kā a'a—(sweet potato) vine that has sprouted rootlets.

[NOTE: The pronunciation of "Ka'a'a" is common for a family bearing the same name.]

'Ili in the ahupua'a of Waikapū.

Variant: Kaa.

94 Kaahu

Kaʻahu

Ka-ʻahu

Literally, the cloak.

"Ancient surfing area, Wailuku qd., Maui." /Place Names (ULUK)/

95 Kaʻahumanu Church

Historic church built upon the site of a small building used by the Reverend Jonathan Smith Green for services.

"In 1832, Queen Kaʻahumanu, an early convert into Christianity, visited Maui, and came to the site of the then new Kaʻahumanu Church, witnessing services being presided by Jonathan Smith Green. Upon seeing this, Queen Kaʻahumanu asked the Congregationalist mission to name the permanent church structure after her...The current structure, the fourth on the site, was built in 1876. It was built to honor Queen Kaʻahumanu's earlier request by Wailuku Sugar Company manager Edward Bailey. It is built in the New England simple style Gothic Architecture." /kaahumanuchurch.org/

96 Kaaikao

Kaʻaikāō / Kaʻaikao

Ka-ʻai-kāō / Ka-ʻai-kao

Pronunciation and meaning undetermined, perhaps: the food baked in the oven without leaf wrapping; or, ka ʻai kao—the goat feed.

The name of a loʻi in the ʻili of Punia, ahupuaʻa of Waikapū.

97 Kaakakai

Kaʻakakaʻi / Kaʻakākai

Kaʻa-kakaʻi / Kaʻa-kākai

Pronunciation and meaning undetermined, perhaps: kaʻa kakaʻi—to pass by in single file line; kaʻa kākai—to braid a handle (of strings or rope); or, an elided version of kaʻa kahakai—to reach the shore.

An intermittent stream, also named Keanakalahu, which begins in the ahupuaʻa of Kailua (Kula), and terminates near Kaʻa in the ahupuaʻa of Wailuku. Perhaps named for the famed kahuna named "Kaakakai," son of Luahoʻomoe.

"Hookahi kahawai o mea[?] Kaakakai ame Keanakalahu...holo aku ke kahawai o Kaakakai kona inoa a hui ae la me ka aina i kapaia Omaopio a haiki loa, ua ike au i keia mau aina ame ke kahawai mahope o ka hiki ana mai o ka poe Kaleponi oia paha ka M.H.1851 a 1852 paha. A kokoke ana ia wa aole au i ike ia Makaku. Ua ike au i ka loko ia ia Kanaha. Ua kauoha R.H. Stanley i keia hoike e hele mai imua o ke [*sic*] Aha e hai i kana mea apau i ike e pili ana ina palena aina o Wailuku ame Kalialinui. [*Ka'akākai and Keanakalahu are one stream… The stream, Ka'akākai is its name, runs and joins the land named 'Oma'opio and greatly narrows; I saw these lands and the stream after the California people arrived maybe around 1851 to 1852. And near that time, I did not see Makakū. I saw the fishpond Kanahā. R.H. Stanley summoned this witness to come before the Assembly to tell everything he knows about the boundaries of the lands of Wailuku and Kali'alinui.*]" /Maly, 2006/

98 Kaakau
See Kaakaupohaku.

99 Kaakaupohaku
Ka'ākaupōhaku
Ka'ākau-pōhaku

Literally, Ka'ākau Stone.

———

"Ancient surfing area, Wailuku qd., Maui." /Place Names (ULUK)/

Variant: Kaakau.

100 Kaakukui
See Keaakukui.

101 Kaalae
See Kaalae & Makaalae.

102 Kaalaea
Ka'alaea
Ka-'alaea

Literally, the ocherous dirt.

———

'Ili in the ahupua'a of Waikapū.

Variant: Kaalea.

103 Kaalaholo
Ka'alāholo
Ka-'alā-holo

Meaning undetermined, perhaps: the rolling basalt stone.

———

High plateau located within ʻĪao Valley, ahupuaʻa of Wailuku.

———————

"Kukaʻe Moku is the old name for Iao needle. On one side there is something like a ridge where there is a stone... It was there an alii hid, the chief who lived above at the place, Kaʻalāholo. Kaʻalāholo is table land on the left hand side of Iao Valley. Kinihapai is behind the needle." /SOM 82/

Variant: Kaalahola.

04 Kaalaino
Kā'alā'ino / Kā'ala'ino
Kā'alā-'ino /Kā'ala-'ino

Pronunciation and meaning undetermined, perhaps: kāʻalā ʻino—intense onslaught of sling stones; or, kāʻala ʻino—spoiled limpet.

———————

ʻIli in the ahupuaʻa of Waiehu, kalana of Waiehu.

Variant: Koalaina.

05 Kaalea
See Kaalaea.

06 Kaaloa
Ka'aloa / Ka'āloa
Ka'a-loa / Ka-'ā-loa

Pronunciation and meaning undetermined, perhaps: kaʻa loa—well traveled; or, ka ʻā loa—the long stone (*see also*: Kaapoko).

———————

Place mentioned in mele within the context of the ahupuaʻa of Waiheʻe.

———————

"Hele haaheo ka uhane, / I ka luna o Kaaloa, / I kilohi iho ko hana, / I ka haki nua a ka lio, / I ka lai o Maunaihi, He lio holo waliwali, / I ke one o Mokapu. [*The spirit goes proudly, / Upon Kaʻaloa, / You gaze down, / While the horse traverses, / Across the tranquility of Maunaʻihi, A horse that travels smoothly, / Upon the sands of Mōkapu.*]" /*Ka Hoku o ka Pakipika*, Buke 2, Helu 9, 11 Kekemapa 1862/

"Me he kuna kuhe la ka wai o Kaaloa, / Ka uliuli lipolipo / O ka wai o Kalaneloko [*sic*].... [*Like a freshwater eel that changes color is the water of Kaʻaloa, / The deep darkness / Of the water of Kalaniloko....*]" /*Ka Nupepa Kuokoa*, Buke 7, Helu 40, 3 ʻOkakopa 1868/

107 Kaapoko
Ka'āpoko
Ka-'ā-poko

From a description for other places of the same name: "*Lit.*, the short stone." /PNOH/

'Ili in the ahupua'a of Waihe'e.

Variant: Kapoko.

108 Kaehu
Ka'ehu
Ka-'ehu

Literally, the spray (of the sea).

Name listed as a shoreline region of the ahupua'a of Waiehu, kalana of Waiehu. Perhaps short for "Ka'ehu a ka Mō'ī." *See also:* Kaehu a ka Moi.

Variants: Kaehu Beach, Kaehu Bay, Ka'ehu Bay.

109 Kaehu/Ka'ehu Bay
See Kaehu.

110 Kaehu Beach
See Kaehu.

111 Kaehu a ka Moi
Ka'ehu a ka Mō'ī
Ka-'ehu a ka Mō'ī

Literally, the sea-spray of the paramount ruler.

The westernmost division of the Wailuku Fishery. From west to east, the divisions of the fishery are: Ka'ehu a ka Mō'ī, Paukūkalo, Malaeha'akoa (Malehaakoa on the original map), Kaihuwa'a, Makawela, Kahului, Pu'uiki, Kaipu'ula, Kanahā, Pala'eke, Kalua, Ka'a, Hopuko'a Nui, Hopuko'a Iki, Papa'ula, Kapahu, Palaha, Wawa'u (Kawau on the original map), Kānepa'ina, and Kahue. /H.K.L. & R.L., 1947/

112 Kahahawai
Kahāhāwai
Ka-hāhā-wai

Meaning undetermined, perhaps: the groping for/in water.

Shoreline region and famed surf in the ahupuaʻa of Waiheʻe.

"Among other southern families of note who arrive at the Hawaiian group during this migratory period *[9–10th century]*, though now it is impossible to place them in their proper order, the legend mentions Kalana-nuunui-kua-mamao, and Humu, and Mau-nua-niho who came from Kahiki (the southern groups), and landed at Kahahawai in Waihee, Maui. Aumu *[sic]* soon returned to Kahiki, being discontented with Kalana, who had taken Kamaunuaniho for a wife." /SOM 11/

"Ancient surfing area, Ka-hakuloa [probably Wailuku] qd., Maui." /Place Names (ULUK)/

13 Kahakapiele
Ka-haka-piele

Literally, the peddler's rack.

ʻIli in the ahupuaʻa of Ahikuli, kalana of Waiehu.

Variant: Kahakupiela.

14 Kahakumaka
Kahakumaka / Kahakūmaka
Ka-haku-maka / Kaha-kūmaka

Pronunciation and meaning undetermined, perhaps: ka haku maka—the raw lump of taro; or, kaha kūmaka—visible mark.

Pond in the ʻili of Pāpahawale, ahupuaʻa of Waiehu, kalana of Waiehu.

15 Kahakupiela
See Kahakapiele.

16 Kahalekulu
Ka-hale-kulu

Literally, the leaky house.

Place mentioned in the ahupuaʻa of Waiheʻe.

"Kahalekulu is as you go up, inland of *[interrupted]*. It is the only place iwa fern is now obtainable." /SOM 47/

117 Kahalulukahi
Ka-halulu-kahi

Literally, the single thunderous roar.

An area above the 'ili of Lo'iloa within 'Īao Valley in the ahupua'a of Wailuku.

"Kaha'i-nui (Kaha'i the strong) is son of Hema, a chief of East Maui living on the hill Kauiki in Hana district, and of Lua (Ula, Ulu)-mahahoa from Iao valley in Wailuku district. He is born in Iao valley at a place called Ka-halulu-kahi above Loiloa at Haunaka." /Beckwith, 1970/

118 Kahekili Highway

Hawai'i Route 340, which begins in the town of Wailuku, heads north into the moku of Kā'anapali, and continues until it terminates in the ahupua'a of Honokōhau (Kā'anapali).

Named for the famed Maui chief Kahekilinui'ahumanu.

Variant: Hawaii Route 340.

119 Kahewa
Ka-hewa

Literally, the offense.

'Ili in the ahupua'a of Wailuku.

120 Kahiki

Meaning undetermined, perhaps: Tahiti, Tahitian; or, "n. A variety of banana, common wild on Maui. Kinds are kahiki hae, kahiki mauki, and kahiki puhi." /HD/

'Ili in the ahupua'a of Wailuku.

121 Kahilinamaia
Kahilinamai'a
Ka-hilina-mai'a

Literally, the striking of/by bananas.

'Ili in the ahupua'a of Waihe'e.

22 Kahimana

See Kuhimana.

23 Kahoana

Ka-hoana

Literally, the grindstone.

'Ili in the ahupua'a of Ahikuli, kalana of Waiehu.

24 Kahoi

Ka-hoi

Pronunciation and meaning undetermined, perhaps: the bitter yam.

'Ili in the ahupua'a of Waikapū.

25 Kahoolewa

Kaho'olewa

Ka-ho'o-lewa

Literally, the ho'olewa ("Hoolewa 1. To cause to swing; to vibrate; to float in the air. 2. To lift up and carry, as between two persons; to carry in a manele or palanquin. 3. To carry a corpse in a funeral procession. 4. To cause a swinging or rotary motion, as in certain forms of dancing." /Parker/).

Ridge that serves as a partial boundary between the moku of Lahaina, Kā'anapali, and Wailuku. In the moku of Wailuku, Kaho'olewa also separates the inland regions of the ahupua'a of Wailuku and Waihe'e.

26 Kahoomano

Kaho'omano / Kaho'omāno / Kaho'omanō

Pronunciation and meaning undetermined, perhaps: ka ho'omano—to cause an increase in quantity; ka ho'omāno—to create, or act like, a dam; or, ka ho'omanō—to act like a shark.

The traditional name of Waihe'e Point in the ahupua'a of Waihe'e.

Variants: Kalaeokahoomano, Waihee Point.

127 Kahua
Kahua / Ka-hua

Meaning undetermined, perhaps: kahua—foundation, site; or, ka hua—the fruit/produce.

ʻIli in the ahupuaʻa of Wailuku.

128 Kahue
Ka-hue

Literally, the gourd.

Kahue is the name of the easternmost division of the Wailuku Fishery. From west to east, the divisions of the fishery are: Kaʻehu a ka Mōʻī, Paukūkalo, Malaehaʻakoa (Malehaa-koa on the original map), Kaihuwaʻa, Makawela, Kahului, Puʻuiki, Kaipuʻula, Kanahā, Palaʻeke, Kalua, Kaʻa, Hopukoʻa Nui, Hopukoʻa Iki, Papaʻula, Kapahu, Palaha, Wawaʻu (Kawau on the original map), Kānepaʻina, and Kahue. /H.K.L. & R.L., 1947/

129 Kahului
Ka-hului

Literally, the hului: "hului. 1. nvi. A kind of bag fish net; to drag such a net." /HD/

Although generalized as a large urban area in the ahupuaʻa of Wailuku, Kahului was originally a region of small fishing villages found mostly in the ʻili of Kaihuwaʻa, ʻOwā, Kalua, and the Kaʻa region around what was once Kahului Bay, now known as Kahului Harbor. Also, Kahului is the name of a beach just south of the western jetty of Kahului Harbor.

"I ke one aloha o Kahului e, Ua haaheo wale i ka ia hukikolo la.... [*Along the beloved sands of Kahului, Made proud through the fish dragged to shore....*]" /*Ka Hoku o ka Paki-pika*, Buke 2, Helu 23, 19 Malaki 1863/

" 'The harbor is formed by two breakwaters extending out over shoals; one northeasterly from the west side, and the other northwesterly from the northeast side [Hobron Point] of the bay.' It is the principal harbor on Maui and can accommodate container ships and cruise ships." /Place Names (ULUK)/

Kahului is also the name of a division of the Wailuku Fishery directly offshore of the ʻili of ʻOwā. From west to east, the divisions of the fishery are: Kaʻehu a ka Mōʻī, Paukūkalo, Malaehaʻakoa (Malehaakoa on the original map), Kaihuwaʻa, Makawela, Kahului, Puʻuiki, Kaipuʻula, Kanahā, Palaʻeke, Kalua, Kaʻa, Hopukoʻa Nui, Hopukoʻa Iki, Papaʻula, Kapahu, Palaha, Wawaʻu (Kawau on the original map), Kānepaʻina, and Kahue. /H.K.L. & R.L., 1947/

Variant: Kaikuono o Kahului.

30 **Kahului Harbor**
See Kahului.

31 **Kaiaha**
Ka'i'aha
Ka'i-'aha

Literally, to direct an 'aha (" 'aha, 3. n. A prayer or service whose efficacy depended on recitation under taboo and without interruption. The priest was said to carry a cord ('aha). (Malo 180–1.) Ua ka'i ka 'aha, the prayer is rendered…" /HD/).

'Ili in the ahupua'a of Waihe'e.

32 **Kaiapaokailio**
See Kalapaokailio.

33 **Kaihumoku**
Ka-ihu-moku

Meaning undetermined, perhaps: the severed nose, or, the prow of the ship.

Place name mentioned in mele within the context of the ahupua'a of Waihe'e. Of note, Kaihumoku is mentioned in at least two mele in conjuction with an area called Mōkapu.

"Me he a-i la no ka nene ke auau, / Ka haki palalahiwa i ke one o Mokapu / Kukaliki ka ii i ke one o Kaihumoku.… [*Like the neck of the* nēnē *goose as it swims, / The indulgent rumbling utterance across the sands of Mōkapu / The gutteral rasp boasting along the sands of Kaihumoku.…*]" /*Ka Nupepa Kuokoa*, Buke 7, Helu 40, 3 'Okakopa 1868/

"Aloha Kaihumoku kahi kaulana oia uka / O Kauahia kai luna o Mokapu kai lalo.… [*Fond memories of Kaihumoku the famed place of those uplands / Kauahia is above and Mōkapu is below.…*] /*Ko Hawaii Pae Aina*, Buke 3, Helu 33, 14 'Aukake 1880/

34 **Kaihuwaa**
Kaihuwa'a
Ka-ihu-wa'a

Literally, the canoe prow.

'Ili in the ahupua'a of Wailuku. Now the site of a phase of the Dream City subdivisions along modern day Kanaloa Avenue.

Kaihuwa'a is also the name of a division of the Wailuku Fishery directly offshore of this 'ili. From west to east, the divisions of the fishery are: Ka'ehu a ka Mō'ī, Paukūkalo,

Malaeha'akoa (Malehaakoa on the original map), Kaihuwa'a, Makawela, Kahului, Pu'uiki, Kaipu'ula, Kanahā, Pala'eke, Kalua, Ka'a, Hopuko'a Nui, Hopuko'a Iki, Papa'ula, Kapahu, Palaha, Wawa'u (Kawau on the original map), Kānepa'ina, and Kahue. /H.K.L. & R.L., 1947/

135 Kaikoo
Kaiko'o
Kai-ko'o

Literally, strong sea.

Name mentioned in the context of the kalana of Waiehu.

"Holu pipio ka wai o Paihi i ka makani / Ua ii mau i ka wai o Kaikoo, / I ke ka alele ia e ke one o Halekii, / Puliki ka aweawe hee i Nakohola, / I ke koali hoomoe ia e ke kaahaaha.... [*The waters of Paihī arch rippling in the wind / Ever gathering the water of Kaiko'o, / As it reels on toward the sands of Haleki'i, / The octopus tentacles embrace Nākohola, / Amidst the morning glory vines flattened by the Kā'aha'aha (wind)....*]" /*Ka Nupepa Kuokoa*, Buke 7, Helu 40, 3 'Okakopa 1868/

136 Kaikuono o Kahului
See Kahului.

137 Kailiili
Ka'ili'ili
Ka-'ili'ili

Literally, the pebble.

'Ili in the ahupua'a of Waiehu, kalana of Waiehu.

138 Kailipoe
Ka'ilipoe / Kāilipoe
Ka-'ili-poe / Kāili-poe

Pronunciation and meaning undetermined, perhaps: ka 'ili poe—the rounded surface; or, kāili poe—runner vine of the *poe* sweet potato.

Name of a site (*kahua*) in the 'ili of Pōhakuokauhi, ahupua'a of Wailuku. Also the name of the wind of that area.

"O Kahekili, aia no ia i Kalanihale makai mai o Kihahale, a maluna aku o ke kahua o Kailipoe i Pohakuokauhi.... [*Kahekili, he was at Kalanihale below Kihahale, above the site of Ka'ilipoe at Pōhakuokauhi....*]" /*Ka Nupepa Kuokoa, Buke 5, Helu 50, 15 Kekemapa 1866*/

Variant: Kilipoe.

39 Kailua
Kai-lua

Literally, two seas.

___

Gulch in the ahupua'a of Waikapū.

___

"A dry gulch bounding the north side of RPG 877, rises at about 3400 ft. elevation under Kapilau Ridge, ends at about 400 ft. elevation." /Place Names (ULUK)/

40 Kaimana
See Kainamu.

41 Kaimuhee
Kaimuhe'e
Ka-imu-he'e

Pronunciation and meaing undetermined, perhaps: ka imu he'e—the underground oven with sliding/crumbling sides, or, the underground oven in which octopus is cooked.

___

An area just inland of the two ponds of Kanahā and Mau'oni in the area of Kahului, ahupua'a of Wailuku.

___

"I ka wa e noho alii ana o Kanenenuiakawaikalu no Maui (ma Wailuku kona wahi noho mau), e noho ana kekahi kanaka kaulana o ia wahi—o Kapoi me kana wahine—ma Kaimuhee, ma uka ae o na wai elua o Kanaha me Mauoni. He mau loko kaulana ia no Wailuku. [*At the time when Kanēnēnuiakawaikalu of Maui was ruling as chief (his permanent residence was at Wailuku), a famed person of that place was living—Kapoi with his wife—at Kaimuhe'e, just inland of the two waters of Kanaha and Mauoni. These are famous ponds of Wailuku.*] /*Ke Au Okoa, Buke 12, Helu 11, 29 Iune 1871*/

42 Kainamu
Kai-namu

Literally, mumbling sea.

___

'Ili in the ahupua'a of Waihe'e.

Variant: Kaimana.

143 Kai o Anehe
Kai o 'Ānehe

Literally, sea of 'Ānehe ("ā.nehe. vi. To come upon quietly, move stealthily, poise" /HD/).

[NOTE: In online database searches, "ka anehe" returned more hits than "ke anehe." As such, it is likely that "anehe" is represented as "'ānehe" in native speech.]

"Kai-o-Anehe, sea from Maalaea to Keoneoio, between Kahoolawe and Molokini." /SOM/

Variant: Anehe.

144 Kai o Nakohola
See Nakohola

145 Kaipuula
Kaipu'ula
Ka-ipu-'ula

Literally, the red gourd.

Place mentioned in mele and mo'olelo within the context of the Kahului region in the ahupua'a of Wailuku, perhaps in the region of Kanahā and Mau'oni.

"O Kaweloikaiehuehu, / Makani aku o Kaipuula, / O-hee aku o Makawela, / Huki kolo aku o Kahului, / Kaa lau ohua aku, / O Kaipuula—la, / Ke lau ahi—la—e. [*Kaweloikaiehuehu, / Wind beyond Kaipu'ula, / Makawela spears octopus, / Kahului fishes with a drag net, / Kaipu'ula pulls in the seine for young fish, / Using a bag net there.*]" /*Ka Hoku o ka Pakipika*, Buke 1, Helu 31, 24 'Apelila 1862/

"Graciously the Oahu princess [Kahamalu'ihiikeao'ihilani] named the pond makai, Kana-ha, in honor of her brother Kanahaokalani, and the mauka pond, Mauoni, the name of her incognito ... The chiefess Kaipuula and her son Pumaia were the custodians of the fish-ponds from the time of K. I & III. The place called Kaipuula is named after the chiefess. Today it is neglected." /SOM 103/

Kaipu'ula is also the name of a division of the Wailuku Fishery. From west to east, the divisions of the fishery are: Ka'ehu a ka Mō'ī, Paukūkalo, Malaeha'akoa (Malehaakoa on the original map), Kaihuwa'a, Makawela, Kahului, Pu'uiki, Kaipu'ula, Kanahā, Pala'eke, Kalua, Ka'a, Hopuko'a Nui, Hopuko'a Iki, Papa'ula, Kapahu, Palaha, Wawa'u (Kawau on the original map), Kānepa'ina, and Kahue. /H.K.L. & R.L., 1947/

46 Kakanilua
Kakani-lua

Meaning undetermined, perhaps: doubly noisy.

———————

Region of sand dunes makai of Wai'ale Pond in the ahupua'a of Wailuku. An ancient battle site, the last battle of which was Kamoku'ilima, fought between Kīwala'ō and Kahekili. Part of this region is included in what is has more recently been referred to as "Wailuku Commons."

———————

"1776 Ke kaua o Ahulau ka piipii i Kakanilua kokoke ma ka puu one o Waikapu, Maui ma waena o Kalaniopuu ame Kahekili, na pukaua o Kalaniopuu 8 haneri ka nui, pau i ka mai e a koe elua. [*1776 The battle of Ahulau ka Pi'ipi'i at Kakanilua near the sand dune of Waikapū, Maui between Kalani'ōpu'u and Kahekili, the officers of Kalani'ōpu'u numbered 800, but were diminished due to a previous epidemic and only two (hundred) remained.*]" / Ka Hoku o Hawaii, Buke 29, Helu 52, 18 Mei 1926/

47 Kakolika
Kakōlika

Literally, Catholic.

———————

Heiau in the ahupua'a of Waihe'e.

———————

"Kakolika Heiau, Walker Site 34. Along road mauka to swamp in cane fields. Site of heiau torn up in cutting road. Inside may still be seen a large rock, the Wawaekanaka Stone (q.v.)..." /Place Names (ULUK)/

48 Kalaeiliili
Kalae'ili'ili
Ka-lae-'ili'ili

Literally, the pebble point.

———————

Shoreline point in the 'ili of Kapoho, ahupua'a of Waihe'e.

49 Kalaeokahoomano
See Kahoomano.

150 Kalaepohaku
Kalaepōhaku
Ka-lae-pōhaku

Literally, the stone shoreline-point.

Area found on the 1885/1903 W.D. Alexander map as being along the southeastern boundary of the ahupua‘a of Waikapū.

151 Kalahape
Kala-hape

Meaning undetermined, perhaps: to forgive transgression, or, to announce inaccurately.

‘Ili in the ahupua‘a of Waiehu, kalana of Waiehu.

152 Kalahihale
See Kalanihale.

153 Kalahiki
Kalāhiki
Ka-lā-hiki

Literally, the approaching sun.

Region just above the juncture of the streams of Kinihāpai and Kapela in ‘Īao Valley, ahupua‘a of Wailuku.

154 Kalanapoe
Kālanapoe
Kālana-poe

Pronunciation and meaning undetermined, perhaps: round sifter, or, rounded bone of the anterior part of the skull.

Village mentioned in context of the ‘ili of Ka‘ohe, ahupua‘a of Wailuku.

"O keia alanui hou, aia no ia mawaena aku o na wahi pana o keia kahawai. E hoomaka ana mai Kuemanu aku, he *Heiau* ia o Kaohe ka aina, o Kalanapoe ke kulanakauhale, a e holo komohana aku ana mai ke kulanakauhale aku o Wailuku. Nolaila, e ka poe kupa kamaaina o ke kahawai o Iao i hele aku ma kahi e, e ike mai oukou ua hiki ke kaa maloko o ke kahawai o Iao, a he nu hou ia au e olelo ae ai e ka mea i ike pono ia wahi. [*This new road, it's between the famed places of this valley. It starts from Kuemanu, that's a* heiau *of the land named Kaʻohe, Kālanapoe is the village, and it goes west from the town of Wailuku. So, those residents familiar with the valley of ʻĪao who went away know that the you can drive into the valley of ʻĪao, and this is the news that I will say, you who know this place well.*] / *Ka Nupepa Kuokoa*, Buke 9, Helu 5, 29 Ianuali 1870/

55 Kalaneloko
See Kalaniloko.

56 Kalani Auwai
Kalani ʻAuwai

Literally, Kalani Ditch.

___

Famed irrigation ditch above the town of Wailuku, ahupuaʻa of Wailuku.

57 Kalanihale
Kalani-hale

Literally, Kalani (the) House/Building.

___

Heiau of luakini category in the ahupuaʻa of Waiheʻe.

" '...a sacrificial heiau at Waihee, known as Kalanihale' was reported." /Place Names (ULUK)/

Also, the name of one of Kahekili's houses in the ahupuaʻa of Wailuku.

___

"Kiwalaʻo donned his royal regalia: Kameeiamoku held his spitoon and Kamanawa carried his kahili. The delegate from Hawaii went up to Wailuku, for at that time Kahekili was living in his house named Kalani-hale." /SOM 110/

Variant: Kalahihale.

58 Kalaniloko
Kalani-loko

Literally, Kalani Pond.

___

Place name mentioned in a mele within the context of the ahupuaʻa of Waiheʻe as "Kalaneloko."

___

"Me he kuna kuhe la ka wai o Kaaloa, / Ka uliuli lipolipo / O ka wai o Kalaneloko [*sic*].... [*Like a freshwater eel that changes color is the water of Kaʻaloa, / The deep darkness / Of the water of Kalaniloko....*]" / *Ka Nupepa Kuokoa*, Buke 7, Helu 40, 3 ʻOkakopa 1868/

Variant: Kalaneloko.

159 Kalaninuineehehe
Kalaninuine'ehēhē
Ka-lani-nui-ne'e-hēhē

Meaning and pronunciation undetermined, perhaps a colloquial elision of: ka lani nui ne'e he'ehe'e—the great chief that marches to flee.

'Ili in the ahupua'a of Waihe'e.

160 Kalanipuu
Kalanipu'u
Ka-lani-pu'u

Literally, Kalani Hill.

Peak (*perhaps* 2,760 feet), present on the 1887 Monsarrat map, from which descends the boundary between the two ahupua'a of Waiehu and Ahikuli, kalana of Waiehu.

161 Kalapaokailio
Kalapaoka'īlio
Ka-lapa-o-ka-'īlio

Literally, the ridge of the dog (Puapualenalena).

Ridge that descends along the north side of the mouth of Waikapū Valley, ahupua'a of Waikapū.

Variant: Kaiapaokailio.

162 Kalauhue
See Lauhue.

163 Kaleholeho
Ka-leholeho

Literally, the callus.

Surf area in the region of Kahului, ahupua'a of Wailuku.

"Ancient surfing area, Ka-hului area, Maui." /Place Names (ULUK)/

64 Kaleia

Kalē'ia

Ka-lē'ia

Literally, the abundance.

Shoreline area found along the front of Keālia Pond, ahupua'a of Waikapū.

65 Kalepa

Ka-lepa

Literally, the lepa ("lepa. 1. n. Flag, ensign, place marked by a flag, tapa cloth on end of a stick, as used to mark a taboo area... 2. Same as lepe 1 ['lepe. n. 1. Hem or fringe, as of a garment; any loose attachment, as of torn cloth or torn flesh.' /HD/] 3. Var. of kepa, notched. 4. Rare var. of lepe, cockscomb." /HD/).

Prominent gulch, stream, and waterfall at the front of Mauna Alani, ahupua'a of Waihe'e.

Also, a shoreline point found at the mouth of the Waiehu Stream in the kalana of Waiehu.

66 Kalepahu

See Halepahu.

67 Kalepelepe

Ka-lepelepe

Literally, the lepelepe ("lepe.lepe. 1. Redup. of lepe 1; fringed... 2. n. Wattles. 3. n. Labia minor... 4. Same as lepelepe-o-Hina." /HD/).

'Ili in the ahupua'a of Waihe'e.

Variants: Kalepelepe 1, 2, 3.

68 Kalepolepo

Ka-lepolepo

Literally, the dirtiness/contamination (as of water).

'Ili in the ahupua'a of Waikapū.

69 Kaloaloa

See Loaloa.

170 Kaloapelu

See Koloapelu.

171 Kalola

Ka-lola

Literally, the sluggish.

An alternative name for the heiau of Halekiʻi in the ʻili of Paukūkalo, ahupuaʻa of Wailuku.

"Halekiʻi is the heiau reserved for females of high rank and is situated on the makai side of the bluff—Kalola is another name. The whole combined in general is Pihana. It is said there is a cave beneath Pihana, and Liliha is the mouth of the cave." /SOM 72/

172 Kalopue

Kalopuʻe

Kalo-puʻe

Literally, taro grown on mounds.

ʻIli in the ahupuaʻa of Waiheʻe.

173 Kalua

Ka-lua

Literally, the pit.

ʻIlikū in the ahupuaʻa of Wailuku.

Kalua is also the name of the smallest division of the Wailuku Fishery found between Palaʻeke and Kaʻa in the Kahului region. From west to east, the divisions of the fishery are: Kaʻehu a ka Mōʻī, Paukūkalo, Malaehaʻakoa (Malehaakoa on the original map), Kaihuwaʻa, Makawela, Kahului, Puʻuiki, Kaipuʻula, Kanahā, Palaʻeke, Kalua, Kaʻa, Hopukoʻa Nui, Hopukoʻa Iki, Papaʻula, Kapahu, Palaha, Wawaʻu (Kawau on the original map), Kānepaʻina, and Kahue. /H.K.L. & R.L., 1947/

Also, shoreline point on the boundary between the ahupuaʻa of Ahikuli and Polipoli in the kalana of Waiehu.

Variant: Kaluaiki [Wailuku].

74 Kaluaoiki
Kalua'ōiki / Kaluaoiki
Ka-lua-'ōiki / Ka-lua-o-Iki

Pronunciation and meaning undetermined, perhaps: ka lua 'ōiki—the narrow pit; or, ka lua o Iki—Iki's pit.

'Ili in the ahupua'a of Wailuku.

75 Kaluaolena
Kalua'ōlena
Ka-lua-'ōlena

Literally, the turmeric pit.

'Ili in the ahupua'a of Ahikuli, kalana of Waiehu.

76 Kaluaolohe
Kalua'ōlohe
Ka-lua-'ōlohe

Meaning undetermined, perhaps: the barren pit (Attested in this citation: "'ō.lohe...Ka lua 'ōlohe o ke ālialia, the barren pit of the salt marsh" /HD/; or, "the robber's hole." /Parker/

Point upon the central-eastern boundary of the moku of Wailuku.

77 Kaluaoopu
Kalua'o'opu / Kālua'o'opu
Ka-lua-'o'opu / Kālua-'o'opu

Pronunciation and meaning undetermined, perhaps: ka lua 'o'opu—the 'o'opu fish pit; or, kālua 'o'opu—to bake 'o'opu fish in the underground oven.

'Ili in the ahupua'a of Wailuku.

78 Kaluli
Kāluli

Literally, to sway.

Destroyed heiau in the 'ili of Pūohala, ahupua'a of Wailuku.

"'Kaluli, Wailuku, at Puuohala. Repaired in time of Kahekili; Kaleopuupuu its priest.' (Thrum) 'Walker Site 42. Now totally destroyed.' (Sterling)" /Place Names (ULUK)/

179 Kamaalaea
See Māʻalaea.

180 Kama Auwai
KamaʻAuwai

Literally, Kama Ditch.

_____

Famed irrigation ditch in the above the town of Wailuku, ahupuaʻa of Wailuku.

181 Kamahoe
Kamāhoe
Ka-māhoe

Literally, the twin.

_____

ʻIli in the ahupuaʻa of Waiheʻe.

Also, a heiau in the same ʻili.

_____

"Ka Mahoe was a heiau. It was also the name of the valley. [Situated] on a knoll...ili and heiau of same name...nothing remained." /Place Names (ULUK)/

182 Kamamao
Ka-mamao

Meaning undetermined, perhaps: the mamao ("mamao. 1. nvs. Far, distant, remote, high in rank; distance...2. n. Third or highest platform of the lana-nuʻu mamao [oracle tower], where the high priest conducted services." /HD/).

_____

ʻIli in ʻĪao Valley, ahupuaʻa of Wailuku.

183 Kamaomao
Kamaʻomaʻo
Ka-maʻomaʻo

Literally, the greenness.

_____

Plains and ao kuewa ("realm of homeless spirits" /HD/) in the moku of Wailuku that is found just inland of the ponds of Kanahā and Mauʻoni, and which stretches southward toward Keālia and Kalepolepo [Kula?/Waikapū?]. The deity of this region is said to be named ʻŌlohe.

_____

"Ma keia hee ana, holo o Kalaiopuu ame na kanaka a pau loa i ke kula o Kamaomao, mawaena o Wailuku ame Kalepolepo. [*In this escape, Kalaiʻōpuʻu and all of his people ran toward the plains of Kamaʻomaʻo between Wailuku and Kalepolepo.*]" /Fornander V5, 455/

"O-lo-he, s. . . . 2. Ke akua o Kamaomao. [*ʻŌlohe, s. . . . 2. The deity of Kamaʻomaʻo.*]" /Andrews/

84 Kamauhalii
Kāmauhāliʻi
Kāmau-hāliʻi

Literally, to add a little more cover (as upon an imu, or upon the ground).

———

ʻIli in the ahupuaʻa of Waikapū.

85 Kamokuʻilima
Ka-moku-ʻilima

Literally, the clump of ʻilima.

———

A name for the 1776 battle in which Kiwalaʻō was defeated by Kahekili at Kakanilua, ahupuaʻa of Wailuku.

———

"1776 Halawai o Kiwalao me ke kapu alii me Kahekili a pauwale ke kaua; o Kakanilua, me Kamokuilima na inoa oia kaua. [*1776 Kiwalaʻō met with royal sanctity in meeting with Kahekili and the war was ended; Kakanilua, and Kamokuʻilima are the names of that war.*]" /*Ka Nupepa Kuokoa*, Buke 4, Helu 29, 22 Iulai 1865/

86 Kanaele
Ka-naele

Literally, the swamp.

———

ʻIli in the ahupuaʻa of Waiheʻe.

Variants: Kanaele 4, Naele.

87 Kanaha
Kanahā
Ka-nahā

Literally, the cracked/shattered.

———

Famed pond in the Kahului/Kaʻa region of the ahupuaʻa of Wailuku once conjoined with the pond of Mauʻoni.

The name of a beach park and area in the Ka'a area, ahupua'a of Wailuku.

"Graciously the Oahu princess [Kahamalu'ihiikeao'ihilani] named the pond makai, Kana-ha, in honor of her brother Kanahaokalani, and the mauka pond, Mauoni, the name of her incognito." /SOM 103/

Kanahā is also the name of a division of the Wailuku Fishery directly offshore of this region. From west to east, the divisions of the fishery are: Ka'ehu a ka Mō'ī, Paukūkalo, Malaeha'akoa (Malehaakoa on the original map), Kaihuwa'a, Makawela, Kahului, Pu'uiki, Kaipu'ula, Kanahā, Pala'eke, Kalua, Ka'a, Hopuko'a Nui, Hopuko'a Iki, Papa'ula, Kapahu, Palaha, Wawa'u (Kawau on the original map), Kānepa'ina, and Kahue. /H.K.L. & R.L., 1947/

188 Kanaha Pond State Wildlife Sanctuary

State wildlife sanctuary located at Kanahā in the ahupua'a of Wailuku.

189 Kanaio
Ka-naio

Meaning undetermined, perhaps: the naio ("naio. 1. Pinworm, as in the rectum; white specks in feces; larvae, as of mosquitos; worm in dung or in taro . . . 2. Inferior taro left in the field after the crop is removed. 3. The bastard sandal-wood (*Myoporum sandwicense*), a native tree, with hard, dark yellow-green wood, scented like sandal-wood . . . 4. Name of a seaweed." /HD/).

Shoreline area found just north of Keālia Pond, ahupua'a of Waikapū.

Also, an 'ili in the ahupua'a of Ahikuli, kalana of Waiehu.

190 Kanehe
See Nehe.

191 Kanepaina
Kānepa'ina

"1. Click beetle or bug (*Elateridae*). 2. (Cap.) Name of a god that sometimes took the form of a click beetle" /HD/; also, *literally*: clicking Kāne.

Kānepa'ina is the name of a division toward the eastern side of the Wailuku Fishery. From west to east, the divisions of the fishery are: Ka'ehu a ka Mō'ī, Paukūkalo, Malaeha'akoa (Malehaakoa on the original map), Kaihuwa'a, Makawela, Kahului, Pu'uiki, Kaipu'ula, Kanahā, Pala'eke, Kalua, Ka'a, Hopuko'a Nui, Hopuko'a Iki, Papa'ula, Kapahu, Palaha, Wawa'u (Kawau on the original map), Kānepa'ina, and Kahue. /H.K.L. & R.L., 1947/

92 Kanoa
Kānoa

"kā.noa n. Bowl, as for kava; hollow of land, pit *(rare)*; circular." /HD/

Ridge that forms the north side of Waiheʻe Valley.

93 Kaohe
Kaʻohe

Ka-ʻohe

Literally, the bamboo.

The name of two ʻili, possibly ʻili lele, in the kalana of Waiehu: one in the ahupuaʻa of Waiehu, one in the ahupuaʻa of Ahikuli.

Also, the name of a large ʻilikū toward the mouth of ʻĪao Valley, ahupuaʻa of Wailuku. This ʻilikū is unique because of its large size, and because its southern boundary lies on the ridge descending from Puʻulio—it sprawls down across the valley floor, crosses the river, and comes to a point at its northern boundary, Kauweloweloʻula.

94 Kaohia
See Ohia.

95 Kaolohe
Kaʻōlohe

Ka-ʻōlohe

Literally, the ʻōlohe (vs. Bare, naked, barren; hairless, as a dog; bald; destitute, needy... 2. nvs. Skilled, especially in lua fighting, so called perhaps because the beards of lua fighters were plucked and their bodies greased; bones of hairless men were desired for fish hooks because such men were thought stronger; also said of hula experts; skilled fighter. 3. vs. Pale... 4. vs. Sick, as after childbirth. 5. n. Ghost; image, as in clouds" /HD/; "O-lo-he, s.... 2. Ke akua o Kamaomao." /Andrews/).

Unidentified region found in mele and story around the region of Kamaʻomaʻo in the moku of Wailuku, perhaps nearer toward Keālia. This name may also be a reference to the deity of Kamaʻomaʻo, ʻŌlohe.

"Uli ka maomao haa ke alialia, / Opu ka hale hau a Kaolohe, / He hale opu mauu nahele-hele, / I ku i ke kaha o Papalekailiu e—ilaila. [*Kamaʻomaʻo is rich and deeply colored and Keālialia sprawls low; / The house formed by the Hau breeze of Kaʻōlohe rises, / It is a house of clumps of grass, / Stood up upon the dry stretch of Papalekailiʻu there.*]" /Hawaiian Historical Society, 2001/

196 Kaonohua
See Kaunuohua.

197 Kaopala
Ka'ōpala
Ka-'ōpala

Literally, the rubbish.

'Ili in the ahupua'a of Waikapū.

Also, a point on the northeastern edge of the ahupua'a of Waikapū, which not only delineates part of this ahupua'a's boundaries, but also serves to demark part of the boundary between the moku of Wailuku and the moku of Kula.

198 Kaopukaula
Ka'ōpūkaula
Ka-'ōpū-kaula

Literally, the string bag.

The name of a gulch in the ahupua'a of Ahikuli, kalana of Waiehu, in which wauke is recorded as having been cultivated.

199 Kaopuohe
See Keopuohe.

200 Kapaaiki
Kapa'aiki

Meaning undetermined, perhaps: the slightly stuck.

'Ili in the ahupua'a of Wailuku.

Variant: Paiki.

201 Kapaaloa
Kapa'aloa
Ka-pa'a-loa

Meaning undetermined, perhaps: the very far border, or, the very steadfast one.

The name of an 'ili, and perhaps 'ili lele, found in the ahupua'a of Wailuku (perhaps related to *Kapaaiki*), as well as an 'ili in the ahupua'a of Polipoli, kalana of Waiehu.

02 Kapahu
Ka-pahu

Literally, the gill net.

———

Kapahu is the name of a division toward the east side of the Wailuku Fishery. From west to east, the divisions of the fishery are: Ka'ehu a ka Mō'ī, Paukūkalo, Malaeha'akoa (Malehaakoa on the original map), Kaihuwa'a, Makawela, Kahului, Pu'uiki, Kaipu'ula, Kanahā, Pala'eke, Kalua, Ka'a, Hopuko'a Nui, Hopuko'a Iki, Papa'ula, Kapahu, Palaha, Wawa'u (Kawau on the original map), Kānepa'ina, and Kahue. /H.K.L. & R.L., 1947/

03 Kapahukauwila
Ka-pahu-kauwila

Meaning undetermined, perhaps: the *kauila* wood drum, or, the kauila wood stake/post.

———

'Ili in the ahupua'a of Waihe'e.

Variant: Paukauila.

04 Kapaka
Kapaka / Kāpaka
Ka-paka / Kā-paka

Pronunciation and meaning undetermined, perhaps: ka paka—the raindrop; or, kā paka—"n. Container for tobacco, pipe, matches." /HD/

———

'Ili in the ahupua'a of Waiehu, kalana of Waiehu.

05 Kapalaaea
See Kapalaalaea.

06 Kapalaalaea
Kapala'alaea
Ka-pala-'alaea

Literally, the daub/smear/dab of ocherous earth.

———

Name of 'ili in the ahupua'a of Wailuku, as well as in the ahupua'a of Waikapū.

Variants: Kapalaaea, Kapalialaea.

207 Kapalaoa
Kapalaoa
Ka-palaoa

Literally, the ivory, or, the sperm whale.

'Ili in the ahupua'a of Polipoli, kalana of Waiehu.

Variants: Kapalaua, Kapalua, Kepalaoa, Kepalaua, Kupalaua.

208 Kapalaua
See Kapalaoa.

209 Kapaliokakae
See Piliokakae.

210 Kapaniwai
See Kepaniwai.

211 Kapanui
Kapa-nui

Meaning and pronunciation undetermined, perhaps: kapa nui—large bank.

'Ili in the ahupua'a of Wailuku.

212 Kapapakoloa
Kapapakōloa
Ka-papa-kō-loa

Pronunciation and meaning undetermined, perhaps: the laying of long sugar cane close together, or, the level ground of long sugar cane.

Point along the northeastern border of the ahupua'a and moku of Wailuku.

Variant: Papakaloa.

213 Kapaohia
See Papaohia.

14 **Kapela Stream**
Kapela
Ka-pela

Literally, the decayed flesh.

———

Tributary of ʻĪao stream, the middle portion of the Wailuku River, found in ʻĪao Valley.

———

"During the four months of Makahiki and harvest season, which began with the rising of Makalii (the Pleiades) in the fall, the populace was allowed to enter ʻĪao Valley to enjoy its delicious shrimp, ʻoʻopu fish, and other delicacies in company with the alii.
But the populace traveled the trail up Kini-hapai (Uplifting of the multitude) stream that flows by the base of Ku Ka Aʻe Moku *[Ku Kaʻe Moku]* (now called the Needle) while the alii followed Kapela stream past Ka Pili o Kakaʻe." /SOM 100/

15 **Kapelakapuokakae**
Kapelakapuokākaʻe
Ka-pela-kapu-o-Kākaʻe

Literally, the sacred remains of Kākaʻe.

———

Famed burial place in the valley of ʻĪao, ahupuaʻa of Wailuku.

———

"Kapela-o-Kakae, name of a large area in Iao Valley. There is one hill in the middle of the land known as Kukaʻe-moku." /SOM 94/

Variants: Kapelaokakae, Pelakapuokakae.

16 **Kapelaokakae**
See Kapelakapuokakae.

17 **Kapilaa**
See Kapilau.

18 **Kapilau**
Ka-pilau

Literally, the stench.

———

Mountain ridge along the boundary between the ahupuaʻa of Waikapū and Wailuku.

Variant: Kapilaa.

219 Kapoho
Ka-poho

Meaning undetermined, perhaps: the *poho* ("poho. 1. n. Hollow or palm of the hand, hollow of the foot, depression, hollow; container, receptacle, pouch, as for tobacco; box, as for matches; hollow of a canoe, divided into three parts (mua, waena, *hope*)...2. nvt. Mortar; to knead, as bread or poi...3. nvt. Patch, as in clothes; a wooden patch inserted into a calabash, as to mend a break; to patch, mend. 4. vt. To belly out, puff out, as clothes on a line or a sail; to hollow or dub out, as a wooden container...5. n. Chalk, chalky white earth, as of limestone. 6. n. A unit of measure equal to half a span (kīko'o). *Rare.* 7. n. A bundle of tapa pieces (mo'omo'o). *Rare.*" /HD/

'Ili in the ahupua'a of Waihe'e.

220 Kapoino
Kapō'ino
Ka-pō'ino

Literally, the disaster.

'Ili in the ahupua'a of Waiehu, kalana of Waiehu.

Variants: Kapoinoiki, Poino, Poinonui.

221 Kapoipoi
Kapo'ipo'i
Ka-po'ipo'i

Literally, the covering/clasping/engulfing; or, Kapo'ipo'i, the proper name of the husband of Waihīnano from the saga of Hi'iakaikapoliopele).

Seaside area along the vicinity of Kaihuwa'a in the Kahului region of the ahupua'a of Wailuku.

"...mawaho aku paha o Kaihuwaa ma kahi i kapaia o Kapoipoi, ua poi ia iho la ka waapa e ka nalu a o ka make iho la no ia, naha ka waapa.... [...*beyond Kaihuwa'a in the area named Kapo'ipo'i, the rowboat was engulfed by the breaking wave and some died; the rowboat was smashed to bits....*]" /*Ko Hawaii Pae Aina*, Buke 8, Helu 4, 24 Ianuali 1885/

"Hoole mai o Waihinalo wahine a Kapoipoi, aole e make kuu alii o oe, ke hai mai nei na kua wahine oia nei. O Walinuu ma laua o Waimaanoanoa [*sic*], o Papa o Hoohoku-kalani, e hoole mai ana, aole e make. Pane mai o Hiiaka i ka hua o ka make. Ua make ke lii nona nei moku. [*Waihinalo, wife of Kapo'ipo'i, refuted this; 'My chief will not die by you,' her goddesses were telling her. Walinu'u and Walimānoanoa, Papa Ho'ohokukalani, they were refuting, he would not die. Hi'iaka responded with the curse of death. The chief to whom this island (Maui) belonged died.*]" /*Ka Hae Hawaii*, Buke 5, Helu 14, 4 Iulai 1860/

"I ke one aloha o Kahului e, / Ua haaheo wale i ka ia hukikolo la, / E aha ana la Waihinano me Kapoipoi e, / E walea nei i ka malu o ke ao la.... [*Upon the beloved sands of Kahului ē, / So proud at the fish caught by seine lā, / What are Waihīnano and Kapo'ipo'i doing ē, / Relaxing under the shelter of the clouds lā....*]" /*Ka Hoku o ka Pakipika*, Buke 2, Helu 23, 19 Malaki 1863/

22 Kapokea
Kapokea / Kapōkea
Kapo-kea / Ka-pō-kea

Pronunciation and meaning undetermined, perhaps: Kapo-kea—White Kapo; or ka pō kea—"Kapokea (kă-po'-ke'ā): the clear night...." /Parker/

———

'Ili adjoining the 'ili of Lo'ikahi in the ahupua'a of Waihe'e. Also, the site of the heiau of Kealaka'ihonua.

23 Kapoko
See Kaapoko.

24 Kapoli
Ka-poli

Literally, the bosom/breast/depression [indentation].

———

An area along the boundary between the moku of Lahaina and the ahupua'a of Waikapū. Currently, the name of a beach park in the Mā'alaea area.

———

"Kapoli. Beach park, Mā'alaea, Maui. Unimproved park on the low cliffs southwest of Mā'alaea Small Boat Harbor. *Lit.*, the bosom. Kapoli is the name of a former spring in the area." /HPN/

25 Kapuakeeo
See Kepuhakeeo.

26 Kapukaulua
Ka-puka-ulua

Literally, the *ulua* fish hole.

———

Shoreline point found along the northeastern border of the ahupua'a of Wailuku. In recent times, the area where the Baldwin Beach Park pavillion is located.

227 Kapuna

Ka-puna

Literally, the spring of water.

'Ili in the ahupua'a of Waihe'e.

228 Kapuoho

Ka-puoho

Meaning undetermined: the puoho ("puoho. nvi. Startled; to cry out in alarm; fright, shock; to explode, as a lava flow; to wake suddenly; sudden appearance, as a burst of fragrance..." /HD/).

'Ili in the ahupua'a of Ahikuli, kalana of Waiehu.

Variants: Kapuohe, Kapuolo.

229 Kauahea

Ka-ua-hea

Literally, the misty rain.

Area in the vicinity of Pihana, ahupua'a of Wailuku, that once served as an encampment for Kahekili's warriors as well as a prison camp during the Territory years of Hawai'i.

"In Kauahea *[S.E. of Iao Stream below Pihana Heiau]* warriors dwelt and were trained in war skills and there was a boxing site in the time of Kahekili. The warriors camped on the level place below. The ridge above is Pihana-ka-lani and Halekii. There were heiaus up there *[Walker Sites 43 and 44]*. This was a very famous place in the time of Kahekili and in the period of Piikea's *[wife of Umi]* brothers *[Lonopiilani and Kihapiilani]*. Kiha is said to have built the heiau of Halekii. After the training was through the warrior was sent out to sea to catch whales. When he had killed a whale he returned and was given a position by the chief." /SOM 114/

"For a number of years Oahu Prison has maintained 4 outside prison camps, which were located on the island of Maui, and 1 at the Waiakea Airport at Hilo, Hawaii. Owing to the necessity for additional housing facilities for county prisoners, the camp at Kauahea, Maui, was evacuated and turned over to the county the latter part of this fiscal year. Men at this camp were transferred to other prison camps." /Annual Report of the Department of the Interior, 1933/

30 Kauahia

Kauahia / Kauʻāhia

Kau-ahia / Kau-ʻāhia

Pronunciation and meaning undetermined, perhaps: kau ahia—set (above) faded; or, kau ʻāhia—placing tinder.

Area mentioned in mele in the context of Mōkapu within the ahupuaʻa of Waiheʻe.

"Aloha Kaihumoku kahi kaulana oia uka / O Kauahia kai luna o Mokapu kai lalo.... [*Fond memories of Kaihumoku the famed place of those uplands / Kauahia is above and Mōkapu is below....*]" /*Ko Hawaii Pae Aina*, Buke 3, Helu 33, 14 ʻAukake 1880/

31 Kauhiana

Kauhiana / Kauhiʻana

Ka-uhi-ana / Ka-uhi-ʻana

Pronunciation and meaning undetermined, perhaps: ka uhi ana—the covering of a cave; or, ka uhi ʻana—the concealment.

Point on the northeastern boundary of the ahupuaʻa of Wailuku.

32 Kauhiloa

Ka-uhi-loa

Meaning undetermined, perhaps: the long uhi ("uhi. 1. nvt. Covering, cover, veil, film, lid, solid tattooing, tent...2. n. Large, bluish-brown birthmark. 3. n. The yam (*Dioscorea alata*)...4. n. Mother-of-pearl bivalve, mother-of-pearl shank...5. n. Turtle shell piece used for scraping olonā. 6. n. Mark made by the gall of raw pūpū ʻawa (a shellfish) on tapa or on the skin as an ornament." /HD/

ʻIli in the ahupuaʻa of Polipoli, kalana of Waiehu.

33 Kauhina

See Kauhiana.

34 Kaula

Kaula / Kaʻula / Kāula

Kaula / Ka-ula / Ka-ʻula / Kāula

Meaning and pronunciation undetermined, perhaps: kaula—rope; ka ula—the flame; ka ʻula—the red appearance; or, kāula—prophet.

ʻIli in the ahupuaʻa of Waiehu, kalana of Waiehu.

235 Kaulehulehu
Kau-lehulehu

Meaning undetermined, perhaps: laid/sacrificed before the multitudes.

An inland point along the northeastern border of the ahupuaʻa of Wailuku.

236 Kaulu
Kaʻulu
Ka-ʻulu

Literally, the breadfruit.

Land listed as being in the ahupuaʻa of Waiheʻe.

"Still farther up was the Kanoa (bowl for kava, hollow of land, pit) of Kane and Kanaloa—a pot hole about 2′ in diameter according to the description on the land of Kaulu. The two gods were accustomed to drink awa at this place. Once they saw down below and Alae at a place now called Alae on that account. One of them threw his arrow (spear?) at it and struck it. The Alae flew against the cliff and where it struck and died is now a hole through which the water now flows." /SOM 29/

237 Kaulupala
Kaʻulupala
Ka-ʻulu-pala

Literally, the ripe breadfruit.

ʻIli in the ahupuaʻa of Wailuku.

238 Kaumuilio
Kaumuʻīlio
Ka-umu-ʻīlio

Literally, the dog oven.

ʻIli in the ahupuaʻa of Waikapū.

239 Kaunoa
Kau-noa

Meaning undetermined, perhaps: to enact freedom from taboo, or, placed without taboo.

Area inland of the Palaha and Wawaʻu region of the ahupuaʻa of Wailuku. This area is also now known by the superimposed name of foreign origin "Spreckelsville."

Kaunoa School: The latter name of the English standard school originally known as Maui Standard School, formed in 1926.

Kaunoa Senior Center: Center for seniors located on the site formerly known as the Maui Standard School and, later, Kaunoa School.

40 Kaunuohua
Ka-unu-o-Hua

Literally, the altar of Hua.

Peak (2,689 feet), ridge, and gulch in the ahupuaʻa of Waikapū.

Variants: Kaonohua, Kaonohue, Kaunohua.

41 Kauoku
Kauʻōkū
Kau-ʻōkū

Pronunciation and meaning undetermined, perhaps: kau ʻōkū—to set a live bird as a decoy; or, an elided version of: kau ʻokuʻu—perched.

ʻIli in the ahupuaʻa of Wailuku.

Variant: Kauoukuu.

42 Kauokuu
See Kauoku.

43 Kaupali
Kau-pali

Literally, set upon the precipice.

ʻIli in the ahupuaʻa of Wailuku.

44 Kaupo
See Puu o Kaupo.

245 Kauwaupali
Kaʻuwaʻupali
Ka-ʻuwaʻu-pali

Literally, the cliff clawing.

Name of the battle between Kamehameha I and Kalanikūpule at what is now Kepaniwai in ʻĪao Valley, ahupuaʻa of Wailuku. "Kepaniwai" and "ʻĪao" are alternative names for this battle.

246 Kauweloweloula
Kauwelowelo'ula / Kauweloweloula
Kau-welowelo-'ula / Kau-welowelo-ula

Pronunciation and meaning undetermined, perhaps: kau welowelo ʻula—[place where the] red streak poised/landed/appeared; or, kau welowelo ula—appearance/rising of streaming flames.

Peak (*perhaps* 3,070 feet) that forms the northern point of the ʻili of Kaʻohe in ʻĪao Valley, ahupuaʻa of Wailuku.

247 Kauwila
Kauwila / Ka-uwila

Meaning undetermined, either: kauwila ("n. 1. A native tree in the buckthorn family (*Alphitonia ponderosa*) . . . 3. Taboo ceremony consecrating a temple; ceremonial readorning of images with feathers. 4. Hard, reddish rock resembling ʻalā. 5. A kind of black, tough sugar cane . . . /HD/); or, the *uila* ("uila. nvs. Lightning, electricity; electric." /HD/).

ʻIli lele in the ahupuaʻa of Ahikuli, kalana of Waiehu.

Variants: Kawila, Kauwilaiki, Kauwilanui.

248 Kawaiola
Ka-wai-ola

Literally, the life-giving waters.

Spring in the ʻili of Waiwela, ahupuaʻa of Wailuku.

249 Kawau
See Wawau.

50 Kawela
See Makawela.

51 Kawelowelo
Ka-welowelo

Literally, the flying streak.

Heiau in the ahupua'a of Wailuku.

"Kawelowelo Heiau. Walker Site 51. Vicinity of Wailuku. Said to have been among those consecrated by Liholiho in his tour of Maui for that purpose about 1801." /Place Names (ULUK)/

52 Kawila
See Kauwila.

53 Kawili
Kāwili

Literally, to mix or blend.

Name of the seaside of the ahupua'a of Ahikuli, kalana of Waiehu.

Variant: Kawili Channel.

54 Keaakukui
Kea'akukui
Ke-a'a-kukui

Literally, the kukui tree root.

'Ili in the ahupua'a of Ahikuli, kalana of Waiehu.

Variant: Kaakukui.

55 Keeau

Place name misinterpreted due to a fold/crease in the original newspaper source as being in the ahupua'a of Waiehu, kalana of Waiehu. No further information available.

256 Keahialoa
Keahialoa / Keahiʻāloa
Ke-ahi-a-Loa / Ke-ahi-ʻā-loa

Pronunciation and meaning undetermined, perhaps: ke ahi a Loa—the fire made by Loa; or, ke ahi ʻā loa—the long burning fire.

Peak (3,548 feet) above the region of Nāpoko, in the kalana of Waiehu.

257 Keahuku
Keahukū
Ke-ahu-kū / Ke-ahukū

Meaning undetermined, perhaps: ke ahu kū—the erect altar; or, ke ahukū—the stoning (to death).

Heiau in the ahupuaʻa of Wailuku.

"Keahuku, Wailuku. No particulars...named among those consecrated by Liho-liho...preceeding [*sic*] the peleleu fleet." (Thrum) ʻWalker Site 45. (Sterling)ʼ " /Place Names (ULUK)/

258 Keahupio
Keahupiʻo
Ke-ahu-piʻo

Literally, the arched mound.

ʻIli in the ahupuaʻa of Wailuku.

Variant: Keahupii.

259 Kealakaihonua
Kealakaʻihonua
Ke-ala-kaʻi-honua

Meaning undetermined, perhaps: the path on which to walk the land.

Large heiau on the shoreline of the ʻili of Kapōkea, ahupuaʻa of Waiheʻe.

60 Kealakapehu
Kealākapehu
Ke-ala-a-Kapehu

Pronunciation and meaning undetermined, perhaps: Kapehu's road.

'Ili in the ahupua'a of Wailuku.

61 Kealia
Keālia
Ke-ālia

Literally, the salt bed.

'Ilikū, pond, and marsh area along the shoreline of Mā'alaea, ahupua'a of Waikapū. Verbiage and illustrations in the Māhele documents indicate that the areas used for salt production were depicted as lo'i, but were simply termed "pa'akai."

62 Kealoha
Ke-aloha

Literally, the love/affection/pity/grace.

Unidentified heiau in 'Īao Valley, ahupua'a of Wailuku.

Interview between Larry Kimura and Joseph Kekaua, Ka Leo Hawai'i radio program. Orthography reflects pronunciation of speaker.

"Ka 'ohana ho'i, ma ko'u makuakāne, wehewehe aku au iā 'oukou, mālama ho'i mākou i ka, 'oia ho'i, ka heiau, ka mea...ka'u mea i mālama me ka'u makuakāne...kēia heiau? 'O ka heiau kēia, 'o ka heiau i kāhea 'ia 'o Kealoha. Kealoha, no 'Īao, ma ka 'ao'ao o ko mākou hale. Aia kēia mau heiau 'elua—heiau wahine, heiau kāne. A ka 'ohana o ka'u makuakāne, 'o ia kāna hana mālama kēia. A na'u i hele waele, kanu nō ho'i nā pua, nā mea like 'ole, kanu i kēlā heiau. A hoihoi ho'i ka'u hana me ka makuakāne i ka heiau no ka mea i leila wau i 'ike ai i nā mea like 'ole...aia nō ke kū nei ma lalo o ke kumu hau. Kēlā manawa a'u i hele ai me nā po'e holoholo, a 'ike wau i kēlā heiau, aia nō ke kū ala ma leila...a, ka pili ho'i o kēia mau heiau i kāhea, i kapa 'ia ai i Kealoha, nānā 'oe 'o ke kāne, like hana 'ia ho'i nā pōhaku like 'ole, a kona home ia. Ka heiau o ka wahine, nānā 'oe i kēlā, nē 'oe a hele a mamao, a i 'ole 'umi paha kapua'i mai kēlā heiau mai, nānā aku 'oe i kēlā heiau, kohu mea he wahine e moe maila i loko. 'O ia ke kumu i kapa 'ia ho'i kēlā heiau, wahine. A kapa 'ia ke kāne, nānā 'oukou he kohu mea ke kāne e kū ana. A 'o ia ke kumu i kapa 'ia, wahine me ke kāne. [*The family, on my father's side, I will explain to you all, we cared for, well, the heiau, the one...that I took care of with my father...this heiau? This is the heiau, the heiau called Kealoha. Kealoha, from 'Īao, on the side of our house. There are these two heiau—female heiau, male heiau. And my father's family, that's what he did, cared for. And I went to weed, plant flowers, all sorts of things I planted on that heiau. And what I did with my father at that heiau was so interesting, because that's where I saw all sorts of things . . . it's there standing under the hau tree. That time I went with the visitors, I saw that heiau; it's standing there . . . and how these heiau are called, named Kealoha: look at the male one, it's like it was made from all sorts of stones, and that's his home. The heiau of the female, look at it; if you go back a ways, maybe ten feet from that heiau, you look at that heiau, it's like it's a women lying there inside. That's the reason that heiau was named female. And the male was named, you all look, it's as if a male was standing. And, that's why it was called female with the male.]"* /Joseph Kekaua, "Ka Leo Hawai'i 212"/

263 Keana
Ke-ana

Literally, the cave.

'Ili in the ahupua'a of Waikapū.

264 Keanakalahu
Keanākalāhū
Ke-ana-(a)-ka-lā-hū

Pronunciation and meaning undetermined, perhaps: ke ana (a) ka lā hū—the day of flood cave.

An intermittent stream, also named Ka'akakai, which begins in the ahupua'a of Kailua (Kula), and terminates near Ka'a in the ahupua'a of Wailuku.

265 Kehei
See Kiheipukoa.

266 Keonekapoo
Keonekapo'o
Ke-one-kapo'o

Literally, the furrowed sand.

Point found just inland of Kapukaulua along the northeastern border of the ahupua'a of Wailuku.

67 Kehoni
Kēhoni
Kē-honi

Literally, to refuse a kiss.

A shoreline area in the 'ili of Ka'āpoko, ahupua'a of Waihe'e.

68 Kehu
Kēhu
Ke-ehu

Literally, the sea-spray.

Famed surf area in the ahupua'a of Wailuku.

"Lea kahela i ke one o Malama, / I ka nome ia e ke one o Maluihi, / I ka noke aihaa ia e ke kai o Kehu, / Ahu kapeke lua i ka nalu o Huiha, / I ka pinai mau ia e ka nalu o Kaakau, / Haki nuanua i ka lae o Hihika.... [*Spreading merrily across the sands of Mālama, / Being slowly consumed by the sands of Malu'ihi, / Vigorously persisted upon by the sea of Kēhu, / Laid completely exposed by the waves of Huihā, / Repeatedly encroached upon by the the waves of Ka'ākau, / Which break along the point of Hīhīkā....*]" /*Ka Nupepa Kuokoa*, Buke 7, Helu 40, 3 'Okakopa 1868/

69 Keokanui
Ke-oka-nui

Literally, the great dregs/sediment.

Supposed 'ilikū in the kalana of Waiehu.

However: "KEOKANUI, - Ili of—CLASS INT. DEPT. YEAR 1861 MONTH Nov. 3th,- In letter from P. Nahaolelua to Min. of Interior, that there is no ili by the above name." /Land Index (HSA)/

70 Keoneula
Keone'ula
Ke-one-'ula

Literally, the red sand/silt.

'Ili at the mouth of 'Īao Valley, ahupua'a of Wailuku.

271 Keopuohe
Keōpū'ohe
Ke-ōpū-'ohe

Literally, the bamboo clump.

_____

'Ili in the ahupua'a of Wailuku.

Variant: Kaopuohe.

272 Kepalaoa
See Kapalaoa.

273 Kepalaua
See Kapalaoa.

274 Kepaniwai
Ke-pani-wai

Literally, the water dam.

_____

Site of the battle of Ka'uwa'upali between Kamehameha I and Kalanikūpule in 'Īao Valley, ahupua'a of Wailuku. "Kepaniwai" is also an alternative name for this battle. The county park, Kepaniwai Park, is now located in this area.

Variant: Kapaniwai.

275 Kepuakeeo
See Kepuhakeeo.

276 Kepuhakeeo
Kepūhāke'eo
Ke-pūhā-ke'eo

Meaning undetermined, perhaps: the indignant belch.

_____

'Ili in the ahupua'a of Wailuku.

Variant: Kapuakeeo.

77 Kiao
Kīʻao / Kiāo
Kī-ʻao / Kia-(a)o

Pronunciation and meaning undetermined, perhaps: kī ʻao—tī with new shoot; or, in regards to another place of a name with the same spelling—"Kiao PEM: The name may once have been Kia-ao (cloud pillar)." /Place Names (ULUK)/

Area mentioned near the ʻili of Koʻiahi, ahupuaʻa of Waiheʻe.

"...someone stole fish from the pond of a land of Waihee close to Kiao, called Koʻahi [*sic*], owned by Alapaʻi Malo-iki..." /SOM 41/

78 Kiha
Kiha / Kīhā

Pronunciation and meaning undetermined, perhaps: "kiha. 1. n. Supernatural lizard (in such names as Kihalani-nui, Kiha-nui-lūlū-moku, and Kiha-wahine); reptile...2. Var. of kihe 1. [kihe. 1. vi. Sneeze...2. n. A small native fern...3. A variety of sweet potato. 4. n. A red seaweed (*Chylocladia* sp.) with narrow cylindrical, branching stems...] /HD/; or, "kī.hā. 1. nvi. Belch, burp; to belch or burp." /HD/

ʻIli in the ahupuaʻa of Ahikuli, kalana of Waiehu.

79 Kihahale
Kiha-Hale

Pronunciation and meaning undetermined, perhaps: Kiha the House (as in, the house named "Kiha").

ʻIli in the ahupuaʻa of Wailuku, presumably located in ʻĪao Valley.

"Eia ua mau kuleana la au e hai aku nei ia olua. Oohia, no Kalainohoino mai koʻu noho ana ma Waikapu nei[.] oia koʻu kuleana i noho ai[.] make o Kalainohoino, noho no wau ma lalo o Keeaumuku [*sic*]. Oohia no nae kuu kuleana mua. o na palena o ohia o Kealia no na ka Paakai a me ke kai a me ke kula o kamaomao, mai ke ala ae a hiki i Kaumuku[,] mai Kaumuku aku a hiki i Kihahale. oia ka palena Oohia. [*Here are the properties I am telling you both about. ʻŌhiʻa, from Kalaʻinohoʻino comes my residence here in Waikapū. That is the property I lived on. Kalaʻinohoʻino died, I lived under Keʻeaumukū (sic). However ʻŌhiʻa was my first property. The boundaries of ʻŌhiʻa are Keālia that has the Salt and the sea and the plain of Kamaʻomaʻo, from the road until Kaumuku, from Kaumuku until Kihahale. That is the boundary of ʻŌhiʻa.*] " /Place Names (ULUK)/

280 Kiheipukoa
Kīheipūkoʻa
Kīhei-pūkoʻa

Meaning undetermined, perhaps: shawl of variegated colors, or, Kīhei reef.

———————

Shoreline area along the southwestern side of Keālia pond in the region of Māʻalaea, ahupuaʻa of Waikapū.

Variant: Kehei.

281 Kiikewe
Kiʻikewe
Kiʻi-kewe

Meaning undetermined, perhaps: crescent-shaped idol.

———————

Shoreline area in the ahupuaʻa of Waiheʻe.

———————

"Nolu mau ke one i Kiikewe i ka makani / Waliwali pepe i ka lomia, / E ka makani Kilioopu.... [*The sands at Kiʻikewe ever yield / Crushed soft as they are kneaded, / By the Kiliʻoʻopu wind....*]" /*Ka Nupepa Kuokoa*, Buke 7, Helu 40, 3 ʻOkakopa 1868/

"17. Haule i Kehoni i Kiikewe / 18. I kapa i Niua ke lii o Hua / 19. Hoi no i uka ka waihona.... [*17. Died at Kēhoni at Kiʻikewe / 18. Along the boundary of Niua was the chief Hua / 19. Taken upland to the sepulcher....*]" /*Ka Naʻi Aupuni*," Buke 2, Helu 64, 16 ʻAukake 1906/

282 Kiiwela
Kiʻiwela
Kiʻi-wela

Meaning undetermined, perhaps: to hold in the arms with passion.

———————

ʻIli in the ahupuaʻa of Wailuku.

Variant: Kiiwela Iki.

283 Kikia
Kikia / Kīkia / Kīkīa

Meaning and pronunciation undetermined, perhaps: kikia—plugged/patched, or stung; kīkia—shot, or expelled/expectorated/spit; or, kīkīa—spouted.

———————

ʻIli in the ahupuaʻa of Waikapū.

84 Kilipoe

See Kailipoe.

85 Kinihapai

Kinihāpai

Kini-hāpai

"*Lit.*, carry multitudes." /PNOH/

Tributary of 'Īao Stream, the middle portion of the Wailuku River, found in 'Īao Valley.

"Kukaʻi Moku* is the old name for Iao needle. On one side there is something like a ridge where there is a stone [*Ka Pili o Kakaʻe?*...]. It was there an alii hid, the chief who lived above at the place, Kaʻalāholo. Kaʻalāholo is table land on the left hand side of Iao Valley. Kinihapai is behind the needle." /SOM 82/

"During the four months of Makahiki and harvest season, which began with the rising of Makalii (the Pleiades) in the fall, the populace was allowed to enter 'Īao Valley to enjoy its delicious shrimp, 'oʻopu fish, and other delicacies in company with the alii.
    But the populace traveled the trail up Kini-hapai (Uplifting of the multitude) stream that flows by the base of Ku Ka Aʻe Moku [*Ku Kaʻe Moku*] (now called the Needle) while the alii followed Kapela stream past Ka Pili o Kakaʻe." /SOM 100/

86 Kiokio

Meaning and pronunciation undetermined, perhaps: kiokio—protruding rock heaps.

'Ili in the ahupuaʻa of Waiheʻe.

87 Kipapa

Kīpapa

"kī.papa 1. nvt. Pavement, level terrace; to pave, lay stones in pavement or terrace; to wall in, as with stones (GP 98). 2. vi. To be close together, as clouds, or as taro neatly packed in a load; to shoot together (see papa 3, Kel. 45). 3. n. A sweet potato..." /HD/

'Ili in the ahupuaʻa of Ahikuli, kalana of Waiehu.

88 Kiwe

Kīwē

Pronunciation and meaning undetermined, perhaps: kī- + wē—to sift.

Shoreline region in the ahupuaʻa of Waiheʻe.

"The traditions as written down by S. M. Kamakau runs thus: 'In the time of Kakaalaneo several foreigners (haole) arrived at Waihee in Maui, two of whom only were or became remarkable, viz: Kukanaloa and Pele, who was Peleie, and the name of the vessel was *Konaliloha*. They landed at Kiwe in the night and when discovered in the morning by the natives, they were taken to the village and fed and brought to the king and the chiefs who treated them kindly and made friends of them (hoopunahele) and admitted them to all the privileges of the kapu. They settled in the country, married some of the chief-women and became progenitors of both chiefs and commoners...'" /Fornander V6, 248/

289 Koalaina

See Kaalaino.

290 Koholaiki

Kohola-iki

Literally, lesser Kohola (reef flat).

Fishing ground off the shore of the kalana of Waiehu. *See also*: Nakohola.

291 Koholanui

Kohola-nui

Literally, greater Kohola (reef flat).

Fishing ground off the shore of the kalana of Waiehu. *See also*: Nakohola.

292 Koiahi

Koʻiahi

Koʻi-ahi

Literally, fire-adze, or fire-colored adze.

ʻIli and pond in the ahupuaʻa of Waiheʻe.

293 Koihale

Koi-hale

Meaning undetermined, perhaps: Koi house/building.

Heiau in the ahupuaʻa of Waiheʻe.

" 'A medium size heiau of about 90 ft. square, still to be seen.' (Thrum) 'Koihale Heiau, Walker Site 30. North side of Waihee stream down by shore. Stones removed to build pens.' (Sterling)" /Place Names (ULUK)/

94 Kolea
Kōlea

"kō.lea 1. nvi. Pacific golden plover (*Pluvialis dominica*), a migratory bird which comes to Hawai'i about the end of August and leaves early in May for Siberia and Alaska ... 4. n. Native species of trees and shrubs (*Myrsine* [*Rapanea, Suttonia*]) with oval to narrow leaves more or less crowded at branch tips, small flowers, and small round fruits among or below the leaves ... " /HD/

'Ili in the ahupua'a of Waihe'e.

95 Koloa
Koloa / Kōloa

Pronunciation and meaning undetermined, perhaps: kōloa—long cane with a crook /HD/; or, koloa—duck.

'Ili in the ahupua'a of Wailuku.

96 Koloapelu
Koloapelu / Kōloapelu
Kolo-a-pelu / Kōloa-pelu

Pronunciation and meaning undetermined, perhaps: kolo a pelu—crawl and turn back; or, kōloa pelu—bent long cane with a crook.

'Ili in the ahupua'a of Waikapū.

[NOTE: In one document, the name Kaloapelu was underlined, and "Koloapelu" written above it.]

Variant: Kaloapelu.

297 Koolau
Koʻolau

"Koʻo.lau n. 1. Windward sides of the Hawaiian Islands...2. *(Not cap.)* Short for koʻokoʻolau." /HD/

———————————

ʻIli in the ahupuaʻa of Waikapū.

298 Kope

"kope 1. nvt. Rake, shovel, dredge; to rake, scratch; scoop, as of a canoe paddle. Fig., to dislike, disregard..." /HD/

———————————

Gulch on the southeast face of Mauna Alani, ahupuaʻa of Kou, kalana of Waiehu.

299 Kou

"kou 1. n. A tree found on shores from East Africa to Polynesia (*Cordia subcordata*)..." /HD/

———————————

Ahupuaʻa in the kalana of Waiehu.

Also, and ʻIlikū in the kalana of Waiehu.

Variant: Ili o Kou.

300 Kuaina
See Kuaiwa.

301 Kuaiwa
Kuaiwa / Kū-āiwa

Pronunciation and meaning undertermined, perhaps: kuaiwa—ninth, or eleven generations back; kū āiwa—to appear divine.

[NOTE: A family with the name "Kuaiwa" pronounces it as "Kuaiwa."]

———————————

ʻIli (possibly an ʻili lele) in the ahupuaʻa of Waikapū.

Variants: Haaiwo, Kuaina.

02 Kuakahanahana
Kuakāhanahana
Kua-kāhanahana

Literally, to hew trees from the forest clearing.

———————

'Ili in the ahupua'a of Waihe'e.

03 Kuanui
Kua-nui

Literally, large beam or tapa anvil.

———————

'Ili in the ahupua'a of Wailuku.

04 Kuemanu
Kue-manu

Literally, to attract petrel birds by imitating their call.

———————

Heiau in the 'ili of Ka'ohe, ahupua'a of Wailuku.

———————

"O keia alanui hou, aia no ia mawaena aku o na wahi pana o keia kahawai. E hoomaka ana mai Kuemanu aku, he *Heiau* ia o Kaohe ka aina, o Kalanapoe ke kulanakauhale, a e holo komohana aku ana mai ke kulanakauhale aku o Wailuku. Nolaila, e ka poe kupa kamaaina o ke kahawai o Iao i hele aku ma kahi e, e ike mai oukou ua hiki ke kaa maloko o ke kahawai o Iao, a he nu hou ia au e olelo ae ai e ka mea i ike pono ia wahi. [*This new road, it's between the famed places of this valley. It starts from Kuemanu; that's a heiau of the land named Ka'ohe. Kālanapoe is the village, and it goes west from the town of Wailuku. So those residents familiar with the valley of 'Īao who went away, know that you can drive into the valley of 'Īao, and this is the news that I will say, you who know this place well.*] /Ka Nupepa Kuokoa, Buke 9, Helu 5, 29 Ianuali 1870/

05 Kuhimana
Kuhi-mana

Meaning undertermined, perhaps: kuhi mana—to delineate a branch in a stream.

———————

'Ili in the ahupua'a of Waiehu, kalana of Waiehu. [NOTE: this 'ili is located at a juncture where the North Waiehu Stream branch joins with the South Waiehu Stream branch to form Waiehu Stream.]

Variant: Kuhimana.

306 Kuipa

Kuipā / Kuʻipā
Kui-pā / Kuʻipā

Pronunciation and meaning undertermined, perhaps: kui pā—fence nail; kuʻi pā—to pound a fence, to join or splice a fence, or to attach the pā net onto a certain type of fishing "bag."

ʻIli, adjoined to the ʻili of Lāʻie, in the ahupuaʻa of Wailuku.

307 Kukaemoku

Kūkaemoku / Kūkaʻemoku
Kūkae-moku / Kū-kaʻe-moku

Pronunciation and meaning undetermined, perhaps: kūkae moku—severed excreta; or, kū kaʻe moku—standing on the projecting broken brow.

Name for the thin ridge within ʻĪao Valley above Kinihāpai Stream. In more recent times, this ridge has been called by the superimposed name of foreign origin "ʻĪao Needle." *See also*: Nanahoa & Puuokamoa.

"Kapela-o-Kakae, name of a large area in Iao Valley. There is one hill in the middle of the land known as Kukaʻe-moku." /SOM 94/

"Luahinepii scaled to the top of Kukaemoku, called Nanahoa, and from its dizzy height dashed herself headlong to the valley beneath, and the waters of Iao were made incarnadine with her blood." /Beringer, 1909/

308 Kukalepa

Kūkalepa / Kūkālepa
Kū-ka-lepa / Kū-kālepa

Pronunciation and meaning undertermined, perhaps: kū ka lepa—the flag stands; kū kālepa—place where traders and merchants stop.

ʻIli in the ahupuaʻa of Wailuku.

309 Kukuialaemaka

See Kukuialaimaka.

310 Kukuialaemoku

See Kukuialaimaka.

11 Kukuialaimaka
Kukuiālaimaka
Kukui-ālai-maka

Literally, kukui trees that obscure the view.

———————

'Ili in the ahupua'a of Waikapū, and the ahupua'a of Waiehu, kalana of Waiehu.

Variants: Kukuialamaka, Kukuialaemaka, Kukuialaemoku.

12 Kukuikomo
Kukui-komo

Literally, kukui [grove/tree] into which one enters.

———————

'Ili in the ahupua'a of Ahikuli, kalana of Waiehu. Also, a heiau in the same kalana.

———————

"Kukuikomo Heiau, Walker Site 40 / Location: On ridge between North and South Waiehu Gulches. Another heiau without walls or platforms." /SOM 58/

Variant: Kukuiokomo.

13 Kukuiokomo
See Kukuikomo.

14 Kula o Puhele
See Kula o Puuhele.

15 Kula o Puuhele
Kula o Pu'uhele
Kula o Pu'u-Hele

Literally, plains of Pu'u Hele.

———————

Presumably the flatland in the vicinity of Pu'u Hele in the region of Mā'alaea, ahupua'a of Waikapū.

———————

"Ia Kihapiilani a me kana wahine e noho nei ma ke alanui ma kahi o kela pohaku o Unula [*sic*] aia hoi hoomaka maila laua nei e iho a hiki ilalo o Kapoli, hele mai la o ke kula o Puhele a mamua aku oia wahi halawai mai la laua nei me kekahi mau kanaka e hele ana no kai o Kamaalaea me na haawe ukana.... [*As Kihāpi'ilani and his wife were sitting on the road in the vicinity of that stone called Unula [sic], they began to descend until they reached below Kapoli, then came until the Plains of Pu'u Hele (Puhele in originial) and*

before they reach there they met with some other people heading toward the sea of Kamāʻalaea
with their belongings....]" /*Ka Nupepa Kuokoa*, Buke 23, Helu 7, 16 Pepeluali 1884/

Variant: Kula o Puhele.

316 Kumukahi
Kumu-kahi

Literally, first origin, or, single tree trunk.

———

ʻIli in the ahupuaʻa of Waiehu, kalana of Waiehu.

317 Kumuwiliwili
Kumu-wiliwili

Literally, wiliwili tree.

———

ʻIli lele in the ahupuaʻa of Waiehu, kalana of Waiehu.

ʻIli in the ahupuaʻa of Wailuku.

318 Kunaheana
See Kuunaheana.

319 Kupaa
Kūpaʻa

Literally, steadfast.

———

Stream in the ahupuaʻa of Waiheʻe.

320 Kupalaua
See Kapalaoa.

321 Kuunahawelu
Kuʻunahāwelu
Kuʻuna-hāwelu

Pronunciation and meaning undetermined, perhaps: descent that tatters the clothing.

———

Name of ʻili—perhaps ʻili lele—in the ahupuaʻa of Ahikuli and Kou, kalana of Waiehu.

22 Kuunaheana
Ku'unaheana
Ku'una-heana

Literally, place where the first war victim was laid as sacrifice.

———————

'Ili in the ahupua'a of Wailuku.

Variants: Kunaheana, Kuunaheana Iki, Kuunaheana Nui.

23 Laaloa
See Loaloa.

24 Lae o Nakohola
See Nakohola

25 Laepohaku o Nakohola
See Nakohola

26 Laie
Lā'ie

"lā.'ie 1. Short for lau 'ie, 'ie vine leaf." /HD/

———————

'Ili in the ahupua'a of Wailuku.

Also, an area in 'Īao Valley found below Ka'alāholo.

———————

"Haalele iho la ia mau wahi a pii aku he ahua ia ahiki iluna, he kahua palahalaha maikai, o Laie makai nei, a o Kaalaholo mauka, he wahi oluolu a maikai loa keia e ku ai kekahi kakela hooluolu, a aole no e nele ke ohohia nui ia e na poe ake e hooluolu i na ola kino. [*We left these places and ascended a rise until, arriving on top, there was a nice flat area, Lā'ie was below, and Ka'alāholo was above; it was a very beautiful and pleasant place where a lovely castle could stand; there would never be a shortage of enthusiasm for it by people who wish to improve their health.*] /*Ka Nupepa Kuokoa*, Buke 37, Helu 5, 4 Pepeluali 1898/

27 Lamalii
Lamali'i / Lamāli'i
Lama-li'i / Lama-ali'i

Pronunciation and meaning undetermined, perhaps: lama li'i—small lama tree, small torch; or, lamāli'i (lama + ali'i)—chiefly torch.

———————

'Ili in the ahupua'a of Wailuku.

Variants: Lamalii Iki, Lamalii Nui.

328 Lanikeha

Lani-keha

Literally, lofty heaven.

___

The name of one of Kahekili's homes in the ahupua'a of Wailuku.

___

"The people of Hawaii lamented greatly. Kalani'opuu grieved over the destruction of his 'Alapa and Piipii warriors. At that time Kahekili was living in his house, Lanikeha, in Wailuku." /SOM 110/

329 Lanihale

Lahi-hale

Literally, house named Lani.

___

Area on the eastern side of Mau'oni Pond, ahupua'a of Wailuku.

330 Lapaleihua

Lapa-lei-hua / Lapa-leihua

Meaning undetermined, perhaps: lapa lei hua—fruit garland ridge; or, lapa leihua—globe amaranth ridge; or, perhaps a misrepresentation of: lapa lehua—*lehua* ridge.

___

Ridge on the Waikapū side of Kahoi, ahupua'a of Waikapū.

331 Lauhue

"lau.hue n. 1. A variety of poisonous gourd; to spread, of this vine." /HD/

___

'Ili in the ahupua'a of Waihe'e.

Variant: Kalauhue.

332 Lehuapueo

Lehua-pueo / Lehu-a-pueo

Meaning undetermined, perhaps: lehua pueo—(tree) ladened with owls; or, lehu a pueo—multitudes of owls.

___

'Ili in the ahupua'a of Waikapū.

33 Lelemako
Lele-mākō

Literally, thick rough-stone altar.

'Ili in the ahupua'a of Wailuku.

Also, a heiau in the same ahupua'a.

"Lelemako Heiau. Walker Site 50. Vicinity of Wailuku. Said to have been among those consecrated by Liholiho in his tour of Maui for that purpose about 1801." /HPN/

34 Lemukee
Lemu-ke'e

Literally, bulging buttocks.

'Ilikū in the ahupua'a of Wailuku.

35 Liliha

Literally, satisfied to the point of nausea, as with rich foods.

Name of the refuse pit of Haleki'i heiau in the 'ili of Paukūkalo, ahupua'a of Wailuku.

"The Luapa'u *[Luapa'ū* (sic) = *refuse pit]* Liliha, once surrounding the heiau [Haleki'i], has been filled with stones… Haleki'i is the heiau reserved for females of high rank and is situated on the makai side of the bluff—Kalola is another name. The whole combined in general is Pihana. It is said there is a cave beneath Pihana, and Liliha is the mouth of the cave." /SOM 72/

36 Limalau

Literally, cooperation.

Area mentioned in mele within the context of the ahupua'a of Waihe'e.

"O ka wai o Wailele, / Amoamo mai maluna, / O ka pua o ke kukui, / Ka'u ia e kilohi nei, / O ka ai hoeha ili, / O ka awa kona inoa, / Ke kahua o Limalau, e polehe [*sic*] ke kai ana…. [*The waters of Wailele, / Twinkling above, / The* kukui *flowers / Are what I am gazing at, / The stroke that pains the skin, / Its name is* 'awa, / *The site of Limalau, Slackens the procession….*]" /*Ka Hoku o ka Pakipika*, Buke 2, Helu 9, 11 Kekemapa 1862/

337 Loaloa

Pronunciation and meaning undetermined, perhaps: loaloa—"elongated garden plot, as for sweet potatoes (so used in 1848 land claims)." /HD/

_____

'Ili in the ahupua'a of Waikapū.

Variants: Kaloaloa, Laaloa.

338 Loikahi
Lo'ikahi
Lo'i-kahi

Literally, singular wetland taro patch.

_____

'Ili, adjoining the 'ili of Kapōkea, in the ahupua'a of Waihe'e.

339 Loiloa
Lo'iloa
Lo'i-loa

Literally, long wetland taro patch.

_____

'Ili found in 'Īao Valley, in the ahupua'a of Wailuku.

340 Lona

"1. n. Block of wood used to support a canoe out of water. 2. Useless, vain. 3. Straight, direct." /HD/

_____

Ridge on the south side of the upper reaches of the 'ili of 'Āwikiwiki in the ahupua'a of Waikapū.

341 Lonoakaulana
Lono-a-kaulana

Meaning undetermined, perhaps: Lono son of Kaulana, or, heard until well known.

_____

'Ili in the ahupua'a of Waihe'e.

42 Luahinepii
Luahinepi'i
Luahine-pi'i

Literally, climbing old woman.

Unawarded 'ili described in Māhele records as being on the south side of the Wailuku River, mentioned in the context of the 'ili of Hala'ula in the ahupua'a of Wailuku.

Perhaps related to the story of the beautiful woman name Luahinepi'i who, distraught at being teased about her unpleasant voice, climbed to the top Nānahoa and leapt to her death.

"Luahinepii scaled to the top of Kukaemoku, called Nanahoa, and from its dizzy height dashed herself headlong to the valley beneath, and the waters of Iao were made incarnadine with her blood." /Beringer, 1909/

Variant: Luahipii.

43 Luahipii
See Luahinepii

44 Lualailua
Luala'ilua
Lua-la'i-lua

Literally, "two-fold tranquility" /PNOH/.

'Ili in the ahupua'a of Waiehu, kalana of Waiehu.

45 Luapuaa
Luapua'a
Lua-pua'a

Literally, pig pit.

'Ili in the ahupua'a of Waikapū.

46 Luapueo
Lua-pueo

Literally, owl pit.

'Ili in the ahupua'a of Waikapū.

347 Maalaea

Māʻalaea
Mā-ʻalaea

Literally, origin of ocherous earth.

———————

Region, perhaps an ʻili, in the ahupuaʻa of Waikapū. Prior to the diversion of the Waikapū River into this region, Māʻalaea, along with the ʻilikū of Keālia, was largely farmed for salt, which was produced in loʻi paʻakai. Also, a newer name for the sea known as Kai o ʻĀnehe.

A story relating to Māʻalaea, shared with the author by Maui kupuna Diane Amadeo, is herein paraphrased: When Pele fled from the Lahaina side, after a fight with Nāmaka-okahaʻi, she created Haleakalā for her family and herself. The favorite food of Pele and her sisters is pēʻū [ceremonially prepared lūʻau leaves cooked with salt]. But on this side of the island, their followers had no salt with which to prepare it. So Pele created Māʻalaea—then called Kamāʻalaea—and then took some salt [of her tears in one version, and some that she had kept since Kauaʻi in another] and created Keālia Pond. The lūʻau for their pēʻū was grown on Puʻu Lūʻau, above Māʻalaea.

Variant: Kamaalaea.

348 Mahalani Cemetery

Maha-lani

Literally, heavenly rest.

———————

Cemetery on the north side of the Waiehu Stream in the ahupuaʻa of Ahikuli, kalana of Waiehu.

349 Mahukaaawe

Mahukaʻawe
Mahuka-ʻawe

Pronunciation and meaning undetermined, perhaps: to flee bearing a burden on the back.

———————

ʻIli in the ahupuaʻa of Wailuku.

Variant: Mahukaawenui.

50 Makaaka

Makaaka / Māka'akā
Maka-aka / Māka'a-kā

Pronunciation and meaning undetermined, perhaps: maka aka—bud protruding from the node of a stalk; or, māka'a kā: *māka'a*—sweet potato sending forth vine-slips.

———

'Ili in the ahupua'a of Waihe'e.

51 Makaalae

Maka'alae
Maka-'alae

Literally, "mud-hen's eyes" /PNOH/.

———

'Ili in the ahupua'a of Waihe'e.

Variant: Kaalae.

52 Makaelelu

Maka'elelū
Maka-'elelū

Literally, cockroach's eyes.

———

'Ili in the ahupua'a of Waikapū.

53 Makahilahila

Maka-hilahila

Literally, bashful eyes.

———

'Ili in the ahupua'a of Waikapū.

Variant: Makahelahela.

54 Makailima

Maka'ilima
Maka-'ilima

Literally, new 'ilima plant shoots, or, center of the 'ilima blossom, or, place where the 'ilima region begins.

———

'Ili in the ahupua'a of Waikapū.

355 Makaku
See Pohaku o Makaku.

356 Makanipalua
Makanipālua
Makani-pālua

"Makani pālua, wind blowing in various directions." /HD/

Sand ridge in the ahupuaʻa of Wailuku.

"...ia manawa i haalele ai ke alii [Kihāpiʻilani] ia Waiehu, o ua kanaka nei ma mua—a mahope mai ke alii, o ko lakou nei hele mai la no ia a hiki i Wailuku, iho pono aku la i kai o Pohaku pii aku la maluna o ke kualapa one o Makanipalua ka inoa, aole i emo, hehi ana na kapuai i ke one hone o Kahului.... [...*at the time the chief [Kihāpiʻilani] left Waiehu, that person was in front—and behind was the chief; they went until they arrived at Wailuku, went straight down toward the sea below Pōhaku, ascended the sand ridge by the name of Makanipālua; in no time, the soles of their feet were treading upon the supple sands of Kahului....*]" /*Ka Nupepa Kuokoa*, Buke 23, Helu 7, 16 Pepeluali 1884/

See also: Puuone and Wao Akua One.

357 Makawela

"maka.wela 1. nvs. Glowing, burning; full of hate, fury, anger. *Fig.* term for the despised kauā, outcasts...2. n. Type of stone from which weights for cowry octopus lures were made. 3. Same as wela 3. (A new field, as of sweet potatoes; a piece of land cleared for planting by burning.)" /HD/

ʻIli in the ahupuaʻa of Wailuku.

Makawela is also the name of a division of the Wailuku Fishery directly offshore of this ʻili. From west to east, the divisions of the fishery are: Kaʻehu a ka Mōʻī, Paukūkalo, Malaehaʻakoa (Malehaakoa on the original map), Kaihuwaʻa, Makawela, Kahului, Puʻuiki, Kaipuʻula, Kanahā, Palaʻeke, Kalua, Kaʻa, Hopukoʻa Nui, Hopukoʻa Iki, Papaʻula, Kapahu, Palaha, Wawaʻu (Kawau on the original map), Kānepaʻina, and Kahue. /H.K.L. & R.L., 1947/

Variant: Kawela.

358 Makole
Mākole

Literally, bloodshot eyes.

ʻIli in the ahupuaʻa of Wailuku.

"Claim No 215. Henry L. Brooks—This is a claim to a certain piece of land at Wailuku, Maui, known by the name of "Makole" together with a certain fishing ground, named "Papaulu [*sic*]." /Foreign Register (KPA)/

59 Malaehaakoa
Malaeha'akoa
Malae-ha'akoa

Meaning undetermined, perhaps: feigning friendship bravely.

Heiau in the 'ili of Paukūkalo, ahupua'a of Wailuku. Located makai of Haleki'i on the south side of the Wailuku River on Nehe Point. Spelled as "Malaihakoa" in some sources.

"Haena ka lae o ke kanaka, / Luu kai o Malaehaakoa, / Ihu kole ula Kaihuwaa i ka makani.... [*The forehead of the person is inflamed, / Diving in the sea of Malaeha'akoa, / Kaihuwa'a is raw-nosed in the wind....*]" /*Ka Nupepa Kuokoa*, Buke 7, Helu 40, 3 'Okakopa 1868/

"Recorded by Walker 1931; '...Heiau sites destroyed on the northeast coast of east Maui...' [Walker 1931]." /State Inventory of Historic Places (SHPD)/

Name (Malaihakoa) recorded for at least one other heiau in Wai'anae Waena (O'ahu).

Malaeha'akoa is also the name of a division of the Wailuku Fishery directly below the heiau. From west to east, the divisions of the fishery are: Ka'ehu o ka Mō'ī, Paukūkalo, Malaeha'akoa (Malehaakoa on the original map), Kaihuwa'a, Makawela, Kahului, Pu'uiki, Kaipu'ula, Kanahā, Pala'eke, Kalua, Ka'a, Hopuko'a Nui, Hopuko'a Iki, Papa'ula, Kapahu, Palaha, Wawa'u (Kawau on the original map), Kānepa'ina, and Kahue. /H.K.L. & R.L., 1947/

Variant: Malaihakoa.

60 Malaihakoa
See Malaehaakoa.

61 Malaihi
Māla'ihi
Māla-'ihi

Literally, sacred garden.

Modern-day region along Malaihi Road in the ahupua'a of Waiehu, kalana of Waiehu. Perhaps named for an original Māhele allottee of the area.

362 Malama
Malama / Mālama

Pronunciation undetermined, perhaps: "malama 1. n. Light, month, moon" /HD/; or, "mā.lama 1. nvt. To take care of, tend, attend, care for, preserve, protect, beware, save, maintain; to keep or observe, as a taboo; to conduct, as a service; to serve, honor, as God; care, preservation, support, fidelity, loyalty; custodian, caretaker, keeper...b. *(Cap.)* Star name. 2. n. Pancreas. 3. *(Cap.)* n. [type of] Stroke in lua fighting." /HD/

Area found to the east of Kanahā, just inland of Ka'a, ahupua'a of Wailuku.

363 Malaukanaloa
Malau-kanaloa

Meaning undertermined, perhaps: malau kanaloa—spoiled young surge wrasse.

'Ili in the ahupua'a of Waihe'e.

364 Malelewaa
Malelewa'a
Malele-wa'a

"*Lit.*, scattered canoes." /PNOH/

Inland area in 'Īao Valley, ahupua'a of Wailuku.

"Malelewaa, land in upland of Iao." /SOM 94/

365 Malena
Mālena

"mā.lena 1. n. Ashes used as medicine, as of bamboo or makaloa reed. 2. vs. Tight, taut. 3. vs. Yellow. 4. Same as 'ōlena, turmeric." /HD/

Heiau in the ahupua'a of Wailuku.

"'Malena, Wailuku. No particulars...named among those consecrated by Liholiho...preceeding [*sic*] the peleleu fleet.' (Thrum) 'Walker Site 48.'" /Place Names (ULUK)/

366 Malu a ka Hekuawa
Malu a ka Hēkuawa

Literally, Shading of the High Cliffside Valleys.

Poetic epithet for the Nāwaiʻehā region.

———————

"Ua olelo ia, ua hiki like na pueo a pau loa i ka po o Kane. Ma na wahi a pau loa a lakou e hoomoana nei. A i ke ao ana o Lono ka hoouka ana o ke kaua ma Wailuku. Aole o kana mai keia hoouka kaua o na pueo me na kanaka a me na alii, a ua nui ka make o kanaka ma ia la ma Na Wai Eha. A ua make hoi o Kapoi a me kana wahine. A no ia luku ana a ka pueo i kapa ia ai ka inoa o Wailuku a hiki i keia la. A ua olelo pu ia no hoi, no ka malu ana o ka la ma ia la no ka paa o ka lewa i na pueo, ka mea i kapa mua ia ai o ka Maluakahekuawa a hiki i keia la. [*It is said that the owls all arrived on the night of Kāne. They were encamped everywhere. The battle was launched in Wailuku at the dawning of Lono. Nothing can compare to the tremendous nature of this war waged between the owls, the commoners, and chiefs and there were many human deaths at Nāwaiʻehā. And Kapoi and his wife were indeed killed. Because of this destruction caused by the owls, this area is called Wailuku until today. Concerning the darkening of the sun on this day because of the great numbers of owls that filled the sky, it is also said that this is the reason that the name Malu-a-ka-hēkuawa (The Shading of the High Cliffside Valleys) was first coined until this day.*] /Ke Au Okoa, Buke 7, Helu 11, 29 Iune 1871/

Maluhia

"malu.hia nvs. Peace, quiet, security, tranquillity, serenity; safety; solemn awe and still-ness that reigned during some of the ancient taboo ceremonies; peaceful, restful." /HD/

———————

Famed fishing ground and stone off the shore of the kalana of Waiehu.

———————

"Pōhaku Maluhia. Fishing site, rock, Waiehu, Maui. Large rock in the ocean off Waiehu that is only visible from shore at low tide when the ocean is calm. During the 1920s a subdivision here was named the Maluhia Beach Lots after the rock, and the church in the middle of the subdivision was called Maluhia Church. Lit., peaceful rock." /HPN/

"Hookapu Kai Lawaia! Ua kapu kuu mau Kai Lawaia apau loa i ikeia ma na inoa pakahi—Maluhia, Waioeo, Aawa, Kohola-iki ame Kohola-nui, na kai lawaia o ke Ahupuaa o Waiehu, Mokupuni a Kalana o Maui. Ua hoolimalima ia e H. N. Birch ke kai lawaia o Maluhia; a o G. P. Kihamahana kaʻu luna kiai no na kai eha i koe iho. Ua mana ia laua ka hooko ana i ke kanawai o ka aina. Lokalia Kananialii Blaisdell. Hono-lulu, Dec. 14, 1906. [*Fishing Ground Prohibition! All of my fishing grounds, the fishing grounds of the Ahupuaʻa of Waiehu, Island and County of Maui, known by the individual names of Maluhia, Waiʻōeo, ʻAʻawa, Koholaiki and Koholanui are off limits. The fishing ground of Maluhia has been rented by H. N. Birch; and G. P. Kihamahana is my over-seer for the remaining four grounds. They have the authority to uphold the law of the land. Lokalia Kananialiʻi Blaisdell. Honolulu, Dec. 14, 1906.*] /Ka Naʻi Aupuni, Buke 3, Helu 4, 4 Ianuali 1907/

Variant: Pohaku Maluhia.

368 Maluhia Beach Lots

Subdivision found upon lands formerly belonging to Lunalilo in the ahupuaʻa of Ahikuli, kalana of Waiehu.

—

"Pōhaku Maluhia. Fishing site, rock, Waiehu, Maui. Large rock in the ocean off Waiehu that is only visible from shore at low tide when the ocean is calm. During the 1920s a subdivision here was named the Maluhia Beach Lots after the rock, and the church in the middle of the subdivision was called Maluhia Church. Lit., peaceful rock." /HPN/

369 Maluihi
Maluʻihi
Malu-ʻihi

Literally, reverent peace.

—

Shoreline area mentioned in the context of Mālama in the ahupuaʻa of Wailuku. Perhaps related to the Oʻahu-born princess Kahamaluʻihiikeaoʻihilani (a.k.a. Kahamaluʻihi) who named the nearby ponds of Kanahā and Mauʻoni.

—

"Lea kahela i ke one o Malama, / I ka nome ia e ke one o Maluihi, / I ka noke aihaa ia e ke kai o Kehu, / Ahu kapeke lua i ka nalu o Huiha, / I ka pinai mau ia e ka nalu o Kaakau, / Haki nuanua i ka lae o Hihika.... [*Spreading merrily across the sands of Mālama, / Being slowly consumed by the sands of Maluʻihi, / Vigorously persisted upon by the sea of Kēhu, / Laid completely exposed by the waves of Huihā, / Repeatedly encroached upon by the the the waves of Kaʻākau, / Which break along the point of Hīhīkā....*]" /*Ka Nupepa Kuokoa,* Buke 7, Helu 40, 3 ʻOkakopa 1868/

"Graciously the Oahu princess [Kahamaluʻihiikeaoʻihilani] named the pond makai, Kana-ha, in honor of her brother Kanahaokalani, and the mauka pond, Mauoni, the name of her incognito." /SOM 103/

370 Malumaluakua
Malumalu-akua

"Malumalu akua, shelter or protection of the gods." /HD/

—

Unidentified heiau attributed to Kahekili for Kāne in the ahupuaʻa of Waiehu, kalana of Waiehu.

—

"Location: Head of south Waiehu Gulch." /SOM 57/

"Malumaluakua, Wailuku. No particulars ... named among those consecrated by Liho-liho ... preceeding [*sic*] the peleleu fleet." /Place Names (ULUK)/

71 Mananole
Mana-nole

"Stream, Wai-luku qd., Maui. *Lit.*, weak branch." /PNOH/

_____

Tributary stream to the Waiheʻe River, the head of which lies below ʻEke Crater.

72 Maniania
Māniania

Literally, "redup. of mania 1. nvi. Shuddering sensation as on looking down a great height, or hearing a saw filed; dizziness; dizzy; to shudder; to be contracted."

_____

ʻIlikū in the ahupuaʻa of Wailuku.

Variant: Manienie.

73 Maniania Ditch

Ditch originating in ʻĪao Valley (Wailuku Ahupuaʻa) that carries water to Waiehu Ahupuaʻa.

_____

"Takes water from Iao Stream at 800 ft. elevation toward Waiehu." /HPN/

Variant: Iao Maniania Ditch.

74 Manienie
See Maniania.

75 Manokohala
See Manukohala.

76 Manoni
See Mauoni.

77 Manukohala
Manu-kohala

Meaning undetermined, perhaps: bird from Kohala.

_____

ʻIli in the ahupuaʻa of Ahikuli, kalana of Waiehu.

Variant: Manokohala.

378 Maui Veterans Highway

The new name of what was once known as Mokulele Highway, Route 311.

"The state Legislature renamed Mokulele Highway, which connects Kahului and Kihei, Maui Veterans Highway last session, and road signs reflecting the new name have gone up." / *The Maui News*, 17 'Okakopa 2017/

379 Maui Waena

Literally, Central Maui.

A synonym for the ahupua'a of Wailuku.

"Ua hoolaha mai ke Kahu Kula Sabati Nui, he aha mele ke wehe ia ana i ke ahiahi Poakahi la 26 ae, no ka pomaikai no o ka hale Kahu o Waihee. Hoolaha mai ke Kahu o ka Makani Kuehu Lepo o Paia he Hoike Kula Sabati na Kula Sabati oia lehelehe o Maui-waena...O ka mea kakau kekahi i kono ia mai e ke Kahu Kula Sabati Nui o Maui waena. He ha'oha'o ko'u, elua Kahu Kula Sabati Nui o na Maui-waena nei. No kela aoao e pili la i ka Mauna Haleakala kekahi, no keia lehelehe e pili nei i na Mauna o Eeka kekahi. Ua kuhihewa paha au. Ea! Ae. 'Elua io no.' [*The Lead Sunday School Pastor publicized that it would be a concert that would be opening on Monday evening, the next 26th, for the blessing of the Pastor's house of Waihe'e. The Pastor of the Kuehu Lepo Wind of Paia announced a Sunday School Performance by the Sunday Schools of that lip of Maui Waena... The author was one who was invited by the Head Sunday School Director of central Maui. I was surprised; there are two Head Sunday School Directors of the places here called central-Maui. One from that side near Mount Haleakalā, and one from this lip near the Mountains of 'E'eka as well. Maybe I was wrong. What! Yes. 'Truly two.'*] /Ka Nupepa Kuokoa*, Buke 38, Helu 2, 13 Ianuali 1899/

380 Mauka Cave

Unidentified cave located in 'Īao Valley, Wailuku Ahupua'a, and found on the "Hydrographic Map of the Island of Maui, Territory of Hawaii." /USGS/

381 Mauna Alani
Mauna Alani

Literally, alani moss mountain.

Prominent mountain that rises above the kalana of Waiehu and the ahupua'a of Waihe'e.

Variants: Maunaalani, Mt. Alani.

82 Maunaihi
   Mauna'ihi
   Mauna-'ihi

   Literally, sacred mountain.

   Prominent sand dune, and burial ground therein, above the 'ili of Kapoho, Lo'ikahi, and Kapōkea, ahupua'a of Waihe'e.

83 Mauna Kane
   See Puukane.

84 Mauna Leo
   See Puu Lio.

85 Mauna Lio
   See Puu Lio.

86 Mauoni
   Mau'oni
   Mau-'oni

   Pronunciation and meaning undetermined, perhaps: to affix that which moves.

   Pond once conjoined to Kanahā Pond in the Kahului/Ka'a region of Wailuku.

   "Graciously the Oahu princess [Kahamalu'ihiikeao'ihilani] named the pond makai, Kana-ha, in honor of her brother Kanahaokalani, and the mauka pond, Mauoni, the name of her incognito." /SOM 103/

   " 'Kapiiohookalani, king of Oahu and half of Molokai, built the banks or kuapa of Kanaha and Mauoni, known as the twin ponds of Kapiioho…The ponds were completed by Kamehamehanui, king of Maui…' (Sterling #103). 'Kiha-a-Piilani is the one who separated the water of the pond, giving it two names [Kanaha and Mauoni].' (Sterling #105)." /Place Names (ULUK)/

   Variant: Manoni.

87 Mehani

   Literally, "1. nvs. Hot, heat, but less hot than 'ena'ena; unapproachable, as of a high taboo chief. 2. vs. Smooth, curved." /HD/

   'Ili in the ahupua'a of Polipoli, kalana of Waiehu.

388 Mokapu
Mōkapu
Mō-kapu

Literally, sacred district.

Area mentioned in mele in the context of Mauna'ihi within the ahupua'a of Waihe'e.

"Hele haaheo ka uhane, / I ka luna e Kaaloa, / I kilohi iho ko hana, / I ka haki nua a ka lio, / I ka lai o Maunaihi, / He lio holo waliwali, / I ke one o Mokapu.... [*The spirit goes proudly, / Upon Ka'aloa, / You gaze down, / While the horse traverses, / Across the tranquility of Mauna'ihi, / A horse that travels smoothly, / Upon the sands of Mōkapu....*] / Ka Hoku o ka Pakipika, Buke 2, Helu 9, 11 Kekemapa 1862/

"Me he a-i la no ka nene ke auau, / Ka haki palalahiwa i ke one o Mokapu / Kukaliki ka ii i ke one o Kaihumoku.... [*Like the neck of the* nēnē *goose as it swims, / The indulgent rumbling utterance across the sands of Mōkapu / The gutteral rasp boasting along the sands of Kaihumoku....*]" / Ka Nupepa Kuokoa, Buke 7, Helu 40, 3 'Okakopa 1868/

"Aloha Kaihumoku kahi kaulana oia uka / O Kauahia kai luna o Mokapu kai lalo. [*Fond memories of Kaihumoku the famed place of those uplands / Kauahia is above and Mōkapu is below.*]" / Ko Hawaii Pae Aina, Buke 3, Helu 33, 14 'Aukake 1880/

389 Mokuhau
Moku-hau

Literally, hau tree grove.

'Ili in the ahupua'a of Wailuku.

390 Mokuilima
See Kamokuilima.

391 Mokulele Highway
Moku-lele

Literally, airplane.

The former name of the Maui Veterans Highway, Route 311.

"The state Legislature renamed Mokulele Highway, which connects Kahului and Kihei, Maui Veterans Highway last session, and road signs reflecting the new name have gone up." / *The Maui News,* 17 'Okakopa 2017/

92 Mookahi
Mo'o-kahi

Meaning undetermined, perhaps: mo'o kahi—single strip of land.

'Ili in the ahupua'a of Polipoli, kalana of Waiehu.

Also, an 'ili in the ahupua'a of Waihe'e.

93 Naele
See Kanaele.

94 Naholomahana
Naholomāhana
Naholo-māhana

Pronunciation and meaning undetermined, perhaps: to flee as a pair.

Gulch and intermittent stream tributary of the Waikapū Stream, in the ahupua'a of Waikapū.

"Intermittent stream rises at about 2600 ft. elevation, joins Waikapu Stream at about 620 ft." /Place Names (ULUK)/

95 Na Hono a Piikea
Nā Hono a Pi'ikea

Literally, the bays of Pi'ikea.

Poetic epithet for the northern region of the moku of Wailuku.

"The valleys on the Lahaina side are known as the valleys of Piilani (Na Hono a Piilani). The valleys on the Waihee side are known as the valleys of Piikea (Piilani's sister), Na Hono a Piikea." /SOM 1/

96 Nakalaloa
Nākalaloa
Nā-kala-loa

Literally, the long house-gables.

Upland tributary of Kapela Stream, the upper portion of the Wailuku River, originating below Pu'ukukui in the ahupua'a of Wailuku. *See also*: Nanahoa.

"['Īao Stream] Stream begins at the junction of Poonahoahoa and Nakalaloa streams at about 1100 ft. elevation, flows to sea. Sometimes called 'Wailuku River' in descriptions of awards." /Place Names (ULUK)/

397 Nakohola

Nākohola

Nā-kohola

Literally, the reef flats.

See also: Koholanui & Koholaiki

———

Shoreline point, also commonly seen as "Lae o Nakohola," "Laepohaku o Nakohola," and "kai o Nakohola," found in the kalana of Waiehu.

———

"Holu pipio ka wai o Paihi i ka makani / Ua ii mau i ka wai o Kaikoo, / I ke ka alele ia e ke one o Halekii, / Puliki ka aweawe hee i Nakohola, / I ke koali hoomoe ia e ke kaahaaha. [*The waters of Paihī arch rippling in the wind / Ever gathering the water of Kaikoʻo, / As it reels on toward the sands of Halekiʻi, / The octopus tentacles embrace Nākohola, / Amidst the morning glory vines flattened by the Kāʻahaʻaha (wind).*]" /*Ka Nupepa Kuokoa*, Buke 7, Helu 40, 3 ʻOkakopa 1868/

398 Nanahoa

Nānahoa / Nānāhoa

Nā-nahoa / Nānā-hoa

Pronunciation and meaning undetermined, perhaps: nā nahoa—the head wounds, or, the defiant ones; or, nānā hoa—to care for a companion, or to look at a companion.

———

Name for the top of the thin ridge of Kūkaʻemoku within ʻĪao Valley above Kinihāpai Stream. In more recent times, this ridge has been called by the superimposed name of foreign origin " ʻĪao Needle." (*See also*: Poonahoahoa, Kukaemoku, & Puuokamoa).

———

"Luahinepii scaled to the top of Kukaemoku, called Nanahoa, and from its dizzy height dashed herself headlong to the valley beneath, and the waters of Iao were made incarnadine with her blood." /Beringer, 1909/

399 Napoko

Nāpoko

Nā-poko

Literally, the short (districts).

———

Perhaps the former name of an ahupuaʻa in what has become the kalana of Waiehu. Now, a collective name for the "short" ahupuaʻa of the kalana of Waiehu: Kou, Hananui, and Polipoli. These ahupuaʻa do not extend to the top of the Wailuku moku. Instead, their uppermost boundaries are along the ridge that separates the ahupuaʻa of Waiheʻe from the kalana of Waiehu.

Another explanation for the *poko* land unit comes from *Hawaiian Antiquities*:

"6. These districts are subdivided into other sections which are termed sometimes *okana* and sometimes *kalana*. A further subdivision within the *okana* is the *poko*." /Malo, 1903/

00 Nawaieha / Na Wai Eha
Nāwaiʻehā / Nā Wai ʻEhā

Literally, the four *wai-*/waters. (Formal name form: Nāwaiʻehā.)

———————

A collective and poetic name for the moku of Wailuku, the four "wai" being the ahupuaʻa of Waikapū, Wailuku, and Waiheʻe; and the kalana of Waiehu.

01 Nehe

"nehe 1. vi. To rustle, as leaves or the sea; rumbling; groping with the hands, as in searching...4. n. Native shrubs and herbs (*Lipochaeta* spp.) in the daisy family, with yellow flowers." /HD/

———————

ʻIli on the south side of the Wailuku River at Nehe Point, ahupuaʻa of Wailuku.

Also, the seaside point of land bisected by the Wailuku River.

Variant: Kanehe.

02 Nelu

"nelu nvs. Flabby fat; soft, as fine, worked-up soil (see ex., mehelu); boggy, marshy, springy, swampy; mire, bog, marsh; soft plumpness." /HD/

———————

Unidentified ʻili in the ahupuaʻa of Waiheʻe.

03 Niu

Literally, coconut.

———————

Area in the vicinity of Pihana, ahupuaʻa of Wailuku. Perhaps near the ʻili of Pāʻūniu.

———————

"The bones of Lono-a-Pi'i were sought out by Kiha-Pi'i-lani in order to desecrate them, and the people of Hawaii dug around Niu close to Pihana in Wailuku in an attempt to find them, but they were never discovered." /SOM 120/

404 Niukukahi
Niukūkahi
Niu-kū-kahi

Literally, lone standing coconut tree.

Famed surf area located somewhere along the shore of the kalana of Waiehu. Perhaps the same as "Nukukahi."

405 Nohoana
Noho'ana
Noho-'ana

Preferred pronunciation and spelling of modern descendants of this 'ili: "Residence, dwelling, seat, mode of life, existence, relationship." /HD/

'Ili in the ahupua'a of Waikapū.

406 Nukukahi
Nuku-kahi

Meaning undetermined, perhaps: single (harbor) entrance, or, single beak.

A fishery and a destroyed heiau in the kalana of Waiehu. Perhaps the same as "Niukūkahi."

"Of this heiau nothing now remains but a heap of stones." /Place Names (ULUK)/

407 Nuukole
Nu'ukole

"Same as hi'ukole, a fish. (hi'u.kole n. A fresh-water 'o'opu fish with a pinkish tail [hi'u kole]. It is taboo to some because it is believed related to the mo'o lizard gods.)" /HD/

Name of the appurtenant fishery of the 'ili of Hāli'ipālahalaha, ahupua'a of Waikapū, in the vicinity of the current Mā'alaea Harbor.

Variants: Anukoli, Nuukoli.

408 Nuukoli
See Nuukole.

09 Ohia
'Ōhi'a

" 'ō.hi'a 1. n. Two kinds of trees: see 'ōhi'a 'ai and 'ōhi'a lehua … 3. n. A native variety of sugar cane … 4. n. A variety of taro. 5. n. A red birthmark, said to be caused by the pregnant mother's longing for mountain apples ('ohi'a 'ai) and eating them. 6. vs. Tabooed, as food patches during famine, so-called because people did not eat from their taro patches, but from upland 'ōhi'a 'ai, ti, and sweet potatoes." /HD/

The name for 'ili in the ahupua'a of Waikapū, Waihe'e, and an 'ili lele in the ahupua'a of Waiehu in the kalana of Waiehu.

Also, the name of an 'auwai in the ahupua'a of Waiehu, kalana of Waiehu.

Variants: Ohianui, Ohiaiki.

10 Olohe
'Ōlohe

" 'ō.lohe 1. vs. Bare, naked, barren; hairless, as a dog; bald; destitute, needy … 2. nvs. Skilled, especially in lua fighting, so called perhaps because the beards of lua fighters were plucked and their bodies greased; bones of hairless men were desired for fish hooks because such men were thought stronger; also said of hula experts; skilled fighter. 3. vs. Pale … 4. vs. Sick, as after childbirth. 5. n. Ghost; image, as in clouds" /HD/; "O-lo-he, s. … 2. Ke akua o Kamaomao." /Andrews/

'Ili lele in the ahupua'a of Waikapū.

Also, the name of the akua of Kama'oma'o.

11 Olokua
Olokua / 'Olokua
Olo-kua / 'Olo-kua

Pronunciation and meaning undetermined, perhaps: olo kua—hill toward the back; or, elided forms of: olo (a)kua—appeal to a deity, or, deity hill; or, 'olo (a)kua—'awa cup of a deity.

Heiau in the ahupua'a of Wailuku.

" 'Olokua, Wailuku. No particulars … named among those consecrated by Liholiho … preceeding [*sic*] the peleleu fleet.' (Thrum) 'Walker Site 46.' " /Place Names (ULUK)/

412 Oloolokalani

Oloolokalani / ʻOloʻolokalani
Oloolo-ka-lani / ʻOloʻolo-ka-lani

Pronunciation and meaning undetermined, perhaps: oloolo ka lani—the heavens resound; or, ʻoloʻolo ka lani—the heavens overflow.

Heiau in the ahupuaʻa of Wailuku.

"Oloolokalani Heiau. Walker Site 54. Vicinity of Wailuku. Said to have been among those consecrated by Liholiho in his tour of Maui for that purpose about 1801." /Place Names (ULUK)/

413 Olopio

Olopio / Olopiʻo
Olo-pio / Olo-piʻo

Pronunciation and meaning undetermined, perhaps: olo pio—prisoner hill; or, olo piʻo—bent hill.

Area in which the famed burial cave of ʻĪao, in the ahupuaʻa of Wailuku, is said to be located.

Also, the name of a heiau said to have been consecrated by Liholiho.

"ʻOlopio, Wailuku. No particulars...named among those consecrated by Liholiho...preceeding [*sic*] the peleleu fleet.' (Thrum) 'Walker Site 47.'" /Place Names (ULUK)/

414 Olopua

"olo.pua 1. n. A large native tree (*Osmanthus sandwicensis*), to 19 m high, in the olive family. It bears narrow or oblong leaves, yellowish flowers, and blue 1.3 cm-long fruits. The hard wood, dark-brown with black streaks, was used for spears, adze handles, and digging sticks." /HD/

Region near the northeastern boundary of the ahupuaʻa and moku of Wailuku. Most likely associated with the landmark Pōhaku o Olopua.

"A place in the vicinity of Village 2 and Puu Nene. Coordinates approximate." /Place Names (ULUK)/

15 Omao
'Ōma'o

"'ō.ma'o 1. nvs. Green, as plants. 2. n. A bundle wrapped in green leaves, as of ti, for carrying food. Rare. 3. n. Hawai'i thrush (*Phaeornis obscurus obscurus*). 4. n. Greenish tapa...6. (Cap.) n. Star name (no data)." /HD/

'Ili in the ahupua'a of Waiehu, kalana of Waiehu.

Variant: Omaa.

16 Onihi

Pronunciation and meaning undetermined, perhaps representative of: 'o nihi—*nihi* (edge, steep).

Ridge that descends from 'Ānāhi in the kalana of Waiehu that separates the upper regions of the two ahupua'a of Hananui and Kou.

17 Ooawa Kilika
'Oawa Kilikā

Perhaps representative of: 'o 'oawa kilikā—moving shower valley.

Valley/gulch in the ahupua'a of Waikapū.

18 Oukea
'Ō'ūkea / 'Ouke'a
'Ō'ū-kea / 'Ou-ke'a

Pronunciation and meaning undetermined, perhaps: 'ō'ū kea—white 'ō'ū bird, or, to perch on a purline; or, 'ou ke'a—protruding purline, or, to pierce with a dart/arrow.

'Ili in the ahupua'a of Wailuku.

19 Owa
'Owā

"'owā Var. spelling of 'oā 1. vi. Split, cracked, burst, grooved; to split, crack."

'Ili lele in the ahupua'a of Wailuku.

A conspicuous 'owā (crack, groove) of this region is exhibited in the natural groove in the high sand dune through which a modern road has been built.

420 Paakukui
Paʻakukui
Paʻa-kukui

Meaning undetermined, perhaps: paʻa kukui—light holder; or, an abreviated form of pāpaʻa kukui—kukui tree bark.

———————

ʻIli in the ahupuaʻa of Wailuku.

421 Paalae
Paʻalae / Pāʻalae
Paʻa-lae / Pā-ʻalae

Pronunciation and meaning undetermined, perhaps: paʻa lae—solidified into a geographic point, or, foundation of the brow of a hill; or, pā ʻalae—mudhen lot.

———————

ʻIli in the ahupuaʻa of Waikapū.

422 Paaole
See Paoole.

423 Paeloko
See Peeloko.

424 Pahaalele
Pāhaʻalele
Pā-haʻalele

Literally, abandoned lot.

———————

ʻIli in the ahupuaʻa of Waiheʻe.

Also, the name of a valley in the same vicinity.

Variants: Pahale, Pahulele.

425 Pahakea
See Pohakea.

426 Pahale
See Pahaalele.

427 Pahapahawale
See Papahawale.

28 Pahihi
Pāhihi

"pā.hihi vi. To spread, as vines; to stream, as water over a cliff." /HD/

'Ili in the ahupuaʻa of Waiheʻe.

29 Pahukahuelo
Pahu-ka-huelo

Meaning undetermined, perhaps: the tail is cut short.

Region mentioned in mele in the context of the northern border of the ahupuaʻa of Waiheʻe. Perhaps: Kapahukauila.

"A ka pali o ka pulehu, / Ka palena o Waihee / Hooihoiho na lio, / Ke kula o Pahukahuelo, / O ka wai o Wailele, / Amoamo mai maluna.... [*At the cliff of Kapūlehu, / The boundary of Waiheʻe / The horses descend, / The plain of Pahukahuelo, / The waters of Wailele, / Twinkling above....*] /*Ka Hoku o ka Pakipika*, Buke 2, Helu 9, 11 Kekemapa 1862/

30 Pahulele
See Pahaalele.

31 Paihi
Paʻihi / Paihī

Pronunciation and meaning undetermined, perhaps: "paʻihi vs. vt. Clear, bright, cloudless" /HD/; or, "paihī n. Trickling water, as down the face of a cliff." /HD/

Name mentioned in the context of the kalana of Waiehu.

"Holu pipio ka wai o Paihi i ka makani / Ua ii mau i ka wai o Kaikoo, / I ke ka alele ia e ke one o Halekii, / Puliki ka aweawe hee i Nakohola, / I ke koali hoomoe ia e ke kaahaaha.... [*The waters of Paihī arch rippling in the wind / Ever gathering the water of Kaikoʻo, / As it reels on toward the sands of Halekiʻi, / The octopus tentacles embrace Nākohola, / Amidst the morning glory vines flattened by the Kāʻahaʻaha (wind)....*]" /*Ka Nupepa Kuokoa*, Buke 7, Helu 40, 3 ʻOkakopa 1868/

32 Paiki
See Kapaaiki.

433 Palaeke
Pala'eke
Pala-'eke

Pronunciation and meaning undetermined, perhaps: pala 'eke—receding seaweed/ sea scum.

___

Pala'eke is the name of a division of the Wailuku Fishery. From west to east, the divisions of the fishery are: Ka'ehu a ka Mō'ī, Paukūkalo, Malaeha'akoa (Malehaakoa on the original map), Kaihuwa'a, Makawela, Kahului, Pu'uiki, Kaipu'ula, Kanahā, Pala'eke, Kalua, Ka'a, Hopuko'a Nui, Hopuko'a Iki, Papa'ula, Kapahu, Palaha, Wawa'u (Kawau on the original map), Kānepa'ina, and Kahue. /H.K.L. & R.L., 1947/

434 Palaelae
Pāla'ela'e

Literally, bright.

___

'Ili in the ahupua'a of Ahikuli, kalana of Waiehu.

435 Palaha

Literally, slick.

___

Palaha is the name of a division toward the east side of the Wailuku Fishery. From west to east, the divisions of the fishery are: Ka'ehu a ka Mō'ī, Paukūkalo, Malaeha'akoa (Malehaakoa on the original map), Kaihuwa'a, Makawela, Kahului, Pu'uiki, Kaipu'ula, Kanahā, Pala'eke, Kalua, Ka'a, Hopuko'a Nui, Hopuko'a Iki, Papa'ula, Kapahu, Palaha, Wawa'u (Kawau on the original map), Kānepa'ina, and Kahue. /H.K.L. & R.L., 1947/

436 Palaie
Pala'ie

"pala.'ie 1. vs. Flexible, inconstant, changeable. 2. nvi. To play the game of loop and ball; the game itself...." /HD/

___

Surf break in the ahupua'a of Waihe'e.

437 Palailaiha
See Paleileiha.

438 Palala
See Papala.

39 **Palalau**
Pala-lau

Pronunciation and meaning undetermined, perhaps: yellowing of a leaf or sweet potato vine.

―――――――

Seaside area along the ʻilikū of Keālia in the ahupuaʻa of Waikapū.

Also, the name of an outlet, "Palalau Outlet," for Keālia pond.

40 **Palaleha**
See Paleileiha.

41 **Palama**
Pālama
Pā-lama

Literally, enclosure of *lama* wood.

―――――――

ʻIli in the ahupuaʻa of Waikapū.

Variant: Palanea.

42 **Palamaihiki**
Pālamaihikī / Pālamaʻihikī
Pālama-ihi-kī / Pālama-ʻihi-kī

Pronunciation and meaning undetermined, perhaps: pālama ihi kī—peeling tī leaf *lama* wood enclosure; or, pālama ʻihi kī—tī leaf hoop (of a royal attendant) *lama* wood enclosure.

―――――――

Heiau in the ahupuaʻa of Wailuku.

―――――――

"Palamaihiki Heiau. Walker Site 53. Vicinity of Wailuku. Said to have been among those consecrated by Liholiho in his tour of Maui for that purpose about 1801." /Place Names (ULUK)/

43 **Palanea**
See Palama.

44 **Paleaahu**
Paleʻaʻahu
Pale-ʻaʻahu

Literally, garment lining.

―――――――

Valley/gulch in the ahupuaʻa of Waikapū.

445 Paleileiha
Pāleileihā
Pā-leilei-hā

Pronunciation and meaning undetermined, perhaps: pā leilei hā—yard in which taro stalks are scattered about; or, an elided version of: palai leha—to glance bashfully.

'Ili in the ahupua'a of Waihe'e and Waikapū.

Variants: Palaleha, Paliliha.

446 Palikau
Pali-kau

Literally, precipice on which to rest or settle.

'Ili in the ahupua'a of Wailuku.

447 Pali Lele o Koae
Pali Lele o Koa'e

Literally, flying cliffs of the *koa'e* bird.

A collective name for the steep cliffs in the back of 'Īao Valley, ahupua'a of Wailuku.

"The circumference of the ridges which encompass Iao Canyons is about twenty miles. They rise up perpendicular all around and are inaccessible except in a few places. And from the summits of these tall, lofty precipes, called 'Pali-lele-o-Koae' or the home of the seabirds, play myriads of tiny waterfalls in the mid-air, which as they reach the bottom, form part of the mighty stream...." /SOM 99/

448 Paliliha
See Paleileiha.

449 Palioa
Palio'a
Pali-o'a

Literally, vertical cliff.

The vertical cliff that forms the southern boundary of the 'ili of Lo'iloa, ahupua'a of Wailuku.

50 Panene

Pānēnē / Pānene
Pā-nēnē / Pā-nene

Pronunciation and meaning undetermined, perhaps: pā nēnē—goose enclosure; or, pā nene—touch of shuddering sensation.

_____

'Ili in the ahupua'a of Waichu, kalana of Waiehu.

51 Paoole

Pao'ole
Pao-'ole

Pronunciation and meaning undetermined, perhaps: pao 'ole—ungouged.

_____

'Ili in the ahupua'a of Waihe'e.

Variants: Paaole, Paooole.

52 Paooole

See Paoole.

53 Papahawale

Pāpahawale / Pāpāhāwale
Pā-paha-wale / Pāpāhā-wale / Pāpā-hāwale

Pronunciation and meaning undetermined, perhaps: pā paha wale—lot of only *paha* plants, or, lot of only uncooked young taro leaves (lot where the taro is only used for leaves?); pāpāhā wale—only by fours; or, pāpā hāwale—to riddle/debate through lies.

_____

'Ili in the ahupua'a of Waiehu, kalana of Waiehu.

54 Papaina

Pāpaina / Pāpa'ina / Pāpā'ina
Pā-paina / Pā-pa'ina / Pā-pā'ina

Pronunciation and meaning undetermined, perhaps: pā paina—pine fence; pā pa'ina—to click or tap; or, pā pā'ina—flat dish upon which food is set to eat.

_____

'Ili in the ahupua'a of Waihe'e.

455 Papakapu
Papa-kapu

Literally, consecrated/tabooed foundation.

'Ili in the ahupua'a of Waikapū.

456 Papala
Pāpala

Literally, *pāpala* tree.

'Ili in the ahupua'a of Waikapū.

Variant: Palala.

457 Papalakailiu
See Papalekailiu.

458 Papalaloa
Pāpalaloa
Pāpala-loa

Literally, tall *pāpala* tree.

'Ili in the ahupua'a of Ahikuli, kalana of Waiehu.

459 Papalekailiu
Papalekāiliū / Papalekaili'u
Papale-kāili-ū / Papale-kai-li'u

Pronunciation and meaning undetermined, perhaps: papale kāili ū—ground oven lining of damp vines; or, papale kai li'u—barrier against the slowly evaporating sea water.

Possibly the strip of dry, higher ground that separates Kama'oma'o from the Kanahā/Mau'oni regions in the ahupua'a of Wailuku.

"I ka wa e noho alii ana o Kanenenuiakawaikalu no Maui (ma Wailuku kona wahi noho mau), e noho ana kekahi kanaka kaulana o ia wahi—o Kapoi me kana wahine—ma Kaimuhee, ma uka ae o na wai elua o Kanaha me Mauoni. He mau loko kaulana ia no Wailuku. I kekahi la, makemake ihola ka wahine a ua Kapoi nei e hele i ke kula i ke poi uhini, a hiki o ia ma ke kula o Papalekailiu. A, ma laila ka hele ana a hiki ma Pohaku o Makaku. A hiki loa aku keeia ma nae aku o laila, he poohaku nui i kapa ia kona inoa o Alaha ma ka aoao e pili laa me Hamakuapoko. Loaa ihola i ua wahine hele poi uhini nei a Kapoi he punana hua pueo ma ka aoao o ua pohaku nei. Ehiku ka nui o na hua ma ka punana. [*At the time when Kanēnēnuiakawaikalu of Maui was ruling as chief (his permanent residence was at Wailuku), a famed person of that place was living—Kapoi with his wife—at Kaimuheʻe, just inland of the two waters of Kanahā and Mauʻoni. These are famous ponds of Wailuku. One day, the wife of this Kapoi wanted to go to the plains to catch grasshoppers, and she arrived upon the plains of Papalekailiʻu. There she continued on until she reached Pōhaku o Makakū. When she was well beyond the easterly side of that area, there was a large rock called ʻĀlaha on the side bordering Hāmākuapoko. This grasshopper-catching wife of Kapoi found a nest of owl eggs on the side of that rock. There were seven eggs within the nest.*]" /*Ke Au Okoa*, Buke 12, Helu 11, 29 Iune 1871/ (A noticeable connection appears to exist with the place name Kaimuheʻe [ka imu heʻe—the oven with sliding sides].)

"Uli ka maomao haa ke alialia, / Opu ka hale hau a Kaolohe, / He hale opu mauu nahelehele, / I ku i ke kaha o Papalekailiu e—ilaila. [*Kamaʻomaʻo is rich and deeply colored, / Keālialia sprawls low, / The ceremonial house of Kaʻōlohe rises, / It is a house of clumps of grass, / Stood up upon the dry stretch of Papalekailiʻu there.*]" /Hawaiian Historical Society, 2001/

60 Papamoku
See Papamuku.

61 Papamuku
Papa-muku

Literally, board cut short.

———

Shoreline point on the boundary between the ahupuaʻa of Polipoli and Hananui in the kalana of Waiehu.

Variant: Papamoku.

62 Papaohia
Papaʻōhiʻa
Papa-ʻōhiʻa

Literally, ʻōhiʻa wood board.

———

ʻIli in the ahupuaʻa of Waiheʻe.

Variant: Kapaohia.

463 Papaula

Papaʻula

Papa-ʻula

Literally, red stratum.

Shoreline area on the eastern end of the ahupuaʻa of Wailuku.

"This point is most likely the site of the fishing ground called "Papaulu" (q.v.) awarded to Henry L. Brooks, LCAw 215." /Place Names (ULUK)/

Papaʻula is also the name of a division of the Wailuku Fishery directly offshore of this region. From west to east, the divisions of the fishery are: Kaʻehu a ka Mōʻī, Paukūkalo, Malaehaʻakoa (Malehaakoa on the original map), Kaihuwaʻa, Makawela, Kahului, Puʻuiki, Kaipuʻula, Kanahā, Palaʻeke, Kalua, Kaʻa, Hopukoʻa Nui, Hopukoʻa Iki, Papaʻula, Kapahu, Palaha, Wawaʻu (Kawau on the original map), Kānepaʻina, and Kahue. /H.K.L. & R.L., 1947/

Variants: Papaulu, Stables Beach.

464 Papaulu

See Papaula.

465 Papohaku

Pāpōhaku

Pā-pōhaku

Literally, stone enclosure/fence.

ʻIli in the ahupuaʻa of Wailuku.

Also, the site of the Maui County Pāpōhaku Park.

466 Papulona

Literally, Babylon.

Area listed as being mauka of the village of Waiheʻe.

467 Paukauila

See Kapahukauwila.

68 Paukukalo
Paukūkalo
Paukū-kalo

Literally, piece of taro.

'Ili in the ahupua'a of Wailuku.

Paukūkalo is also the name of a division of the Wailuku Fishery directly offshore of this 'ili. From west to east, the divisions of the fishery are: Ka'ehu a ka Mō'ī, Paukūkalo, Malaeha'akoa (Malehaakoa on the original map), Kaihuwa'a, Makawela, Kahului, Pu'uiki, Kaipu'ula, Kanahā, Pala'eke, Kalua, Ka'a, Hopuko'a Nui, Hopuko'a Iki, Papa'ula, Kapahu, Palaha, Wawa'u (Kawau on the original map), Kānepa'ina, and Kahue. /H.K.L. & R.L., 1947/

69 Paulahi
See Paulani.

70 Paulani
Pau-lani

Literally, completely consumed by the heavens/high chief.

'Ili in the ahupua'a of Waihe'e.

Also, a heiau "'[s]aid to have been built by Kamehameha about 1819 on ruins of temple built by Kahekili to Kane.... [n]ear head of road leading mauka from Waihe'e....' [Walker 1931]." /State Inventory of Historic Places/

Variants: Paulaui, Paulahi.

71 Paulaui
See Paulani.

72 Pauniu
Pa'uniu / Pā'ūniu
Pa'u-niu / Pā'ū-niu

Pronunciation and meaning undetermined, perhaps: pa'u niu—soot from burning coconut; or, pā'ū niu—coconut (leaf) skirt.

'Ili in the ahupua'a of Wailuku. Perhaps named for the woman named Pā'ūniu, famed in the narrative of Kūapī'ei.

"O Ku ka makuakane, o Hinahele ka makuahine, hanau mai na laua he kaikamahine, o Pauniu kona inoa, a ma ia hope mai, hanau mai la o Kuapiei he keikikane, a hanai ia iho la oia a nui. Eono paha makahiki, aole i paa kahi malo i ka hope, ia manawa, iho aku la o Ku, kona makuakane i ka lawai-a, no ka mea, he kanaka lawai-a nui oia na Olopana, ke ʻLii ia ia o Maui a puni, a i ka makuakane i hiki ai i kahakai, hoolale ae la oia i na mea a pau, he lawai-a huki kolo i kai o Kahului, a o ka lawai-a aku la no ia a komo na waa eha i ka i-a. [*Kū was the father, Hinahele the mother, born was their daughter, her name was Pāʻuniu, and afterward, born was Kūapīʻei, a boy, and they were raised until big. Perhaps at six years, he (Kūapīʻei) was still unclad by malo, at that time Kū, his father, went down to fish because he was an important fisherman for ʻOlopana, the Chief of all of Maui, and when the father got to the shore, he readied everything to fish by dragnet in the sea of Kahului, and they fished until four canoes were filled with their catch.*]" /*Ke Au Okoa*, Buke 1, Helu 22, 18 Kepakemapa 1865/

473 Pealoko
See Peeloko.

474 Peeloko
Peʻeloko

Peʻe-loko

Literally, Peʻe pond.

Pond and area in the ʻili of Puʻulolo, ahupuaʻa of Waiheʻe.

Variants: Pealoko, Paeloko.

475 Peepee
Peʻepeʻe

Literally, to hide.

ʻIlikū in the ahupuaʻa of Wailuku.

Variant: Pepee.

476 Pelakapuokakae
See Kapelakapuokakae.

477 Pepee
See Peepee.

78 Pihana

Literally, completion.

———————

Human sacrifice temple on the ridge of the sand dune overlooking the Wailuku River in the ahupuaʻa of Paukūkalo. An alternative name used by some residents is "Piʻihana."

———————

"'Pihana Heiau, Walker Site 43. West [*sic*, North] side of Iao Stream on the sand ridge about half a mile from the sea…A large heiau partly eroded away by the action of Iao Stream…its floor being about 70 feet above the stream bed on the Southeast…The undisturbed side of the heiau proper is about 300 feet in length.' (Sterling) 'Its construction is credited to the traditional Menehunes who are said to have brought all the stones therefor [*sic*] from Paukukalo beach and erected it in one night.' (Thrum)" /Place Names (ULUK)/

Variant: Piihana.

79 Piihana

An alternative name used by some residents for the heiau complex of Pihana. *See also*: Pihana.

80 Piilani
Piʻilani
Piʻi-lani

Literally, heavenly ascent; also, Piʻilani, the name of the aliʻi who first united the island of Maui under one government.

———————

ʻIli in the ahupuaʻa of Waiehu, kalana of Waiehu.

81 Piipii
See Pikoku & Pohaku o Piipii.

82 Pikoku
Pikokū
Piko-kū

Meaning undetermined, perhaps: standing *piko* taro, or, pierced navel.

———————

ʻIli in the ahupuaʻa of Waikapū.

Variant: Piipii.

483 Piliokakae
Piliokāka'e
Pili-o-Kāka'e

Literally, place where Kāka'e clung.

Storied area just above the juncture of the streams of Kinihāpai and Kapela in 'Īao Valley, ahupua'a of Wailuku.

"Loaa i ka eha a ka Pauda. Ma ka la 11 o Dekemaba o ka A.D. i hiamoe aku la, ia makou no e hana ana i ua alanui nei, a ma kahi *pana* i kapaia ka pili o Kakae, loaa iho la kekahi o ko'u mau hoa paahana i ka eha a ka Pauda, o Mokeha kona inoa, o ka hana a keia kanaka, o ka eli i lua iloko o ka pohaku a hookomo hoi i ka pauda malaila.... [*Injured by Gunpowder. On the 11th of December of this past year, while we were working on that road, at a* famed site *called the pili o Kāka'e, one of my coworkers was injured by Gunpowder; his name was Mokeha, his task was to dig a hole into a boulder and put gunpowder in there....*]" /*Ka Nupepa Kuokoa, Buke 9, Helu 5, 29 Ianuali 1870*/

"O Iao ke anahuna kaulana o Maui, aia ma Olopio a pili ma ka aoao o ka pili o Kakae i Kalahiki, ua oleloia aia iloko o ka wai ka puka komo, a o ka lua o ka puka, aia i ka pali laumania ma ka aoao hema. He anahuna kaulana loa i ka wa kahiko, aia mailaila [*sic*] na'lii Moi kaulana a pau loa, ka poe mana, ka poe ikaika, na kupua, ka poe kaulana e pili ana i na Moi i hana i na hana kupua.... [*'Īao is the famed burial cave of Maui, it is at Olopio near the side of the pili o Kāka'e at Kalāhiki, it's said that the entrance is in the water, and the second entrance is in the steep cliff on the south side. It was a very famous burial cave, all of the famous Kings, the supernatural people, the powerful people, the demigods, and all of the famous people connected to the Kings who accomplished miraculous acts are there....*]" /*Ke Au Okoa, Buke 6, Helu 25 6 'Okakopa 1870*/

Variants: Kapaliokake, Piliokakai.

484 Piliokakai
See Piliokakae.

485 Pilipili

Literally, clinging.

Name of 'ili found in the ahupua'a of Waiehu, kalana of Waiehu, as well as in the ahupua'a of Waikapū.

86 Poaiwa
Pō'aiwa / Pōā'iwa
Pō-'aiwa / Pōā-'iwa

Pronunciation and meaning undetermined, perhaps: pō 'aiwa—ninth night; or, pōā 'iwa—robbed by the 'iwa bird/thief.

'Ili, heiau, and pu'uhonua in the ahupua'a of Waiehu, kalana of Waiehu.

87 Pohakea
Pōhākea
Pōhā-kea

Literally, white stone, or, limestone.

'Ili (adjacent to the 'ili of Pōhakuuli) in the ahupua'a of Wailuku.

Also, a valley/gulch along the boundary between the ahupua'a of Waikapū, moku of Wailuku, and the moku of Lahaina.

88 Pohaki
See Pohoiki.

89 Pohakiikii
Pōhāki'iki'i
Pōhā-ki'iki'i

Meaning undetermined, perhaps: tilted boulder.

Landmark above Ka'ōpala on the boundary between Pūlehunui (Kula) and the ahupua'a of Wailuku.

Variant: Pohaku.

90 Pohakoi
Pōhāko'i / Pōhākō'ī
Pōhā-ko'i / Pōhākō'ī

Pronunciation and meaning undetermined, perhaps: pōhā ko'i—adze (sharpening) boulder; or, pōhākō'ī—rock avalanche.

'Ili in the ahupua'a of Waikapū.

491 Pohaku

Pōhaku

Literally, boulder.

___

The name of a sea in the ahupuaʻa of Wailuku.

___

"...ia manawa i haalele ai ke alii [Kihāpiʻilani] ia Waiehu, o ua kanaka nei ma mua—a mahope mai ke alii, o ko lakou nei hele mai la no ia a hiki i Wailuku, iho pono aku la i kai o Pohaku pii aku la maluna o ke kualapa one o Makanipalua ka inoa, aole i emo, hehi ana na kapuai i ke one hone o Kahului.... [*at that time the chief (Kihāpiʻilani) left Waiehu, that person was in front—and behind was the chief; they went until they arrived at Wailuku, went straight down toward the sea beyond Pōhaku, ascended the sand ridge by the name of Makanipālua; in no time, the soles of their feet were stepping upon the supple sands of Kahului....*]" / *Ka Nupepa Kuokoa*, Buke 23, Helu 7, 16 Pepeluali 1884/

492 Pohakukapu

Pōhaku-kapu

Literally, sacred boulder.

___

Famous landmark in the vicinity of Kamaʻauwai in the ahupuaʻa of Wailuku.

493 Pohakukupukupu

Pōhakukupukupu

Pōhaku-kupukupu

Meaning undetermined, perhaps: pōhaku kupukupu—boulder covered with *kupukupu* ferns, or, boulder rising conspicuously high.

___

ʻIli in the ahupuaʻa of Wailuku.

494 Pohakuloa

Pōhakuloa

Pōhaku-loa

Literally, long boulder.

___

ʻIli in the ahupuaʻa of Waikapū.

95 Pohakulua
Pōhakulua
Pōhaku-lua

Meaning undetermined, perhaps: second boulder, or, boulder found in/taken from a pit.

'Ili in the ahupua'a of Ahikuli, kalana of Waiehu.

96 Pohaku Maluhia
Pōhaku Maluhia

Literally, Maluhia Boulder.

Site in the ahupua'a of Ahikuli, kalana of Waiehu.

"Pōhaku Maluhia. Fishing site, rock, Waiehu, Maui. Large rock in the ocean off Waiehu that is only visible from shore at low tide when the ocean is calm. During the 1920s a subdivision here was named the Maluhia Beach Lots after the rock, and the church in the middle of the subdivision was called Maluhia Church. Lit., peaceful rock." /HPN/

97 Pohakunahaha
Pōhakunāhāhā
Pōhaku-nāhāhā

Literally, cracked boulder.

Inland point along the border between the ahupua'a of Kou, kalana of Waiehu, and the ahupua'a of Waihe'e.

Also, an inland point along the northeastern border of the ahupua'a of Wailuku.

98 Pohakunui
Pōhakunui
Pōhaku-nui

Literally, large boulder.

'Ilikū in the ahupua'a of Polipoli, kalana of Waiehu.

Also a large boulder in the 'ili of Kapoho, ahupua'a of Waihe'e.

"Most of Kapoho [Waihe'e] was once a fishpond with the entrance near a rock, Pohakunui." /SOM 24/

499 Pohaku o Ioleakalani
Pōhaku o ʻIoleakalani

Literally, ʻIoleakalani's boulder.

Landmark just before the northeastern boundary of the ahupuaʻa of Wailuku.

500 Pohakuokauhi
Pōhakuokauhi

Pōhaku-o-Kauhi

Literally, Kauhi's boulder.

ʻIli in the ahupuaʻa of Wailuku.

Variant: Pohakuuhi.

501 Pohaku o Makaku
Pōhaku o Makakū

Literally, Makakū's Boulder.

Survey landmark just inland of the ponds of Kanahā and Mauʻoni in the ahupuaʻa of Wailuku.

"I kekahi la, makemake ihola ka wahine a ua Kapoi nei e hele i ke kula i ke poi uhini, a hiki o ia ma ke kula o Papalekailiu. A, ma laila ka hele ana a hiki ma Pohaku o Makaku. A hiki loa aku keeia ma nae aku o laila, he poohaku nui i kapa ia kona inoa o Alaha ma ka aoao e pili laa me Hamakuapoko. Loaa ihola i ua wahine hele poi uhini nei a Kapoi he punana hua pueo ma ka aoao o ua pohaku nei. Ehiku ka nui o na hua ma ka punana. [*One day, the wife of this Kapoi wanted to go to the plains to catch grasshoppers, and she arrived upon the plains of Papalekailiʻu. There she continued on until she reached Pōhaku o Makakū. When she was well beyond the easterly side of that area, there was a large rock called Alaha on the side bordering Hamakuapoko. This grasshopper-catching wife of Kapoi found a nest of owl eggs on the side of that rock. There were seven eggs within the nest.*]" /Ke Au Okoa, Buke 12, Helu 11, 29 Iune 1871/

Variant: Pohaku o Manaku.

502 Pohaku o Olopua

Literally, Boulder of Olopua.

Point found along the northeastern border of the ahupuaʻa Wailuku.

03 **Pohaku o Piipii**
Pōhaku o Piʻipiʻi

Literally, Piʻipiʻi's boulder.

_____

Point found along the northeastern border of the ahupuaʻa Wailuku.

04 **Pohakupa**
Pōhakupā
Pōhaku-pā

Literally, flat-topped boulder.

_____

Inland point along the border between the ahupuaʻa of Kou, kalana of Waiehu, and the ahupuaʻa of Waiheʻe.

05 **Pohakupukapuka**
Pōhakupukapuka
Pōhaku-pukapuka

Literally, stone with many holes, or, perforated rock.

_____

ʻIli in the ahupuaʻa of Wailuku.

06 **Pohakuuhi**
See Pohakuokauhi & Pohakuuli.

07 **Pohakuuli**
Pōhakuuli
Pōhaku-uli

Literally, dark boulder.

_____

ʻIli (adjacent to the ʻili of Pōhākea) in the ahupuaʻa of Wailuku.
Variant: Pohakuuhi.

08 **Pohoiki**
Poho-iki

Literally, small depression/hollow.

_____

ʻIli in the ahupuaʻa of Wailuku.
Variant: Pohaki.

509 Pohuea
See Poohuea.

510 Poino
See Kapoino.

511 Polea
Pōlea / Pōleʻa

Pronunciation and meaning undetermined, perhaps: "pō.lea vs. 1. Sunken in, as the lips and cheeks of a toothless person. *Rare*. 2. Blurred, as eyes of a diver. *Rare*" /HD/; or, pō leʻa—delightful night.

ʻIli in the ahupuaʻa of Waiehu, kalana of Waiehu.

512 Poliala
Poliʻala
Poli-ʻala

Literally, fragrant bosom/embrace.

Storied hill, and its surrounding region, in the ahupuaʻa of Waiehu, kalana of Waiehu.

513 Polipoli

"poli.poli 1. n. A soft, porous stone as used for polishing or for octopus lure sinkers 2. vs. Rounded, of an adze. (Malo 51.)" /HD/

Ahupuaʻa in the kalana of Waiehu.

514 Poohahoahoa
See Poonahoahoa.

515 Poohuea
Poʻohuʻea / Pōʻohuea
Poʻo-huʻea / Pō-ʻohu-ea

Pronunciation and meaning undetermined, perhaps: poʻo huʻea—exhumed skull; or, pō ʻohu ea—obscured by rising mist.

ʻIli in the ahupuaʻa of Ahikuli, kalana of Waiehu.

Variant: Pohuea.

16 Poonahoahoa
Poʻonāhoahoa
Poʻo-nāhoahoa

Literally, fractured skull.

Upland tributary of Kapela Stream, the upper portion of the Wailuku River, originating below Puʻukukui in the ahupuaʻa of Wailuku. (*See also*: Nanahoa).

"[ʻĪao] Stream begins at the junction of Poonahoahoa and Nakalaloa streams at about 1100 ft. elevation, flows to sea. Sometimes called 'Wailuku River' in descriptions of awards." /Place Names (ULUK)/

Variant: Poohahoahoa.

17 Poopuupaa
Poʻopuʻupaʻa
Poʻo-puʻu-paʻa / Poʻo-puʻupaʻa

Meaning undetermined, perhaps: poʻo puʻu paʻa—occupied hilltop; or, poʻo puʻupaʻa—head of a female virgin.

Puʻuhonua of the ahupuaʻa of Waiheʻe.

"O ko Maui poe Puuhonua, o Lahaina kekahi, a o Olowalu kekahi, a o Poopuupaa ma Waihee kekahi. Ma ia mau wahi no e pakele ai na kanaka ke komo. [*Maui's places of refuge were Lahaina, as well as Olowalu, and also Poʻopuʻupaʻa at Waiheʻe. These places are where people could become exempt from persecution upon entry.*]" /Ka Nupepa Kuokoa, Buke 42, Helu 3, 15 Ianuali 1904/

18 Popoie
Pōpōʻie
Pōpō-ʻie

"*Lit.*, ʻie vine cluster." /PNOH/

Surf break in the ahupuaʻa of Waiheʻe.

519 Puaanui
Puaʻanui
Puaʻa-nui

Literally, large pig.

"At Puaanui, near the site of the present Wailuku mill, was where the victims for sacrifice were kept, in the time of Kahekili." /SOM 107/

520 Puakala
Pua-kala

Literally, *kala* flower.

Region listed in the area of the kalana of Waiehu.

"The canefields now extend throughout this region, continuously from Waihee on the lower slopes; but above Waiehu and Puakala from the upper roads following the irrigation ditches well toward the upper limits of the cane, a few old plantations still persist." /SOM 49/

521 Puakea

"pua.kea 1. nvs. Pale-colored, especially a tint between white and pink, as sunset clouds; the color of a buckskin horse . . . 2. vi. To spread, as a ship's sails or as fog." /HD/

ʻIli in the ahupuaʻa of Wailuku.

522 Puako
Puakō
Pua-kō

Literally, sugar cane blossom/tassle.

ʻIli in the ahupuaʻa of Wailuku.

523 Puali
Pūʻali

"pū.ʻali 1. n. Warrior, soldier, so called because Hawaiian fighters tied (pūʻali) their malos at the waist so that no flap would dangle for a foe to seize; army, host, multitude . . . 2. nvt. To gird tightly about the waist, as of malo-clad warriors, or as corseted women; compressed, constricted in the middle; grooved, notched; irregularly shaped, as taro; notch; tight belt . . . 3. n. Isthmus. 4. n. Slender abdominal stalk on a wasp's body . . . 6. n. Irregularly shaped ravine. 7. n. A vague term for an adopted man or boy who had no servants." /HD/

Unidentified 'ili attributed in the Māhele databases as being in the ahupua'a of Wailuku, belonging to H. Kalama, and in Waihe'e to V. Kamāmalu.

24 Pualinaapau
See Pualinapao.

25 Pualinapao
Pū'alinapao
Pū'alina-pao

Pronunciation and meaning undetermined, perhaps: pū'ali + -na pao—elongated furrows left after the ground was scooped out.

'Ili in the ahupua'a of Waikapū.

Variant: Pualinaapau.

26 Puanea

"pua.nea vs. Mournful." /HD/

'Ili in the ahupua'a of Waihe'e.

27 Pueokaia
Pueokāia
Pueo-kāia

Literally, fast asleep owl.

The name of a hill on the eastern side of the ahupua'a of Wailuku, inland of Wawa'u. This hill was named after Pueokāia, the husband of 'A'apueo.

"O keia Pueo wahine no uka o Kula, o Aapueo kona inoa, a ku kapa la no kona inoa i kekahi Ahupuaa malaila, o Aapueo ka inoa a hiki i keia la, a o kela Pueokaia hoi, ke kane a ia nei, o kona wahi noho mau, he wahi puu mauka ae o Awau [*sic*], i ke kaha o Wailuku, a ua kapaia ka inoa o ia wahi puu o Pueokaia a hiki i keia la. [*This female owl from the uplands of Kula, her name was 'A'apueo, and her name stands as the name for a certain ahupua'a there, its name is 'A'apueo until today, and that Pueokāia, he was her husband, his place of residence was a small hill inland of Awau (sic, Wawa'u) upon the dry plains of Wailuku, and the name of that small hill is Pueokāia until today.*]" /*Ke Au Okoa*, Buke 7, Helu 11, 29 Iune 1871/

Variant: Puuokaia.

528 Pueololo
See Puulolo.

529 Puhau
Pūhau

"pū.hau n. Cool spring." /HD/

_____

'Ili in the ahupua'a of Waikapū.

530 Puhaualu
See Puhauolu.

531 Puhauohe
See Puhauolu.

532 Puhauolu
Pūhau'olu
Pūhau-'olu

Literally, cool, pleasant spring.

_____

'Ili in the ahupua'a of Waihe'e.

Also, archaeological site in the same ahupua'a.

_____

"Wawaekaaaka...At Puhauolu, Waihee, said to date from Kahekili's time, long ago demolished, save a mound of stones which mark its site." /Thrum, "Hawaiian almanac and annual for 1909"/

Variants: Puhaualu, Puhauohe, Puhouohu, Puhouou.

533 Puhele
See Puu Hele.

534 Puhiawaawa
Puhiawaawa
Puhi-awaawa

Pronunciation and meaning undetermined, perhaps: blown into the valley, or, to burn the valley.

_____

An 'ilikū, and perhaps an 'ili lele, in the ahupua'a of Wailuku, and an 'ili in the ahupua'a of Waikapū.

Variant: Puhiawawa.

35 Puhinale
See Puuhinale.

36 Puhouohu
See Puhauolu.

37 Puhouolu
See Puhauolu.

38 Puhouou
See Puhauolu.

39 Puki
See Puuki.

40 Punia

"punia 1. Pas/imp. of puni 1–4. ('puni 1. vs. Surrounded, controlled; overcome, as in battle or by emotion; to pervade, gain control of; to enclose . . . 3. vs. Deceived, deluded; to believe a lie . . .) 2. n. Head cold. 3. n. A kind of coconut, the husk of which is chewed for its sweet juice." /HD/

ʻIli in the ahupuaʻa of Waikapū.

Variants: Puuia, Puniha.

41 Puohala
See Puuohala.

42 Puuhanau
Puʻuhānau
Puʻu-hānau

Literally, birth hill.

Place mentioned in mele within the context of the ahupuaʻa of Waiheʻe.

"O ka luna o Wailele, / Puliki ana ka uhane, / I ka pua o ke kuikui, / Kuhihewa aku no au, / A he pua rose oe naʻu, / I kui ai a lawa, / I lei hololio, / I ka lai Puuhanau. . . . [*The top of Wailele, / The spirit clings, / At the* kuikui *blossom, / I am mistaken, / You are a rose blossom that I / Strung until complete, / A horse-riding garland / In the calm of Puʻuhānau. . . .*] /*Ka Hoku o ka Pakipika*, Buke 2, Helu 9, 11 Kekemapa 1862/

543 Puu Hele
Pu'u Hele

Literally, Traveling Hill.

_____

Hill and landmark in the ahupua'a of Waikapū, found near the southwestern border of the moku of Wailuku.

Variant: Puhele.

544 Puuhinale
Pu'uhīnale
Pu'u-hīnale

Literally, thin/sickly hill.

_____

An inland point along the northeastern border of the ahupua'a of Wailuku.

Variant: Puhinale.

545 Puuia
See Punia.

546 Puuiki
Pu'uiki
Pu'u-iki

Literally, small hill.

_____

Pu'uiki is the name of a division of the Wailuku Fishery found just east of what is now called Hobron Point. From west to east, the divisions of the fishery are: Ka'ehu a ka Mō'ī, Paukūkalo, Malaeha'akoa (Malehaakoa on the original map), Kaihuwa'a, Makawela, Kahului, Pu'uiki, Kaipu'ula, Kanahā, Pala'eke, Kalua, Ka'a, Hopuko'a Nui, Hopuko'a Iki, Papa'ula, Kapahu, Palaha, Wawa'u (Kawau on the original map), Kānepa'ina, and Kahue. /H.K.L. & R.L., 1947/

547 Puu Kane
Pu'u Kāne

Literally, Kāne Hill.

_____

Peak along Kaho'olewa Ridge, between the ahupua'a of Wailuku and the kalana of Waiehu.

Variants: Mauna Ka-ne, Puukane, Puukani, Puu Kani.

48 Puukani / Puu Kani
See Puu Kane.

49 Puuki
Puʻukī
Puʻu-kī

Literally, ti plant hill.

ʻIli in the ahupuaʻa of Wailuku.

Variant: Puki.

50 Puukoa
See Puukoae.

51 Puu Koae
Puʻu Koaʻe

Literally, *koaʻe* bird hill.

A point consisting of a cinder hill along the eastern boundary of the moku of Wailuku. Also, the name of the road that once passed through that area.

"Mai laila mai hoi holo aku la a loaa o Puukoae, he puu aa nae ma kela wahi i oleloia ae la o Puukoae. He alanui o Puukoae he holoia no e ka lio maluna oia wahi aa. [*From there continue along until reaching Puʻu Koaʻe, there is a cinder hill at that place said to be Puʻu Koaʻe. Puʻu Koaʻe is a road traversed by horse over that cindery place.*] /Maly, 2006/

Variant: Puukoa.

52 Puu Kuma
Puʻu Kuma

Literally, Kuma Hill; meaning of "kuma" undetermined, perhaps: dark; moss-covered; pitted or cracked.

Storied hill and heiau site above the ʻili of Pāhihi, ahupuaʻa of Waiheʻe.

Variants: Puukuma, Puukumu.

53 Puukumu
See Puu Kuma.

554 Puuleo

See Puu Lio.

555 Puu Lio

Pu'u Lī'ō

Pronunciation and meaning undetermined, perhaps: terror hill.

———————

"A point on the Wailuku/Waikapu boundary, elevation about 3130 ft., marking the transition between Kalapaokailio ridge and Kapilau ridge." /Place Names (ULUK)/

"In confusion and fear, the Mauians tried to escape by climbing the steep slopes of Mauna Leo, only to be destroyed. At that time the name of the mountain changes from Leo to Lio [lī'ō], meaning 'terror.' The cliffs of Mauna Lio were named Pali Kau-a'u [*sic*], or 'clawing-frantically.' " /Ashdown, *Honolulu Star-Bulletin*, 24 Iulai 1960/

Variants: Mauna Leo, Mauna Lio, Puuleo.

556 Puulolo

Pu'ulolo / Pu'ulōlō
Pu'u-lolo / Pu'u-lōlō

Pronunciation and meaning undetermined, perhaps: pu'u lolo—coconut sponge hill, coconut flower sheath hill, *lolo* ceremony hill, ti root liquor hill; pu'u lōlō—crazy hill; or, a contraction of pu'u olōlo—oblong/elongated (sweet potato) hill.

———————

'Ili in the ahupua'a of Waihe'e.

[NOTES: This is the 'ili in which the pond named Pe'eloko/Paeloko is found, and from where Māui harvested the coconut fibers for his rope to snare the sun. As such, the coconut-related names may apply. Alternatively, because the next 'ili over is Waioka'ona'ona (Water of Intoxication?), the name related to ti root liquor may also be valid. Also, the variation "Pueololo (Pu'e-olōlo?)" may allude to elongated planting mounds. Lastly, the *lolo* ceremony is performed at canoe launchings, and, interestingly, one of the original allotees of this 'ili was Pi'imaiwa'a.]

Variant: Pueololo.

557 Puunene

Pu'unēnē
Pu'u-nēnē

Literally, nēnē goose hill.

———————

The name of a once-prominent hill inland of Wawa'u, near the northeastern boundary of the moku of Wailuku. The region now known by the superimposed name of foreign origin "Spreckelsville" may also have been called Pu'unēnē.

Also, small unincorporated town once centered on the Puʻunēnē Sugar Mill, along the Spreckelsville Railroad line, near the northern region of Kamaʻomaʻo, ahupuaʻa of Wailuku.

"Spreckelsville is made up of Russian Village, Japanese Village, Hawaiian Village, Cod Fish Village." /Place Names (ULUK)/

"Puunene is made up of Yung Hee Village, Alabama Village, Spanish B Village, Sam Sing Village, McGerrow Village." /Place Names (ULUK)/

58 Puuohala
Puʻuohala
Puʻu-o-Hala

"Lit., hill of pandanus" /HD/, or, Hala's hill.

ʻIlikū in the ahupuaʻa of Wailuku.

Also, an ʻili lele found just makai of the ʻili of Keahupiʻo in the ahupuaʻa of Wailuku.

Variants: Puohala, Puuokala.

59 Puuokaia
See Pueokaia.

60 Puuokala
See Puuohala.

61 Puuokamoa
Puʻuokamoa
Puʻu-o-ka-moa

Literally, hill of the chicken.

A name for the landmark in the valley of ʻIao, ahupuaʻa of Wailuku, also now referred to by the superimposed name of foreign origin " ʻIao Needle." *See also*: Kukaemoku & Nanahoa.

62 Puu o Kaupo
Puʻu o Kaupō

Literally, Kaupō's Hill.

Peak along the ridge that separates the two ahupuaʻa of Waiehu and Ahikuli in the kalana of Waiehu.

563 Puuone
Puʻuone
Puʻu-one

Literally, sand dune.

———————

Area just north of the western jetty of Kahului Harbor in the ahupuaʻa of Wailuku. *See also*: Wao Akua One and Makanipalua.

564 Puuone Hills
Puʻuone Hills
Puʻu-one Hills

Literally, Sand Dune Hills.

———————

A portion of the extensive natural, lithified sand dune system, also referred to by the superimposed name of foreign origin "Sand Hills," which extends north from the ahupuaʻa of Waikapū through the Kakanilua region, and veers east below modern-day Wailuku town. The ʻili of ʻOwā runs across and along this region in the ahupuaʻa of Wailuku.

565 Puuopalili
Puʻuopalili
Puʻu-o-palili

Literally, Palili's (stunted taro shoot) hill.

———————

ʻIli in the ahupuaʻa of Waiehu, kalana of Waiehu.

Variant: Pauopalili.

566 Puupili
Puʻupili
Puʻu-pili

Literally, *pili* grass hill.

———————

Point along the northeastern boundary of the moku of Wailuku.

67 Puu Pio
Puʻu Pio / Puʻu Piʻo

Pronunciation and meaning undetermined, perhaps: puʻu pio—prisoner hill, or whistle hill; or, puʻu piʻo—curved hill.

––––––––––––

Peak above the valley of Waikapū, on the south side of Nāholomāhana Gulch.

68 Sand Hills

A superimposed name of foreign origin commonly recognized as being the portion of the extensive natural, lithified sand dune system below modern-day Wailuku town and extends toward Kahului Harbor.

Another "Sand Hills" is found on early maps of the ahupuaʻa of Waikapū.

Variant: Puuuone.

69 Spartan Reef

A superimposed name of foreign origin for the reef off the shoreline of Papaʻula, toward the eastern end of the moku of Wailuku.

70 Spreckelsville

A superimposed name of foreign origin for an area inshore of of Papaʻula and Wawaʻu, toward the eastern end of the moku of Wailuku. This area is also called Puʻunēnē (not to be confused with the current town of Puʻunēnē).

––––––––––––

"[Baldwin Park] Community park between Village 5 and Yung Hee Village in Puunene." /Place Names (ULUK)/

71 Stables Beach
See Papaula.

72 Ukihi
ʻŪkihi

"ʻū.kihi 1. nvi. Cold sores, any sores about the corners (kihi) of the mouth; to have such. Fig., to talk too much. 2. n. Name of a bird (no data)." /HD/

––––––––––––

ʻIli in the ahupuaʻa of Waiehu, kalana of Waiehu.

Variant: Ukiki.

573 **Ukiki**
See Ukihi.

574 **Ulukua**
Ulukua / 'Ulukua
Ulukua / Ulu-kua / 'Ulu-kua

Pronunciation and meaning undetermined, perhaps: ulukua—agitated; ulu (a)kua—
deity inspiration; or, 'ulu kua—hewn breadfruit tree.

———————

Heiau in the ahupua'a of Waihe'e.

———————

"Ulukua Heiau, Walker Site 28 and 29. North side of Waihee stream two sites with same
name on either side of the road. Both destroyed." /Place Names (ULUK)/

575 **Umieu**
'Umi'eu

Meaning undetermined, perhaps: 'Umi'eu (a proper name of a person), or 'umi 'eu—
to repress mischief.

———————

'Ili in the ahupua'a of Wailuku.

Variants: Imiau, Umiheu.

576 **Umihale**
'Umihale
'Umi-hale

Literally, 'Umi house.

———————

The name of one of Kahekili's houses in the vicinity of Kāilipoe, in the 'ili of Pōhakuokauhi, ahupua'a of Wailuku.

———————

"One of the warriors who served the two masters, Kahahana and Ka-hekili, was a certain
lesser chief (*kaukauali'i*) named Ka-pohu. Ka-hekili built himself a chief's house called
'Umi-hale on the *mauka* side of Ka'ilipoe, *makai* of Kihahale." /SOM 124/

577 **Waepae**
See Waiopae.

578 **Wahanemaili**
See Wahineomaili.

79 Wahineomaili
Wahineomā'ili
Wahine-o-Mā'ili

Meaning undetermined, perhaps: woman of/from Mā'ili.

———

'Ili in the ahupua'a of Waikapū.

Variant: Wahineomaile.

80 Waiaka
Wai-aka

Pronunciation and meaning undetermined, perhaps: reflective water.

———

'Ili in the ahupua'a of Wailuku.

81 Waialae
See Waiale.

82 Waiale
Wai'ale
Wai-'ale

Literally, rippling water.

———

A large freshwater pond, now a reservoir, located amongst the sand hills in the Kakanilua region south of the 'ili of Kalua, ahupua'a of Wailuku.

Also, an 'ili in the ahupua'a of Polipoli, kalana of Waiehu.

Variants: Waialae, Waiuli.

83 Waialua
Waialua
Wai-a-Lua

Meaning undetermined, perhaps: wai a Lua—waters belonging to/used by Lua.

———

Unidentified 'ili in the ahupua'a of Waihe'e. Perhaps in the vicinity of 'Eleile, near the juncture of the Waihe'e and Mananole streams.

———

"There were two young women, perhaps in very ancient times, who belonged to that cave [at 'Eleile]. Eleile was the younger sister and she was prettier. The older was Wailua. Their work was tapa making in this cave. One night they were washed out by the water because there was a stream alongside of the cave. When this happened and it stormed, the water flowed until it reached these women, Eleile and Wailua, and that is why it became the water of Eleile. After this time the people took the umbilical cords to hide in that cave. Those who could hold their breath dived down and hid the piko." /SOM 18/

Variant: Wailua.

584 Waiaolohe
Waia'ōlohe
Wai-a-'ōlohe

Meaning undetermined, perhaps: waters of the expert, waters in which one bathes nude, or waters used by 'Ōlohe (proper name).

'Ili in the ahupua'a of Waihe'e.

585 Waiauiki
Wai-au-iki

Literally, small current water.

'Ili in the ahupua'a of Wailuku.

Variant: Waiauniki.

586 Waiaukuu
Wai'auku'u
Wai-'auku'u

Literally, black-crowned night heron waters.

'Ili in the ahupua'a of Waihe'e.

587 Waiehu
Wai-ehu

Literally, misty water.

Kalana and streams in the moku of Wailuku. This kalana consists of five ahupua'a: Waiehu, Ahikuli, Polipoli, Hananui, and Kou. Waiehu is one of the four "wai" of Nāwai'ehā.

588 Waiehu Camp

Plantation camp upland of the Māla'ihi area.

89 Waihalulu

Wai-halulu

Literally, roaring water.

The name of ʻili found in the ahupuaʻa of Waiheʻe and Waikapū.

90 Waihee

Waiheʻe

Wai-heʻe

Literally, flowing dripping water.

Ahupuaʻa and river in the moku of Wailuku. Waiheʻe is one of the four "wai" of Nāwaiʻehā.

91 Waiheʻe Point

See Kahoomano.

92 Waiheʻe Reef

Broad name for the fishing grounds that lie roughly between the shoreline point of Kahoʻomano in the ahupuaʻa of Waiheʻe to the shoreline of the ahupuaʻa of Kou, kalana of Waiehu.

93 Waihinanoakapoipoi

Waihīnanoakapoʻipoʻi

Waihīnano-a-Kapoʻipoʻi

Literally, Waihīnano (wife) of Kapoʻipoʻi (Waihīnano is featured in the saga of Hiʻiakaikapoliopele).

Seaside area in the Kahului region of the ahupuaʻa of Wailuku. Perhaps the whole, or poetic, name for the area of Kapoʻipoʻi. *See also*: Kapoipoi.

"...komo i ke kai holu o Kahului, lele po no [*sic*] i uka, ua pau e na kaa hoolimalima i ka poe lele mua, kau kahi paiki i ke kua(,) pekipeki wawae i ke one o Kahului a hiki i Waihinanoakapoipoi. Loaa mai i na lio e kai mai ana, motio pololei no Wailuku.... [...*entered into the swaying sea of Kahului (Bay), promptly disembarked onshore, the rental vehicles were already rented to those who disembarked first, put a small bag on back, trudged along by foot on the beach of Kahului until reaching Waihīnanoakapoʻipoʻi. We were picked up by horses coming our way, dashed straight for Wailuku....*]" /*Ka Nupepa Kuokoa*, Buke 31, Helu 19, 7 Mei 1892/

"Hoole mai o Waihinalo wahine a Kapoipoi, aole e make kuu alii ia oe, ke hai mai nei na kua wahine oia nei. O Walinuu ma laua o Waimaanoanoa [*sic*], o Papa o Hoohoku-kalani, e hoole mai ana, aole e make. Pane mai o Hiiaka i ka hua o ka make. Ua make ke lii nona nei moku. [*Waihīnalo wife of Kapoʻipoʻi refuted this: 'My chief will not die by you,' her goddesses were telling her. Walinuʻu and Walimānoanoa, Papa, Hoʻohokukalani, they were refuting, he would not die. Hiʻiaka responded with the curse of death. The chief to whom this island (Maui) belonged died.*] / Ka Hae Hawaii, Buke 5, Helu 14, 4 Iulai 1860/

"I ke one aloha o Kahului e, / Ua haaheo wale i ka ia hukikolo la, / E aha ana la Waihi-nano me Kapoipoi e, / E walea nei i ka malu o ke ao la.... [*Upon the beloved sands of Kahului ē, / So proud at the fish caught by seine lā, / What are Waihīnano and Kapoʻipoʻi doing ē, / Relaxing in the shelter of the clouds lā....*]" / Ka Hoku o ka Pakipika, Buke 2, Helu 23, 19 Malaki 1863/

594 Waikai
See Waikani.

595 Waikani
Wai-kani

Literally, noisy water.

———————————

'Ili in the ahupuaʻa of Wailuku.

Variants: Waikai, Waikini, Waikaninui, Waikaniiki, Waikani uuku.

596 Waikapu
Waikapū
Wai-ka-pū

"Lit., water [of] the conch." /PNOH/

———————————

Ahupuaʻa and stream in the moku of Wailuku. Waikapū is one of the four "wai" of Nāwaiʻehā.

Variant: Waikapu nui.

597 Waikini
See Waikani.

598 Waikuli
See Ahikuli.

99 Wailaahia

Waila'ahia

Wai-la'ahia

Literally, consecrated water.

'Ili in the ahupua'a of Polipoli, kalana of Waiehu. Perhaps named after a man of the region, Waila'ahia, who along with his wife, Halelau, were the first priests of the akua, Kūho'one'enu'u.

00 Wailele

Literally, waterfall.

An upland region mentioned in mele in the context of the ahupua'a of Waihe'e.

"A ka pali o ka pulehu, / Ka palena o Waihee / Hooihoiho na lio, / Ke kula o Pahu-kahuelo, / O ka wai o Wailele, / Amoamo mai maluna.... [*At the cliff of Kapūlehu, / The boundary of Waihe'e / The horses descend, / The plain of Pahukahuelo, / The waters of Wailele, / Twinkling above....*] /*Ka Hoku o ka Pakipika*, Buke 2, Helu 9, 11 Kekemapa 1862/

"Akahi au a ike ia Mookahi kahi a ke aloha i noho ai / Kuu hoa mai ka piina ikiiki o Wailele / Lele ka uhane haalele i ke kino.... [*I have just seen Mo'okahi where love dwelt / My companion from the stifling ascent of Wailele / The spirit leaps and departs from the body....*]" /*Ko Hawaii Pae Aina*, Buke 3, Helu 33, 14 'Aukake 1880/

01 Wailua

See Waialua.

02 Wailuku

Wai-luku

Literally, waters that destroy.

The name of one of three moku of West Maui, as well as the name of an ahupua'a and river in the same moku. Wailuku is one of the four "wai" of Nāwai'ehā.

"Wailuku is the county seat and principal town on Maui." /Place Names (ULUK)/

"Wailuku, Waikapu, Waiehu and Waihee were independent, belonging to no Moku. On the map it was necessary to form a new district and call it Wailuku, Nawaieha, the four waters, being too combersome [*sic*] and ill understood." /Place Names (ULUK)/

From a name chant for Lonoikamakahiki by Kaikilani: "Kahua ao lele Wailu-ku–e.... [*Wailuku is a region of drifting clouds–ē....*]" /Fornander V 4, 305/

"Ua olelo ia, ua hiki like na pueo a pau loa i ka po o Kane. Ma na wahi a pau loa a lakou e hoomoana nei. A i ke ao ana o Lono ka hoouka ana o ke kaua ma Wailuku. Aole o kana mai keia hoouka kaua o na pueo me na kanaka a me na alii, a ua nui ka make o kanaka ma ia la ma Na Wai Eha. A ua make hoi o Kapoi a me kana wahine. A no ia luku ana a ka pueo i kapa ia ai ka inoa o Wailuku a hiki i keia la. A ua olelo pu ia no hoi, no ka malu ana o ka la ma ia la no ka paa o ka lewa i na pueo, ka mea i kapa mua ia ai o ka Maluakahekuawa a hiki i keia la. [*It is said that the owls all arrived on the night of Kāne. They were encamped everywhere. The battle was launched in Wailuku at the dawning of Lono. Nothing can compare to the tremendous nature of this war waged between the owls, the commoners, and chiefs and there were many human deaths at Nāwai'ehā. And Kapoi and his wife were indeed killed. Because of this destruction caused by the owls, this area is called Wailuku until today. Concerning the darkening of the sun on this day because of the great numbers of owls that filled the sky, it is also said that this is the reason that the name Malu-a-ka-hēkuawa (The Shading of the High Cliffside Valleys) was first coined until this day.*]" /Ke Au Okoa, Buke 7, Helu 11, 29 Iune 1871/

603 Wailuku Commons

A superimposed name of foreign origin for the area makai of Wai'ale Pond that includes the regions of Kakanilua and Kama'oma'o in the ahupua'a of Wailuku, and which extends toward Kahului along the 'ili of Kalua.

604 Wailuku Fishery

A collective name for the appurtenant fishery of the ahupua'a of Wailuku. On the west, this fishery's boundary is a seaside point/stone below Pu'u o Kaupō on the western boundary of Wailuku Ahupua'a, and its eastern boundary is Kapukaulua. From the shoreline, the fishery extends one geographic mile into the sea. The entire fishery, about 4,950 acres, was once granted to Claus Spreckels, Grant 3343.

From west to east, the divisions of the fishery are: Ka'ehu a ka Mō'ī, Paukūkalo, Malaeha'akoa (Malehaakoa on the original map), Kaihuwa'a, Makawela, Kahului, Pu'uiki, Kaipu'ula, Kanahā, Pala'eke, Kalua, Ka'a, Hopuko'a Nui, Hopuko'a Iki, Papa'ula, Kapahu, Palaha, Wawa'u (Kawau on the original map), Kānepa'ina, and Kahue. /H.K.L. & R.L., 1947/

605 Wailuku River
Wai-luku

Literally, waters that destroy.

_____

The river system of the ahupua'a of Wailuku that originates in 'Īao Valley.

Hakuao is the main branch of the Wailuku River that flows past Piliokākaʻe in ʻĪao Valley, ahupuaʻa of Wailuku.

"[ʻĪao] Stream begins at the junction of Poonahoahoa and Nakalaloa streams at about 1100 ft. elevation, flows to sea. Sometimes called 'Wailuku River' in descriptions of awards." /Place Names (ULUK)/

"During the four months of Makahiki and harvest season, which began with the rising of Makalii (the Pleiades) in the fall, the populace was allowed to enter ʻĪao Valley to enjoy its delicious shrimp, ʻoʻopu fish, and other delicacies in company with the alii.

But the populace traveled the trail up Kini-hapai (Uplifting of the multitude) stream that flows by the base of Ku Ka Aʻe Moku [*Ku Kaʻe Moku*] (now called the Needle) while the alii followed Kapela stream past Ka Pili o Kakaʻe." /SOM 100/

06 Waioeo

Waioʻeo / Waioeʻo / Waiʻōeo
Wai-o-ʻEo / Wai-o-(a)eʻo / Wai-ʻō(w)eo

Pronunciation and meaning undetermined, perhaps: wai o ʻeo—waters of ʻEo (proper name); or, elisions of: wai o aeʻo—waters of the *aeʻo* bird; or, wai ʻōweo—reddened waters.

Shoreline area and fishing ground in the ahupuaʻa of Waiehu, kalana of Waiehu.

07 Waiohia

Waiʻōhiʻa
Wai-ʻōhiʻa

Literally, ʻōhiʻa tree water.

Gulch and streambed that originates in the ʻili of ʻOmaʻopio (Kula) and enters the southeastern area of the ahupuaʻa of Wailuku between Puʻukoaʻe and Kaluaʻōlohe.

08 Waiolimu

See Auwaiolimu.

09 Waiokaonaona

Waiokaʻonaʻona
Wai-o-Kaʻonaʻona / Wai-o-ka-ʻonaʻona

Meaning undetermined, perhaps: wai o Kaʻonaʻona—Kaʻonaʻona's waters; or, wai o ka ʻonaʻona—liquid of the drunkard, or, water of the bad smell.

ʻIli in the ahupuaʻa of Waiheʻe.

610 Waiopae
Wai'ōpae
Wai-'ōpae

Literally, shrimp water.

'Ili in the ahupua'a of Waihe'e.

Variants: Waepae, Waipae, Waipai.

611 Waipae
See Waiopae.

612 Waipai
See Waiopae.

613 Waipukua
Wai-pukua

Meaning undetermined, perhaps: water offered at the close of a ceremony.

'Ili and pu'uhonua in the ahupua'a of Waihe'e.

614 Waiuli
See Waiale.

615 Waiwela
Wai-wela

Literally, hot water.

'Ili in the ahupua'a of Wailuku found just across the river between the heiau of Pihana and Malaeha'akoa.

616 Wao Akua One

Literally, sand region inhabited by *akua*.

Term applied to at least part of the Pu'uone region in the ahupua'a of Wailuku. *See also*: Puuone and Makanipalua.

617 Wawaekaaaka
See Wawaekanaka.

18 Wawaekanaka
Wāwaekanaka
Wāwae-kanaka

Literally, human foot.

The name of an adze-grinding boulder found within a demolished heiau in the ʻili of Pūhauʻolu, ahupuaʻa of Waiheʻe.

"The rock had been used for adze grinding. It got its name from a tradition that a certain chief was chasing some soldiers to kill them and one got his foot caught in the rock...." /SOM 22/

"Kakolika Heiau, Walker Site 34. Along road mauka to swamp in cane fields. Site of heiau torn up in cutting road. Inside may still be seen a large rock, the Wawaekanaka Stone (q.v.)...." /Place Names (ULUK)/

Variant: Wawaekaaaka.

19 Wawau
Wawaʻu

Meaning undetermined, perhaps: to grate.

Shoreline area toward the northeast boundary of the moku of Wailuku.

"Wawau...Point near Spreckelsville, Maui. This name is probably cognate with an old name for Raʻi-ātea in the Society Islands, for an inland area at Vai-taha, Tahuʻata, Marquesas, and for Vavaʻu, an island in the Ton-gan group." /PNOH/

Paraphrasing of a moʻolelo told to the author by Maui kupuna Diane Amadeo: there was a group of people who came from Sāmoa that landed at Wawaʻu. They went and stayed up at ʻOmaʻopio, then moved over to Pūlehunui. Finally, they moved to Kahi-kinui where they stayed.

Wawaʻu is also the name of a division toward the east side of the Wailuku Fishery. From west to east, the divisions of the fishery are: Kaʻehu a ka Mōʻī, Paukūkalo, Malaehaʻakoa (Malehaakoa on the original map), Kaihuwaʻa, Makawela, Kahului, Puʻuiki, Kaipuʻula, Kanahā, Palaʻeke, Kalua, Kaʻa, Hopukoʻa Nui, Hopukoʻa Iki, Papaʻula, Kapahu, Palaha, Wawaʻu (Kawau on the original map), Kānepaʻina, and Kahue. /H.K.L. & R.L., 1947/

Variants: Awau, Kawau.

CHAPTER 5

PAPA KUHIKUHI

This chapter serves as an index for place names that have been grouped into the individual kalana and ahupua'a of each of the three moku of Maui Komohana. The listings create a lei—in the form of a clockwise circuit—around nā Mauna o 'E'eka, which begins with the moku of Lahaina (commencing from the ahupua'a of Ukumehame and continuing northwest until the kalana of Lahaina). Next comes the moku of Kā'anapali (commencing from the ahupua'a of Honokōwai and continuing north and east to the kalana of Kahakuloa). Closing the lei is the moku of Wailuku (commencing from the ahupua'a of Waihe'e and continuing south to the ahupua'a of Waikapū).

LAHAINA MOKU

Ukumehame Ahupua'a

Aalaloloa, Anehe, Anehenehe, Anu, Auau, Aweoweoluna, Haai, Halepohaku, Hanaula, Hanaulaiki, Haui, Hawaii Route 30, Hikii, Hokuula, Hona, Honoapiilani Highway, Hono o na Moku, Kaalaino, Kaheawa, Kai o Anehe, Kai o Haui, Kalanipapa, Kalawea, Kamaalaea, Kamanawai, Kamaohi, Kapoli, Kapoulu, Kaulu, Kaunukukahi, Kealaloloa, Keanapaakai, Keawanui, Keekeenui, Keekenui, Kekenui, Keonepohuehue, Koai, Lae o Opihi, Lahaina, Lahaina Pali Trail, Luau, Maalaea, Maalaea Small Boat Harbor, Makahuna, Makaiwa, Makenewa, Malalowaiaole, Manawainui, Manawaipueo, Manuohule, Maomao, McGregor's Landing, McGregor Point, Mokumana, Ohia, Old Lady's, Opihi, Opunaha, Pali, Papawai, Pioneer Mill Company, Pohakea, Pohakuloa, Puaaloa, Puahoowali, Puako, Puamana, Puehuehu, Puhako, Puu Anu, Puu Hona, Puu Kauoha, Puu Luau, Puu Moe, Scenic Lookout, Ukumehame, Ulaula, Umulau, Uwai, Wash Rock.

357

Olowalu Ahupuaʻa

Auau, Halepohaku, Haui, Hawaiikekee, Hawaii Route 30, Hekili, Honoapiilani Highway, Hono o na Moku, Kailiili, Kai o Haui, Kalolopahu, Kaluaaha, Kaluaaho, Kaluaana, Kaluaha, Kaluakanaka, Kamani, Kawaialoa, Kawailoa, Kilea, Kuekue, Lae o Hekili, Lahaina, Liha, Lihau, Lihauwaiekeekeikalani, Mopua, Nalowale, Olowalu, Olowalu Gap, Olowalu Lanakila Church, Olowalu Massacre, Olualu, Paumaumau, Pioneer Mill Company, Punahoa, Puu Kilea, Puukoleaohilo, Puukoleohilo, Puukoliohilo, Puukoliolio, Puuokapolei, Puu Ulaula, Ulaula, Unahi, Wailoa.

Launiupoko Ahupuaʻa

Auau, Awalua, Haui, Hawaii Route 30, Helu, Hipa, Honoapiilani Highway, Hono o na Moku, Kai o Haui, Kapuali, Keahuiki, Kulanaokalai, Lahaina, Launiupoko, Liha, Lihau, Lihauwaiekeekeikalani, Luakoi, Mahanaluanui, Nalimawai, Olauniupoko, Onehali, Pahee, Pioneer Mill Company, Puhiaama, Puu Hipa, Puu Papai.

Lahaina Kalana

Aaka, Ahikuli, Aimakalepo, Akau, Aki, Akiaiole, Akiaole, Akiakaiole, Akinui, Aki Uuuku, Alamihi, Alanuikikeekee a Maui, Alio, Anapenape, Anapuka, Apaa, Apahua, Apuakaiao, Auau, Aupokopoko, Auwaiawao, Auwaimalino, Auwaiowao, Awalau, Ball Mountain, Banyan Tree Park, Belekane, Beretane, Beretania, Breakwalls, Crater, Crater Camp, Eleluli, Hahakea, Halaaniani, Halakaa, Hale Aloha, Halehuki, Halekaa, Halekamani, Halekumukalani, Halekumulani, Halelua, Hale Mahina, Haleokane, Halepai, Halepai Palapala, Halepiula, Haleu, Halipiula, Halona, Halulukoakoa, Hanaia, Hanakaoo, Hanakapuaa, Hanaukapuaa, Harbor Left/Right, Haui, Hauola, Hawaii Route 30, Helu, Hema, Holanui, Holili, Honoapiilani, Honoapiilani Highway, Hono o na Moku, Hoolili, Hoomanamana, Huemiemi, Iki, Ilikahi, Kaakau, Kaalo, Kaaula, Kahala, Kahau, Kahea, Kahili, Kahinahina, Kahoma, Kahoolewa, Kahua, Kahuaiki, Kainehe, Kai o Haui, Kaiwihole, Kaiwiholi, Kalehua, Kalimaohe, Kalolo, Kaluaehu, Kalualepo, Kaluaokiha, Kamaiki, Kamakalaukalo, Kamani, Kamehameha Iki, Kamohomoho, Kanaha, Kapaahu, Kapahumanamana, Kapaulu, Kapauma, Kapewakua, Kapualiilii, Kapukaiao, Kapunakea, Kau, Kauakahikaula, Kauaula, Kauheana, Kaukahoku, Kaukaiweli, Kaukaweli, Kaulalo, Kauohiokalani, Keaaula, Keahua, Keahuakamalii, Kealii, Keana, Keawaiki, Keawawa, Keekeehia, Kelawea, Keonepoko, Kiholaa, Kilolani, Kiolani, Keoihuihu, Koheeleele, Kokonamoku, Kokoonamoku, Kooka, Kopili, Kuemiemi, Kuholilea, Kuhua, Kukuikapu, Kulahuhu, Kuliole, Kumuula, Kumuwi, Kunamoe, Lahaina, Lahaina Fort, Lahainakai, Lahainalalo, Lahainaluna, Lahainaluna High School, Lahainawaena, Laina, Lainapokii, Laiolele, Lapakea, Leilehua, Lele, Lelekahauli, Loinui, Loko Alamihi, Loko o Nalehu, Luaehu, Luakoi, Luakona, Mahikuli, Makailii, Makaiwa, Makalaukalo, Makila, Makiwa, Mala, Malu Ulu o Lele, Manoa, Maria Lanakila, Maunaanu, Maunahoomaha, Maunaihi, Maunakui, Miana, Moalii, Moanui, Mokahi, Mokuhinia, Mokuula, Molakia, Mooahia, Mount Ball, Muliwaikane, Nakalepo, Nalehu, Ohia, Opaeula, Paeohi, Pa Hale Kamani, Pahalona, Pahoa, Pahu-manamana, Paiula, Pakala, Panaewa, Papalaau, Papalaua, Pa Pelekane, Papiha Cemetery, Papu o Lahaina, Pauma, Paunau, Paupau, Pawakua, Pelekane, Piilani Auwai, Pioneer Mill Company, Pohakunui, Pohaku o Wahikuli, Polaiki, Polanui, Polapola, Pools, Puaa, Pukalele, Punawai, Puopelu, Puou, Puuhale, Puuheehee, Puuhoowali, Puuhulilole, Puuiki, Puuki, Puukolii, Puu Laina, Puunau, Puunoa, Puu Papai, Puupiha, Puu Ulaula, Puuwaiohina, Raheina, Shark Pit, Uhailio, Uhao, Unahiole, Uo, Wahikuli, Wahine Pee, Waianae, Waianiokole, Waianukole, Waianukoli, Waianuukole, Waiie, Waiieiki, Waikapu, Waikeekeehi, Waikekeehi, Wailehua, Waimana, Wainalo, Wainee, Waiokama, Waiola, Waiolimu, Waipaahao, Wanapa.

KĀʻANAPALI MOKU

Honokōwai

Aipohopoho, Aipopo, Aliʻi Kahekili Nui ʻAhumanu Beach Park, Amalu, Analoa, Auwailimunui, Black Rock, Haena, Hawaii Route 30, Honoapiilani Highway, Honokawai, Honokowai, Honokōwai Beach Park, Hono o na Moku, Ilikikoo, Kaainaiki, Kaainanui, Kaanapali, Kaanapali Church, Kaawaiki, Kaelepuni, Kahekili Beach Park, Kahiku, Kaioo, Kaleinaakauhane, Kananau, Kaneauau, Kapaloa, Kapili, Kapunakea Preserve, Ke Alanui Kikeekee a Maui, Kekaa, Kipapa, Kou, Kuhuwa, Laau, Lahuiokalani Kaanapali Congregational Church, Leinakauhane, Limalau, Loainalu, Loinui, Maele, Maile, Makaa, Makahiki, Makahiku, Momole o Kekaa, Moomuku, Na Hono a Piilani, Na Pali Po i ka Ohu, Naunaunawele, Naunaunahawele, Nukunukuapuaa, Ohia, Onepeha, Palaha, Papanahoa, Papaolena, Papaolina, Popohaku, Poehu, Pohakea, Pohakiki, Pohakuowahineomanua, Poohumoi, Poopohaku, Puu Kekahi, Puulena, Puweu, Uilikiko, Ulukikoo, Waihale, Waikiki, Wainalo, Wainalu, Wanaloa.

Māhinahina

Aipuaa, Haelaau, Hailaau, Hawaii Route 30, Honoapiilani Highway, Hono o na Moku, Kaanapali, Kaanapali Pohaku, Kaawaiki, Kahina, Kahoolewa, Kapalua West Maui Airport, Kauhilua, Kaukini, Kekaalaau, Kikikihale, Kuaaimano, Laeokama, Mahinahina, Mahinahina Camp, Na Pali Po i ka Ohu, Paupolo, Pohaku o Kaanapali, Puweu.

Kahana

Hawaii Route 30, Hihiho, Hinapikao, Hoaka, Honoapiilani Highway, Hono o na Moku, Kaanapali, Kaanapali Pohaku, Kaape, Kahakapuaa, Kahana, Kahanaiki, Kahanaiole, Kahananui, Kahuna, Kaia, Kalaeiliili, Kalaeokaea, Kalaeokaia, Kalakahi, Kaluailio, Kapohale, Kaulalewalewa, Kaulalewelewe, Keaakukui, Kolekole, Kukuikanu, Kukuiolono, Kumukahi, Kupoupou, Likipu, Na Pali Po i ka Ohu, Ohia, Opihi, Pakei, Pohaku o Kaanapali, Pohale, Pulepule, Puu Kalakahi, Uhali.

Mailepai

Halelani, Haua, Hawaii Route 30, Honoapiilani Highway, Hono o na Moku, Kaanapali, Kahalua, Kaia, Kalaeokaia, Kanaele, Kaopala, Kaulu, Kaumuokama, Kukaua, Mailepai, Mailepai Point, Makaulii, Na Pali Po i ka Ohu, Ohia, Pahuaa, Pahukauila, Puu Makina, Uahaili.

ʻAlaeloa

Alaeloa, Haukoe, Hawaii Route 30, Honoapiilani Highway, Hono o na Moku, Kaaio, Kaalo, Kaanapali, Kahoomano, Kalaekole, Kalena, Kaluaomano, Kaopala, Kapuaa, Keonenui, Keonohuli, Manaaiole, Manawaikalupe, Nalowale, Na Pali Po i ka Ohu, Niholau, Olohe, Ouohau, Puu Heewale, Puu Makina, Puu Nene, Puu o Kalauliko, Waikala, Waikulu, Waikalupe.

Honokeana

Apakawaha, Elekii, Fleming's Beach, Haukoi, Hawaii Route 30, Honoapiilani Highway, Honokeana, Hono o na Moku, Kaanapali, Kaelekii, Kahuki, Kalelo, Kaluaniha, Kaluaniho, Kaluanui, Kaluaoopu, Kaolapalapa, Kaukeke, Keoa, Kiiakapapa, Kuamopua, Kuamoopua, Lapamuku, Manaaiole, Na Hono a Piilani, Naio, Na Pali Po i ka Ohu, Ouolii, Papano, Pohakuloa, Pukaulua, Waikala, Waikulu.

Nāpili

Aikahi, Elekii, Hawaii Route 30, Hawea, Hawea Point Light, Hokuanui, Honoapiilani Highway, Hono o na Moku, Iuao, Kaanapali, Kaekaha, Kaelekii, Kahalua, Kahao, Kahauloa, Kaholua, Kaieie, Kalama, Kapalua, Kapalua Lighthouse, Kapua, Keauhou, Keaukaia, Kue, Kukuokaawe, Kuunaakaiole, Mahana, Na Pali Po i ka Ohu, Napili, Pailolo, Punaholo, Waiakeakua, Waikeakua, Waiokeakua, Waipae, Waipueo.

Honokahua

Ahuakolea, Anakaualehu, Anamoo, D. T. Fleming's Beach County Park, Haawekaula, Hanaloa, Haohao, Haunaku, Hawaii Route 30, Hawea, Hokolo, Honoapiilani Highway, Honokahua, Hono o na Moku, Ihukoko, Iole, Kaanapali, Kaekaha, Kahanalo, Kahanaloa, Kahoolewa, Kalaepohaku, Kalakahi, Kalana, Kalokoloko, Kaluakanaka, Kanuku, Kaolina, Kaonahi, Kaulalewalewa, Kaulalewelewe, Kaulu, Kaunahi, Kiowaiokihawahine, Laa, Luapuna Bay, Mahana, Mahoe, Makaluapuna, Makaoioi, Maunalei Arboretum, Mokupea, Moomuku, Na Hono a Piilani, Naio, Nakalalua, Nalaalono, Namalu, Nanahu, Na Pali Po i ka Ohu, Ohia, Oneloa, Opukaha, Pailolo, Paina, Pakala, Paliuli, Paopao, Pehukanukunuku, Pineapple Hill, Pohakuloa, Pohina, Poopueo, Pua Ka Huahua, Pukukui, Puu Kahuahua, Puulu, Violet Lake, Wahalau, Waiuli, Walahaha.

Honolua

Aimaia, Alaelae, Hawaii Route 30, Hikiapo, Honoapiilani Highway, Honolua, Honuaula, Hunonaaahu, Kaanapali, Kaea, Kaeo, Kahauiki, Kahikinui, Kahoolewa, Kahooulu, Kalaepiha, Kalila, Kaluaniho, Kaluanui, Kamane, Kaolina, Kapaeulua, Kapahaoholo, Kauhihonohono, Kauhipilo, Kauhipueo, Kauila, Kaulukanu, Kauwahine, Keahikauo, Keonehelelei, Kihapiilani Trail, Kiki, Kuakepa, Kukaekanu, Kukaenui, Kukuikanu, Kulaokaea, Lipoa, Makuleia, Malili, Malo, Manawaikaha, Maumea, Maunalei Arboretum, Miloiki, Mokuleia, Moomaka, Na Hono a Piilani, Naioio Pahahao, Na Pali Po i ka Ohu, Pahahao, Pahala, Paiala, Pailolo, Pakahea, Pakihi, Papahao, Papua, Pohakuiolea, Puakea, Puhalakau, Puiwa, Puu Kaeo, Puu o Kaopuu, Wahikolokolo, Waioio, Waipapa, Waiuli.

Honokōhau

Akaluaiki, Akaluanui, Akhluaiki, Anakaluahine, Apopo, Eke, Eke Crater, Elekini, Hawaii Route 30, Hawaii Route 340, Heakalani, Honoapiilani Highway,

Honokahau, Honokohau, Honokohau Falls, Huakukui, Iliilikea, Kaanapali, Kaehaiko, Kaehakiko, Kaeo, Kahalamanu, Kahekili Highway, Kahoolewa, Kaihukiako, Kaimooalii, Kalalalaolao, Kalaulaolao, Lalaulaula, Kamoouli, Kaneloa, Kaneneilio, Kanounou, Kaolanakaloa, Kapaaukini, Kapalaalaea, Kapaukua, Kapuakea, Kaulanakaloa, Kaulanakoloa, Kawaipeke, Keahau, Keaahau, Keahua, Keamoalii, Keanaakaluahine, Keawalua, Kepuhi, Kihapiilani Trail, Kikalahai, Kiowaiokihawahine, Kiula, Kuimooalii, Kulaokalalaolao, Kula o Kalaulaolao, Kumukea, Lae Kunonou, Maepono, Mailapa, Maipono, Maiu, Maluaka, Manienie, Manokiei, Mauna Eeke, Na Hono a Piilani, Naipono, Nakalele, Nākālele Lighthouse, Na Pali Po i ka Ohu, Niula, Niuula, Ohiapoko, Opopo, Paaukini, Pahua, Pailolo, Panioi, Paulole, Pauoa, Pipipi, Pohakuiolea, Pohakupule, Pua Melia Home, Puawa, Punaha, Punalau, Puu Eke, Puu Kaeo, Puu Kilea, Puuloli, Uau, Violet Lake, Waiakeakua, Waikeakua, Waiokeakua, Waiuli.

Kahakuloa Kalana

Aawaiki, Aawanui, Ahoa, Ahoaiki, Alaapapa, Alapapa, Auwaipaki, Awalua, Camp Maluhia, Eke, Eke Crater, Eliwahine, Hainau, Hakuhee, Hale, Haleino, Haleokane, Hanonana, Haunaa, Hawaii Route 340, Heinau, Hononana, Hoomanunu, Hulu, Kaakua, Kaanapali, Kaauwaipaki, Kaehaiko, Kaehakiko, Kaemi, Kahakahalani, Kahakuloa, Kahakuloa Game Management Area, Kahakuloa Head, Kahakuloa Homesteads, Kahanahana, Kahau, Kahekili Highway, Kahilianapa, Kahuku, Kaihukiako, Kaikaina, Kaimalolo, Kainui, Kakapa, Kalanikawai, Kalaniwai, Kalaoa, Kalauhulu, Kamani, Kamoa, Kanaele, Kanea, Kanehalaoa, Kaneola, Kanoa, Kanukuokeana, Kaohe, Kaopilopilo, Kapa, Kapalalau, Kapaloa, Kapelekai, Kapolalau, Kapuaikahi, Kapulehu, Kapuna, Kauila, Kaukini, Kaulu, Kaulunai, Kaulunui, Kaunuwahine, Kawaihae, Kawaiopilopilo, Kawelokio, Keahialoa, Keahikano, Keahikauo, Keahinaluahine, Keahupuaa, Kealakahakaha, Keana, Keanae, Keikapalani, Keikipalani, Kihapiilani Trail, Kipu, Koaeloa, Kuewa, Kuewaa, Kuhaa, Kuhakea, Kuhanahana, Kukaeaoa, Kukuikapu, Kukuimamalu, Kukuipuka, Kulaloa, Kulanaumeume, Kupaa, Kuulu, Lae Kahilianapa, Lahoole, Lamahihi, Lanihili, Lanilili, Lanipanoa, Lapaiki, Leinaha, Lelepaua, Luapuaa, Mahele, Mahinanui, Makahuna, Makalina, Makaliua, Makamakaole, Makawela, Malalokai, Malama, Malu, Maluhia, Mana, Maopo, Mauakini, Mauna Eeke, Maunaohuohu, Maupo, Moho, Mokeehia, Mokolea, Moomuku, Na Hono a Piilani, Naio, Nalowale, Namahana, Na Pali Po i ka Ohu, Niu, Noni, Ohia, Omaolehulehu, Opilopilo, Opuupuu, Owaluhi, Paehala, Pailolo, Pakao, Pakolo, Palaala, Palau, Palauhulu, Palaula, Papanalahoa, Papanahoa, Pauhulu, Paulae, Paulai, Pawili,

Peekoa, Piilani, Piliamoo, Pipipi, Poelua, Pohakukani, Pohakuloa, Pohakuo-holonae, Pohaku o Kane, Polanui, Polua, Puawa, Puekahi, Pueno, Pulehu, Puloi, Punanakuhe, Punauekuhe, Puu Eke, Puu Haunaka, Puu Haunako, Puu Kahulianapa, Puu Koae, Puu Kukae, Puulae, Puu Makawana, Puu Olai, Puu Olelo, Sugarloaf, Uau, Umi, Waialae, Waiaololi, Waihali, Waihapapa, Waikalae, Wailena, Waiokila, Waiolai, Waiololi, Waipili, Waipiliamoo.

Wailuku Moku
Waiheʻe

Ahuakolea, Alae, Aliele, Halelani, Halepahu, Halepaka, Hawaii Route 30, Hawaii Route 340, Holili, Honoapiilani Highway, Hoolele, Hoolili, Huakolea, Huluhulupueo, Kaalae, Kaaloa, Kaapoko, Kahahawai, Kahalekulu, Kahekili Highway, Kahilinamaia, Kahoolewa, Kahoomano, Kaiaha, Kaihumoku, Kaimana, Kainamu, Kakolika, Kalaeiliili, Kalaeokahoomano, Kalahihale, Kalaniloko, Kalanihale, Kalaniloko, Kalaninuieehehe, Kalauhue, Kalepa, Kalepahu, Kalepelepe, Kalopue, Kamahoe, Kanaele, Kanoa, Ohia, Kapahukauila, Kapaohia, Kapoho, Kapokea, Kapoko, Kapuna, Kauahia, Kaulu, Kauwila, Kealakaihonua, Kehoni, Kiao, Kiikewe, Kiokio, Kiwe, Koiahi, Koihale, Kolea, Kuakahanahana, Kupaa, Lauhue, Limalau, Loikahi, Lonoakaulana, Makaalae, Malaukanaloa, Malu a ka Hekuawa, Mananole, Mauna Alani, Maunaihi, Mokapu, Mookahi, Naele, Na Hono a Piikea, Nawaieha, Nelu, Ohia, Paaole, Paeloko, Pahaalele, Pahale, Pahihi, Pahukahuelo, Pahulele, Paihi, Palaie, Palailaiha, Palaleha, Paleileiha, Paliliha, Paoole, Paoooole, Papaina, Papaohia, Papulona, Paukauila, Paulahi, Paulani, Paulaui, Pealoko, Peeloko, Pohakunui, Pohakupa, Poopuupaa, Popoie, Puanea, Pueololo, Puhaualu, Puhauohe, Puhauolu, Puhouohu, Puhouolu, Puhouou, Puuhanau, Puu Kuma, Puukumu, Puulolo, Ulukua, Waepae, Waiaolohe, Waiaukuu, Waihalulu, Waihee, Waihee Reef, Wailele, Wailua, Waiokaonaona, Waiopae, Waipae, Waipai, Waipukua, Wawaekaaaka, Wawaekanaka.

Waiehu Kalana

Aawa, Ahikuli, Alakaha, Alapaka, Anahi, Aukanaha, Auwai Ohia, Halawa, Halelau, Halelena, Hananui, Hanohano, Hawaii Route 30, Holawa, Holoikauai, Honoapiilani Highway, Honohono, Honuhonu, Kaakukui, Kaalaino, Kaehu, Kaehu Bay, Kaehu Beach, Kahakapiele, Kahakumaka, Kahakupiela, Kahekili Highway, Kahimana, Kahoana, Kahoolewa, Kaikoo, Kailiili, Kai o Nakohola, Kalahape, Kalanipuu, Kaleholeho, Kaluaolena, Kanaio, Kanehe, Kaohe, Ohia, Kaopukaula, Kapaaloa, Kapaka, Kapalaoa, Kapalaua, Kapoino,

Kapuoho, Kauhiloa, Kaula, Kawila, Kawili, Keaakukui, Keeau, Keahialoa, Keokanui, Kepalaoa, Kepalaua, Kiha, Kipapa, Koalaina, Koholaiki, Koholanui, Kope, Kou, Kuhimana, Kukuialaemaka, Kukuialaemoku, Kukuialaimaka, Kukuikomo, Kukuiokomo, Kumukahi, Kumuwiliwili, Kupalaua, Kuunahawelu, Lae o Nakohola, Laepohaku o Nakohola, Lualailua, Mahalani Cemetery, Malaihi, Malu a ka Hekuawa, Maluhia, Maluhia Beach Lots, Malumaluakua, Manokohala, Manukohala, Mauna Alani, Mehani, Mookahi, Na Hono a Piikea, Nakohola, Napoko, Nawaieha, Niukukahi, Nukukahi, Ohia, Omao, Onihi, Pahapahawale, Palaelae, Panene, Papahawale, Papalaloa, Papamoku, Papamuku, Piilani, Poaiwa, Pohakulua, Pohaku Maluhia, Pohakunahaha, Pohakunui, Pohakupa, Pohuea, Poino, Polea, Poliala, Polipoli, Poohuea, Puakala, Puu o Kaupo, Puuopalili, Ukihi, Ukiki, Waiehu, Waiehu Camp, Waikuli, Wailaahia, Waioeo,.

Wailuku

Ae, Ahuakokole, Ahuakokoli, Ahuena, Ahuka, Ahuwahine, Aipaako, Alaha, Auhaka, Awau, Baldwin Beach Park, Black Gorge, Dream City, Eleele, Eleile, Eliile, Haakupu, Hakuao, Halaula, Halekii, Halekou, Halelani, Halemano, Haliau, Haliiau, Happy Valley, Haunaka, Hawaii Route 30, Hei, Hihika, Hiiwela, Hoaloha Park, Holu, Honoapiilani Highway, Honuakaua, Hopoi, Hopukoa, Huiha, Iao, Iao Makai, Iao Maniania Ditch, Iao Needle, Iao (Stream), Imiau, Kaa, Kaahu, Kaahumanu Church, Kaakakai, Kaakau, Kaakaupohaku, Kaalaholo, Kahalulukahi, Kahekili Highway, Kahewa, Kahiki, Kahoolewa, Kahua, Kahului, Kahului Harbor, Kaihuwaa, Kaikuono o Kahului, Kailipoe, Kaimuhee, Kaipuula, Kakanilua, Kalahihale, Kalahiki, Kalanapoe, Kalani Auwai, Kalanihale, Kalola, Kalua, Kaluaoiki, Kaluaolohe, Kaluaoopu, Kaluli, Kama Auwai, Kamamao, Kamaomao, Kanaha, Kanaha Pond State Wildlife Sanctuary, Kanehe, Kaohe, Kaopala, Kaopuohe, Kapaaiki, Kapaaloa, Kapaliokakae, Kapaniwai, Kapanui, Kapapakoloa, Kapela Stream, Kapelakapuokakae, Kapelaokakae, Kapilaa, Kapilau, Kapoipoi, Kapuakeeo, Kapukaulua, Kauahea, Kauhiana, Kauhina, Kaulehulehu, Kaulupala, Kaunoa, Kauoku, Kauoukuu, Kaupali, Kaupo, Kauwaupali, Kauweloweloula, Kawaiola, Kawela, Kawelowelo, Keahuku, Keahupio, Kealakapehu, Kealoha, Keanakalahu, Keonekapoo, Kehu, Keoneula, Keopuohe, Kepaniwai, Kepuakeeo, Kepuhekeeo, Kihahale, Kiiwela, Kilipoe, Kinihapai, Koloa, Kuanui, Kuemanu, Kuipa, Kukaemoku, Kukalepa, Kumuwiliwili, Kunaheana, Kuunaheana, Laie, Lamalii, Lanikeha, Lanihale, Lelemako, Lemukee, Liliha, Loiloa, Luahinepii, Luahipii, Mahukaawe, Makaaka, Makaku, Makanipalua, Makawela, Makole, Malaehaakoa

Malaihakoa, Malama, Malelewaa, Malena, Malu a ka Hekuawa, Maluihi, Maniania, Maniania Ditch, Manienie, Manoni, Maui Veterans Highway, Maui Waena, Mauka Cave, Mauna Kane, Mauna Leo, Mauoni, Mokuhau, Mokuilima, Mokulele Highway, Na Hono a Piikea, Nakalaloa, Nanahoa, Nawaieha, Nehe, Niu, Olokua, Oloolokalani, Olopio, Olopua, Oukea, Owa, Paakukui, Paiki, Palamaihiki, Palikau, Pali Lele o Koae, Palioa, Papalakailiu, Papalekailiu, Papaula, Papaulu, Papohaku, Paukukalo, Pauniu, Peepee, Pelakapuokakae, Pepee, Pihana, Piihana, Piliokakae, Piliokakai, Pohakea, Pohaki, Pohakiikii, Pohaku, Pohakukapu, Pohakukupukupu, Pohakunahaha, Pohaku o Ioleakalani, Pohakuokauhi, Pohaku o Makaku, Pohaku o Olopua, Pohaku o Piipii, Pohakupukapuka, Pohakuuhi, Pohakuuli, Pohoiki, Poohahoahoa, Poonahoahoa, Puaanui, Puakea, Puako, Puali, Pueokaia, Puhiawaawa, Puhinale, Puki, Puuhinale, Puu Kane, Puukani / Puu Kani, Puuki, Puukoa, Puukoae, Puu Lio, Puunene, Puuohala, Puuokaia, Puuokamoa, Puuone, Puuone Hills, Puupili, Sand Hills, Spartan Reef, Spreckelsville, Stables Beach, Umieu, Umihale, Waiaka, Waialae, Waiale, Waialua, Waiauiki, Waihinanoakapoipoi, Waikai, Waikani, Waikini, Wailuku, Wailuku Commons, Wailuku River, Waiohia, Waiuli, Waiwela, Wao Akua One, Wawau.

Waikapū

Ahuakolea, Aikanaha, Aikanaka, Anehe, Anukoli, Aoakamanu, Auwailimunui, Auwailimuuuku, Auwaiolimu, Auwakamanu, Awakamanu, Awikiwiki, Haaiwo, Haaua, Halepalahalaha, Haliaipalala, Halipalahalaha, Haliipalahalaha, Haliipalalii, Hawaii Route 30, Honoapiilani Highway, Hoopahelo, Huakolea, Kaa, Kaaa, Kaaikao, Kaalaea, Kaalea, Kahoi, Kaiapaokailio, Kailua, Kai o Anehe, Kalapaokailio, Kaleia, Kalepolepo, Kaloaloa, Kaloapelu, Kamaalaea, Kamaomao, Kamauhalii, Kanaio, Ohia, Kaolohe, Kaonohua, Kaopala, Kapalaaea, Kapalaalaea, Kapilau, Kapoli, Kaumuilio, Kaunuohua, Kealia, Keana, Kehei, Kiheipukoa, Kikia, Koloapelu, Koolau, Kuaina, Kuaiwa, Kukuialaemaka, Kukualaemoku, Kukuialaimaka, Kula o Puhele, Kula o Puuhele, Laaloa, Lapaleihua, Lehuapueo, Loaloa, Lona, Luapuaa, Luapueo, Maalaea, Makaelelu, Makahilahila, Makailima, Malu a ka Hekuawa, Maui Veterans Highway, Mokulele Highway, Naholomahana, Nawaieha, Nohoana, Nuukole, Nuukoli, Ohia, Olohe, Ooawa Kilika, Paalae, Pahakea, Palailaiha, Palala, Palalau, Palaleha, Palama, Palanea, Paleaahu, Paleileiha, Paliliha, Papakapu, Papala, Piipii, Pikoku, Pilipili, Pohakea, Pohakoi, Pohakuloa, Pualinaapau, Pualinapao, Puhau, Puhele, Puhiawaawa, Punia, Puu Hele, Puuia, Puuone Hills, Puu Pio, Sand Hills, Wahanemaili, Wahineomaili, Waihalulu, Waikapu, Waiolimu.

Bibliography

Maps

Alexander, A.C. *Olowalu Plantation Maui.* Hawaii Territory Survey, 1906. MAP.

Alexander, W.D. *Kahului Harbor and Adjacent Coast Line Maui.* Hawaiian Government Survey, 1881. MAP.

———. *Town of Lahaina Maui.* Hawaiian Government Survey, 1884. MAP.

Alexander, W.D., et al. *Maui Hawaiian Islands.* Hawaiian Government Survey, 1885. MAP.

———. *Maui Hawaiian Islands.* Hawaiian Government Survey, 1885 & 1903. MAP.

Alliance of Maui Community Associations. *Maui Maps – 1800's and 1900's.* https://maui-communities.weebly.com/19th--20th-century-maps.html. WEBSITE.

Bailey, C.T. *Topographic Map of the Island of Maui – Maui County, Hawaii.* U.S. Geological Survey, 1930. MAP.

Baldwin, D.D. *Map of the Ahupuaa of Wahikuli.* 1865. MAP.

Bier, James A. *Hawai'i Maui The Valley Isle – Seventh Edition.* Honolulu: University of Hawai'i Press, 2002. MAP.

Boothe, Glendon E. *U.S. Coast and Geodetic Survey Register No. 4465.* 1929. MAP.

Brigham, William T. "W.T. Brigham on Hawaiian Volcanoes." *Notes one the Volcanoes of the Hawaiian Islands.* Boston: Riverside Press, 1868. MAP.

C.J.W. (Tracing). *Map of Spreckelsville Plantation,* 1893. MAP.

Dana, James D. "History of Changes in the Mt. Loa Craters; by James D. Dana." *The American Journal of Science.* Connecticut: J.D. & E.S. Dana, 1888, p. 169. MAP.

Danforth, F.A., et al. *Hawaii (Island and County of Maui) Kahului Quadrangle – Kahului Hawaii Edition of 1925.* Territory of Hawaii, 1925. MAP.

Dove, Chas. V.E. *Public Lands Map No 9a – Kahakuloa Valley – Kahakuloa Maui.* Commissioners of Public Lands, 1896. MAP.

Duncan, C., and Shishido, F. *Honokohau Valley – Detail Survey – Section 1, Section 2, Section 3, Section 4,* no date. MAPS.

Earthwalk Press. *Island of Maui Topographic Recreation Map.* Earthwalk Press, 2003. MAP.

Gauger, J.C. *Maui – North Coast – Kahakuloa Pt. to Maliko.* Department of Commerce and Labor Coast and Geodetic Survey, 1912. MAP.

———. *Maui – North Coast – Kahului Harbor and Vicinity.* Department of Commerce and Labor Coast and Geodetic Survey, 1912. MAP.

———. *Maui – Northwest Coast – Kekaa Pt. to Kahakuloa Pt.* Department of Commerce and Labor Coast and Geodetic Survey, 1912. MAP.

Google Earth. *Various locations on West Maui,* https://earth.google.com/web/. WEBSITE.

Ho, Ah Leong. *Map Showing the Land Holdings of Baldwin Packers, LTD. in Kaanapali, Lahaina, Maui. T.H.* 1940. MAP.

Iao, Joseph, and Hawaii Territory Survey. *Map of the Ahupuaa of Waikapu – Wailuku District, Maui.* Territory of Hawaii, 1925 & 1930. MAP.

Kalama, Samuel P. *A Map of the Hawaiian Islands According to the Latest Surveys.* London: Royal Geographical Society, 1838. MAP.

———. *Na Mokupuni o Hawaii nei.* Lahaina: Kulanui Lahainaluna, 1837. MAP.

Makalena. *Wailuku Maui.* Hawaiian Government Survey, 1866. MAP.

Martin, W.F. *Hydrographic Map of the Island of Maui Territory of Hawaii.* U.S. Geological Survey, no date. MAP.

Maui Chamber of Commerce. *Island of Maui.* 1956. MAP.

May, James (Tracing). *Map of Waihee Kuleanas Maui T.H.* Taxation Map Bureau, 1875 & 1930. MAP.

Monsarrat, M.D. *Map of a Portion of Wailuku Maui.* 1882. MAP.

———. *Waiehu Maui Dec. 1887.* 1887 & 1889. MAP.

Old Maps Online. *Maps of Maui County,* https://www.oldmapsonline.org/map/usgs/5644746. WEBSITE.

Perkins, Frank W. *Hawaiian Islands Maalaea Bay Maui I.* Treasury Department U.S. Coast and Geodetic Survey, 1900. MAP.

——— *Hawaiian Islands Vicinity of Kahului Maui I.* Treasury Department U.S. Coast and Geodetic Survey, 1899. MAP.

H.K.L. & R.L. *Hawaiian Islands, Map 4 of 27: Ahupuaa of Wailuku and its appurtenant Fishery, Grant 3343 to Claus Spreckels; &, Wailuku Fishery, Island of Maui.* Public Archives of Hawaii, 1947. MAP.

State of Hawaii Department of Accounting and General Services. *Maui Maps,* http://ags.hawaii.gov/survey/miscellaneous-maps/maui-maps/. WEBSITE.

Stearns, Harold T. *Geologic and Topographic Map – Island of Maui Hawaii.* Geological Survey United States Department of the Interior, 1942. MAP.

———. *Plate 2. Map of the Island of Maui, Hawaii, Showing Points of Geological Interest.* Geological Survey United States Department of the Interior, 1942. MAP.

Territorial Survey Office. *Tax Map 2nd Division.* Taxation Maps Bureau, 1932. MAP.

Topozone. *Hawaii Topographic Maps,* Topozone, https://www.topozone.com/hawaii/. WEBSITE.

Towill, R.M. *Title Map – Wailuku Sugar Company.* 1937. MAP.

United States Department of the Interior Geological Survey. *Topographic Map of the Island of Maui – Maui County, Hawaii.* Denver: Geological Survey. 1954, 1956, & 1957. MAPS.

Wright, Geo. F. *Lahaina Town – Lahaina, Maui, T.H.* no date. MAP.

Wall, Walter E. *Honokowai Government Remnants.* Hawaii Territory Survey, 1922. MAP.

———. *Pa Pelekane and Vicinity – Lahaina Maui.* Hawaii Territory Survey, 1910, 1912, & 1915. MAP.

White, Trumbull. "Book IV. The Hawaiian Islands." *Our New Possissions. Four Books in One.* Chicago: National Educational Union, 1898, p. 628. MAP.

Wright, George F. *Kauaula Valley – Lahaina, Maui, T.H.* 1916. MAP.

Wright, George F., and Mosarrat, M.D. *Kauaula Valley – Lahaina, Maui, T.H.* 1916. MAP.

TEXT RESOURCES

Alexander, T.M. "The newly discovered Crater of Maui." *The American Journal of Science and Arts*, editors and proprietors James D. Dana and B. Silliman, 1874, pp. 525–526.

Andrews, Lorrin. *Dictionary of the Hawaiian Language.* Honolulu: Henry M. Whitney, 1865.

Andrews, Lorrin, and Parker, Henry H. *A Dictionary of the Hawaiian Language.* Honolulu: The Board, 1922.

AVAKonohiki.org, www.avakonohiki.org. WEBSITE.

Bailey, Charles T. *Indices of Awards Made by The Board of Commissioners to Quiet Land Titles in the Hawaiian Islands.* Honolulu: Star-Bulletin Press, 1929.

Bailey, Edward. *Hawaii Nei. An Idyll of the Pacific Isles.* Michigan: Samuel C. Andrews, 1879.

Beckwith, Martha. *Hawaiian Mythology.* Honolulu: University of Hawaii Press, 1970.

Beringer, Pierre N. "A Tourist's Paradise." *The Overland Monthly, Vol. LIV—Second Series: July-December 1909.* San Francisco: The Overland Monthly Co., 1909.

Bernice Pauahi Bishop Museum. "Na Malihini Kaahele i ka Moku o Keawe." *Nupepa Kuokoa*, 4 Feb 1898. TRANSCRIPT.

Bird, Isabella L. *The Hawaiian Archipelago: Six Months Amongst the Palm Groves, Coral Reefs, and Volcanoes of the Sandwich Islands.* London: John Murray, 1906.

Camp Maluhia, Boy Scouts of America Aloha Council, https://www.scoutinghawaii .org/camp-maui. WEBSITE.

Clark, John R.K. *Hawai'i Place Name: Shores, Beaches, and Surf Sites.* Honolulu: University of Hawai'i Press, 2002.

Coulter, John Wesley. *A Gazetteer of the Territory of Hawaii.* Honolulu: University of Hawai'i, 1935.

Dana, James D. *United States Exploring Expedition During the Years 1838, 1839, 1840, 1841, 1842: Geology.* Philadephia: C. Sherman, 1849.

Dega, Michael F. "An Archaeological Monitoring Plan for the Proposed Central Maui Regional Park, Wailuku and Waikapu Ahupua'a, Wailuku District Island of Maui, Hawai'i." 2014.

Engledow, Jill. "Old School Spirit," *Nō ka 'Oi Maui Magazine*, https://www .mauimagazine.net/old-maui-high-school-history/. WEBSITE.

Fitzpatrick, Gary L. *The Early Mapping of Hawai'i.* Honolulu: Editions Limited, 1986.

Fontaine, Mark A.F. "Two Views of Ancient Hawaiian Society: A Thesis Submitted to the Graduate Division of the University of Hawai'i at Mānoa in Partial Fulfillment of the Requirements for the Degree of Master of Arts in History." 2012. THESIS.

Forbes, Charles N. "The Genus *Lagenophora* in the Hawaiian Islands, with Descriptions of New Species." *Occasional Papers of Bernice P. Bishop Museum.* United States, Bishop Museum Press, 1918.

Fornander, Abraham, and Thrum, Thomas G. *Fornander Collection of Hawaiian Antiquities and Folk-lore, Volumes 4, 5, & 6.* Honolulu: Bishop Museum Press, 1916–1917, 1918, 1919–1920.

Government Records, Hawaii State Archives Digital Collections, https://digitalcollections.hawaii.gov/greenstone3/library?fbclid=IwAR26wc3tINCzw-BkkjMpQUvMLnGAx8_AJb271F_8Lg5zyOxFM5fk5WnRm30. WEBSITE.

Guerriero, Diane, et al. *Draft Archaeological Inventory Survey Report for Several Parcels of Land Situated within Waikapū Ahupua'a; Wailuku District Pū'ali Komohana Moku.* 2013.

Guppy, H.B. *Observations of a Naturalist in the Pacific between 1896 and 1899.* New York: The MacMillan Company, 1906.

Hale Alii Honolulu. *Buke Kakau Paa no ka Mahele Aina i Hooholoia iwaena o Kamehameha III a me na Lii a me na Konohiki ana Hale Alii Honolulu.* Honolulu: Archives of Hawaii, 1924, 1848.

Hawaii Aviation (An Archive of Historic Photos and Facts), "Kapalua Airport (West Maui)," https://aviation.hawaii.gov/airfields-airports/maui/kapalua-airport-west-maui/. 2021. WEBSITE.

Hawai'i, State of. *Mahele Book 1848.* Honolulu: Kodak Hawaii, Ltd., 1971, 1924, 1848.

Hawaii Supreme Court. "Horner v. Kumuliilii." *Reports of Decisions Rendered by the Supreme Court of the Hawaiian Islands.* United States: H.L. Sheldon, 1897.

Hawaiian Historical Society. *Na Mele Aimoku na Mele Kupuna a me na Mele Ponoi o ka Moi Kalakaua I, Dynastic Chants, Ancestral Chants, and Personal Chants of King Kalākaua I.* Honolulu: Hawaiian Historical Society, 2001.

Hawaiian Place Names, Ulukau: The Hawaiian Electronic Library, http://ulukau.org/cgi-bin/hpn?e=p-omahele--00-0-0--010---4------0-0l--1haw-Zz-1---20-about---00031-001-10escapewin-00&a=p&p=about&c=mahele&cl=&d=&l=en. WEBSITE.

Highways Division, County of Maui, https://www.mauicounty.gov/557/Highways-Division. WEBSITE.

Hiking Trails, Kapalua, https://www.kapalua.com/activities/hiking-trails. 2017. WEBSITE.

Hillebrand, William. *Flora of the Hawaiian Islands: A Description of Their Phanerogams and Vascular Cryptogams.* Germany: Williams & Norgate, 1888.

Ho'olaupa'i, www.nupepa.org. WEBSITE.

Hosmer, Ralph S. "Committee on Forestry, Board of Agriculture and Forestry," *The Hawaiian Forester and Agriculturist,* 1908, pp. 65–72.

Ickes, Harold L. *Annual Report of the Department of the Interior, 1933.* Washington: United States Government Printing Office, 1933.

Imada, Lee. "Highway name change honors Maui veterans," *The Maui News,* https://

www.mauinews.com/news/local-news/2017/10/highway-name-change-honors
-maui-veterans/. WEBSITE.

Ka'ahumanu Church, Ka'ahumanu Church, https://www.kaahumanuchurch.org.
WEBSITE.

Ka'iwakīloumoku Hawaiian Cultural Center, www.kaiwakiloumoku.ksbe.edu. 2020.
WEBSITE.

Kamakau, Samuel M. *Ruling Chiefs of Hawaii (Revised Edition)*. Honolulu: Kamehameha Schools Press, 1992.

———. *Tales and Traditions of the People of Old: Nā Mo'olelo a ka Po'e Kahiko*. Honolulu: Bishop Museum Press, 1991.

Kepano's Combined Hawaiian Dictionary for browsers, trussel2.com. WEBSITE.

Kīpuka. www.kipukadatabase.com. WEBSITE.

Krauss, Robert W. "A Taxonomic Revision of the Hawaiian Species of the Genus
Carex," *Pacific Science, Vol IV*. 1950.

Kuihelani, H. *Royal Patents L.C. Awards Nos. 420, 453 & 5228 – Kuihelani Wailuku
and Waikapu – Maui – Plans and descriptions*. Dept. of Land and Natural Resources, 1851 & 1975.

Lahaina Restoration Foundation, www.lahainarestoration.org. 2020. WEBSITE.

Lahuiokalani: A Church With the Gift of Hawaiian Hospitality, Lahuiokalani Ka'ānapa-
li [*sic*] Congregational Church, UCC, http://lahuiokalani.org. 2019. WEBSITE.

Malo, Davida. *Hawaiian Antiquities: Moolelo Hawaii*. United States: Hawaiian
Gazette Company, Limited, 1903.

Maly, Kepa. *He Mo'olelo no Maui Hikina–Kalialinui i Uka a me Nā 'Āina o Lalo, A
Cultural-Historical Study of East Maui–the Uplands of Kalialinui, and the Lands
that Lie Below, Island of Maui*. Hilo: Kumu Pono Associates LLC, 2006.

———. *Volume 1 (Part 1): He Wahi Mo'olelo no Kaua'ula A me Kekāhi 'Āina o Lahaina
i Maui, A Collection of Traditions and Historical Accounts of Kaua'ula and Other
Lands of Lahaina, Maui*. Hilo: Kumu Pono Associates LLC, 2007.

———. *Volume 1 (Part 2): He Wahi Mo'olelo no Kaua'ula a me Kekāhi 'Āina o Lahaina
i Maui, A Collection of Traditions and Historical Accounts of Kaua'ula and Other
Lands of Lahaina, Maui*. Hilo: Kumu Pono Associates LLC, 2007.

Mather, Helen. *One Summer in Hawaii*. New York: Cassell Publishing Company,
1891.

Mauna Kahālāwai Watershed Partnership, https://www.maunakahalawai.org.
WEBSITE.

Maui County Parks, County of Maui, https://www.mauicounty.gov/287/Maui
-County-Parks. WEBSITE.

Minor light o Maui – Nakalele, HI, Lighthousefriends.com, https://www
.lighthousefriends.com/light.asp?ID=919. WEBSITE.

Moffat, Riley M., and Fitzpatrick, Gary L. *Mapping the Lands and Waters of Hawai'i:
The Hawaiian Government Survey*. Honolulu: Editions Limited, 2004.

———. *Surveying the Mahele: Mapping the Hawaiian Land Revolution*. Honolulu:
Editions Limited, 1995.

Nā Puke Wehewehe 'Ōlelo Hawai'i, wehewehe.org. WEBSITE.

Newell, C.M. *Kamehameha, the Conquering King: The Mystery of His Birth, Loves and Conquests.* New York and London: G.P. Putnam's Sons, 1885.

Nimmo, H. Arlo. "Pele's Journey to Hawai'i: An Analysis of the Myths." *Pacific Studies: Vol. 11, No. 1–November 1987.* Brigham Young University – Hawaii Campus, 1987.

Nu'uhiwa, Kalei. (2021, June 5). *Add this to your dictionary cause it doesn't just mean dirty or filthy. Mahalo. 'Eka'eka Spelled ' E K A ' E K A Smoky gray, as clouds agitated by the onset of a storm. Just think Harry Potter clouds. ~ MARAKI 24, 1866 Now you know. Use it.* [Status update]. Facebook. https://www.facebook.com /halaulanipapa/posts/10208088237599129

Oliveira, K.R. Kapā'anaokalāokeola. "'Ohu'ohu 'O Kahakuloa Ku'u Kulāiwi, A Thesis to the Graduate Division of the University of Hawai'i in Partial Fulfillment of the Requirements for the Degree of Master of Arts in Geography, University of Hawai'i, 1999. THESIS.

Olowalu Lanakila Hawaiian Church, https://olowalulanakilahawaiianchurch .wordpress.com. WEBSITE.

Papakilo Database, www.papakilodatabase.com. WEBSITE.

Pukui, Mary K., and Elbert, Samuel H. *Hawaiian Dictionary – Revised and Enlarged Edition.* Honolulu: University of Hawai'i Press, 1986.

Pukui, Mary K., et. al. *Nānā i ke Kumu, Vol. 1.* Honolulu: Hui Hānai, 1979.

——— *Place Names of Hawaii – Revised and Expanded Edition.* Honolulu: University of Hawai'i Press, 1976.

Rock, Joseph F. "A Monographic Study of the Hawaiian Species of the Tribe *Lobelioideae* Family *Campanulaceae.*" *Memoirs of the Bernice Pauahi Bishop Museum: Volume VII., Number 2.* Honolulu: Bishop Museum Press, 1919.

Rosser, W.H. *The Seaman's Guide to the Islands of the North Pacific with an Appendix on the Winds, Weather, Currents &c., of the North and South Pacific.* London: James Imray and Son, 1870.

Sanborn Maps, Library of Congress, https://www.loc.gov/collections/sanborn-maps/ ?fa=location:hawaii&sp=1. WEBSITE.

Shapiro, Michael. *Violent Cartographies.* Minneapolis: University of Minnesota Press, 1997.

Sterling, Elspeth P. *Sites of Maui.* Bishop Museum Press, 1998.

Tanigawa Lum, A. U'ilani, and Rivera, Keely S. Kau'ilani. *Malu 'Ulu o Lele: Maui Komohana in* Ka Nupepa Kuokoa. Lahaina: North Beach-West Maui Benefit Fund, 2020.

Tau'a, Keli'i, and Kapahulehua, Kimokeo. "INTERVIEW: Earl Ray Kukahiko, By Keli'i Tau'a and Kimokeo Kapahulehu, Oct 12, 2005." *Kahoma (Thin or Hollow): Final Report, Appendix E. Cultural Impact Assessment.* 2005. REPORT.

The Nature Conservancy – Hawai'i Operating Unit. "Kapunakea Preserve West Maui, Hawai'i: Final Long-Range Management Plan Fiscal Years 2016–2021." 2015. REPORT.

Thrum, Thos. G. *Hawaiian Almanac and Annual for 1884.* Honolulu: Thos. G. Thrum, 1884.

————. *Hawaiian Almanac and Annual for 1897*. Honolulu: Thos. G. Thrum, 1897.

————. *Hawaiian Annual for 1924*. Honolulu: Thos. G. Thrum, 1923.

————. *The Hawaiian Annual 1909*. Honolulu: Thos. G. Thrum, 1909.

————. *The Hawaiian Annual 1910*. Honolulu: Thos. G. Thrum, 1910.

————. *The Hawaiian Annual 1911*. Honolulu: Thos. G. Thrum, 1911.

————. *The Hawaiian Annual 1912*. Honolulu: Thos. G. Thrum, 1912.

————. *The Hawaiian Annual for 1921*. Honolulu: Thos. G. Thrum, 1920.

Ulukau, www.ulukau.org. WEBSITE.

United States Board on Geographic Place Names. *Decisions on Names in the United States*. Washington, D.C.: Department of the Interior, 1954.

United States Department of the Interior National Park Service. "National Register of Historic Places Inventory – Nomination Form: Hale Pa'i Hawaii Site Number 50-03-1596." 1975. APPLICATION.

US Army Corps of Engineers. "Appendix A Literature Search/Annotated Bibliography," *Maui RSM Plan*, https://rsm.usace.army.mil/Hawaii/documents/maui/plan/Maui_RSM_Appendices.pdf. WEBSITE.

Van, James. *Sites of Oʻahu: A Guide to Hawaiian Archaeological Places of Interest*. Honolulu: Bishop Museum Press, 1991.

Young, Peter T. *Images of Old Hawaiʻi*, 1 June 2020, imagesofoldhawaii.com/. WEBSITE.

Nupepa (Hawaiian-Language Newspapers)

Honolulu Star-Bulletin, newspapers.com, 1960.

Ka Elele, papakilodatabase.com, 1844, 1845.

Ka Hae Hawaii, papakilodatabase.com, 1858, 1860.

Ka Hoku o Hawaii, papakilodatabase.com, 1926, 1945.

Ka Hoku o ka Pakipika, papakilodatabase.com, 1862, 1863.

Ka Lahui Hawaii, papakilodatabase.com, 1876, 1877.

Ka Lanakila, papakilodatabase.com, 1909.

Ka Lei Rose o Hawaii, papakilodatabase.com, 1898.

Ka Leo o ka Lahui, papakilodatabase.com, 1894.

Ka Nai Aupuni, papakilodatabase.com, 1868, 1907.

Ka Nupepa Kuokoa, papakilodatabase.com, 1862, 1863, 1864, 1865, 1866, 1867, 1868, 1869, 1870, 1871, 1875, 1877, 1878, 1883, 1884, 1892, 1894, 1895, 1899, 1902, 1914, 1918, 1919, 1924, 1926.

Ke Alakai o Hawaii, papakilodatabase.com, 1930.

Ke Aloha Aina, papakilodatabase.com, 1901.

Ke Au Okoa, papakilodatabase.com, 1865, 1866, 1867, 1869, 1870, 1871.

Ke Kumu Hawaii, papakilodatabase.com, 1835.

Ko Hawaii Paeaina, papakilodatabase.com, 1878, 1879, 1883, 1885, 1887, 1890.

Ko Hawaii Ponoi, papakilodatabase.com, 1873.

Kuokoa Home Rula, papakilodatabase.com, 1912.

The Honolulu Advertiser, newspapers.com, 1957.

The Maui News, newspapers.com, 1902, 1903, 2017.
The Pacific Commercial Advertiser, 1864.

ADDITIONAL

Amadeo, Diane Nāpua. Personal Communications between Aunty Di and Pueo Pata. 1991–2005.
Holt, Hōkūlani. Personal Communications between Kumu Hula Hōkūlani Holt, PhD, and Pueo Pata. January 21, 2022.
Ka Leo Hawaiʻi 212 (Joseph Kekaua), Ulukau, Kaniʻaina, http://ulukau.org/kaniaina/ ?a=d&d=A-KLH-HV24-212&e=-------haw-20--1--txt-tpIN%7ctpTI%7ctpTA %7ctpCO%7ctpTY%7ctpLA%7ctpKE%7ctpPR%7ctpSG%7ctpTO%7ctpTG %7ctpSM%7ctpTR%7ctpSP%7ctpCT%7ctpET%7ctpHT%7ctpDT%7ctpOD %7ctpDF----------------. WEBSITE.
Ka Leo Hawaiʻi 378 (John Nākoa), Ulukau, Kaniʻaina, http://ulukau.org/kaniaina/ ?a=d&d=A-KLH-HV24-378&e=-------haw-20--1--txt-tpIN%7ctpTI%7ctpTA %7ctpCO%7ctpTY%7ctpLA%7ctpKE%7ctpPR%7ctpSG%7ctpTO%7ctpTG %7ctpSM%7ctpTR%7ctpSP%7ctpCT%7ctpET%7ctpHT%7ctpDT%7ctpOD %7ctpDF----------------. WEBSITE.

ABOUT THE AUTHOR

Cody Kapueola'ākeanui "Pueo" Pata began his formal education in Hawaiian knowledge, language, and culture in 1991, under Kumu Hula Nona Mahilani Kaluhiokalani and Kupuna Diane Nāpua Amadeo. In 1992, his journey to becoming a Kumu Hula was initiated by renowned Hula Master George Lanakilakeikiahiali'i Nā'ope. Throughout the course of his learning, Pueo would also be sent by these three key figures to learn directly from Kumu Hula Ke'ala Kūkona, Kumu Hula Jay Jay Ahulau Akiona, Kupuna Eleanor Makida, and Hula Master Hilda Keana'āina. Traditional education of this kind often found Pueo living with some of his masters for extended periods of time, and working very closely for, and with, all seven of his teachers through a variety of experiences. Although he was classically graduated as a Kumu Hula in the fall of 2001, and as a Haku Mele in the spring of 2003, he continued to learn directly from all of his mentors until the ends of their lives—the last of whom passed in 2011.

Pueo's foundation for Hawaiian worldview, values, language, and culture was laid by these esteemed po'e kumu, and it is upon this foundation that his career as a Kumu Hula, Haku Mele, a Hawaiian language and culture teacher, consultant, researcher, musician, entertainer, and artisan is built. Since 1993, he has taught Hawaiian language and culture through various public and private educational systems, which include the Pūnana Leo O Maui, the Pākōlea A+ Program of the Kula Kaiapuni O Maui, the Hawaiiana Club of Lahainaluna High School, Kamehameha Schools Maui High School, Papahana Kuaola, and his own Hālau Hula 'o Ka Malama Mahilani. As an award-winning Hawaiian music entertainer, Pueo has released three solo albums, and has been featured on 20 other music projects to date.